"For anyone who wished to grow up in a functional family with the guidance of loving elders this is your sneak preview into such a world. You can become virtually immersed in it, moved by it and perhaps transformed by it. Your surrogate wise guide is a child psychologist who can pour his knowledge into his own history and help galvanize your spirit and behavior."

—Erika Meir, Yoga Instructor

"…a nostalgic trip from childhood to adulthood providing answers to the stumbling blocks we all face on our journey. I recommend it highly"

—Jerry Kramer,
Retired High Tech Engineer,
Plant Manager

May, 1961, 1ˢᵗ date

THE CLASSROOM OF LIFE

*Tools and Skills to Overcome
Obstacles and Adversity*

ANTHONY J. CEDOLINI

Dr. Anthony J. Cedolini
P.O. Box 20531
San Jose, CA 95120
https://www.drtonycedolini.com/contact

Website: https://www.drtonycedolini.com
Cover design by Don Barnes

ISBNs:
Hardcover 978-1-64184-647-9
Paperback 978-1-64184-648-6
eBook 978-1-64184-649-3

DEDICATION

It is with great gratitude that I dedicate this book to my parents, grandparents, siblings, a dedicated and darling wife, my loving in-laws, cousins, and of course, to my children and their children. May you and all children, parents, and relatives enjoy a peaceful, loving, giving, and successful life. May we all work together as brothers and sisters to leave this world a better place.

CONTENTS

ACKNOWLEDGEMENTS

I need to acknowledge, first and foremost, my wonderful wife, Clare. Her total support and the hundreds of hours of assisting and editing has made this major undertaking happen. I am blessed to have her by my side and can't thank her enough. I love you, Clare!

I'm indebted to an amazing mentor and prime mover, Sharon CassanoLochman. She took my initial draft and turned it into a very respectable book. Sharon's confidence in my work provided the momentum needed to finish improving my writings. Her many hours languishing over my verbosity and over-the-top chapters were incredible. She was like a dietician slimming down an obese patient. Her remarks and helpful suggestions were priceless. My over-the-top thank yous!

I am forever grateful to nephew Don Barnes, a gifted artist and graphic designer, for his assistance in preparing the design, layouts, composition, and website. He was an inspiration and rescuer when computer obstacles stalled my progress. His selfless devotion and generous dedication to my four-and-a-half year project will forever be cherished.

I cherish and thank my entire family for their unwavering support, understanding, encouragement and love. They were not only my audience; they were my *raison d'etre*. Without you, my existence and purpose would be simply elusive.

In addition, I acknowledge my enduring friends, colleagues, and all of the many gifted mentors who provided their support, guidance, and love along the way. Because of them and all of my varied life experiences, I feel so very fortunate to have lived most of my preconceived dreams and aspirations.

It has been through easy access to information, books, libraries, research studies, and periodicals that has allowed for this mountainous pursuit. The many boxes of inspirational quotes, articles, and stories contributed the material that provided validity. I am especially indebted to the profound words of the wisest and most astute minds of the past three millennia. I value those 3,500 years of incredible wisdom. Their shared treasures will continue to resonate for many future generations.

It may have been Leo Tolstoy that said it best, "The key to success in life is using the good thoughts of wise people"

DESIDERATA

As an undergraduate University student of the socially-conscience 1960s generation, a historical 17th century document dated 1692, found in old St. Paul's Church in Baltimore, Maryland, captivated my attention. The astute words, although more than 300 years old, held a resonating, compelling, meaningful, and inspiring message—indeed, a formidable road map offering personal guidance and direction.

Follow the star of Desiderata towards a life of quiet happiness.

Begin your journey here.

"Go placidly amid the noise and haste, and remember what peace there may be in silence. As far as possible without surrender be on good terms with all persons. Speak your truth quietly and clearly; and listen to others, even the dull and ignorant; they too have their story.

Avoid loud and aggressive persons, they are vexations to the spirit. If you compare yourself with others, you may become vain and bitter; for always there will be greater and lesser persons than yourself. Enjoy your achievements as well as your plans.

Keep interested in your own career, however humble; it is a real possession in the changing fortunes of time. Exercise caution in your business affairs; for the world is full of trickery. But let this not blind you to what virtue there is; many persons strive for high ideals; and everywhere life is full of heroism.

Be yourself. Especially, do not feign affection. Neither be cynical about love; for in the face of all aridity and disenchantment it is perennial as the grass.

Take kindly the counsel of the years, gracefully surrendering the things of youth. Nurture strength of spirit to shield you in sudden misfortune. But do not distress yourself with dark imaginings. Many fears are born of fatigue and loneliness. Beyond a wholesome discipline, be gentle with yourself.

You are a child of the universe, no less than the trees and the stars; you have a right to be here. And whether or not it is clear to you, no doubt the universe is unfolding as it should.

Therefore be at peace with God, whatever you conceive Him to be, and whatever your labors and aspirations, in the noisy confusion of life keep peace with your soul.

With all its sham, drudgery, and broken dreams, it is still a beautiful world. Be cheerful. Strive to be happy."

INTRODUCTION

I AM THE CHILD

*"I am the child. All the world waits for my com-
ing. All of earth watches with interest to see what
I shall become. Civilization hangs in the balance.
For what I am the world of tomorrow will be.
I am the child. I have come into your world
about which I knew nothing. When I came,
I know not. Why I came, I know not.
I am the child. You hold in your hands my destiny. You determine largely whether I shall succeed or fail. Give me, I pray you, those things
that make for happiness. Train me, I beg you,
that I may be a blessing to this world."*
—Author Mamie Cole

"I expect to pass through the world but once; Any good thing therefore that I can do, or any kindness that I can show to any fellow-creature, let me do now; let me not defer or neglect it, for I shall not pass this way again."

—*Attributed to Stephen Grellet*

PREFACE

As a young man and new father, almost 55 years ago, I had a dream of being able to assist my children in understanding some of the obstacles and hard work necessary in growing up.

Wouldn't that be a noble goal?

As my naïveté lessened and the years passed, I realized that most of my learning had required immersion and active participation with life. My personal growth had included painful falling, failing, and too many mistakes to count. I learned that the most crucial life lesson, and a critical step for growth and maturity was to get back up!

There are so many other dimensions in learning life's lessons. Layered among trials and tribulations are the rules of conduct, establishing a moral compass, expanding social skills, developing emotional maturity, maintaining an open mind, and an understanding of the importance of their application in everyday life.

I decided to collect and save as much canned knowledge as possible in hopes that someday I would share my collection with my children.

Years passed. The saved snippets of wisdom from the mental giants from centuries ago eventually grew into countless boxes of quotes, stories, books, seminars, notes, and memorabilia—a golden treasure continuously refreshing, feeding, and rekindling my dream. I had amassed a treasure chest of rare stones and priceless antiquities. To this day, I am overwhelmed and humbled by the immensity of the hidden treasures of the millennia.

Now, over 50 years later, my message has evolved into a passion for the love of life.

—Tony Cedolini

THE ROAD AHEAD

Dear Grandchildren,

I write this to my darlings because life is a series of challenges. I am your Poppie, and with your first breath, I have lovingly prepared the road ahead for your journey of life. Over 20 years ago, when first grandchild Bobby was born in 1994, I began writing this book. Unfortunately, it took decades to finish.

As I enter the winter of my life, some 22 years later than my first letter, I begin the final chapter, my winter pilgrimage, and the last attempt to complete this life-long dream.

Fifty-plus years have gone by so quickly. My brain feels like a cement mixer. How could I forget the unexpected death of my dearest friend, business partner, and brother, Billy, at age 26? How could I forget the daily early-morning car rides and chats with my dad delivering newspapers, my first bicycle; or the early adolescent epiphany, sobbing in my basement consumed with self-pity? Receiving my first baseball trophy from Dizzy Dean, or the birth of our first child, or the thrills of parenthood, or the pain and frustrations of my youngsters' adolescent years—or the death of a parent, favorite aunt or uncle?

This is life.

May my messages carry you through the challenges of life.

May my words embrace you during your darkest moments and provide clarity through uncertain times.

I have only one request—that you absorb, assimilate, and save what is useful to you; reject what you find useless. This book is not a novel, but an intense and frank course on the love of life.

Your life, like mine, will be filled with sorrow, joy, mistakes, hellos and goodbyes, exhilaration, creativity, failures, tears of joy, and sincere happiness.

I cannot imagine anything different.

So, my darlings, this is your short course on life.

Be aware of the natural beauty that surrounds you. Your love of Mother Nature will serve you well, especially when the minor quakes of life strike. Worship Mother Nature, for she will indeed carry you amidst her vast beauty and never-ending serenity.

Recognize your senses. With your sense of vision, see beyond the immediate. Smell the sensuous scents of flowers, trees, spices, fruits, the morning dew, and the gentle evening breeze. Hear the vibrant sounds of sinuous streams, waterfalls, raging rivers, breaking waves, songs of birds, the breathing of a newborn, the falling raindrops, and soft snow billowing in the wind. Feel the eagerness of your pets snuggling next to you. Savor the friendly arm on your shoulder, the quiet kiss, the passionate hug, and the effects of a kind smile.

Minimize your fears. Don't let fear detour you; most things in life need to be experienced. The most difficult journeys are often the most successful. Enjoy your successes and learn from your mistakes. Worrying, sulking, complaining, or bragging will only waste your time. Accept your consequences by taking responsibility for your actions. Move forward without unrealistic fear.

Time is very short. Time wasted today can result in a repetition of lost days. The sooner you value your time, the more you will appreciate that it is the most limited of all resources. It is impossible to control time, and worse yet, it is finite. It has a termination date.

You will encounter pain. Most painful experiences have a purpose and result in a valuable learning experience. Since everything in life is temporary, whether it is pain or pleasure, it will not last forever. However, it will provide you with an indelible memory. Overcoming personal difficulties is the hallmark of progress. You are always progressing and becoming even when the road gets very bumpy. Bruises heal, and your strength will be renewed. Each struggle is simply another step forward on your journey.

The only thing you will ever fully control is you. You are neither indispensable nor indestructible. The sooner you understand that nothing lasts forever, the sooner you will appreciate yourself and others and work toward making yourself and the world a better place. It is important to remember that no person can make you happy. Only you can do that!

You must learn to let go! During my worst depression after the unexpected death of my best friend and brother, Billy, I learned this precious antidote. People are always more important than things or possessions. Yes, friends may disappoint you, and you need to be alert that some people have a motive for their actions. Sometimes their motives are honorable and supportive. Sometimes the opposite is true. You will learn this with time, experience, and reasonable caution. Regardless, always honor your word. Be good to others; follow the Golden Rule, but not blindly. Be honest and trustworthy; set a good example. Forgive yourself and others and let go of grudges.

Never allow yourself to be bored. Bored people are indeed boring. Remember that you have thousands of choices. No one with a brain should ever find him or herself bored. Also, the most boring word in all languages is the word "I." Use it sparingly!

Fill your life with passion and love. Young love and even mature love are sometimes transient. Your loved ones can come and go, or even worse, leave this world, and your sadness and pain will cause tears and sorrow. Your pet may be your first loss. Your tears of love and loss are necessary. Although time might heal, your memories will inevitably remain. Appreciate the love you had without exaggerating it or deprecating it. But please allow love for others and allow them to love you with all their heart. Especially love your family.

Gift yourself a formal education. As you have undoubtedly observed, some successful people did not receive a bona fide formal education. However, formal and informal education remains a prudent and honorable means of developing knowledge, awareness, and sensitivity. If successful, formal education can assist in developing an open and informed mind, a work ethic, and personal discipline. Formal education should always run parallel with hands-on volunteer work in your community. Working with, helping, and understanding others, particularly needy individuals, is paramount and indeed the finest of all curricula. Every piece of knowledge gained becomes another coping skill that can be added to your expanding toolbox.

Character is critical. Achieving the various values of character will ultimately provide you with freedom and will eliminate the need for irrational fear and worry. Be yourself; humility and simplicity are the keys to happiness. My role is to assist and support you in finding the value of a good, productive, and satisfying life. Hopefully, I can help you learn the value of hard work, persistence, kindness, and all the many behaviors that constitute character.

Your future is something you create. It is not fate or destiny, and it begins as a blank canvas. You get to paint and sketch your life portrait as either a classic masterpiece or a lost piece of art. You have now embarked on a long, arduous, and uncharted journey. You have no clues, no discernible direction, no navigational aids, and you begin with tabula rasa. All that you know is that you are bound for unknown destinations during unknown times.

There are many directions and some fundamental rules to follow. When your points of reference are obscure or your journey stalls, there may be a means to assist you in finding markers and landmarks. Be careful not to be slowed by poor choices, congestion, or speed traps. It's your journey, and it's your ultimate decision that will expedite your trip.

Soon you will learn that there will be many false starts, potholes, dead ends, washed-out bridges, punctured tires, shortcuts, missed turns, and long-cuts. Each will prompt thinking, understanding, and decision-making. Surely, there will be specters of light and periods of blackouts, moments of glory, and times of despair. All that you know is that once the trip has begun, you must continue each moment regardless of whether you choose to or not.

You begin with no worldly possessions but a modicum of love and support. There will be benefits and rewards, disappointments and setbacks, vistas, and sensational sunsets, but you will have lived and survived the journey of life. Realistically, that's the metaphor of life.

You can't control life or others; you can only control yourself.

If life is as good to you as it has been to me, you'll enjoy all of the many benefits and beauties of your travels. I hope that you will indulge yourself with love, humor, learning, family, friends, mentors, enthusiasm, and wisdom, for then you will genuinely experience the meaning of success.

There is no rush, no hurry.

Take your time and enjoy your life journey. Especially make time for your family and the people you will forever remember, for many of them will no longer be there at the end of your journey—Savor the many unforgettable memories through life. Time can be your greatest ally or your deadliest enemy. Treasure it as you would your most precious possessions. Live life to its fullest. Gather success and give love; you, too, can leave behind beautiful memories to those who will take their journey after yours.

I define success as true personal happiness.

Your forever loving Poppie

A LIFE OF LOVE
AND HAPPINESS

"The family is both the fundamental unit of society as well is the root of culture. It . . . is a perpetual source of encouragement, advocacy, assurance, and emotional refueling that empowers a child to venture with confidence into the greater world and become all that he can be."

—*Marianne E. Neifert*

BLISSFUL TOGETHERNESS

My first personal renaissance occurred in my early 20s. It started with a budding romantic relationship with my future wife, Clare, that culminated in our marriage in 1964. Three years later, in 1967, with the inspired awe of first-time parents, we welcomed our darling firstborn, Maria, into the world. Parenthood brought much joy and adventure, as well as the seriousness of responsibility and the new reality of nurturing and caring for a child full time. Becoming a husband, then a father, were the most significant positive events of this epiphany. It only continued to unfold further as our enthusiasm was further enhanced by planning for another child. At that moment in my life, I realized that family was not just important; it was *everything*.

Balancing our first child, graduate school, and my full-time work while Clare did substitute teaching was challenging. Learning to operate on limited sleep was another hurdle. Graduate school was not just an academic full load of classes, but also meant writing a master's thesis. This included conducting an experimental study to test my hypothesis, collect the data, and write up the results. Early mornings were a combination of studying, writing, and enjoying our new gift of joy, Maria. Evenings after a day at work, I first focused on holding and playing with our new arrival, then back to studying. Some days I would take our little Maria to a graduate class. Fortunately, she would slumber in her bassinet while I gently rocked it with my foot. Those responsibilities brought our family closer together than ever before. Not to say there weren't many other logistical, social, and emotional obstacles to overcome. Yet, it remains one of the most joyous moments of my life. I was so deeply in love with parenthood, regardless of smelly diapers, interrupted sleep, or a rush to work and school. Thank God my mother-in-law lived close by and frequently came to our rescue. Without her and my father-in-law's support, life would have been desperate.

We loved the exciting adventure of parenting and began planning for the next addition to our family. When our adorable second child, Antonia, was born in 1971, we began notifying family and friends. I proudly called my brother, Billy, my dearest best friend and best man at our wedding. He was now living in Boise, Idaho. He was ecstatic over the news and thrilled to be an uncle again. He said he would take care of some business and leave in a day or two. Two days later, while I was working my second job assessing a youngster, I received the most dreaded phone call of my life. The highway patrol notified me that my 26-year-old brother had been involved in a head-on auto accident and was dead. I was devastated. I quickly went into denial. Surely this was a dream; it could not have happened. It took several days and an open coffin to allow reality to sink in. My most ghastly and persistent feeling was that if I had not called him then, perhaps he would have left later and still be alive. For many years I carried the immense weight of lingering guilt. I'll share my three-year depression in the chapter that addresses depression.

Unfortunately, our joy over our adorable new baby was dampened by that tragic event. Over time, we made every effort to ameliorate the sad association. She was such a good and cuddly baby; we did not want her to feel our sadness. At that time, we were temporarily satisfied that our family was complete. However, a few years later, my brother-in-law Nick's wife Mary gave birth to a beautiful baby boy, Joey. This gave Clare a renewed enthusiasm. In late 1975, her "baby fever" transmitted to me. It aroused a rebirth of strength in both of us, and we were now ready to expand our family. We decided to add another member to our delightful family of four. Our first and only dear son, Peter, another joyful miracle, came into our world in 1976. Our family was now complete. Little did we know the challenges ahead of us.

The basic unit of life, the family, is the key to happiness and success or the key to conflict and failure. Of all creation, humankind has the gift of free will and decision-making. Consequently, our basic family unit was not only critical for survival; it was an essential building block for peace and harmony. If there is anything I value and respect most, it is family. All other primary institutions and relationships pale in comparison to the family.

Perhaps needless to say, my background was heavily grounded in family. *Family is always first and foremost!* As our family grew to three children, our family dynamics changed. Juggling work with the needs of three different independent personalities, each with different interests and unique needs, we all needed to make significant adjustments to our time and resources. For instance, it was not only far more expensive, but each child required transportation to activities that eventually became a blur. Now, our family unit needed to work together, solve problems together, love each other unconditionally, support each other, and help each other as its sole priority in life.

When the basic tenets of the family give way to personal temptations, hostility, unresolved problems, ongoing conflict, and discord, the family unit becomes imbalanced. In turn, it also harms our neighbors, village, city, country, and world.

Taking full responsibility for the family becomes our prime priority.

Since Stanford University was nearby and its Psychology Department was a legend. I was fascinated by an iconic study by Dr. Lewis Terman, professor emeritus at Stanford University. He began the most extensive longitudinal study ever conducted in the annals of family research. Even more surprising, some 80 years later, his study continues. His most significant finding was that the key factor in the development of trust, faith, confidence, and happiness is a strong family. Family is the security blanket and supportive refuge for children, future generations, towns, villages, and countries.

Family is, of course, a team sport. It involves give-and-take, sharing and compromising, and above all, ongoing communication. Disagreements are inevitable. However, they are challenging opportunities to deal with unresolved and reoccurring problems. Do not allow squabbles to fester or damage your relationships. It is wise to remember that silence can often be golden. In any disagreement with loved ones, it is best to deal with only the current situation. Bringing up the past is distracting and futile. There are times that recesses and breaks are necessary, especially during the turbulent years of adolescence. Ultimately, self-reliance and independence are the single most important gifts a parent can give a child.

As a young man, I marveled over families who seemed so mature, happy, and balanced. These families were frequently in the news. For instance, the Roosevelts, Kennedys, Clintons, Bushs, Nixons, Popes, rulers, religious leaders, heroes, and prophets made impressive and heroic news stories. However, over time we have learned through books, newscasting, and investigations that much of what had been said was nothing more than fluff. And, when I looked deeper into their private lives, I discovered the fallacies of my Pollyannaish thinking. Like most, I had my rose-colored glasses on, and I had interpreted these significant individuals as nearly perfect. Now, we are all comforted in knowing that every family has skeletons in their closets. I am thoroughly convinced that when you shake a family tree, you'll find some rotten fruit on the ground. I'm sure that mathematicians using sophisticated logarithms can agree with the laws of probability; find the expected percentage of chance events that will be predicted to occur in a typical extended family.

Thus, it is not surprising that there is not a single family that I have either known or read about that doesn't have some problems or deep dark secrets. For some, you can be assured that the news media within minutes will disclose such problems or secrets. For others, perhaps decades or centuries later, after biographers had previously painted a very rosy, euphemistic past, will repaint the ugly truth.

The reality is that no family or individual is perfect. Everyone has faults.

We are simply products of an imperfect world.

We need to understand and take the good with the ugly because upon self-examination, we too have our hidden faults and shrouded secrets. Surely life will always throw you curves, but acceptance, understanding, and love should remain focused on the wonders and beauty of your family. With this attitude, the flaws of your immediate family will be tempered and never expand to a size that constitutes rejection, disbandment, or abdication.

Communication and problem resolution remain critical tools in maintaining family balance. Paying close attention to love, bonding, acceptance, shared understanding while maintaining limits, rules of conduct, reciprocal sharing, and individual responsibility will be keys to minimizing family failures. An ounce of prevention will always provide the pound of cure. Establishing reasonable limits and codes of conduct of acceptable behavior will be necessary for all parents. Your role in creating a very definitive family creed will enhance harmony, balance, and responsibility. The relatively simple family creed below, found many years ago, was our family's starting point.

A FAMILY CREED

If you open it, close it.
If you turn it on, turn it off.
If you unlock it, lock it.
If you break it, repair it.
If you can't fix it, call in somebody who can.
If you borrow it, return it.
If you use it, take care of it.
If you make a mess, clean up.
If you move it, put it back.
If it belongs to someone else,
and you want to use it, get permission.
If you don't know how to operate it, leave it alone.
If it doesn't concern you, don't mess with it.

It is important to remember that living in a tight family circle allows you to learn the strengths and weaknesses of each family member. As with food or drink, you can use your judgment to savor the good or bask in weakness, overindulgence, and temptation. It is very easy to press hot buttons, whether they enhance or despoil what we already learned. Once you know each family member intimately, their strengths and weaknesses become apparent. Of course, this knowledge can allow for playing these individuals like a fiddle or acknowledging weaknesses without exacerbating them.

It is always best to build rather than destroy. My son-in-law Bob is a master at pressing positive hot buttons. He purposefully looks for something endearing to say, even if it is, "That shirt looks good on you." In his very first remarks, he never hesitates to say something praiseworthy, pleasant, and positive. It is no wonder that he started as a salesman for one of the largest private companies in the world and now is an executive vice-president. This does not mean it should always be Pollyanna and that sensitive issues shouldn't be addressed and approached. However, like finding compliments, you need considerable thought, sensitive planning, and, if possible, consultation with a neutral third party. These extra moments allow for guidance, careful timing, and constructive feedback. When ready to discuss thorny issues, get to the point with sensitivity. Avoid repetitive nagging or good-intentioned reminders; they become trite, incisive, and frequently unwanted. Face it, do it, and don't dance around problems. If presented sincerely, a wise family member can recognize their transgressions. They, in turn, will learn from your modeling. Confronting with poise and planning will add to your repertoire and result in a smoother journey. Remember, if you want to accelerate change in others and yourself, pay close attention to positive behaviors by acknowledging them; avoid focusing on negative behaviors. Real change and confidence occur when you catch people in the positive act of doing things right, rather than wasting time paying attention to negative behaviors!

Like my grandmother, some grandparents can be quiet and inspiring behind the scenes yet have no difficulty giving unconditional love, affection, and wisdom. Having had only one grandparent, I was so fortunate to have a loving grandmother, Angelina Cristadoro, who made up for the three grandparents I was never able to know or appreciate. Now, as a most fortunate grandparent myself, I must admit it's one of the most fulfilling and rewarding roles that anyone could have ever hoped.

PERSONAL GLIMPSES

All of the platitudes preached over the years are only validated by "the proof is in the pudding." We never know until much later that our painstaking efforts of doing right are indeed genuinely right. As a parent, we often look for feedback to clarify and validate our parental efforts. Were our efforts worthwhile and appropriate?

The note below was written by our middle child, Antonia, a few years ago, after she had become a parent. It reflected my feelings, hopes, and dreams as a struggling parent during all those uncertain years. I am sharing it verbatim. It remains a nostalgic and meaningful moment that I will always remember and cherish.

Below is Antonia's note.

"My Dearest Parents,

I wanted to take a moment to remind you both that family is everything to us. With family, we will get through all of life's trials and triumphs TOGETHER! Our family was built on that very concept, and it is a theme that will continue for many generations. Thank you for setting an example of love and commitment to one another and our entire family. We are ONE, and we are BLESSED! We love you both so much, and we are here to love and support you through whatever is in store for us. With the love of a family, anything and all things are possible. Thank you for instilling these values in us. We love you. XOXO"

Love Antonia & John, Clare, and Mia

I end this very nostalgic chapter with my final insights about family. Yes, there comes a time when we know everything, and our parents are rather slow and ignorant. It usually occurs in mid- to late-teen years, but fortunately, it is not a fatal disease.

As mentioned earlier, a family is a team sport. It requires cooperation—and sometimes it's only semi-cooperation—to work successfully. Could there be an institution that is more important than family? Immediate family is the fundamental unit of all humanity. It is so important to remember that family is the single most crucial support system. It ultimately contributes to your freedom, happiness, and success.

I sincerely believe that you should always depart one's loved ones, whether by phone, email, or in-person, with a hug and an expression of love. Remember, a hug and a kiss are free; they require no batteries, are fully returnable, reduce stress, and generates blissful togetherness. It is important to remember that it could be the very last time you will ever see or speak to them. It is our sacred family ritual—whether in person or not, we always conclude with I love you!

"A friend is a person with whom I may be sincere. Before him I may think aloud."

—*Ralph Waldo Emerson*

THE CHAOS KIDS

Welded together in both fame and chaos, Billy, Jacob, and I made up "The Terrifying Preschool Triumvirate." We received accolades of praise after picking a bouquet of our neighbor's irises and presenting them to our mothers, our idea of atonement for our sinful shenanigans. But most of the time, we were "Hell on Wheels" or "The Chaos Kids," as described by some of our elderly neighbors. Even as an adult, I still look down embarrassingly at my feet when my mother recounts some of our more infamous tales.

I remember playing pirates with long sharp sticks, thinking we were indestructible. We fabricated eye patches, a fake peg leg, and an arm hook. We learned the term *en garde* and felt compelled to fight competitively until victory was achieved. Indeed, a miracle that even with our constant flailing, we never severely injured ourselves, or, God forbid, lost an eyeball as predicted by adult onlookers.

Our backyard neighbor, a recent dental school graduate, lived with his sickly mother. He was continually hollering at us not to use his backyard as a quick path to the small grocery store at the corner of his street for fear that we'd create a trail. I was known to frequent the store for five cents' worth of baloney, which worked out to be about four to five thin slices—just enough to make sandwiches for lunch.

One day we discovered that the dentist was having a white picket fence installed between our backyards. The triumvirate put their heads together and decided to retaliate by burning down the new fence. We collected paper and bits of wood, found some long stick matches, and watched with glee as the smoke billowed. Fortunately, my mother saw the smoke and extinguished it. She forced me to apologize to the neighbor and made sure he remained as our family dentist.

Years later, I realized that he never gave me Novocain.

To this very day, I find myself unconsciously stiffening and anxiously grabbing the armrests each time I'm in the dental chair. I still remember the forlorn and excruciating pain experienced while drilling my cavernous cavities without the use of Novocain! I faintly remember hearing his admonition, "Eating candy causes cavities."

Ironically, Jacob entered the seminary many years later and became a priest. Eventually, I lost contact with him. Billy and I renewed our friendship, and he and his wife came to visit us in 2015. I reminded Billy about the fence and fire. While our wives laughed in horror, we reminisced about our past foibles. Conversely, we recalled our most loving kindergarten teacher, Mrs. Mason, our daily naps, and chocolate milk.

Friends like Billy and Jacob are those who radiate warmth, trust, understanding, unconditional acceptance, and have the listening ears of an elephant. They accept you for what you are and allow you to be yourself, even during the most difficult times. Friends recognize your strengths, and they know your vulnerabilities. Humor, fun, even momentary craziness are allowed and reciprocated. Empathy and honesty are shown by action, not always by words. They are indeed, as Emerson suggested, a friend is one before whom I think aloud.

Friends can sometimes say or do hurtful things, but they are tolerated, especially when apologies are forthcoming. We all know that relationships are imperfect; thus, tolerance, understanding, and acceptance should be understood. Often unwritten and unvoiced, the permanence of such a relationship withstands periodic tsunamis. These turbulent tides will, without warning, show up and temporarily sweep you off your personal shores.

THE MAGIC OF FRIENDS

Friendships start with a smile, grows with hugs, and ends with tears. Good friends are hard to find, harder to leave, and impossible to forget!

Friends are the additional siblings that our mother forgot to give us.

Perhaps the most significant balance between sharing and receiving is this resulting beautiful relationship. Friendships develop maturity, sensitivity, empathy, self-awareness, confidence, honesty, sharing, intellectual stimulation, and most notably, good health.

Best friends are your comrades in arms, your confidants, and your confessors. Your friends are one of your most valuable gems, brighter than a star, strong as a diamond, wear the wings of an angel, and fit as comfortable as an easy chair. Best friends are like spring after a turbulent winter or sweetness after a series of bitter experiences.

Initially, good friends do not magically arrive at your doorstep like a lost puppy. They are carefully hand-picked by you or by them, knowing that what is waiting is the beginning of an electrical and inspiring relationship. As your friendship grows, it develops deep roots. Each of you soon recognizes the needs and wants of the other. And yes, when in need, a good friend will magically call or arrive at your doorstep.

Each time you make new friends, you benefit from their knowledge and wisdom. Besides, a new set of eyes and ears can provide you with valuable feedback. True friendship allows you adequate distance, and intimate friends withhold the damage of negative value judgments. Paradoxically, this distance-yet-closeness begets personal freedom. With an acknowledging smile, a sincere handshake, a meaningful hug, and a friendly wink, the close connections tighten, allowing honest sharing, thus magnifying happiness while dissolving loneliness. They offer the prevailing affection, love, and counsel in the absence of family.

Friends bring with them not only joy but intangible gifts. They keep their word, ameliorate our excesses, share, and listen. They are open and willing and honest and provide constructive feedback. They help you become a better person. Their approval and cheery words are music to your ears, and there are few problems that you cannot solve together. Good friends voluntarily give and receive willingly, without ever sending a bill, keeping a tab, or expecting compensation. True friends will respect your political, social, religious, and philosophical differences. Not only do they bring out the best in you, but they also relieve your stress and reduce your burdens. One of the finest benefits of true friends is their willingness to tell you things others are embarrassed or fearful to share.

Friends provide us with the human contact, trust, and support necessary for our sustenance. We need friends to share our private thoughts, listen and maintain confidentiality, understand us, give honest feedback, and provide counsel. Of utmost importance is that friends are there when we need them because they are an additional lifeline. On the other hand, sociologists, psychologists, and criminologists recognize that loners are at high risk for poor health, depression, suicide, or homicide.

So, how does one win friends? To gain friends, you need to reach out and be a friend! If you can provide support by listening, understanding, sharing, and developing trust, you will ensure that others will reciprocate in due time.

Making friends seems rather complicated at first, but with observation, learning, and experience, it can become second nature. Smiling and greeting others with a glint of enthusiasm and sincere interest is difficult to beat. Being fair, honest, open, humble, and able to praise others are excellent appetizers to friendship. Sincerely looking for the best in others and displaying it always gets positive results. Accepting people for who they are regardless of their exterior, social class, or position is essential. Focus on their interests and avoid boring them with excessive details about yourself. Make others feel important by remembering their names and some of the things they have shared with you. Don't be standoffish, but instead warmly recognize and acknowledge them when the next opportunity presents itself. As you get to know each other, remember that a good sense of humor can cement your bonding.

It is important to remember that the foundation of all trusting relationships is to be yourself. As your comfort level feels more secure, you will be able to share your innermost feelings, fears, concerns, and insecurities, as well as your desires, goals, and most pleasant memories. If expressed with genuine sincerity, gentleness, and trust, your friendship will grow exponentially. Keeping friends requires not only treating them with respect and kindness but also maintaining self-control, confidentiality, and gentility.

Being a good friend requires that you like and appreciate yourself. Censor your critical comments of yourself and others to avoid becoming a beacon of ongoing complaints and disappointments. Yes, please share, but excess in any form is ultimately fatal. A balanced relationship avoids excessive negativity, or conversely, excessive superlatives.

Friends are like a new California home that develops cracks caused by tremors and intermittent jolts. Friendships incur the same kinds of jolts as time wears on. Conflicts and minor battles are inevitable. Picking your battles eventually helps win the war. Some people who come into your life are indeed true blessings, and others merely become life's lessons. During these tumultuous times, you will be able to determine if your current relationship is going to become a genuine friendship or not. Usually, the difference between true friends and false impostors is tested by adversity. The true friend remains staunch and unshakable during crises. False friends become shaken and quickly find escape routes.

Ultimately, after observing and getting to know someone, you may discover their shortcomings—or even worse, their toxicity, compelling you to make a tough decision. Diplomacy, kindness, and thoughtfulness will be needed during those transformative moments.

Maintaining friendships can sometimes be difficult, especially if patience, empathy, and understanding are not your virtues. You must maintain contact, even if many miles separate you. All relationships need continuity and renewal. Being sensitive during trying times—whether they are your dark days or theirs—keeps friendships afloat. There will always be crises such as illnesses, political calamities, aging, recessions, hormone imbalances, financial woes, and unexpected deaths. It is during those times that your friendships may be tested. Stop, think, and carefully watch your words during those distressing periods. Sometimes sincere heartfelt apologies are necessary.

Even the best of relationships do not bring together two perfect people. Each must learn to live with each other's imperfections. However, if you focus on their shortcomings, you will especially have difficulty rallying and admiring their wonderful attributes and accomplishments. Remaining forever cheerful is not always possible, but being frequently grouchy, such as the Sesame Street character named Oscar, does not promote friendship longevity. Besides Oscar, who enjoys unhappy people?

Learning to forgive each other is necessary, but repeated episodes of discontent and lack of appreciation can make enemies of friends. True friendship is always the union of two individuals willing to forgive each other. One must understand that you can assist in making friends or making enemies. The choice is yours.

THE DARKER SIDE OF FRIENDSHIP

All relationships, particularly the most intimate ones, will experience obstacles and bumps along the way. Each can damage or even destroy a beautiful friendship. You are bound to experience most of these down cycles. They include such things as major disagreements, especially political or religious, hitting below the belt with hurtful comments, insinuations, or accusations. Also, hurt feelings due to neglect, unkind and mindless mistakes, lopsided jabs at known vulnerabilities, and insatiable demands. Sometimes the bumps might be overuse of another's time or resources, fair-weather friending, rigid rules or narrow-mindedness, the need always to be right, or maintaining a game of one-upmanship. Still further, conflicts can be a result of repetitive suggestions on how *you* should change *your* behavior, unending reminders, traditional backseat driving, and bullying. The list goes on and on! Pay attention; it may save your friendship or end it.

My wife and I were friends with another couple. They lived close, so it was easy to get together. After spending many hours with each other, Clare and I began to feel disenchanted with each visit. The husband had a great sense of humor and was a happy-go-lucky guy. He worked for me for over three years, and we enjoyed many hilarious Laurel & Hardy moments. He was a supreme joy to be around. On the other hand, his wife was argumentative, a know-it-all, contrary, arrogant, and quite frankly toxic. She needed to be right, and with her shrill and strident voice would take charge of any conversation. Her need to control—regardless of subject—often caused us to capitulate only to her assaultive language. Eventually, Clare and I had to make a decision; do we fish or cut bait? Fortunately, our timing was perfect. We were able to move to a new house several miles away. It was easy to go our separate ways and find new neighbors and friends in our new abode.

I am forever grateful for Billy and Jacob. They set the foundation for my personal initiation and experimental course on developing true friendships and the reminder that a good friend is a grand gift. We are so lucky to have these wonderful gifts. They epitomized the beautiful definitions and expressions of true friendship.

MOTHER TERESA'S GUIDE TO LIVING

Perhaps the most famous humanitarian of the past half-century is Mother Teresa. She remains one of my greatest heroes and a model of remarkable altruism. She was born in Macedonia to a very wealthy family. Mother Teresa grew up observing the immense discrepancy between her family's wealth and the majority of her people. As a result, she later dedicated herself to the vows of charity and poverty. Mother Teresa won the Nobel peace prize in 1979. She was nominated and canonized a Catholic saint by Pope Francis as Saint Teresa of Calcutta. She has become the pinnacle of inspiration and hope. After sharing her life in hospices and caring for the sick and dying, this remarkable lady shared her cogent guide on living. It is with great pleasure that a paraphrase of the sign on the wall at the children's home in Calcutta be shared:

ANYWAY

"People can be illogical, unreasonable, and self-centered. Love and trust them anyway!

If you do good, people may accuse you of having selfish, ulterior motives. Do good anyway!

If you are successful, you will also win some false friends and true enemies. Succeed anyway!

The good you do today will be forgotten tomorrow. Do good anyway!

Honesty and frankness make you vulnerable. Be honest and frank anyway!

The biggest man with the biggest ideas can be shot down by the smallest man with the smallest mind. Think big!

People favor underdogs, but they follow only top dogs. Fight for underdogs anyway!

What you spend years building may be destroyed overnight. Build anyway!

People really need help but may attack if you do help them. Help people anyway!

Give the world the best you have, and you may get kicked in the teeth. Give the world the best you have anyway!"

from The Paradoxical Commandments,
Dr. Kent M. Keith

"We all participate in weaving the social fabric; we should, therefore all participate in patching the fabric when it develops holes."
—Anne C. Weisberg

THE GOLDEN RULE

As a youngster attending St. Ambrose Catholic School, I first learned the term, Golden Rule. My teachers, parents, and relatives had frequently reminded me to always think about my actions and their effects on others. Perhaps the term Golden Rule wasn't voiced, but the idea was clearly conveyed. Dad was sometimes off with the military, leaving me to set the mature example for my younger brothers. Especially since I was the eldest brother, it was essential that I take responsibility for myself. It took until third grade for my dad to etch this maxim into my thick skull.

Picking on my brother, Billy, was both a time-filler as well as sport.

One day while we played hide-and-go-seek, he found a large green Army trunk in which to hide.

I discovered where he was hiding. I sneaked up and pressed the large brass lock shut.

He started yelling and slamming the inside of the trunk.

I tried to open it, but it was locked shut. Quickly, I called for Mom. She ran across the street and down to the mechanic at the corner garage. He came running with some tools and was quickly able to unhinge the large lock.

When my dad came home that night, my mother immediately shared the trunk story.

My father promptly took me by the arm and led me to the trunk. He put me inside and closed the trunk. It didn't take long to become frightened and horrified to be in a confined solitary space with limited movement and air. When my dad determined that the lesson was learned, he unlocked the trunk.

At that moment, I began to feel sincere empathy and the consequences of my impulsive actions.

It took many years for me to truly grasp *Do unto others as you would have them do unto you*, but this was a harsh initiation to connecting those dots. Now, I am a vociferous proponent in advocating, sometimes preaching, that all relationships demand equanimity. My Golden Rule is, *All matters must result in a fair and equal win-win compromise. No one should ever walk away as a loser!*

Since time immemorial, all cultures developed their own moral code. For simplicity's sake, I'll call it a religious creed. My first-grade nun at St Ambrose said that the very first creed ever recorded was called the Golden Rule. It very simply stated, "Do unto others as you would have them do unto you." Basically, treat others the way you would like to be treated. My teacher said that if everyone followed that rule, we could all live forever in harmonious peace. I sincerely believe she was right.

However, time passed, populations exploded, and organizations expanded. The Golden Rule became more confusing and less pious. For example, additions were applied, such as an eye for an eye, a tooth for a tooth. While taking a college class, I soon discovered the reasons why. There is a sociological truism, The longer an organization exists, the further it gets from its original purpose. Humanity can be kind and gentle, but also capable of being evil. This certainly applies to religions, politics, social orders, economies, ideologies, and forms of government. Thus conflicting negative additions and deletions were tagged onto rather simple and appropriate aphorisms, like the Golden Rule or Ten Commandments. Instead of relying on a simple moral code, you could now be considered an outsider, non-believer, or critic. If so, you might be excluded, imprisoned, beaten, stoned, or even killed. As you mature, you will need to make many important decisions. What will be your ethical and moral code of conduct? Will it be the Golden Rule and follow the Judeo-Christian's Ten Commandments, or will you seek another consistent set of standards. You might be inspired by an Eastern religion or philosophy or whatever you choose. Your choice of creed, personal ideology, guiding rules, values, and actions will depend on you. Once chosen, your moral compass will guide you and provide you with not only direction but profound philosophy of life. Woven throughout this book, you will discover many opportunities to clarify, set, and fine-tune your moral compass.

THE
MEANING
OF LIFE

KICKSTART TO MOMENTUM

Not many years ago, my wife and I traveled to the Far East. Besides seeing many large cities, we visited various outlying areas where people lived a Spartan existence. On one occasion, we were transported by bus to a smaller town for an authentic homemade meal. After disembarking the bus, we began walking to an area where we would catch a rickshaw. It would take us to a private residence for a personal taste of local food and culture. On our walk, we were immediately accosted by peddlers trying to sell their wares. One fellow zoomed in on us; he had a package of various-sized silk bags. He was very respectful but was noticeably anxious to make a sale.

We politely declined, thanked him, and resumed walking with our group. He politely rejoined us again, gesticulating and cajoling us along the entire walk to the rickshaw. We continued listening to his riveting requests and responded with polite refusals. The bags that initially began at an exorbitant price, about $100, was slowly shrinking.

Seeking an opportunity to terminate our insistent salesman, I said, "I'll give you $10."

He shook his head and continued his spiel.

We still respectfully refused. We did not need the bags other than to buy more unnecessary things to carry home. We climbed into our rickshaw, and off we sped.

About five minutes into the trip, I looked over my shoulder, and to my amazement, there was the same man, now riding an old beat-up bicycle.

He continued gesticulating with his bike filled with his wares. He went on and on and in a friendly but persistent manner, now starting at $50 ... then $40 ... soon $30, and finally $20.

As we exited the rickshaw and approached the house, he said, "Okay, $10, okay, okay $10, okay."

We were overwhelmed and in complete surprise at his salesmanship and willingness to complete a sale. As an added reward for his persistence and determination, we added a few extra dollars. The hungry and highly motivated salesman left, entirely satisfied, smiling, and whistling as he drove his dilapidated bike away.

In all of my 78 years, I have never experienced a higher level of both drive and determination. He was indeed the epitome of motivation!

Without the fuel of motivation, your journey stands still. Discipline, preparation, confidence, hard work, and perseverance, coupled with the fires of incentive, are the perfect formula for personal success. If you have a personal incentive, namely, an internal one, it is the basic definition of motivation. A belief in oneself sprinkled with enthusiasm will ignite your internal fires. Of course, you need a purpose for your impetus. For instance, if your target is a scrumptious meal, then an appetite and spices are your metaphorical fuel. Or, if your goal is a delicious loaf of bread, the metaphorical yeast (motivator) allows it to rise. Being sated, too comfortable, or fearful are the three biggest obstacles that will cause you to miss your meal. Likewise, the most important ingredient in the pursuit of happiness is a persistent internal struggle to compete with yourself, the real yeast of a fulfilling life. Motivation kick-starts you, but the momentum of your internal competitiveness keeps you on target.

For example, researchers have found that personal and work-related satisfaction are far more intrinsically rewarding to those very high achievers than money or external gratification. For many, monetary rewards are motivators, but the Warren Buffets and Bill Gates of the world are just as happy and prosperous without them. They both have pledged almost all of their earthly possessions to helping others and improving the world. I applaud and admire them immensely for their altruism, but also because in the process, they have expressed personal happiness and satisfaction.

Personal satisfaction remains the cornerstone and prime motivator of your success and happiness.

Retrospectively, it is my conviction that everyone develops their own unique personal motivators. There is no doubt that parents, relatives, teachers, and neighbors provide the initial stimulus, guidance, and direction. Having special people believing in you because they "knew you could" is the spark that eventually starts your engines while building your confidence.

In my case, there were many supporting actors and actresses. First and foremost was my mother, Mary, who was indefatigably energetic and invariably supportive, even when it was not earned. My grandmother was the most accepting person I have ever known. Her unrelenting and unconditional love, kindness, and support were forever forthcoming. She has always conveyed the message, "You will be a blessing to this world. Godda bless!" My father knew that if I wanted something, I would be willing to work for it. He knew earning things was far superior to magic. He always fortified my motivation with a carrot, not dissimilar to a horseman who puts a carrot on the end of a long stick, just barely out of the reach of the horse's mouth. The cast of supporting characters goes on and on, including my wife, uncles, aunts, cousins, teachers, mentors, etc. It does take a village!

Fortunately, I had many awakeners as well as ongoing stressors to keep me motivated and on task.

Another interesting source of motivation is the naysayers. The more I was told I couldn't, shouldn't, can't, the more determined I became. However, if I didn't have the constant support from my mom, the carrot from my dad, or grandma's constant confidence boosts, my level of desire would have been marginal. There is a great deal to be said about the doubters. In looking back, the supportive forces overwhelmed the naysayers, but paradoxically they both combined to provide me with supercharged fuel.

Like me, you will find boulders and obstacles that provide renewed motivational fuel on your journey. Motivation gets you going, but naysayer bumps become your supercharged fuel along your way.

Don't be afraid to question the motives of others. Sometimes their motives are competitive and envious, which can provide you more of an incentive. Sometimes, even more than your best supporters. Remember, your supporters fill your tank with confidence and trust. Like a savings account in which you regularly make deposits and build up a cash reserve, your supporters regularly fill you with the confidence needed to overcome adversity. Use your supporters' deposits to overcome obstacles. You will learn that those whose motives are cooperation and win-win solutions are your real friends and supporters. Put your trust behind them, and let your ambition lead the way.

MOTIVATION - PERSONAL GLIMPSES

Often, I envied my brother's ability to take things apart and meticulously put them back together. I was great at taking things apart, but seldom able to put them back together. I was frequently reminded of my unfinished work. Often, when my mom asked me to fix something, it would remain broken. Billy would come along, rescue the item, and magically make it work.

When I was in high school, I needed to save money for college, so I desperately put away as much as I could. My Uncle John, a skilled WWII airplane mechanic, was now a very competent lift truck mechanic. He took me under his tutelage and convinced me that I could learn mechanics.

Uncle John not only tapped into my motivation to save money, but also sensed my lacking confidence in mechanical things—a subject I had failed miserably.

From that day forward, my attitude changed dramatically. It is funny how epiphanies occur and how motivation springs from the strangest of events. For years I had resented my lack of mechanical ability and believed it could never be developed. But a combination of my hunger for savings and a wonderful uncle's willingness to take me in his stead sparked many memorable moments. It became yet another iconic epiphany.

The skills I learned from Uncle John started with taking apart my 1954 Ford engine, rebuilding it, and then putting it back together. He also taught me how to maintain my car in pristine condition at a fraction of the typical costs. That car not only ran well but lasted through my college years. Thank you, Uncle John.

OPPORTUNITY

Skeptics and naysayers suggest that opportunities are few and far between. My solid belief is that opportunities arrive each day. Like my youth, you have lots of energy and motivation to find opportunities. Currently, the most successful here in Silicon Valley have been the young 20- to 30-year-olds. They have achieved phenomenal success by their creative drive, focus, and willingness to take on a challenge. They were indeed motivated. Many, although financially wealthy, share their wealth with nonprofits, education, and the search for cures for debilitating diseases. I am very proud to say that this new generation of technical giants and entrepreneurs have transcended their predecessors' stereotypes. Not only have they found high-tech discoveries that have transformed the world, but they have also given back to the world benefits seldom bestowed by any previous nouveau riche. Probably the single most critical attribute of these opportunists is an "I can" attitude.

You will find that one of the fascinating parts of studying human nature is that life is a series of paradoxes. For example, most people see problems as major obstacles. However, problems are simply opportunities in a disguised costume. Of course, solving problems involves time, energy, and hard work. The great inventors, thinkers, explorers, and academic heroes all realized that hard work was involved. Most recognized the risks but had little concern about them. Instead, they decided to take on the challenge by not fishing in the safe harbor, but venturing out to fish with the sharks. Venture out, dare to challenge yourself, and I'll provide the carrot; you provide the motivation.

The successful can turn problems into personal opportunities by taking advantage of their talents while developing new skills in the process. Unused talents provide little to those who fail to see the face of opportunity. You must understand that fear is a significant source of lost opportunity. The successful do not fear risk as an obstacle standing in their way. Instead, they see it as a catalyst for a supreme opportunity.

Don't be afraid. Go for it!

Many modern ads and articles point out that we enjoy classical music from a very famous composer who was deaf, or contemporary piano music by a blind man. A famous woman, Helen Keller, became an incredible success and contributed to humanity, even though she was unable to speak, hear, or see. If you allow yourself to be hoodwinked by fear, stopped or diminished by an "I can't" attitude, your potential will lie dormant. You can be assured that someone else with less skill and ability will act on that same opportunity and find the required solution.

If you are fortunate to have all of your senses, keep your eyes open, your ears focused, your spirits high, and your appetite hungry with peak motivation. If you keep your mind open, an opportunity will knock at your door daily.

Remember, people with far fewer physical attributes have run marathons, climbed mountains, and like President FDR, led men and women through the gruels of wars. There are many stories of individuals who have been able to turn lemons into lemonade. Those who have turned their handicaps into assets have made the world a better and safer place.

Opportunities exist.

Opportunities will always exist.

Having confidence and an "I can" attitude can conquer all.

Every significant discovery made was once considered an impossible obstacle. Hordes of great minds could not fathom the possibilities of a newfangled device. They prematurely denounced it. Only those who had the foresight, confidence, and creativity could see a unique opportunity beyond the puzzling challenge. You, like the gifted pioneers, can bring to the world a revolutionary discovery.

Remember, I will always have your back. Keep your mind and eyes open, never give up hope, maintain your resolve, and rise above the naysayers that rattle your cage.

"Forgiveness is the way to true health and happiness."
—Gerald Jampolsky

THE PATH TO TRUE HAPPINESS

Forgiveness is a tool that will not only save you thousands of hours of pain and suffering but will also bring you peace and happiness. Such a simple word as forgiveness gives way to a far more complex understanding of anger, fear, listening, ego, criticism, impatience, and the need to let go. Each of these items is a flashpoint and tool discussed in other chapters. However, dismissing the pressure that weighs on your mind is neither easy nor simple.

When I was about nine years old, I remember walking on the sidewalk up Longview Terrace. I was somewhat overweight and wearing husky clothes. I can't say that I felt particularly big and strong. Except for make-believe fighting with Billy and Jacob, I never learned to be particularly aggressive. At that time of my life, my confidence level was mediocre at best. As I proceeded to walk, I felt alone and somewhat fearful. Soon, I saw another boy on the other side of the street walking in my direction. To this day, I don't know what caused him to cross the street and start calling me names. However, I do remember cowering as he approached. I didn't recall seeing him around our neighborhood. He approached me, calling me a sissy, and then began pushing me. He grabbed me by the neck and threw me to the ground.

I didn't fight back.

After he knew he had shown his dominance, he walked away. I never forgot his angry look or face. He was bigger than me but not much older. From that day forward, his face became fixated in my mind. I dusted myself off and made a personal pledge. Having been so humiliated, I promised myself that I would pay him back until he cried. Many months passed, my waistline shrunk, my fat turned to muscle, my confidence grew, and I was ready. Every day while walking or riding my bike I would look for him. I was going to give him the beating of his life. For over two years, I was ready and convinced that the vendetta would finally be put to rest.

The day came.

There he was, coming toward me. I was ready and eager for revenge.

I prepared myself, ready to launch—then I stopped, regained my composure, and said, "I've been waiting for two years for this moment. You probably don't remember me. We encountered each other a few years ago. I've wanted to pay you back so bad I could taste it".

At that moment, all I could see was a wimpy kid, not the big bully I imagined.

I said, "I can kick your ass, but after seeing you, I have decided to forget it. Get your ass out of here, and I'll go my way. But if I ever see you bullying somebody else, I won't walk away."

I stood my ground.

I forgave.

No one would ever again intimidate me.

It was my very first memory of forgiveness.

Let me first share some background information. Humanity is bounded by numerous mistakes of judgment, especially in relationships of the heart. To gain peace and happiness, we must come to grips with our imperfections and ultimately admit our wrongdoings. We often need to swallow our pride. It's been said that no one in the history of humankind has ever choked to death by swallowing their pride. Since time immemorial, a person's ego has been his salvation, as well as their demise. Most of us are unable to learn that cleansing one's mind is not primarily for the one scorched, but even more for the scorcher. It is one of life's most precious teaching moments because it allows you to move on rather than to remain stuck!

And as a psychiatrist Gerald Jampolsky said, "Forgiveness allows us to release the past and let go of our fears of the future." It truly is the way to true health and happiness.

It's important to remember that the past is unchangeable and irreversible; however, forgiving offers you multiple benefits. It releases the burdens you carry each day, it clears your mind, strengthens your resolve, rests the soul by substituting peace, heals the wound, and extinguishes the ongoing anger of a cold war. Most of all, it rekindles kindness, love, and happiness.

Some of us fear that absolving others is a form of weakness, yet in reality, it is a genuine form of implacable strength. Sipping good wine is a personal passion. I recall the phrase, "Sour grapes make a lousy wine." Likewise, a sour, unrepentant attitude makes for poor bedfellows.

In an interesting and eye-opening article cited in "Bits and Pieces" from the After Hours Inspirational Stories website, a metaphor on forgiveness was discussed. Recounting the metaphor and putting in my own words suggested the following: Take potatoes and label each one with the name of each person who has fallen out of your good graces. Gather all the potatoes and place them in a potato sack. Keep the sack with you for one week. Take it everywhere you go. Have it with you at all times. Carrying this burden, which will eventually grow sprouts, fester, and soon develop a foul smell. It will provide you with not only a burden of weight, but a putrid stench. The constant smell is a reminder of all those who have disappointed, angered, or who have hurt you. As you will soon realize, these unpleasant memories will create ongoing anguish and unhappiness. Unburdening yourself of the heavy sack will be analogous to giving forgiveness to each person that each potato represents. This weight lifted from your shoulders will free you from the load of daily internal turmoil. Only true exoneration allows harmony and peace.

Think about it. Vengeance is far too heavy a burden for you to carry endlessly. Carrying that sack of potatoes will eventually slow you down to a standstill.

Forgiveness does not necessarily ensure that incident will be forgotten. It is important for you to remember that forgiving is a significant learning moment and needs to remain a tool in your repertoire for future reference. Yes, kudos to those able to forgive without remembering, but also laudatory are those who can give or receive absolution without forgetting. Yet, even worse are those who magnify and preserve their betrayals, treachery, and perfidies, while maintaining a vendetta for reprisal. An eye for an eye never buries the original problem. It only exacerbates blindness!

Above all, we must first learn to forgive ourselves because unless we do, we will succumb to the same burdens and vices of the unforgiving. By letting go, it relinquishes the past, and it gets you into the illuminated present. Tears of forgiveness can fill a pond of peace, harmony, and goodwill.

A person I found most inspirational about the process of apologizing was Dr. Randy Pausch, author of the powerful book "The Last Lecture." It's a small book that I unequivocally recommend reading. Dr. Pausch says:

"Apologies are not pass/fail. I always told my students: when giving an apology, any performance lower than an 'A' really doesn't cut it. Half-hearted or insincere apologies are often worse than not apologizing at all because recipients find them insulting. If you've done something wrong in your dealings with another person, it's as if there is an infection in your relationship. A good apology is like an antibiotic; a bad apology is like rubbing salt in the wound. Proper apologies have three parts: What I did was wrong; I feel badly that I have hurt you; how do I make this better?" Please take heed; forgiveness is a tool that will free you of the heavy burden and expedite your journey!

"Holding on is believing that there is only a past; letting go is knowing that there is a future."

—*Daphne Rose Kingma*

FREEDOM FROM GRIEF

My very first thought about letting go immediately centered around the loss of my beloved brother.

When Billy died unexpectedly, I suffered through varying degrees of depression for three years. My brother certainly didn't want me to experience pain and sorrow. He would have preferred to be remembered as a loving legacy as I, in turn, enjoyed the remainder of my life. It took me those three years to let go of the guilt and sadness that overwhelmed me. Although those shackles are gone, I regularly reflect on my deep feelings and memories of our life together. Releasing yourself from the pain of grief is difficult.

My brother knew he was loved deeply, and my regrets have faded.

Instead, he would be saying, *Remove all the ancient and rusty shackles of depression you carried with you after my death. Please find freedom from grief and bondage and instead enjoy your remaining years knowing I will always be with you and will never stop loving you. I remain in your heart forever.*

One of the most crippling human emotions is one's inability to let go. Hanging on or hindering the unleashing of things longer than needed leads to unhappiness, depression, or even suicide. When letting go, you will go through depressive episodes, become angry, and often lonely. If you handle it empathetically, you will accept the consequences, often with an attitude of self-discovery and willingness to move on.

The impermanence of life guarantees there will be a loss—the loss of relationships, possessions, pets, and loved ones.

Eckhart Tolle sums it up quickly, "The mind is a superb instrument if used rightly. Used wrongly, however, it can become very destructive."

Giving up on the past and letting go is painful. However, the present is all you have, and actually all you will ever have.

Be present in all that you do because the past is a canceled check, while the present is the cash currently in your hands. Use your currency wisely. Spend it now, savor it, because it too will eventually disappear.

The death of a loved one, especially a spouse, parent, child, or sibling, requires substantial time to understand, assimilate, and adjust. Detaching from a job, friend, or short- term relationship is somewhat easier to overcome. Although time is required to soothe and assimilate a loss, eventually letting go allows for positive mental and physical health.

Liberating yourself from things can also become problematic. Whether they are articles, cash, real estate, or securities, your attachment to possessions can be obsessive. Greed and excessive control can become toxic due to power and ego needs. They can motivate you to acquire and control possessions, or even worse, to control other people. Your rationale for over-attachment may be your insecurity.

Regardless of the motivation, over-attachment to things can become as much a disease as an inveterate collector of woodcarvings, antique furniture, and cars. I, the obsessed collector, know the potential for problems.

Letting go has been tough for me.

After many years, it has finally become a welcome relief. Planning for disposal, giving away possessions, or donating have resulted in renewed peace of mind, balance, and contentment.

My wife's grandfather Pasquale, who possessed old-world Italian wisdom, frequently commented to his wife, "Rosie, what are we going to do, save it for the rats?"

For years I had avoided unfettering my obsessive collecting, but those simple words regularly resonated in my ears. Eventually, they led to another of my many epiphanies. Saving and recycling items for this book to create a guide for others serves better than collecting dust.

Letting go involves the ability to stop arguing with yourself, whether due to anger, depression, or fear of reprisal. The need to win or be right is admirable, but only if it results in a win-win conclusion. Unburdening your shackles also includes the need to be in control. Your ego will not allow you to be wrong or lose control, even if it means losing a close relationship. Once again, the inability to let go can result in pain and turmoil. Indeed, those with a need to control people, situations, events, colleagues, conversations, driving, and games will spend their lives in isolation and despair. The only true control you have is self-control.

Instead, you will bring balance, peace, and harmony to your life by going with the flow.

LETTING GO OF LOVE

I'll now share my most intimate thoughts with you, both from my heart and my personal experiences. Sometimes the most challenging part of love is letting go. Developing love and respect for another person often begins as a budding relationship in an attempt to determine mutual interests, comfort levels, compatibility, flexibility, commitment, and trust. Ultimately, real intimacy is achieved. Sometimes relationships take off and grow like plants in a fertile garden. Other times, relationships wither and slowly die. All forms of love need room to breathe and space to grow. When it becomes clear that you need space and breathing room, decisions should be mutually understood and decisive. Providing personal space by unlocking a relationship is usually tricky.

My early childhood encounters included the loss of my first dog, Blackie, later the suicide death of a second-grade friend, and several moves to new houses that included letting go of friends, school, and neighborhoods. However, the move to the country allowed our family to acquire a puppy. Unfortunately, only a few months later, we lost my dog. It was hit by a speeding car when it unknowingly darted into the street. The dog, a German shepherd named King, died in my arms. That event remains agonizingly memorable. I can still remember sitting in a pile of sand sobbing a pond of tears.

About five years later, in 1959, our family moved to California at the end of my junior year in high school. It again resulted in a loss of friends, school, and a comfortable neighborhood. It, too, caused both pain and many new adjustments. Also, the loss of early girlfriends and buddies caused additional hurt and further adaptation. Yes, these were all painful, but actually they turned into precursors of what would become the most difficult of life's realities, the death of brother Billy. My beloved brother's sudden death, followed by my dad's death, was particularly distressing and gut-wrenching. Then a few years later, the death of my darling Grandma Angelina. Life has little permanency, so you must either adapt or succumb. Learning to let go became one of my most essential tools in dealing with life's lessons. Life of any kind on Mother Earth eventually expires. Like my Boy Scout motto, *be prepared*. You will need to learn to cope and adapt because there will always be unpredictable and inevitable outcomes.

Please remember, your heart must let go of what the hands long to hold.

"To be old and wise, you must first be young and stupid."
—*Author Unknown*

THE FOUNTAIN
OF KNOWLEDGE

Wisdom: the purpose of your journey.

I have spent most of my life as a serious student of the maestros of wisdom. I hoped that just a tiny bit of their sagacity might somehow rub off. I share their knowledge because their maxims have remained alive in perpetuity. The fact their wisdom lives on is the verification of both their value and validity. The profound words from the Bible, the Golden Age of Greece, the Roman Empire, the Renaissance, and throughout history remain epigrams of literary genius. The profound and penetrating words of these scholars are critical to this chapter. This chapter is relatively short, even though the wisdom included is long and deep. Please savor their witty remarks. Consider them intellectual nourishment tools to ponder along your long journey.

Some 3400 years ago, The Oracle of Delphi was the most important venue in all of ancient Greece. Surrounded by a sacred spring, Delphi was considered the center of the world. It was *the* font of all erudition.

It was here that the classic Greek writers of the Golden Era of Greece began their saga of philosophical enlightenment. They included Aristotle, Diogenes, Euripides, Ovid, Plato, Plutarch, Sophocles, and others. Those undisputed and infallible Oracles of Delphi served the Greeks for 1800 years, from 1400 B.C. until 400 A.D. Except for the Old Testament, it all began in Delphi.

By reducing the complex into simple terms, real enlightenment blossoms.

A short sentence can sum up a complex concept, resulting in a priceless message or lesson. Obtaining wisdom is similar to a chemist constructing a new compound. Use your scientific tools by combining your attention, recognition, assimilation, experiences, and mistakes to create the final distillation: YOUR WISDOM!

Uncovering and discovering the hidden golden words of icons ignites enlightenment—the final step to intellectual maturity. A single quotation can become a powerful declarative statement. It has the impetus to convey a momentous epiphany. Carefully watch and listen—and birth wisdom! The examples of "savvy sagacity" are sprinkled below:

2,700 YEARS OF "OLD WORLD" WISDOM THE FIRST 700 YEARS

The wise can capitalize by connecting all the dots. All learning is interconnected and can lead to wisdom. The wisest of all are those able to borrow from other disciplines, experiences, knowledge, and prior understanding. It is the product of distilling complex interconnected elements into their simplest forms, resulting in a brief, compelling, and profound message. Here are some selected examples:

> *"Better are loaves when the heart is joyous, than riches in unhappiness."*
> —*Amenemope (c.1000 B.C.)*

> *"The oldest, shortest words—"yes" and "no"—are those which require the most thought."*
> —*Pythagoras (c580-500 B.C.)*

> *"The greatest griefs are those we cause ourselves."*
> —*Sophocles (c496-406 B.C.)*

> *"Waste not fresh tears over old griefs."*
> —*Euripides (c480-406 B.C.)*

> *"Know thyself."*
> —*Plato (c427-347B.C.)*

> *"Learn to be silent. Let your quiet mind, listen, and absorb."*
> —*Pythagoras*

PLATINUM PLATITUDES

Over the years, I have saved various quotes in a file I call *My Platinum Platitudes*. Each of these quotes has added special meaning to different parts of my life. I want to share some of them with you as they were originally conceived:

"A scholar knows no boredom."
—*John Paul Richter*

"It is not the strongest of the species that survives, nor the most intelligent that survives. It is the one that is most adaptable to change."
—*Charles Darwin*

"The greatest tragedy in life is people who have sight but no vision."
—*Helen Keller*

"All knowledge is connected to all other knowledge. The fun is making the connections."
—*Arthur Aufderheide*

"A dog teaches a boy fidelity, perseverance, and to turn around three times before lying down."
—*Robert Benchley*

"Some people are always grumbling because roses have thorns; I am thankful that thorns have roses."
—*Alphonse Karr*

"Don't find fault. Find a remedy."
—*Henry Ford*

THE WISDOM OF HUMANITARIANS

Humankind has known many humanitarians over the ages. Some have won Nobel Prizes; others have made contributions to a more safe and sane society. All have exerted valiant efforts to make the world a better place. Most humanitarians have gone quietly about their concern for others and have not sought recognition. Through their humanitarian efforts and good example, they have unwittingly given us many gold nuggets of advice. I've selected a few worth sharing. They will hopefully inspire you and help you make a better life. They will also provide clarity and value to your journey.

"Knowledge comes but wisdom lingers."
—*Alfred, Lord Tennyson*

"Be the change you want to see in the world."
—*Arleen Lorrance (widely attributed to Mahatma Gandhi)*

"Be kind and merciful. Let no one ever come to you without coming away better and happier.
—*Mother Teresa*

POLITICAL WISDOM

We seem to be frequently in the twilight of another contentious political election and debate. Humor and satire are both the equalizers and the palliative prescriptions for most political affairs.

I have selected a few stellar quotes that might lighten the seriousness of the voting cubicle.

> *"Those who are too smart to engage in politics are punished by being governed by those who are dumber."*
>
> —*Plato*

> *"A politician is a fellow who will lay down your life for his country."*
>
> —*Tex Guinan*

> *"Instead of giving a politician the keys to the city, it might be better to change the locks."*
>
> —*Doug Larson*

> *"Politics is the gentle art of getting votes from the poor and campaign funds from the rich, by promising to protect each from the other."*
>
> —*Mark Twain*

THE WISDOM OF ERMA BOMBECK

Erma Bombeck was one of my favorite journalists and humorists. She was born in Ohio in 1927 and died at age 69 in San Francisco. Erma never failed to entertain and enlighten me. I religiously read her column and loved her homespun humor. She was scintillating, motivating, deliriously witty, and whimsical. Here's Erma:

> *"When humor goes, there goes civilization!"*

"The only reason I take up jogging is so that I could hear heavy breathing again."

"My theory on housework is, if the item doesn't multiply, smell, catch fire, or block the refrigerator door, let it be. No one else cares. Why should you?"

"It's not until you become a mother that your judgment slowly turns to compassion and understanding."

"Stop sweating the small stuff!! Don't worry about who doesn't like you, who you are, or who's doing what. Instead, let's cherish the relationships we have with those who do love us. Let's think about what God has blessed us with and what we are doing each day to promote ourselves, mentally, physically, and emotionally. Have a great day and know that someone loves you."

MY DEAR MOTHER'S MOST FAVORITE QUOTES

Mom frequently had some old adage, saw, song, or quote. I can't say it was a literal translation, but it always conveyed a meaningful thought or proverb. Here are three quotes that are the literal reproductions. As she reached her nineties, she kept reminding me that she was always trying to put smiles on sober faces and that her current job was to bring them inspiration.

"We were put on this earth for one purpose, and that is to make it a better place. We should, therefore, be contributing members of society. And if the earth, as a result of our having been on it, is a better place than it was before we came, then we have achieved our destiny."

—*General James Doolittle*

"What you are is God's gift to you. What you make of yourself is your gift to God."

—*Author Unknown*

"Aspire to inspire before you expire."

—*Anonymous*

Thanks, Mom and Dad, you remain my dearest inspirators and my greatest supporters. I never doubted your devotion and love for my family and me. You are my pillars of strength!

I love you!

A more comprehensive anthology that captures the iconic quotes from the most ardent thinkers of the past millennia entitled "THE WISDOM OF THE AGES" is available by going to https://www.drtonycedolini.com/wisdom-of-the-ages

REACHING
YOUR DREAMS

"I suppose it is tempting, if the only tool you have is a hammer, to treat everything as if it were a nail."

—*Abraham Maslow*

TOOLS NEEDED FOR EACH BEND IN THE ROAD

Young, naive, rambunctious, and high strung as I was, my mother and father had their work cut out. During those young and tender years, I remember the blunt and harsh realities of growing up. The discipline of the '40s and '50s invariably involved corporal punishment, both at home and at school. That's how the tools of life were quickly inculcated.

The tool of choice in our family was *the wooden spoon*.

In little time, the simple threat of its appearance would immediately dissuade my questionable behavior. I attempted to hide the spoon several times. The result was not pleasurable because it was soon replaced by another larger one. I must admit it did change the course of my behavior quite successfully. That tool taught me quickly to heed life's lessons. It was the initiation of preparing for my new toolbox. Soon my tools would not be the instrument of punishment, but purpose. I was now ready to navigate my future with all the things necessary for my important odyssey.

On my sojourn, I learned to carry many tools, otherwise called strategies. They are my metaphoric language for my means of assistance, like a tow truck waiting along the road. Each tool's strategy will aide you in overcoming each of life's challenges

I discovered first and foremost that if I didn't pay close attention by focusing carefully along my circuitous route, I would be forever lost. Paying close attention was my first priority. This was my very first tool: focused attention. It meant to watch out, danger might be lurking, and this time it's not a wooden spoon.

Life is a scary journey.

My new adventure was stalled and wracked by frequent mistakes. Each day I would refocus on the multiple errors caused by my naiveté. Routine adaptation was needed for the unsuspecting altitude changes, the strange bends in the road, the rivers and chasms to be crossed. All were challenging and dangerous. The first tool, focused attention, was soon followed by another tool, adaptation.

Adaptation enables forward momentum.

I was initially terrified by this new set of learning experiences that I had not been aware of or prepared to undertake. Survival was at stake. Either I stopped to pick up new strategies or succumbed to the vexations of this new terrain.

Your journey will demand that you acquire all of the necessary tools that will assist in making your trip successful. Focused attention and adaptation are your first two biggies!

This book is your toolbox, your tow truck sitting in wait.

Each chapter provides assistance and instructions to guide and secure your journey safely. Without strategies, you will not go very far. Use them wisely, and you will be guaranteed a successful voyage into the unknown. You will encounter missteps, obstacles, roadblocks, blowouts, and dead ends. You will often need to go back and review the instructions for their use. Some strategies may be inadequate for the task at hand; others will need to be adapted. As time passes, you will learn to develop and master all of the tools available to you.

Remember, the learning curve is not straight up, but has multiple ups and downs along the way.

Your available strategies will get you past the various bumps and diversions on the road. Sometimes it will feel like a momentary stop to change a tire; other times, you will feel like you're lost in a dense forest. However, having at your disposal a road map and a toolbox with instructions, you won't be lost for long.

Thus, I will be spending a significant amount of time identifying the various tools you will need to navigate the obstacle course called life. Each chapter will clarify those necessary for your journey. For example, they will include focused attention, learning, love, support systems, adaptation, coping with stress, humor, and many more. They are necessary to travel toward your personal goals successfully. Each chapter will provide ample opportunity to scroll through the various skill sets and the strategies needed. The more you have and the more often you practice and sharpen them, the better the results.

I refer not to mechanical tools but to intellectual and psychological strategies needed to achieve a rich, fulfilling life. Assess each tool and, at your discretion, determine its viability. There will be some that will not fit your particular likes, personality, or needs. You can either discard them or put them in abeyance until required. You will find that some of the more useful tactics will resolve problems; others need only be used to cope or counteract stressful situations. Assimilate them and save them in your mental toolbox. Carefully choose them in order of priority. Place your preferred tools and their associated quotes in your virtual toolbox. Visit your toolbox often to review and reacquaint yourself with them. Sharpen your memory by regularly visiting and reviewing them. Keep your tool chest open because you'll never know when you need a special tool. They are your only insurance policies necessary to enhance the quality of your life.

Finally, the most critical of all tools is learning. It is the generic mother of all your utensils. Learning involves memory; the more learning and relearning that occurs, the more you will remember which tool you will need next. It is important not to allow your mind to remain idle or wander continuously. Learn as much as you can; it will ultimately be your salvation. Not only will learning assist you in problem-solving, but it will pave the way toward facing the increased challenges you will soon face. Focus intently and avoid unnecessary distractions. Allow for new and exciting thoughts, flashes of creativity, collections of wisdom, and profound knowledge. Write or copy your most essential thoughts and associated quotes for quick reference points. Then put them in your veritable mental tool chest.

Similarly, author James Baldwin wrote, "The world is before you, and you need not take it or leave it as it was when you came in."

Likewise, I've taken it on as my mission to help you and others join forces to make this a better world. By combining your energy with others, the synergy will be magical and earth-moving. You must not pass through Mother Earth without making every attempt to leave it a better place. Thus, my original objective was to develop, sharpen, and perfect my strategies before passing them on to you. You can then further refine your selections and place them in your virtual toolbox. For me, identifying the tools was relatively easy; learning to use them was far more difficult. Even more mind-boggling was to know which one to use and when and where to use it. Organizing and filling the toolbox will be followed by utilizing them to hurdle each obstacle.

The wisdom of the great minds of the ages will provide different fits, allowing you to pick and choose the best one. I'm sure that sometimes you will feel like a safecracker trying to listen and focus on the turning dials to crack the safe. Once you open the safe, the age-old treasures will abound before you, and their words of wisdom will speak for themselves. Gather and harbor all the tools needed; enjoy your trip!

BE PREPARED
"THAT'S WHY PENCILS
HAVE ERASERS"

My first exposure to being prepared was at age seven, when Cub Scouts entered my life. I was young and naïve but determined to win my Bear, Wolf, and Lion Badges. My cub master guided our group in achieving those badges, along with the silver and gold arrows accompanying each badge. My mother diligently sewed on each award. I still remember beaming when my chest was covered with badges and arrows. I felt like the Mad Magazine cover, Alfred E. Neuman, with his iconic smug smile. Cub Scouts was mainly a precursor for the greater seriousness of being elevated to the big leagues, Boy Scouts. All of a sudden, at age ten, I was a real Boy Scout. Now, as a heavyweight, the operative words were *Be Prepared*. They were extremely important words if you were to maintain your Boy Scout status. Every solemn meeting began with "Be Prepared," with emphasis on developing citizenship, confidence, and leadership skills. Now in the big league, we always had to create a plan of action, no matter the hike, or activity. It was our calling card.

You never achieved a higher designation or merit award without preparing a successful plan of action.

By successful planning and preparation, winning and achieving will become your twin rewards. Luck, chance, or wishing will never compete with diligent forethought.

As a student and later an employee, I invariably planned for each assignment. The finished product was often completed well ahead of schedule. My final graduation into planning and preparation was in ROTC, Army officer training. There we were taught not only of its logistical significance, but that preparedness needed became the difference of life and death. Even today, my mind ruminates, *Be Prepared!*

Planning and preparation will be required tools for you to successfully navigate the many milestones of your lengthy journey. When anyone decides to take a long trip, seldom does it begin immediately. For a successful and enjoyable short sojourn or long voyage, careful plotting will be required. On the other hand, your journey, if successful, will take many decades. For you to impulsively take off without purpose is irrational and unwise. A long and tedious trip requires crystal clear purpose. You will need to be well organized and anticipate possible problems.

Clarifying your purpose needs to be preceded by careful analysis. Why am I on this journey? What sites do I want to visit? While going to school, what do I hope to accomplish? What things in my life do I want to explore? Where, when, or how will my dreams be realized? Every major and minor visit on your journey needs thought and purpose. Remember, the operative words are *Be Prepared*.

> *"By failing to prepare, you are preparing to fail."*
> —*Anonymous*

A colleague, Dr. Bob Bainbridge, modified and simplified Ben Franklin's quote to read even more succinctly: "If you fail to plan, you plan to fail."

Both quotes emphasized the same basic message: planning is crucial for successful living. Once heard, it became our family's gold standard at home and work.

All of us have witnessed impetuous and uninformed decisions that result in personal disasters. Whether you do things without thinking or do them without evaluating the circumstances of the moment, your life can turn dismal. These somewhat capricious capers can cause injury and sometimes death.

It will take you years of practice and tons of consequences to learn those critical lessons. A friend jokingly shared, "Some men only get the learning connection the hard way; by urinating on an electrical fence."

Most admissions to local hospitals or prisons are from the schools of hard knocks. Some never learn and end up in morgues. This could have been averted if careful thought preceded action. Planning prepares for action. Yes, you will make mistakes; but avoid repeating the same mistakes.

My former sixth-grade elementary teacher would say admonishingly, "That's why pencils have erasers."

All of my children regularly heard my admonition; *If you fail to plan, you plan to fail.*

It sometimes was uttered spontaneously, but usually when they hadn't planned for a test, report, or trip. They heard it so much they derisively began reminding me for my transgressions. Even with insight and careful thought, there are always potential external forces that can cause your finest plans to implode.

The following was originally written by the famous Scot poet Robert Burns in 1785, "The best-laid schemes o' mice and men Gang aft a-gley, An lea'e us nought but grief an' pain for promis'd joy."

Almost two centuries later, John Steinbeck, one of the West's foremost authors, summed Robert Burns' quote even more succinctly, "The best-laid plans of mice and men often go awry."

Yes, even thoughtful planning can go awry.

Sometimes all-powerful Mother Nature interferes; other times, it is purely serendipitous. There may have been a flaw in the plan, or perhaps there were no alternative plans. Regardless, the results end up being a sack instead of the expected touchdowns. However, do continue to prepare your plan, and then work your plan, even though you may sometimes fail to score the winning touchdown.

A PERSONAL GLIMPSE

Almost 40 years ago, after writing my book on stress, I was blatantly reminded of my own words about planning, preparation, and prevention. I had to swallow a little crow, namely, *Do as I say and not as I do.*

I had not listened to my dentist and his dental assistants, who had warned me for several years. They strongly suggested, then urged me to take better care of my teeth. They even gave me special tools and instructions on what I needed to do to prevent serious gum problems. Of course, my resistance was denial and rationalization. When I looked into the mirror, my teeth looked great. I didn't have any pain or discomfort; however, there was evidence of swelling and bleeding after brushing. Surely I didn't need to floss, Water-Pik, or use a sonic toothbrush. To me, it was a waste of time. I especially didn't have time for all those other silly things they had instructed me to do daily!

Then one day, I began to have pain in a rear molar. Each day the pain increased, and so did my bad breath. After two months of what I considered the most excruciating pain I have ever felt, I reluctantly visited my dentist. I soon swallowed all pride for not following a plan of preventative measures. They had previously implored me to follow a plan and had even given me the tools to accomplish it. My embarrassment and apologetic behavior equalized the situation. After the tooth was pulled and the pain finally gone, I carefully examined the tooth. It was a very large molar with huge roots. On the roots were very thick coats of black plaque that had built up over the years. It was like the barnacles covering the bottom of a transit ship.

After that harrowing experience, I now brush, floss, Water Pik, and then finish with my sonic toothbrush. It takes at least 20 minutes each day, but I now have a plan. In addition, I make sure that I have an ample supply of tools, both at home and when I go on trips. I now go to the dentist every three months for intense teeth cleaning, examination, and sometimes x-rays. My swollen, bloody gums and bad breath have vanished, and so has the pain. Fortunately, I still have all of my remaining teeth. According to the dental hygienist, my teeth have never looked so good. My cousin Louis, a practicing periodontist, said that inflamed gums that bleed after brushing are a red flag and early warning signs of impending periodontal disease. He also said that it is a precursor to more serious health problems and, frequently, an indication of stress. Perhaps writing the book on stress may have had some personal implications? My message to you: Please, I implore you to make every effort to prevent periodontal problems.

As my Boy Scout Pledge, *Be Prepared*—please always prepare a plan and not just to prevent periodontal problems, but to address all your activities. A tool in time will keep the doctor away!

The above is only a snippet of the consequences that occur from a lack of preventative action. Any attempt to recall the many times I lacked planning during my young years, as well as later, is now impossible. But I can assure you, there were some. My learning curve took many twists and turns. As I age, just remembering where I last placed my keys, where I placed a pertinent piece of paper, why I went into my pantry, or . . . or . . . still follows me like a dark shadow. Don't fret. There will be days and times when your very best-laid plans will amount to wasted energy.

As my mother said, "Son, don't be afraid to smile and laugh at yourself. We are all imperfect."

Once asked by my religious mentor, "Tony, don't you think you should start thinking about the Hereafter?"

My response was quick and thoughtful, "Of course I do, at least several times a day! I go into the pantry, go down to the garage, or find myself in my clothes closet. And I ask myself, "What am I here after?"

As your mentor, I can guarantee you only one thing; levity will extend your life!

"To be is to do!"

—*Socrates*

MAKE HAY WHILE THE SUN SHINES

My dad grew up during the Great Depression. His father, my namesake, died in the Spanish Flu Epidemic of 1918, when my father, the eldest child, was just five years old. From the time he was in high school and almost to his death, he worked two and three jobs to support his family. He wanted his family to have the things he was unable to have as a child.

Time and hard work were valuable tools for both his survival and success.

His favorite comment was, "You're never going to get anything done with your hands in your pockets. You need to make hay while the sun shines."

His other reminder was, "God only helps those who help themselves."

Although at the time I didn't always appreciate the reminders, however, I seldom ever followed with a disrespectful rejoinder. I am forever grateful to my dad for having instilled that same work ethic. Consequently, my children, relatives, and friends have heard me parrot dad's phrases often.

Worrying or having good intentions about something will never change that something. In the meantime, you torture yourself mentally and emotionally until taking action. It begins with a decision followed by a resolve to move forward.

You can't harvest a crop of hay if it hasn't been planted.

Good intentions and worry waste time.

Without planning and follow-through, frustration, and worry abound. Incomplete tasks leave you tired and depressed.

Procrastination, the converse of action, is the epitome of frustration and despair.

Procrastination is not the only delay, but it frequently denies the need to proceed forward. In Italian, tomorrow is *domani*. In Spanish, *mañana*.

Every language has a word that expresses putting things off until tomorrow. Tomorrow is yet another day, so why do it now. It's a great way to avoid moving ahead. By further delaying and procrastinating, you will develop internal frustration, fear, and worry. Each delay wreaks havoc on your mind and body.

Action requires thought, purpose, planning, preparation, and motivation.

Motivation is rooted in anticipation of success and benefits from an "I can do" attitude.

But what of fate or destiny?

The word destiny is tossed around like a soccer ball. It is shocking how many people feel that their lives are destined. If things were destined, wouldn't you lack freedom and free will? To conceive that all things are predictable and prearranged is irrational. Man is far more wise and intelligent than to think that life's outcomes are cast in cement. To believe that you have no responsibility for your deeds is unequivocally ludicrous. Your responsible decision-making creates; fate does not!

Some people enjoy talking about what they plan to do but are unable to finalize their plans. Their words are hollow attempts to rationalize their thoughts to themselves and others. Their delay conveys bold and noble intentions but lacks real integrity. For instance, I cannot begin to count the number of times friends and family have announced that they would stop smoking or lose weight. Empty promises with no substance.

Several of my mentors have reminded me many times of the old phrase: Words are cheap; they are a dime a dozen!

Actions do speak much louder than words.

On the other hand, your actions are priceless.

As my mom would say, "The proof is in the pudding." If you contradict your message with empty words, you will lose credibility and respect, not only from others but from yourself. Your loved ones, colleagues, and friends will soon discount your communications if they perceive them as hollow.

Keep your promises.

Promises will remain vacuous if your anticipated outcome never comes through. Your word is your coveted pledge to do, not merely to say.

Conversely, words can be motivators. Praise and encouragement are action words that instill confidence. Many people owe their success and happiness to someone who took the initiative to share their thoughts with words of praise. Words of encouragement, trust, and confidence will inspire and motivate. They help you and others discover and bolster innate and undiscovered possibilities. They kick-start and reinforce your positive efforts.

Action phrases like, *use it before you lose it*, or *make it possible, before it becomes impossible,* reflect reality. These expressions acknowledge that you possess the native ability to create success by realizing your potential. This recognition of success will motivate you to raise your bar. In a similar vein, exercise and an active lifestyle also promote good health and conditioning. Take constructive action; use it before you regret it.

It is not unusual to hear that success and happiness are a result of luck or chance. Some believe that they come from divine intervention or miracles. I believe that only you can make things happen. You are solely responsible for creating your paradise or your wretched inferno. Like destiny, the believers of pure chance convey a message of irresponsibility and lack of control.

Personal freedom and responsibility are critical to action outcomes!

As mentioned earlier, my dad always had a handy response; "God only helps those who help themselves."

Attitude and motivation are the components that dictate the results of planned actions. If you believe in yourself, your confidence and optimism will trump pessimism and fear. Happiness does not need to be the focus; instead, it is usually the byproduct of your achievements guided by your positive attitude. Opportunity doesn't automatically open its doors. It operates on the same paradigm of natural consequences—vision, followed by a plan, propelled by motivation, and sprinkled with optimism. Taking decisive action will guarantee positive results. As you continue, all of your prior experiences spiced with hope, vision, and judgment will provide you with the necessary tools and ingredients to reignite your momentum.

CAVEATS

Fear often stops action in its tracks. Lack of confidence, laziness, daydreaming, indecision, complaining, whimpering, and excuses are all symptomatic of fear. Too often, fear paralyzes thinking and results in indecision and an inability to act. Dealing with difficulty can result in you either becoming defensive or offensive. Playing defense begs for safety and security. Taking the offensive, although risky, can score the ultimate touchdown. Being on the offensive begets results. Defensive withdrawing from action due to anticipatory fear begets your disappointment and paralysis.

Excuses are another form of delay and denial. Words like *I don't have the time*, or *I'm tired,* or *maybe tomorrow,* are all good excuses to avoid moving forward. Again, frustration and despair from inaction will lead you to further paralysis and misguided energy.

Perhaps I've become an old fuddy-duddy, but I get irritated when I hear the words *I'll try*, or *I'm trying*, I believe that you either act or don't act, you either do or you don't do, you are either proactive or inactive. Trying is often a cop-out. It's a way of rationalization, like covering your fanny. Trying is wishing, not doing. It is a means of allowing chance, destiny, karma, or any other handy rationalization to excuse your behavior. Another ploy is pretending to act. Instead, it's a mirage of frenzied motion, rather than the required action. I much preferred responses like *I will, I can, I shall,* or *I will get it done.*

Excuses are the most typical rationalizations, and they abound. Sometimes, they are abstract and theoretical, but most times, they are concrete and real. Prepare yourself in life for every conceivable excuse. They can be very clear-cut or clouded in mystery, intrigue, and conveniently disguised. Over time, you will hear or use every possible reason for avoiding responsibility. *The devil made me do it,* or *I don't believe that it's my fault.* Rationalizations are simply avoidance techniques to cover up the real reason for deflecting blame. They are like the excuses both girls, boys, men, and women used to avoid intimacy, commitment, and maturity.

Be alert by recognizing excuses quickly. Otherwise, you will find yourself confused by another's intent and motives. Please remember that everyone has a motive; it may be a hidden agenda, not wanting to be exposed. Be vigilant and attentive because you will learn a great deal about another's character by their use of excuses. In the process, you will also learn a lot about yourself by exploring your use of excuses. These caveats will prove valuable on your sojourn.

Your deeds define you. You cannot hide behind the fact that your actions—diligence and its results determine your character. Talk is cheap. It is your actions that delineate who you are. Your entire reputation lies transparent to your audience of friends, family, and neighbors. If your behaviors show kindness, restraint, and respect for others, you will be lauded. If, however, you act with impulsiveness, disrespect, and a lack of sensitivity, you may wallow in despair.

SUMMARY

Instead of standing on the sidelines, you can have great moments if you are willing to take action. Any lack of it will slow your progress. To avoid roadblocks and unnecessary stop signs, initiate, don't withdraw. Ultimately, the result is either an expected success or a correctable mistake. Regardless, it is an action rather than inaction that produces a result.

Mistakes are learning moments.

Mistakes are far superior to the paralysis of fear, which defines inaction. Making mistakes averts fear and indecision while providing valuable feedback.

If you are unsure and waver, you will always settle for less than what you rightfully deserve. How can you ever achieve success and happiness if you feel you deserve less? Put the bar at a reachable level, and you will aspire to reach that level and nothing less.

"All roads that lead to success have to pass through hard work boulevard at some point."

—*Eric Thomas*

NOSE TO THE GRINDSTONE

Your father, mother, grandfather, grandmother, or great-grandparents came to this country to make a better life for their families. A strong work ethic was necessary to ensure their freedom, happiness, and success. Husbands and wives all toiled cooperatively for the future of their respective families. For every comfort afforded to their families, an industrious sacrifice was required.

The American work ethic has defined our country as the most industrious and successful nation in the world.

Your productive output will eventually become a large part of your character and personality. It is an essential tool necessary to develop your independence, responsibility, and freedom. When you feel you have done your very best, you cannot avoid the confidence, joy, and self-satisfaction that follows.

As our late President Harry Truman once said, "There ain't no such thing as a free lunch."

Anything received for nothing, ultimately, is worthless.

Some have suggested that fate is genuinely your future. Your success is actually a result of hard work. It does not come from luck or destiny. It is not happenstance, but a means to an end. Luck might sometimes land a job, but keeping it involves thoughtful, hard work, and focused action. Fortuity is for gamblers; success in life comes from keeping your nose to the grindstone. Of course, liking what you do and doing your best helps move the needle of fate. Unless no other choices exist, continuing to plod at something with little personal value does not engender strong motivation and purpose. Sometimes your ancestors toiled long hours, but they envisioned a better future for their loved ones. As a result, they became determined to make their toils worthwhile and focused on their family's future. They worked hard to provide an opportunity for their children to survive and prosper. The results are self-evident!

Without work, there would be little purpose in life.

How can one continue to extract without ever replenishing?

How can one expect to earn freedom, gain confidence, or secure happiness without earning it?

Progress means giving up a piece of you. Yes, fighting your way up can be stressful, even in a civilized world. Work and life are forever bonded as conjoined twins. They both serve themselves and others. Your labor can't slay the Grim Reaper but can forestall him. Temper your weaknesses and vices by replacing them with pride and healthful energy—the most successful look forward to the benefits of assiduous efforts.

However, there exists a startling statistical caveat. It is not surprising that by the end of the third generation, inheriting a family fortune usually results in indigence. This sudden lack of motivation occurs as soon as one's work ethic fades, and the heirs decide to live off their inheritance without providing for it. Unfortunately, reality dictates that you can't continue to take without giving.

COPING WITH WORK

Enjoying your work keeps you happy and motivated. If you do not enjoy it, you will need to change your attitude or change your job. Your labor will take up the majority of an average week. If you are unhappy or overly stressed, it requires a serious re-evaluation. Family and close personal friends should remain your highest of all priorities. However, job imbalance can have significant effects on your family.

Researchers and employees now realize that the notion that the more stress one has at home, the more it affects one's work life and threatens one's job is a fallacy. It is actually the converse. Job tension accounts for at least 50% of an individual's total stress. Job distress is more frequently the real culprit in causing family and personal problems. This reality is in contrast to what most people believe. It is very important to evaluate how much job stress causes you to lose your balance, both at home and at work. If this is the case, you will receive subtle feedback from your body, fellow employees, and loved ones. It's at that time that action should be taken.

Learning to cope with the pressures of your vocation is by choice, passion, or necessity. If by choice or passion, your stress will result from how much pressure you allow. If you are genuinely passionate about your toil, you will engender a need for perfection and accomplishment. As in all endeavors, to be optimally efficient you will need to provide a balance between work, family, and fun.

On the other hand, if your job is not fulfilling and not your primary choice, it can become humdrum, non-motivating, repetitive, often difficult, and very stressful. There will be obstacles and missteps until you either change your job or your attitude towards it. If you know it is only temporary employment until you reach the next rung of success, it will sustain you during those less inspirational days, months, or years.

My first jobs were picking fruit and vegetables. It was followed by delivering newspapers at 5 a.m. each morning, seven days a week. It was later an evening job working at the American Can Company for five summers while attending high school and college. Finally, it was an evening job at a supermarket while in graduate school. Each occupation taught me to do my very best and progress forward. But they also taught me what I didn't want to do for a living. When I found my real passion, it was a job that I not only appreciated, but no longer felt like work. Instead, it was my chosen profession. Each day, with rare exceptions, it brought me happiness and joy!

Expect that some things may erode, collapse, explode, or disappear during your quest for your ideal job, but never give up hope for a brighter tomorrow. Things can always be worse; you could be unemployed! Do your best and achieve personal satisfaction with as much enthusiasm as you can muster. Avoid apathy or lack of attention to detail. If you allow too much emphasis on dissatisfaction, it will rust your mind and disturb your thinking. It can cause mental paralysis. Keep your head up, be persistent, and persevere.

Be your own very best friend by providing yourself with personal pep talks. Solicit the support of those you love and admire, and remember that:

> *"Work banishes those three great evils: boredom, vice, and poverty."*
> —*Voltaire*

When you feel stressed, the best antidote is humor. When humor is injected into the workplace, not only does productivity increase, it decreases stress, and morale is reincarnated. Humor fosters creativity, retains sanity, increases work relationships, and reduces sick time. The bottom line is that the funny bone and productivity intersect and synergize. Schedule time for fun and humor, both in the workplace and outside it. Activities such as trips, wine tasting, bowling, chess, or board games provide relief from stress. Outdoor sports like baseball, basketball, golf, or tennis are also great diversions from job stress. You need fun and humor to maintain your sanity and balance because you will sometimes live in an insane world. Work diligently, but don't take your job too seriously while taking yourself too lightly!

PERSONAL GLIMPSES

The quote by Thomas Edison, "I never did a day's work in my life. It was all fun." is not entirely accurate for everyone.

Some of my initial jobs were not a fun day at the amusement park. I started working for pay at age eleven. My first job was picking raspberries and blackberries for a local farmer. I remember coming home each night after a grueling ten to twelve hours, dirty and exhausted. Yes, I ate almost as many raspberries as I put into the cardboard cartons, but it was hard labor. Admittedly, I was among many friends and contemporaries, including my brother, Billy. We laughed and joked. It made our job more fun than initially perceived. At the end of each six-day week, we each netted about six to eight dollars in total. It was our first taste of work and a grand opportunity to appreciate school and family.

Perhaps, as Khalil Gibran states, "Work is love made visible."

Yes, perhaps, but so are the calluses, dirty hands, aching bones that go along with it. My dad was a very astute man. He nudged us to work because he knew from his own experiences that it would open our eyes to the real world and assist in future decision making. His father had died at age 28, when my dad, the eldest of three, was only five years old. From the time he was nine till his death, he managed to have two or three jobs to support his mother and two sisters and support his three sons and wife. Throughout his life, he continued to assist his mother and sometimes-needy siblings.

I'll never forget the day I told my father I wanted to go to a private, parochial college-prep high school. He said, "You'll have to earn your tuition by getting a paper route. I will help you when I can, but you will have to fund it yourself."

With a nostalgic heart, I recall the many mornings getting up at 5 a.m. and delivering newspapers. Then every Friday night collecting $.25 from each of my 50 or more newspaper subscribers. As much as it was difficult, it was also love. I will never forget my dad's sacrifices, or the unspoken love attached to those wonderful reminiscent days.

My father was implicitly conveying that all work is fruitful, but choosing your occupation is far more satisfying. Having a mental tape measure to evaluate various types of jobs is invaluable. Learning the value of hard labor and what it brings is one of life's lessons. In retrospect, I found those years to be the most valuable learning moments of my life.

Some forty years ago, while taking a sabbatical leave and writing a book on stress, I found some fascinating statistics. Researchers had found that those individuals who had the greatest control over their lives and jobs experienced the least amount of stress and lived the longest of all. Not surprisingly, they were the individuals who had chosen their professions and had been quite successful at them. In particular, symphony conductors, college professors, and CEOs' topped the list. Not only had they perfected their professions, but they had chosen them. These successful and long-living folks had become passionate about their chosen fields and were in control. Secondarily, famous statesmen, noted professional sports players, and well-known scientists followed closely behind. They also enjoyed great success and longevity. If you want supreme success and happiness, along with a fulfilling life, take control of your future and profession.

A CAVEAT

This may seem idealistic and somewhat unrealistic, but liking what you do and making a living at it is an outstanding ethic. Yes, you will need to experience jobs that are intermediate stepping-stones to finding your life's work, but don't ever give up your hope and desire for a job that is truly fun and exciting. When you find it, you'll awake each morning aglow, anxiously awaiting your next challenge and the self-satisfaction that it includes. Choose a career that in retrospect, you would work for free, even if you had not been offered a salary.

A rather important caveat needs to be included. Americans are perceived as perennially busy. Consequently, we toil longer hours, take fewer vacations, and with more occasional pauses than almost all other advanced societies. Even our leisure is filled with pressing responsibilities and endless activity. We are in perpetual motion, completing to-do lists, stopping and starting, commuting, multi-tasking, doing odd jobs, and working very long hours. We often spend too much time struggling. Even on holidays, I was frequently obsessed with work activities. Our frenetic pace has caused us to have less longevity than most European nations and many other civilized countries. You need to add a little frivolity and self-indulgence without guilt. Don't forget humor, play, laughter, and spontaneity; they provide a balance between work and play. Also, we live in a global economy, where jobs change frequently, and new skills are required. Keep learning and thinking; otherwise, your job could become extinct.

Peter Drucker predicted, "In about five years, there will be two types of CEOs: those who think globally and those who are unemployed."

"They are able who think they are able."

—*Virgil*

WALKING TALL

While working on this chapter about personal change, my son Peter volunteered to share a story.

"Since change is so difficult to achieve, it will require a little humor," he said.

His story follows.

A Buddhist monk and a Hare Krishna walked into an Italian restaurant, Mangia Mi, and ordered a Double Meatball Panini to go.

The server said, "That will be a total of $12.50."

So, the monks handed him a $20 bill. The young cashier proceeded to put the money in his pocket.

"What about my change?" asked the monk.

"Change?" the cashier replied. "Change comes from within!"

Individual power, control, choice, responsibility, and ongoing change will be crucial to your successful voyage. Without them, you may as well pack up your tent because you will be doomed to fail. You will soon be the locksmith, able to unlock these valuable tools.

Having inner confidence and trust in yourself is the essence of personal power.

The "I can" attitude will be your foundation and your saving grace.

If you are active, not passive, have recognizable self-respect, and respect others as equals, you will be well on your way. Listen, understand others, and always be willing to negotiate fairly. Your new confidence will allow you to think before acting. You will then be able to control yourself and your choices. Thinking before acting will save relationships and will enable you to communicate without fear or anxiety. It will further build and bond your relationships. These enduring relationships will ultimately provide your most significant support system.

Walking tall does not mean displaying arrogance.

Your actions should reflect humility, kindness, empathy, and warmth. They resonate with internal control, not outward domination, bullying, and bluster. Instead of bold strength and over-aggressiveness, building confidence will help you be more gentle, patient, and humble. Your persona of strength and self-assurance will shine as you walk into a room or join a new group.

Seldom held in high esteem are the flashy egomaniacs or loud, boisterous clods.

The person who exhibits inner strength elicits the respect and attention of others. They exude a comfortable persona who do not rely on fluff. As you move from adolescence to adulthood, these softer yet healthier characteristics will slowly prevail.

Your body movements and gesticulations confirm your confidence. The best use of power is to share it, not hoard it. The most beautiful thing about confidence and a positive attitude is that you are in control. No one can take it away from you.

Patience and calmness are the ability to wait, remain calm, and let timing be your ally.

Powerless people are those who choose to live and act like victims. Being weak may primarily be due to lifestyle and dependency. Helpless are those who have not learned the raw strength of personal dominion. Self-strength does not mean manipulative or destructive control over other people. Personal strength is power over your thoughts, words, attitudes, choices, and actions. Equally important, it will enable you to stand tall and take full responsibility for your actions and behavior.

Your potency is not innate. No, it is something that you will need to learn through supportive modeling, reading, schooling, and lots of practice.

Honor your strength, not by bullying your fellow man, but by owning responsibility for your actions. You must be consciously vigilant of your every action and not asleep at the switch. Making positive choices and decisions leads to a healthier life and a much-improved world.

Below are two quotes that further clarify the concept of personal power written by some of the greatest minds of our time. They are both clarifying and compelling statements.

"Between stimulus and response, there is space. In that space is your power to choose your response. In your response, lie your very growth and your freedom."
—*Rollo May*

"The most common way people give up their power is thinking they don't have any."
—*Alice Walker*

The mind is the seat of strength and the prime source of action. If your mind is confident and comfortable, you can think through options and move to responsible behavior. Your capabilities will allow you the freedom to put purpose into your life without fear. That strength of thought moves mountains and will help create shortcuts on your journey.

Although paradoxically, personal power does not mean wealth; those who possess it do not seek wealth, however usually by default obtain it. History is rife with stories of great wealth. Unfortunately, many whose prime focus was greed ended unhappily. On the other hand, some of the wealthiest Americans have been the most generous. One of America's most significant philanthropists was John D. Rockefeller, Jr. He gave the equivalent of almost ten billion dollars in today's dollar equivalence. Billionaires Warren Buffett, Bill Gates, MacKenzie Scott and Priscilla Chan have donated to education, medical research, and poverty almost 90% of their entire fortunes. In interviews with them, they are humble, egalitarian, sincere, and empathetic.

Don't seek wealth as your prime goal in life.

Instead, the most important thing to give the world is to give your very best. Give it everything you've got to be the best you can be. Reach out for a better life and a better world. You will be handsomely rewarded.

CONTROL

You can hardly expect to be happy and prosperous if you are weighed down by feelings of anger, victimization, fear, and resentment. If you feel you are stuck like a broken record, you are experiencing the red flags of indecision. You need to stop, take a break, and determine how to regain your self-control. As a critical first step, it is necessary to know what you can control and what you cannot. If you have the control needed to solve a problem, then you simply need to take the next and final step—*choose wisely*. Change can only occur when you make thoughtful decisions.

You cannot control the weather, other people, or their actions. You cannot prevent unexpected tragedies or Mother Nature's natural disasters.

You only control your reaction to the uncontrollable.

You can only control yourself.

You are the only one on earth that has sole control of your life.

Personal control requires the development of an active conscience because it gives you guidance and direction. This moral compass helps you determine whether something is good or bad, ethical or unethical, right or wrong. It is your inner voice of experience and wisdom. It enables you to share your insecurities with trusted others and gain control over fears, anxieties, and uncertainties. Being in control requires understanding yourself, especially your frailties. To manage yourself, you must clarify your expectations. Otherwise, your journey will be directionless and haphazard.

CHOICE

I heard somewhere that the average person makes almost 1,000 decisions every day. Most are two-part options of yes or no, but some are multiple-choice, requiring deep thought and careful decision-making.

Almost everything in life offers opportunities for prudent decision-making.

There are very few must do's. Some options are self-evident because they lead to a dead-end or danger. But many require careful consideration, thought, research, and reevaluation. If you genuinely control your conscious thoughts and ultimate choices, you begin to set your priorities based upon your decisions.

Having the freedom of both thought and action allows for either growth or dangerous regression.

You have the option to decide whether you will control yourself or not. When you choose not to maintain control, you decide by default that someone else will decide for you. At that point, you have lost personal control. That's why there are lawyers, jails, counselors, police officers, judges, and psychiatric hospitals. They take control when a person chooses not to take responsibility for his/her actions. For example, when a student loses control, he or she permits the teacher to take charge. Hundreds of research studies have similarly concluded that control over one's destiny is a key to success and longevity.

Your control syncs with responsibility by saying in true Harry Truman style, "The buck stops here!"

When you control your destiny, you don't need to blame others for your mistakes and failures.

The most successful people have control over their future because they understand that they are fully responsible for their actions.

The very first selection to make each day will determine the kind of day you will have. Choose an attitude of "Life is beautiful," or conversely, choose "Another day, another struggle." You can choose your attitude, regardless of your circumstances.

Your daily choices determine your happiness and survival.

You can choose to be peaceful or choose to be cranky. You can choose to control your day or let your day control you. You and only you are at the helm. Don't ever give away your freedom, your attitude, or your ability to make choices!

Decisions, decisions, decisions!

Please remember that decisions are based on the value you place upon yourself. If you feel omnipotent and invulnerable, you will sometimes drive too fast, drive under the influence, or have one-night stands. Experience develops judgment, but prudence is achieved by observing others, making foolish mistakes. Vicariously learning from others' poor choices can save you from the evils of your poor decision-making. As a teenager, I took unnecessary risks, like playing football on frozen fields with no shoes, causing bruises and frostbite. I have driven when I was exhausted or had one drink too many, and watched my beloved puppy get hit and killed because I chose not to put her on a leash. On the other hand, I am very grateful for having learned from these errors of judgment while watching others make more serious mistakes. Those vicarious experiences saved me much grief, poor judgment, and perhaps death.

To further clarify, there is a considerable difference between choice and chance. Avoiding decisions and leaving your life to chance is begging the question. I have known people who have lived a life with a *che sarà a sarà*, Italian for a whatever will be, will be, attitude.

Living life by chance can be scary, risky, and sometimes fatal. Unfortunately, taking a chance, like passing on a two-lane road, or taking unknown drugs, or having unprotected sex are all playing the game of chance called Russian roulette. I had the horrifying experience of discovering that my brother had been killed in a head-on accident. He was the driver in the safe lane when somebody was passing on a two-lane road. It was a devastating experience and one that I'll never forget. Yes, living on the dark side, a life of chance, can lead to danger and death. There will always be forks in the road that require decisions. Make them cautiously.

Remember, your selections determine your destiny.

One of the most challenging things I encountered as a child was assertiveness. As a young man, rather than be empowered to choose a direction, a place, an activity, or a restaurant, it was easier to let another person decide. My passivity became self-evident. By slowly garnering self-confidence, power, and self-control, although alien, I began asserting myself. Becoming assertive and learning to be a victor rather than a victim was painful, but of absolute necessity.

Again, as time passed, every time I participated in joint decision-making, I felt more comfortable. Sometimes I was faced with a very dogmatic participant. After a few urination contests, it became easier to say a firm no and go my own way. The learning curve is not a straight ascent. It twists and turns. As the eldest son, it was easy for me to assume a dominant role, yet it was necessary to adapt. There were times where group decisions became the majority rule. I accepted the majority rule with as much grace as I could engender. Sometimes my selection did not necessarily appeal to the majority. It taught me new degrees of tolerance and sensitivity.

If you prefer to be happy, confident, and maintain a positive attitude, your selections need to be weighed along with others' intentions. The choices you make will define you. If the choice or compromise is successful, it is called growth; if unsuccessful, it is called *experience*!

RESPONSIBILITY

You may not be responsible for your genes, your parents, or your relatives, but that is where it all ends. Life cannot provide total freedom without the assumptive responsibility. To be successful and happy, you must be accountable for all of your actions. Freedom requires taking ownership. Taking control of your life is your most important responsibility.

Taking responsibility means owning up to your actions. Excuses, denial, and alibis are the first line of defense by the irresponsible.

It was all her fault; I didn't do it; I had no other choice. Not me! He started it!

These are the typical defenses to shield, demure, and ward off the embarrassment of being caught red-handed. It certainly applies to social relationships. We are responsible for the things we say and do to others. Any person involved in problematic situations must understand that the enemy can be within. You and only you are responsible for your words and actions; remember, the buck stops with you!

Finally, placing responsibility and trust upon another becomes the real acid test. At the age of eleven, I was asked if I wanted to earn some money during my summer vacation. Without much thought, I readily accepted. My brother, Billy, quickly joined me. My dad was soon dropping my nine-year-old brother and me at a farm on the outskirts of Rochester, New York, at 6:30 in the morning. We worked until 6:00 every night, every day except Sunday for two solid weeks. Our job was to pick raspberries. The good news was I had my first job, and I could eat as many raspberries as I wanted. The bad news was that raspberries were difficult to pick because they were full of thorns. Besides, it was hot and humid, and we worked over 60 hours per week. At the end of two weeks, I probably had eaten many more raspberries than I turned in. My brother and I collected a total of fifteen dollars each for over 120 hours of work. What resulted was a lesson in appreciation and an understanding of an occupation I was determined to avoid in the future.

At age twelve and a half, after graduating from 8th grade, I decided to go to a private college-prep high school. Enthusiastically, I announced to my dad, "Dad, I want to go to Aquinas Institute next year; I've just been accepted."

My dad's rather terse response was, "Then you'll have to pay for the tuition yourself!"

After considering my alternatives, I applied for a paper route and was soon rewarded with a route in our general neighborhood. I'm usually near tears when I think about what followed.

My dad sat down with me and announced, "Anthony, okay, you've done your part. I'm proud of your initiative. I'd like to make a deal with you. If you take this job seriously and get up at 5:00 a.m. every day, I'll help drive you each morning. When I can't, your mom can pinch-hit."

As you might know, Rochester, New York, is in the snow belt and like Buffalo, Watertown, and Syracuse, receives copious amounts of snow each winter; actually, sometimes in fall and spring, too, ranking Rochester in the top three nationally in annual snowfall. My sweet, loving dad kept his promise. We would wake up at 5:00 a.m., I'd pack the old '54 Willy's with newspapers, and we would slide through the snow. Sometimes there was a chill factor of fifteen degrees below zero. Worse yet, I would trudge between tall drifts of snow from house to house, street to street, until my 50-plus house route finished each morning. Mom would periodically pinch-hit, too. I can't thank them enough for teaching me the value of work, the value of money, trust, and responsibility that they had thrust upon me. It became a labor of love and the single most learning experience of my young life, as challenging as it was. It was indeed a valuable epiphany into young adulthood.

CHANGE

When you can listen, understand, and accept yourself, you can proceed to real self-change. It takes serious commitment, a high degree of motivation, and hard work to effect personal change. When you start considering how little opportunity you have to change others, you realize that it is even more difficult to change yourself, even with a carefully laid out plan.

Instead, following Yogi Berra's comical advice, "When you come to the fork in the road, take it." At every fork, you'll have a two-choice decision to make.

You can face the problem head-on and change, or you can conveniently avoid change. Fortunately, you have at your immediate disposal the most sophisticated and complex computer sitting right under your hat.

You will realize that by changing yourself, you can significantly affect others behavior; namely, your loved ones, friends, neighbors, and an ever-expanding world. As I mentioned earlier, your self-image and demeanor are closely related. Your self-image predicts and perpetuates your behavior. To change your behavior, you need to change the self-image pictures and replace the negative photos and the associated words attached to them. Visualize and repeat the new statements at least ten times a day.

I can still remember the story of Ben Franklin that I read early in my career. Ben Franklin realized that he had thirteen different things about himself that needed to be changed as a young adult. He was determined to change his mistaken ways and replace them with new, more constructive behaviors. He decided that to be successful, he could only change one action at a time. He established a very systematic plan and mastered the entire thirteen items. Ben prioritized them from highest to lowest. He worked on the most challenging and highest priority first. His biggest challenge was to increase his efficiency by not wasting his time. It took almost four years to master all thirteen items. But as history reflects, Ben Franklin became an extremely successful man who indeed used his time wisely.

Ben Franklin's story reminded me that it's easy to blame others for our shortcomings. Instead of turning the spotlight on others, you are better served by focusing your attention on yourself. When you look into the mirror, you need to also look at your shortcomings. Perhaps changing your attitude from blame to self-change will extinguish your anger and resentment. You should replace those negative feelings with self-forgiveness for any prior transgressions. Change, along with taking full responsibility for your behavior, regains your power, clarifies your direction, and motivates you for a successful sojourn.

Self-change is forever adapting to a new situation; changing is dynamic, not static. It is evolutionary, but potentially powerful. Unlike Ben Franklin, it has taken me decades to see real personal change. Changing my attitude, especially acceptance, unconditional love, understanding individual differences, political thinking, humility, and even my willingness to change, have taken decades of ongoing revision and refinement. Change is necessary and adapting to change is inevitable. I can confidently say that I am not the man I was at 21 years old, at 42, or 62. I don't wait until an emergency or crisis occurs; I prepare for it. I find that life and change are a direct corollary to writing; I'm continually revising and tearing up my latest draft.

SUMMARY

You will always find cycles of economic ups and downs, political snafus, catastrophes, crises, and conflicts on your journey.

As Auntie Mame said, "Life is a banquet, and most damn fools are starving to death."

Remember, you do not need to live in a self-inflicted prison when an overflowing garden paradise exists. You will need to control your attitude because attitude will give you altitude. Appreciate and give thanks daily.

Manage both your input and your output.

Control yourself and your two lips.

Guard your tongue.

Exercise your power, control your destiny, make self-improvement choices, take responsibility for your actions, and change those things that delay your journey. Don't just look to make it through the day; visualize the paradise you can have each day. Like writing a book, plan your goals, break them into bite-size pieces, and schedule your time. Accordingly, take a break now and then. Revise each draft until you are ecstatic, and then rejoice. When stuck, remember change means reversing, not rehearsing your failures. Don't let the little things, the trivia, upset your day. And if you wake up late, burn your toast, break a shoelace, spill your coffee, stain your new shirt, hit a traffic jam, remember, you can always re-start your day. Self-actualizing is your ability to detach yourself from the negativity of life, change your attitude, and proceed full speed ahead.

"If a man does not keep pace with his companions, perhaps it is because he hears a different drummer. Let him step to the music which he hears, however measured or far away."
—*Henry David Thoreau*

A BLANK CANVAS

If creativity was not included in this treatise, I would be remiss in its shameful omission. With the exception of humanistic characteristics, creativity is the most fascinating of all human qualities. From a young age, I was intrigued, awestruck, and overwhelmed by the minds of Leonardo da Vinci, Thomas Edison, Michelangelo, Henry Ford, Albert Einstein, Galileo, Isaac Newton, Walt Disney, and many others. It wasn't just the level of their intellectual prowess, but their creative imaginations, insatiable curiosity, and the intuition needed to understand and solve complex problems. Creators focus on innovation rather than imitation. Almost as fascinating was the study of their backgrounds, personality development, education, motivation, and perseverance.

My dad had a touch of creativity. I remember when he was at Bausch & Lomb (B&L), he would occasionally come home with a surprise in his hand. It was a letter from an executive staff member at B&L congratulating him for an outstanding suggestion. Each time he would unveil a check as a cash award for his ingenuity. We looked forward to a special treat, usually at Don & Bob's for white hot dogs or hamburgers with their special hot sauce. Or, if it was a big bonus, a Sunday dinner at a white tablecloth Italian restaurant downtown. He was so proud he would beam for a week. Eventually, after achieving several suggestion awards, he received a letter from the CEO. It gave words of praise for his cost-saving ideas and designated VIP status. Usually, that meant a promotion and pay increase. My very quiet and humble dad never made much of a big fuss but carried a slightly smug grin for weeks.

Probably one of the most fascinating things about creative individuals is their motivation. Most would think that creative individuals are primarily motivated by money and fame. Paradoxically, research shows their motivation is precisely the exact opposite. Parenthetically, their rewards are similar to that of a jig-saw puzzle. Each step, whether the results are either positive or negative, is to complete another piece to the puzzle. Their curiosity to solve and create closure is far more rewarding than money or material things. In fact, most are shy and reclusive. They do not enjoy being in the limelight but prefer anonymity. Curiosity is the motivation and their satisfaction is problem-solving, and becomes the greatest internal reward of creative geniuses. My dad fit the stereotype to a T.

Renowned painter, sculptor, raconteur, and scientist Leonardo da Vinci, a formidable Renaissance Man, was also an architect, engineer, botanist, draftsman, futurist, and inventor extraordinaire. As an illegitimate child, he was not afforded a formal education and was often considered feverishly independent, a real loner. Most creative individuals find great pleasure in their loneliness and unique differences. Interestingly, many of the most famous creative minds over the centuries were homeschooled or self-educated. For instance, Benjamin Franklin was homeschooled. Thomas Edison, a very poor student, was also homeschooled by his mother. After a series of serious behavioral problems at school, Edison's mother removed him and terminated his formal education. Other examples included Isaac Newton, Albert Einstein, and Gregor Mendel. Research studies have consistently found that by the time a youngster reaches 4th grade, their creativity scores are negligible. It is assumed that the rules, rigidity, and a structured school environment destroy the students' creative juices.

Like his creative colleagues, Leonardo was besieged by unlimited energy, incredible curiosity, and little sleep. He, like Thomas Edison and Henry Ford, attributed their creativity and perseverance to frequent naps that renewed their energy and refreshed their imaginative thinking. Leonardo resembled many Nobel Prize winners who are able to combine multiple disciplines in order to visualize the big picture. This skill enabled him and others to create and solve very perplexing problems by knowing and combining many different scientific disciplines simultaneously. Their curiosity allowed them to delve into the intricacies of things, resulting in innovative theories, discoveries, inventions, artwork, and engineering achievements.

Leonardo da Vinci prided himself on his ability to know *how to see.* He said that the typical person looks without seeing, hears without listening, breathes in without awareness of aroma or fragrance, eats without tasting, touches without feeling, and talks without thinking!

Many people consider da Vinci the founder of aviation in the 15th Century. Aviation was not taken seriously until the 20th Century, some 500 years later. Yet Leonardo had already conceived of airplanes, helicopters, and even parachutes hundreds of years earlier. Today we take aviation for granted, even though discovered less than 100 years ago. It has propelled us to the moon and outer space. Galileo, another creative genius, would be equally surprised by our current state of Astronomy and Astrophysics. Creative minds are now exploring new galaxies, black holes, the expansion of space, and the discovery of the smallest particles previously unknown until a few years ago.

My dad often reminded me of Leonardo. He was quiet, artful, curious, and creative. During his work with optics and nuclear engineering, he received many awards and commendations for his creative solutions. He, like most inventive personalities, was never happy until he felt the accomplishment of solving a problem. My dad would frequently say that problems were just opportunities that needed simple creative solutions. What I have marveled most about creative people was their undying and untiring need to see change, improvement, modification, adaptation, or new use. Some discoveries were made somewhat accidentally, like the serendipity of the x-ray discovery by Madame Curie. Or, the accidental discovery of Alexander Graham Bell's telephone, when he was trying to invent a hearing aid for his wife. Most were accomplished by persistence and a desire to create, such as the many inventions of Thomas Edison. All of which resulted in significant benefits to society.

I have the firm belief that almost everyone has a touch of creativity, just waiting to explore and explode. Being in awe of the highly creative, I have been most curious about their personalities. There are many opposing characteristics that you should become aware of, review, and recognize. With such an understanding, you might recognize your own capabilities. Perhaps you may be able to ignite your creativity and help better your world.

Dr. Mihaly Csikszentmihalyi studied creative people for over three decades. He stated that creative individuals have ten antithetical traits. He concluded creative people are first and foremost paradoxical personalities. Creative individuals:

- Have intense energy yet are quiet and unassuming. They maintain laser-beam focus.

- Are creatively smart but also naïve; immature and childlike, e.g., Mozart.
- Combine fun and playfulness with moments of both seriousness and irresponsibility.
- Alternate between imagination and fantasy in an attempt to create a new reality.
- Are humble and proud, not arrogant, and may also be self-deprecating and shy.
- Are able to shift from extrovert to introvert like a chameleon, simultaneously.
- Escape from rigid conventional stereotyped gender roles, tending towards androgyny.
- Because they are very open and sensitive, they suffer more pain from lack of appreciation and criticism.

In Rabinov's words, "Inventors have a low threshold of pain. Things bother them. They are vulnerable, especially after devoting so much time and passion."

What is so interesting is the number of paradoxes represented by creative and inventive personalities. It seems that paradoxes are like a germinal seed ready to explode and re-create. These contradictions—sometimes called oxymorons—allow for the opening of new horizons of growth and discovery. Paradoxes are a set of profound phenomena; they are the yin and yang, the very balance of all creation. Remember that you indeed have a spark of creativity. Don't allow others to have such an influence that they snuff out your touch of genius. Make every attempt to maintain undeterred your curiosity and imagination.

Since the beginning of time, fear, embarrassment, and criticism have been major deterrents to creative and inventive thinking. Your limitless potential will frequently be challenged by the closed-mindedness of others unwilling to accept original thinking or individual differences. Maintaining the status quo is the human cry of the majority.

As a matter of fact, in 1899, the Commissioner of the US patent office announced, "Everything that can be invented, has been invented."

Novel ideas are easy to kill, and so are the comments that accompany them. Unless unduly confident, great ideas either lay dormant or are easily snuffed out by the know-it-alls. Some of the glaring examples of these foot-in-mouth disasters are best illustrated by these two classic statements:

> *"The wireless music box has no imaginable commercial value. Who would pay for a message sent to nobody in particular?" This was the response to David Sarnoff's effort to raise investment capital for the radio in 1921.*

> *"This telephone has too many shortcomings to be seriously considered as a means of communication. The device is inherently of no value to us." Western Union internal memo, 1876.*

Living here in the heart of Silicon Valley, the home of the nation's creative brain trust, is forever fascinating. Like most other communities, it has not always welcomed creative and inventive thought. Times have certainly changed. Silicon Valley is now the center of divergent thinkers and the home of the most advanced high-tech organizations in the world. Living here for more than a half-century has caused me to feel awestruck by the incredible transformation of technology, social interface, and scientific discovery, and all at lightning speed.

Like Walt Disney, the dominant corporate theme in Silicon Valley is now playfulness and fun. Google, Apple, Facebook, Adobe, Cisco, eBay, Intel, LinkedIn, Netflix, Oracle, Pandora, Yahoo, and all the other major innovative companies feel that fun stimulates the creative imagination. Their corporate environments are so reminiscent of the venue found in young children during their most expansive creative period.

Cooperative playfulness is what researchers have found to create the kinds of innovations and inventions that will propel us into the future. They are like children who engage in open possibilities, allowing for exploratory play, having infinite numbers of choices that give rise to brainstorming, constructive feedback, and ultimately innovative products. These companies take imagination seriously and avoid the destructive forces of embarrassment, insecurity, and lacking trust. They instead not only allow but strongly support risk-taking. Social scientists have found that the symbols, logos, and names expressed by these innovative companies are symbols of imaginative, creative thinking. Visiting these companies is like going to a creative kindergarten. Their workplace is replete with specially-designed study corrals, group settings for creative group problem solving, play areas, comfortable and aesthetically pleasing furniture, and recreational facilities.

I sincerely hope this review of creativity will give you the following takeaways:

- Allow for divergent thinking by thinking outside the box.
- Keep an open mind and allow your relaxed mind to think and create!
- Bite your tongue before saying discouraging or disparaging remarks to alien ideas.
- Don't allow fear, intimidation, embarrassment, or criticism to deter you.
- Don't ever give up!
- Maintain a level of fun and playfulness.
- Remember, either I or someone else will be on the sidelines, cheering you on.

If you can, think of something no one else has, that would do something no one else has considered; write about a subject that is different from any other, break a barrier that no one else has; create a true original in music, art or science; or teach others how they can change their world for all of our benefit. That's your creative challenge. Go for it!

"If your life is marked by an unselfish determination to inspire or better the lives of others, you'll probably never get rich or leave a fortune. But you'll certainly leave the world better than you found it and make an investment that will last for all eternity."
—*Three Minutes a Day, Vol. 4*

A LOVING TORCH LEFT BEHIND

I must leave you with hope. Having happiness and success does not mean that your life is perennially blessed or that you are destined to achieve great things. Happiness is not counted in dollars or gold. It is instead a life measured in accomplishments benefiting others and your world. Success is not what you have done for yourself, but what others have gained by your brief stop and involvement in their lives. The medals, trophies, recognition, degrees, or designations you have earned will probably be long forgotten. What lives on are not the tangibles, but instead, the intangibles that can go on ad infinitum—your lofty reputation, your persona, your integrity, your idiosyncratic uniqueness, your legacy.

Life without hope seems empty and finite. You will feel splendidly fulfilled if you leave a legacy on our wonderful planet.

Perpetuity is the words, messages, stories, and memories exported to others.

There are so many messages that make life immortal. Your values are the most critical intangibles you can transmit to future generations. Living by the values of excellence will prepare you to internalize them and pass them on to future generations. They are the elements of a good and enduring life. During your journey, develop the values of integrity, honesty, courage, helpfulness, and compassion. They will stiffen your character, guide you, and prepare you for a successful journey.

I will never forget the day that my son announced that he had decided to come out of the closet and declare his sexuality. My wife and I were both initially shocked and dismayed.

In a fit of anger, I said, "Peter, how could you do this to us? I had always felt that you would be our only chance for the Cedolini family surname to survive."

Selfishly, I thought that with no other males in our immediate family progeny, the Cedolini name would die forever. Besides my brother, there are no other families in the United States with the same surname. As I impetuously cried for clarification, I was struck with my extreme short-sightedness and selfishness.

I could not accept one of life's inimitable realities.

My expectations and fantasies were unrealistic.

Both my wife and I had to face facts. We were relieved to find support from our immediate family and friends, who had already known. We had been naïvely not processing, nor understanding, and we were long overdue to face reality. My anger and disappointment proved to be from my short-sighted misconceptions. In my naiveté, I had regarded Peter's behavior as a deliberate act of rebellion and self-destructive. Time, introspection, support, and research taught me the fallacy of my thinking.

I had ignored all of the obvious signals that were displayed repeatedly; denial was my major misperception.

My immature macho ego was dissolved in short order; fortunately, love and support eventually supplanted it. What reasonable parents must realize is that life is not perfect; there are always surprises. It doesn't matter which country or region of the world that one encounters; there will always be a population whose diverse DNA creates individual differences. We eventually realized that humans are as serendipitous as the planet Earth.

In our awakening, we see the special gift of our son—a wonderful son who has deep love, a most profound mind, and a great appreciation of natural beauty, art, and the humanities.

Sharing our knowledge and our experiences are not only ways to achieve immortality, but an opportunity to allow others to see life as it exists, without embellishments or fantasies. Life is indeed a walk on an unknown path, yet it can be so healing. If you can accept reality, survive the obstacle course, absorb the pain, and embrace its outcomes, you will overcome your misperceptions and ignorance. These life experiences are indeed the opportunities to share your knowledge and wisdom so you can leave your footprint for those to savor and rejoice as your everlasting legacy.

I am convinced that there is nothing more intoxicating than perpetuity.

Of all the tender, heartfelt emotions that make life so worthwhile, unconditional love stands out as the one most important and lasting gift I want to leave with you on your continued journey. Without love, your life will never be complete. Hopefully, you will encounter love from your parents, siblings, grandparents, relatives, and close friends. Most importantly, your journey will also include other extraordinary people who will become the loves of your life. May your loving torch give you light and inspiration, and may it reign forever in the hearts of those you have touched and cherished, for that is the immortality called perpetuity.

TO REMEMBER ME

When your journey ends, you will leave your experiences, both beautiful and ugly, on the altar of dust. Prepare to share your travels and wisdom with others. It will elevate your journey to perpetuity.

"Success is inevitable if the passion for your work exceeds your diligent efforts."

—Author Unknown

THE CHASE FOR SUCCESS

If achieving personal success and happiness is your goal, you will need to add a massive dose of enthusiasm to each day of your life. If you're looking for job advancement, you must love what you do and passionately pursue it. If you regularly wake up dulled and unenthusiastic, you will need to rethink and readjust the course of your journey.

When I interviewed the top 20 corporations in Silicon Valley, the most frequent comment from human resources managers was, "Those employees on the fast-track have a very positive attitude, are enthusiastic, and are passionate about their work."

It doesn't matter what field you're in, business, academia, art, music, construction, or high tech; each requires enthusiasm to reach the top rungs of job success. It does not necessarily mean moving into management or executive positions. Find your comfort level in your chosen field—whatever or wherever that may be.

The difference between happiness and success is that happiness is an ongoing goal; each success is the by-product of that goal. Both mean sacrifice, hard work, and determination. It is not automatic. Your eventual achievement begins with a dream, a vision of what you can do to make your world better. Yes, the dream or vision starts with you having the leading role, but ends with you as a supporting actor.

At a relatively young age, I had a reoccurring dream of what life would be like in my future. I visualized a house, a wife, and the family living in a happy valley. As time passed, detailed pictures of the house, the wife, and the family came into my imagination and dreams. I saw myself contributing to my community and hoping to leave it just a touch better than when I arrived. At that time, there was no realization of what it would take to fulfill these dreams. The best part was the hope for a better future for me, my family, and my fellow neighbors. In my dreams, I saw myself relishing a life of joy, contentment, and satisfaction.

In my mind's eye, they were all signs of ultimate success. Those were the simple days of milk and honey, where one's imagination is filled with joy and hope. However, I sincerely believe those regularly-visited images provided the foundation for a fulfilling life. Time passed, and even after the roughest and toughest of days, my visual foresight remained as solid as granite. I allowed no one to diminish those rose-colored scenes. My dreams became the bricks of my new foundation as

I would drift off each night into somnolence. Even after a harrowing day, if I let my mind go, it would often turn to the pictures of what a glorious future might bring. I believe that visualizing future images of happy days allows those dreams to become a reality eventually.

Of course, success doesn't mysteriously show up at your back door. It takes hard work to put forth your very best efforts.

> *"Frustration . . . although quite painful at times, is a very positive and essential part of success."*
> —*Bo Bennett*

Once again, success is also paradoxical. It is not a final destination but an ongoing part of your journey. Indeed, there will be moments of temporary highs, such as hitting a home run, having cookies and tea with your elderly neighbor, acing an examination, getting a hug, a kiss from your grandma, or an "I love you" from some of the loves of your life. But, once more, there will be momentary disasters from which you'll need to recover. Success is evasive; its permanence is sustained only by your inner spirit. Remember, it remains elusive. If you consider it your terminal point, you are mistaken. The magic is in the chase and not the end of the rainbow. When you think you are there, you are not!

To succeed, you must first believe that you can. Evaluate any fears that may cause interference. Without a winning attitude, repeated achievements are impossible.

Knowing what it takes and the direction you choose will be the equation for a winning formula. There will be no fairy godmothers, no genies, no Jiminy Crickets to direct you; it will rely on your motivation. Only you can make it happen. You undoubtedly will sometimes get discouraged but avoid dropping out or quitting; that's not what winners do.

"The road to success is always under construction."
—*Today's Chuckle, 1963*

Survey after survey has repeatedly concluded that good health, a happy family, and a satisfying job are far more critical than expensive luxuries. Your real worth and value cannot ride on your material wealth. Your actual value and true reward are your real worth, without including financial assets. Paradoxically, truly successful people have a chance in their favor. They work hard, are persistent, have the right attitude, love others, and usually find themselves, by default, financially comfortable. If your priorities are people, you will be a grand winner of all that life has to offer. Getting along with others, caring for your brethren, and respecting them will undoubtedly result in untold happiness and continued success. An ounce of love will produce pounds of joy. You can only help yourself succeed when you help others succeed.

STRATEGIES FOR SUCCESS

There are a multitude of strategies that will assist you in your journey to personal and job success. Some have already been mentioned in previous chapters. Carefully review each one. Pick the top five and write them down and visualize them. Keep a ready copy nearby for your regular review. Rotate each next five, until you feel you have mastered them all.

Here's the summary and laundry list:

- Recognize yourself as unique and capable. Avoid comparing yourself to others, and be reminded that mistakes are the stepping stones to success.
- Catch yourself and reward yourself and others for acts of doing things right. Don't rush or hurry; take life slow and easy and count your blessings along the way.
- Believe in love, hope, and charity.
- Always be yourself; authenticity is important, duplicity deceives.
- Go with the flow, don't fight life, and cooperate.
- Don't pursue pure pleasure; pursue meaning and engagement.
- Visualize your dreams, repeat positive affirmations regularly.
- Control your input by valuing the positive and locking out the negative. Be resilient.
- Remember that personal change only occurs by reversing, not rehearsing your failures.

- Don't worry, be happy!
- Attempt to be physically fit.
- Strive to obtain as much knowledge and education as possible. Knowledge ensures power.
- Be active, develop hobbies and social interactions, and volunteer for community assistance.
- Anything worthwhile doing is worth doing well.
- Be responsible for all your actions by not making up excuses. Live honestly and keep your promises. Remember, these will be the hallmark of your character.
- Face your fears! The sooner you can overcome them, the sooner your journey will resume.
- Leave your worries behind.
- Make every attempt to follow your strengths and passions in choosing your career. Enjoy your work.
- Share your attention, time, and skills with others. Selfishness, egotism, and greed are enemies of success.
- Don't waste your time fighting ghosts or conditions you cannot change.
- Be sensitive to others by thinking, by listening intently and not over-talking. Remember, two ears always trump one mouth.
- Resolve conflicts, problems, and minor quarrels as quickly as you can. Don't allow them to fester or become bed partners, for they will cause you sleepless nights. Focus on today. Yesterday

was a canceled check, and tomorrow is only a promissory note.

- Others can take responsibility for their problems. Don't add them to your laundry list.
- Your journey is essentially endless, keep growing each day!
- Remember, only you can ultimately choose to be happy, kind, loving, and successful! Using the above strategies, you will find Lady Luck at your side and success at your back.

"Your success and happiness lie in you . . . Resolve to keep happy, and your joy and you shall form an invincible host against difficulty."
—*Helen Keller*

THE FINAL SOLUTION

After researching the origin of what I consider the finest of all definitions of success.

"To laugh often and much; to win the respect of people and the affection of children; to earn the appreciation of honest criticism and endure the betrayal of false friends; to appreciate beauty; to find the best in others; to leave the world a bit better, whether by a healthy child, a garden patch or redeemed social condition; to know even one life has breathed easier because you lived. This is to have succeeded."
—*Bessie Stanley*

SURRENDERING TO SERENITY

"Nothing is so contagious as enthusiasm; It is the real allegory of the tale of Orpheus—it moves stones, it charms brutes. Enthusiasm is the genius of Sincerity, and Truth accomplishes no victories without it."

—*Edward George E.L. Bulwer-Lytton (1ˢᵗ baron)*

SAVORING LIFE'S PRECIOUS MOMENTS

My mother, an excellent example of passion and enthusiasm, is possessed with a zest for life. Even as she approaches 102, she remains relentless in pursuit of a meaningful and spirited life. She enthusiastically shares her enjoyment of life each day. It doesn't matter whether you are family, friend, peer, or stranger. Not only does she remain joyful, but she gives thanks in prayer each day for being blessed with another gift of time. Her motto is, "Every day I must inspire before I expire!" My mother is a firm believer in Maya Angelou's quote, "Try to be a rainbow in someone else's cloud."

Learned or inherited, I have been blessed with her innate zeal for life.

Enthusiasm is the fire that motivates and molds the future. It is contagious and builds exponentially. It is the key to your nirvana.

Life without passion and enthusiasm equates to living with mediocrity, dullness, and boredom.

The word enthusiasm comes from the Greek word "enthousiasmos," meaning "the God or power within us," Enthusiastic individuals have an inner spirit that's a source of their inspiration. There are few things more welcoming than an impassioned person who can enthusiastically instill motivation and gusto into either the simplest or the most challenging situations.

PASSION

Passion is a driving force and one of the greatest joys of life. It is powerful!

A life without it is like a tree without water.

Without ardent zeal, life remains without much purpose or meaning. Please follow your passion by making every moment of your life exhilarating.

Exuberance for those things you fervently believe will empower you to walk on hot coals. Put high spirit in your step and move into the world of responsible enjoyment. I am not suggesting pure self-pleasure, but the unparalleled enjoyment of your surroundings, family, friends, a field of endeavor, friends, and the natural beauty of Mother Nature. Let your passion consume you, and let your enthusiasm explode. You will undoubtedly be handsomely rewarded with giant goosebumps of excitement.

Likewise, you must love what you do and passionately pursue it, particularly your job, where you will spend the majority of your adult life. If you wake up dulled and unenthusiastic, you will need to reconsider how you want to spend the remainder of your work life. It doesn't matter what field you're in, business, academia, art, music, construction, or high tech; each requires vivacity to gain and maintain job happiness and success. It does not necessarily mean moving up to the top of the ladder or even staying where you are. Find your comfort level and bring passion and enthusiasm to your workplace. You will be rewarded by bringing calm and peace to your daily toils.

> *"Passion is more important than intelligence and the most significant factor in job success."*
> —*Anonymous*

DEALING WITH PASSION AND ENTHUSIASM

Unexpressed feelings and attitudes are like caged wild animals. They are fighting to get out. Once let out, these intense feelings can be directed with zestful zeal. These crushing emotions are like wild stallions; they need to be saddled and ridden until they are broken. Don't be afraid to express those exhilarating feelings but learn to modulate them over time with gentle care, caution, and eventual satisfaction. You don't break a wild stallion overnight. Calmness will eventually prevail.

"Enthusiasm for life is the most important of all attitudes."
—Author Unknown

Apathy is the antonym and counterweight of enthusiasm. It negates positive feelings and is the antithesis of deep, devoted emotional zeal. You can't negotiate or buy enthusiasm. You must develop it through your concerted efforts. It is learned and earned! Passion is not a gratuity or entitlement for living, but a purposeful goal that will jet propel your journey.

PERSONAL GLIMPSES

At age fifteen, in the summer of 1958, our family visited my long-lost Uncle John. He had moved to California after WWII. Our family fell in love with California. To our surprise, my father decided to find employment and relocate us to San Jose. He went to work as a nuclear engineer for General Electric in January 1959. We moved after my junior year of high school in June of 1959. I was sixteen years old, and little did I know what was on the horizon. As I look back, the luckiest and most profound event in my entire life was moving to California. At the time, I didn't know it, but we bought our new house directly across the street from the future love of my life. Nor did I know she would also provide the genesis of my unparalleled passion and enthusiasm.

There was a period in my late adolescence and young adulthood when life was rather bland and unexciting.

It was the passive period of my life. My nose was to the grindstone at school, at work, and in ROTC., training to be an Army officer. But the wild stallions were revolting. I had not wanted to let them out for fear that my life might become out of control. Then came romance! It was not until I was age nineteen and in college that the girl-next-door asked me to her school dance. For the very first time, I was besieged by butterflies fluttering frantically in my frenetic tummy. My testosterone was at peak performance and primed; my passion consumed me. No, this time it wasn't infatuation. I was sure it was true love.

I could no longer contain the zeal of those inner beasts. My passivity turned overnight to exaltation. The quiet turned to aggression, jealousy, and elation. The hunger to fulfill my heart's delight was ignited like an atomic explosion. The chains of restraint were released. I was bitten by cupid and hell-bent in love. I was determined to do everything in my power to perfect not just a friendship but a lifelong relationship. We fell in love, and after a three-year courtship were married in August 1964. It was the very best thing in my entire life. This ebullience remains after 56 years. Calmness now prevails, but the coals remain crimson.

Once the gates were open and the wild stallions made their way to the treasures of Mother Nature, there was no holding back. Life was resurrected, the renaissance was ignited.

My glowing zeal opened the doors to serendipity. I went on to graduate school, worked 36 hours a week, and became the only part-time worker in the Lucky Store chain to be officially named "third man" (third in charge). The store was called "Gemco," one of the largest combined grocery/department stores in California. My enthusiasm and passion were in high gear. I thoroughly enjoyed both the work and my fellow workmates as I continued to follow my dream. Not only had I transferred universities to be close to her, but my dream was modified. I had been a pre-med student. Now, how could I afford to attend medical school and have a wife, too? Once more, serendipity struck! A professor from the Psychology Department visited our class. Dr. John MacRae spoke about a new Master of Science program specializing in School Psychology that was to begin the following year. There was a growing need for school psychologists, and San Jose State University had been chosen to begin an intense 60-unit Master's program. This new curriculum would result in a one-year internship, and then final certification and credentialing. There was only one more major obstacle: I was in Army ROTC. and scheduled for Fort Lewis, Washington, that summer before my marriage.

At that time, the Vietnam War was beginning, and we were in training for guerrilla warfare. I had mixed emotions, looking forward to marrying my sweetheart, yet fearing going off to the state of Washington to train, then to war thousands of miles from home. My ambivalence was creating enormous stress. Ironically, I had developed a 1½-inch growth on the back of my left marching foot. When I visited my local orthopedist, I suggested that he also x-ray my back. I frequently encountered serious back problems during high school football, but like most exuberant and unthinking football players, I ignored it and played through it. I would wait until the end of the season to rest my back. Following an exam and x-rays, my doctor scheduled a consultation. Upon my return, he announced that not only would my walking and marching be impaired, but that I had a severe congenital lumbar problem.

He quickly concluded, "You have a congenital disability of L5 and L6 and will never be accepted into active duty in the Army."

I was immediately relieved. Although I love my country and was willing to risk my life, the thought of being thousands of miles away from my new bride weighed heavily. I met with my commanding officer, explained the results, and handed him the doctor's report. He requested a second opinion from the Army's Letterman Hospital in San Francisco. A few weeks later, I was in a long queue awaiting x-rays and an examination from the Army orthopedic specialist.

While waiting, I was interrupted several times by a big heavyset master sergeant. He repeatedly and somewhat brusquely said, "Hey, mother f—, I don't know why you're wasting your time waiting in line. You're gonna be just like the other guys in line and me; in good ol' Army green."

My anxiety heightened, and I proceeded with the exams and x-rays. Upon return two weeks later, I was scheduled to receive a summary of the results. The full-bird Colonel, an Army orthopedist, asked me to come in and sit down. He began slapping x-rays on an illuminated glass screen.

Before he could finish, I blurted out, "There it is—a unilateral defect, lumbar area!"

Surprised, he said, "How did you know?"

In my excitement, I quickly answered, "You know I was a pre-med student!" Both tears of joy and a tinge of sadness filled my eyes as I drove back from San Francisco.

The remainder is history, and over 56 years later, I'm able to share this story. Yes, life is indeed beautiful, but there are always obstacles and bumps on one's journey. Fortunately, the passion and enthusiasm were so resplendent that they can never be forgotten in those divine days. Sometimes, fortuity meets reality, and joie de vivre, hope, and destiny results!

> *"One cannot have a lukewarm life. You have to live life with passion."*
>
> —*Antonia Pantoja*

> *"If you have health, you probably will be happy, and if you have health and happiness, you have all the wealth, you'll need, even if it is not all you want."*
>
> —*Elbert Hubbard*

MANGIA MANGIA HEALTHFUL LIVING

As a child, my parents, friends, and extended family could not believe how much I could eat. They were sometimes horrified when I took my fourth helping of veal cutlets or ate my third Don and Bob's quarter-pound hamburger. Not surprisingly, I came from an Italian-American family that not only encouraged a good appetite but continuously reminded me MANGIA! MANGIA! (EAT! EAT!).

My grandma Angelina would smile and pat me on the back when I accepted her delicious second, third, or fourth helpings. She was an accomplished self-made chef who worked in a posh restaurant. Even though she spoke broken English and was designated a cook by her employer, she cooked like Julia Child. I knew no one who ever turned down Grandma's meals. Her meals were peasant dishes, highly nutritious, but relatively simple. Her comfort foods included homemade chicken soup with vegetables and pastina, pasta con broccoli, pasta e piselli (peas), pasta fagioli (white beans), pasta aglio e olio (olive oil and garlic), spingi (fried dough), cardone (stalks similar to artichoke), spaghetti and meatballs with a Bolognese sauce that included both hamburger and pork, Melanzane Parmigiana (eggplant), stuffed artichokes, calamari, fish stew, fried codfish, tender, tasty roasts, and much more.

Each recipe had a touch of heaven with sprinkles of love and spiced with angel wings.

As I write, nostalgic shivers and warm fuzzies run up and down my spine.

My parents, aunts, uncles, cousins, grandchildren, and now great-grandchildren have adopted Grandma's simple recipes. My dad and mom had side jobs working in restaurants. After completing his BA and working in finance for seven years, my son decided to go to culinary school and currently has two restaurants called Mangia Mi. My cousins in Rochester, New York, own Pasta Villa, a popular Italian restaurant in the metropolitan area. Our extended family consists of amateur chefs, and many are food connoisseurs. All thanks to my most wonderful grandma. She always took the time to share her food and allow us to prepare meals with her guidance. My grandma's cooking continues to be a topic of conversation at almost all of our extended family gatherings.

Seldom a week goes by that I have a *"voglia,"* a craving, for one of grandma's comfort foods. When those cravings overwhelm me, it's off to the refrigerator and stove. Comfort foods provide me with good health and security, quiet repose, unification, hope, happiness, and always a bit of tangible love. Usually, it's a peasant dish of pasta with vegetables doused in olive oil and garlic, but sometimes it involves an extensive number of pots and pans. For instance, it includes another special dish that my grandmother and dad made called Caponata, a southern Italian vegetarian dish. It includes eggplant, onions, garlic, olives, pine nuts, celery, fresh tomatoes, mushrooms, peppers, oregano, basil, capers, and a touch of balsamic vinegar sautéed in extra-virgin olive oil. By the time I finish, I will have made two huge pots. I then bottle it, freeze it, and share it with our family and friends at the Italian-American Heritage Foundation. It's just one of those fun nostalgic trips to my past, enveloped by hugs and kisses from Grandma Angelina. I must add my wife and her family as almost mirror images to mine.

Our Sunday rituals have lasted for many of my 78 years. They remain not only happy childhood memories, but I also continue to look forward to them with great delight. These festive feasts included mounds of pasta, heavenly aromas, bottles of wine, and soft music, all in the comforting bliss of a unified family. When we share these Sunday food and wine experiences, we all raise our glasses and say, "Salute!" It is a traditional appreciation not only for the occasion, but to toast our lost family members and the good health of those who remain. During those special meals, everyone is encouraged to share their thoughts and the most recent happenings. They are often lengthy and loud discussions. We try to avoid controversial issues; however, sometimes, it is necessary to discuss them. There is nothing more heartwarming or stomach-satisfying than sharing those special loving meals. I hope to close my eyes on my very final day, visualizing those etched nostalgias and magical moments.

Your choice of food, friends, and environment is critical to your physical and mental fitness. You can't control your genes or DNA, nor can you manage all the microorganisms or potentially dangerous extraneous events that you will encounter. Also, you can't control Mother Nature, only your lifestyle and the conditions that surround it. Your future is dependent upon your ability to control the physical, social and psychological factors under your sphere of influence. If you are the master of your environment, you can be assured of the benefits of excellent wellness. Once more, the keys are in your hands; unlock the doors to a sound and fulfilling life.

Health and happiness are strongly correlated. Happy people are usually healthy people. The relationship is called the circle of a good life; regardless of whether happiness affects health or health affects happiness, they are intimately tied together. The combination of physical, mental, and social well-being constitutes robust fitness. It is a result of self-managing those challenges discussed throughout this book. Your well-being is directly related to your ability to understand, assimilate, and make conscious decisions about food, social relationships, and daily difficulties. It is dependent upon your ability to adapt, change, and cope with your environment.

A fit mind and body constitute homeostatic balance. They allow you to cope with physical, social, and psychological insults.

It seems that each decade, the pundits recommend a different health focus or fad. In the 1980s, the buzzwords were low-fat diets; a decade or more later, it became the low-carb diet. Recently, it is a high-protein diet. Why protein? Because athletes and bodybuilders want bigger muscles and higher performance. Like other fads, there is a downside to each. For example, animal protein can cause various organ problems, especially heart and kidney dysfunction. Researchers have attempted for many years to tease apart the various low-fat, low-carb, and high-protein diets. Each includes a myriad of foods, such as meat, dairy, fish, legumes, fortified foods, vegetables, fruits, and other miscellaneous plants that constitute each diet.

The only repeatedly consistent diet recommended by medical experts is the Mediterranean Diet. It is primarily composed of fruits, vegetables, legumes, whole grains, fish, nuts, poultry, low sodium, olive oil, and a little wine.

All reputable health organizations recommend regular exercise, a balanced diet, social support, and stress management. However, exercise is the most neglected of all recommendations. It will improve your balance, emotional mood, muscle tone and provide supplemental social support if enjoyed with others. It is good for both mind and body. Exercise can also be accomplished by walking, gardening, dancing, working out, etc. Pick your favorite daily activity and put it on your day-to-day To-Do list.

In reviewing the most recent health recommendations, the UCLA "Healthy Years" published the article "Go Out and Play." They said, "Fresh air and a change of scenery are just a few of the reasons that being active outdoors does the mind, body, and spirit good." Consider the outdoors as your recreation facility or big workout room. It invigorates, increases vitamin D, keeps joints and muscles fit, and is a venue second to none. UCLA's suggestions included cycling/biking, swimming, hiking, geocaching (outdoor treasure hunting), and paddle boarding. Needless to say, whatever exercise activity you choose will be a far better break from being frozen in front of a television or computer. Regardless of where you exercise, your ultimate goal is to stay fit. Avoid an overly sedentary lifestyle and maintain a reasonable body mass.

There are some basic elements that I'd like to suggest in order to gain and maintain good health. They include:

- Drink a lot of water.
- Eat your breakfast like a king, lunch like a princess, and dinner like a beggar.
- Eat as much food as possible from trees and plants. Eat fewer foods made in factories.
- If appropriate, a glass of wine is recommended.
- Involve yourself in more sports and more active playing in your life.
- Read as much as you can about wellness.
- Invest in at least seven hours of sleep every night.
- Take a 15- to 30-minute walk each day or a minimum of 30 minutes of some kind of exercise.
- Make time for contemplation, meditation, or prayer for at least 5 to 10 minutes a day.
- Remember, no one is responsible for your health but you.
- The secret of secrets is that you *can* remain physically fit.

Except for your mental faculties, without physical health, your journey may be doomed. Helen Keller was an exceptional individual whose determination, persistence, and perseverance overcame the handicaps of blindness, deafness, and initial muteness. Regardless of your self-determination, perseverance, persistence, or lack of physical handicaps, you will face many obstacles. Your mastery of all the tools mentioned throughout this book will be your ticket to a balanced life. Adding those tools and the health and happiness tools of this chapter will not only extend your life but provide you with soundness of mind and body.

PERSONAL GLIMPSES

I have known many friends and family who have overcome major difficulties. They were able to turn their negative environments into positive outcomes by choice, not destiny; by strength, not capitulation; by determination and persistence, and most of all, by adaptation. My mother grew up without a mother and spent many years in an orphanage. My dad lost his dad at age five due to the 1918 flu pandemic. He grew up without a father and with a mother who barely spoke English. She needed to support her three children, age five and younger. They struggled and persevered. Their life tragedies strengthened them, and they became motivating forces for a better life. Their resolve awakened and forced them to adapt, accept, and appreciate life as their most precious gift. I silently applaud them every time I pass their photos in our hallway. Their stories are not rare, but replete in the lives of many whose misfortunes were ultimately blessings in disguise. Health is the ability to overcome adversity. There is no doubt that diet, exercise, sleep, and medical interventions cannot be disregarded, but your knowledge and conscious decisions ultimately will determine your health.

"Prepare for mirth, for mirth becomes a feast."
—*William Shakespeare*

JEST FOR THE HEALTH OF IT

I get more pleasure out of humor than any other subject—except love. It is the other love of my life. Everyone who knows me well knows that without wit and jest, my life would be bland, boring, and lackluster. Comedy and its subsequent laughter are some of the most powerful tools that one can possess. Unquestionably these potent tools are required for survival from the stressful effects of our current world and its accelerated high technology. Also, humor easily dissolves our regular annoyances as well as our day-to-day petty issues.

BEGIN BY LAUGHING AT YOURSELF

At 101, my mother continues to say that laughing at herself saves her the embarrassment of having to excuse her behavior. She says, "Try laughing at yourself. Try it, you'll like it!"

Now that she has reached the centenarian status, her ʳt-term memory has decidedly diminished. When I convey a date or time that she doesn't remember, she chuckles and says, "I don't remember; that's my middle name."

Most people find that laughing at oneself is a much better response than self-condemnation or self-guilt. It also conveys a valuable virtue—humility. The foibles of life can be chuckled away by, first and foremost, laughing at oneself. Truly mature persons can laugh at themselves in the presence of others and enjoy its benefits while experiencing a good laugh. It makes problems less serious and provides another moment of fun and laughter.

> "To make mistakes is human, to stumble is common-
> place, to be able to laugh at yourself is maturity."
> —William Arthur Ward

Humor comes in many shapes and sizes. Sometimes it's just a play on the truth. It can be a look at the bizarre or a trip into your inner sanctum. It can be triggered by satire or even a look at the silly realities of contemporary society. Sometimes it is buffeted with embellishments or exaggerations; sometimes the blatant truth; sometimes a complete contradiction, or strange certainties, or threat, or fear, or misdirection. The punchline is the surprise and usually results in a guffaw. Laughter provides you the distance to step back, observe, and enjoy your world.

Humor is the emotional opposite of depression!

The World Health Organization has predicted that by the year 2022, depression will be the second major cause of death in the United States. Levity is a potent tool and antidote for depression.

Ironically and sadly, as I was writing this chapter, I received an email. Gayle Kramer, a dear friend and wit extraordinaire, had succumbed to cancer. I met Gayle some 50 years ago. She was concerned with the lack of attention given to intellectually gifted students. With her at the helm, we and two others created a private, nonprofit program for the intellectually talented that was called Lyceum of Silicon Valley. At that time, Silicon Valley was in its infancy. Yet, it was a budding and veritable brain trust. It is not surprising that some of these young brainsters later shaped our high-tech valley. Gayle's sense of humor was just what the doctor ordered. My wife, children, and friends spent many hours belly-busting from her laconic and hilarious wit. She might say, "Silicon . . . you know . . . that's a silly crook," or she might say to parents, "you know intellectual giftedness always skips a generation!" Sometimes at 3 a.m., after a hilarious but long evening, Gayle was known to say, "Tony, it must have been a very scintillating evening; you fell asleep an hour ago!" We will miss her greatly. I thus dedicate this chapter to my dear and talented friend Gayle Kramer.

Comedy not only forces you to think differently, but it is also a medium for creativity. Hilarity stretches your mind and connects related and unrelated verbal associations. It expands your horizons and creates unlimited black cranial holes to explore further and discover. Humor is considered by most professionals to be the most effective antidote to stress. It represents the David in the story of Goliath because it delivers a deathblow to the torment of unrelenting tension. It provides the magical pinch of spice to the entrées of life's daily stress. We are often surprised to see tense moments negated by a simple touch of witticism. Not only does it eliminate the seriousness and dangers of stress, but levity also converts it into enthusiastic energy and new opportunities to step out of a funk.

We have all experienced a very tense situation shifting from near morbidity to hilarity in a matter of seconds, all by a carefully chosen quip or cleverly-placed joke. Those abrupt comedic moments of mood-shifts miraculously cleanse the air. I had the opportunity to know intimately two friends aged 97; a mother who is currently age 101, and a 102-year-old aunt, as well as a few elderly acquaintances. They all can be described as happy, laughing at the silliest of things, giggly, and fun to be around. Their overall demeanor seemed to be *might as well laugh and enjoy, rather than sulk and be somber*. My observations found them enjoying life and work, not bothered by the mundane trivialities that often create obstacles. Probably my biggest revelation was that they were almost all frequent gigglers. They and comedians like George Burns and Bob Hope lived long and enjoyable lives because they found the fountain of youth in a bottle of witticisms.

NORMAN COUSINS

Laughter is the best antidote for the temporary poison of stress. Humor can heal and extend one's life by balancing seriousness with hilarity. Norman Cousins, in his famous book, *Anatomy of an Illness*, illustrated how it saved his life. Norman, a famous writer and editor of the New York Post and Saturday Review, was diagnosed with ankylosing spondylitis by his friend and family physician. At that time, it was thought to be a terminal illness. He decided that since he had been given only months to live, that he would make them the best months of his life.

Norman realized that the hospital costs would be more expensive than a stay at New York's finest, the Waldorf-Astoria Hotel. He checked into a suite and invited his friends and relatives. It was his opportunity to enjoy the finest of food, drink, and entertainment, as well as to say his final goodbyes. With a smile on his face, he proceeded to purchase the most hilarious movies of the time. The flicks included the Marx Brothers, Amos and Andy, Dean Martin and Jerry Lewis, the Three Stooges, Laurel and Hardy, Abbott and Costello, the Bowery Boys, et al.

As he and his friends visited, they watched these outrageously funny movies, hysterically laughing while savoring fine food and drink. Norman soon was surprised to discover that ten-minute belly laughs gave him two hours or more of pain relief. After three months of belly-laughing, enjoying belly-loving delicacies, and visiting with his friends, he again saw his family physician. Norman went through an extensive series of medical tests and returned for the bad news. His physician was baffled and could not believe the results.

This supposedly incurable disease was not only in remission, but undetectable.

As a matter of fact, Cousins lived another 28 years! Norman was so astonished and so appreciative that he decided to dedicate the rest of his life to sharing his good news.

Comedy had indeed saved his life!

He spent the remaining of his year's life teaching the benefits of humor to students at the UCLA.'s School of Medicine. He soon became the most respected and popular professor there.

During his stay at UCLA, he wrote a famous treatise on levity and its effect on the psyche and the extension of physical health. The book was *Anatomy of An Illness*. It described Cousins' humor-cure from the throes of death. It became a best seller and is still widely read. In this book, Norman shared a hilarious story, which I especially enjoyed. It involved his friend and mentor, Bennett Cerf, an inveterate joke collector, publisher, and author. Cerf came to the aid of Cousins, who was about to give a significant speech. He appeared far too nervous and serious. Norm asked Cerf if he could think of a comical story, perhaps one he may have recently encountered. Bennett replied that a week earlier, Gen. Dwight D Eisenhower was installed as the new president of Columbia University. Cerf was about to give an introductory speech, and seeing his nervousness, Eisenhower suggested a technique that always worked for him. "I look around at the audience and visualize everyone in their old, tattered underwear. When you speak, try this technique." A few weeks later, in St. Louis, Cousins shared the Eisenhower story. Although the speech went well, his anecdote failed to get the response intended. After the lecture, he was puzzled until a fellow shared, "Are you sure about the General Eisenhower story? Did it really happen to you?"

Cousins responded, "Of course it did."

"That's very strange," the man replied, "Bennett Cerf lectured here last week and said it happened to him!"

Another similar anecdote is the story of comedian Stan Silliman. He'd been diagnosed with cancer at age 55 and had six operations, radiation, and 24 MRIs. He considered comedy as his salvation. Like Norman Cousins, he had not only survived over 20 years, but wrote eight humor books and continues to entertain in hospitals as well as stand-up comedy venues. According to him, he was thrilled and rewarded by others' laughter, especially his darling wife's.

THERAPEUTIC HEALTH
BENEFITS OF HUMOR

The mind indeed is the best apothecary of all, and humor is its best medicine. The therapeutic benefits of it are well-documented and are as old as humanity.

The Old Testament (Proverbs 17:22) attests to it, "A merry heart doeth good like a medicine."

Humor may not be a cure-all, but the many benefits of it are almost endless. It is the supreme elixir and the closest thing to the fountain of youth. No, it can't stop the clock, but it relaxes and stretches "Father time" and extends life's terminal time clock. Coincidentally, many famous comedians live well into their nineties. Two centenarians mentioned above, Bob Hope and George Burns, immediately come to mind. Humor is a significant health benefactor. It boosts memory, brings people together, and stimulates the brain. It is infectious, entertaining, relieves tension, inoculates the immune system, accelerates friendship, enhances love, solves problems, suppresses stressful events, aids our communication skills, shrinks the complex, and creates a common bond among different groups of people. The list can go on and on.

Below are some of the acknowledged benefits from research studies, anecdotal data, and consensus:

- Laughter assists the vascular system by dilating blood vessels and reducing blood pressure.
- Biofeedback studies have demonstrated that the human body's muscle stress can be reduced.
- Researchers found the connection between the stress hormone cortisol and memory and learning. Memory was enhanced by 33%-48% by the introduction of levity.
- Studies have found that watching humorous films or live performance reduces pain and the need for stronger analgesics. Hilarity reduces pre-operative anxiety and post-operative pain.
- Laughter reduces epinephrine associated with hypertension and arrhythmias.
- Humor affects our panic or threat responses by allowing the amygdala to release oxytocin, helping us cope with stressors.
- Social scientists point out that laughter strengthens interpersonal relationships, teamwork, diffuses interpersonal conflicts, increases trust, and allows for physical and emotional attraction.
- Laughter simulates a physical workout.
- Laughter increases the body's ability to fight disease by increasing T cell production.
- Laughter stimulates the immune system by activating the thymus, causing it to work at peak

levels. Endorphins are released in well-being and relaxation. Similarly, levity reduces the stress hormones cortisol and adrenaline.

- Laughter allows more oxygen to the brain and vital organs, making cheeks rosy and displaying a healthy complexion.
- Scientific studies find that the brain's response to humor is very fast. The left hemisphere immediately displays electrical activity and analyzes the joke, while the right hemisphere gets the joke. The limbic system becomes happily excited, causing the motor sensations to smile and laugh.
- Several types of headaches are caused by constricted blood vessels and reduced oxygen. The result is the pulsing and throbbing symptoms of a headache. Humor dissipates headaches.
- Many studies have found that smile and laughter intensity is related to longevity. Those who smiled more lived an additional seven years.

SOCIAL AND EMOTIONAL BENEFITS OF HUMOR

There is a consensus that the most effective means of social success is humor. Two-thirds of women listed it as the most important trait in a potential mate. When we take ourselves or our current situation too seriously, we are doomed to stress and social/emotional conflicts.

When things seem to be coming apart, calmness and a sense of humor will often save the day. Walking away with a satisfied smile and a feeling of relief is possible when panic is replaced by confidence and contentment.

Besides the health benefits mentioned above, wittiness has a substantial impact on work, productivity, personal insight, social media, creativity, and ultimate survival. It is a boon to society. Studies have consistently found that laughter in the workplace results in more job productivity, longer voluntary work hours, camaraderie, company loyalty, increased problem-solving, and creativity. Workers who found more fun in their jobs were less anxious and less bored with their labors.

It is not surprising that the top companies in the world, such as Apple, Google, and Facebook, have been so spectacularly successful in such a brief period of time. As I write, Apple is currently the wealthiest company in the world. Other high-tech companies such as Google, Yahoo, and Facebook, have also, in just a few years, far exceeded innovations and productivity than the highly conservative companies in existence for more than a century. Having a relaxed workplace where laughter is encouraged appears far more productive than the constraints of a necktie, suit, and somewhat staid environments that discourage frivolity. Certainly, hilarity needs to be balanced with the semblance of structure. This equilibrium is necessary to propel corporate productivity, even in the most liberal of work environments.

However, the motto of success seems to be: "Let's get serious about humor!"

So, try to make work and family life fun. There seems to be an obvious corollary; *the family that plays and laughs together stays together.* You cannot have compatibility and accomplishment without having some form of fun. Peters and Waterman, in their famous book, *In Search of Excellence*, point out that the nation's best-run companies allow their employees to enjoy and have fun in their workplace. Many of these same organizations promote levity by bringing in humorists, posting daily cartoons, jokes, and quotes, or have after-work happy hours.

Joel Goodman, the founder of the Humor Project, says that humor creates inverse paranoia, "You begin to feel that the world is out to do you good!" He says that hilarity is not only the best medicine; it's the least expensive and the quickest acting. All humorists agree that it is the single best method in the development of personal relationships. It often leads to love. It releases the grip of anger, stress, and depression.

All good comedians and salespeople know the power of persuasion through the effectiveness of levity. Laughter opens the doors of the mind, heart, and pocketbooks. Humor is truly a universal language in all areas of our world. It breaks tension; it equalizes socioeconomics; it serves political purposes and cuts cultural and religious barriers. The lightness of jest allows us to become all brothers and sisters in the family called *humanity*. It diffuses and unites, and it has more explosive power than a nuclear bomb. For your survival, understand it, develop it, and use it frequently. It is your biggest tool for success and happiness.

Many comedians and cartoonists readily admit that they had complicated lives as children. Charles Schulz of Charlie Brown and Snoopy fame admitted that he developed jest to help him cope with the frustrations and feelings of helplessness. Likewise, the inimitable Robin Williams often considered his form of comedy relief as therapeutic.

TYPES OF HUMOR SATIRE

A relatively sophisticated type of humor is called satire. I am a dyed-in-the-wool lover and confirmed believer in its value. Satire is defined as the use of buoyant levity to exaggerate, ridicule, criticize, berate, or expose current conditions or well-known people, especially political or luminary types. Satire is a form of gray or dark humor. Often, it is found in the form of a joke, derision, carica-ture, mockery, or a roast. Please pardon my momentary indulgence by taking you a short walk back in time.

Although often purported to be founded by the Greeks, snippets of satire go much farther back in time. Ancient cave writings sometimes depicted the incipi-ent satire. However, it was the Romans who created the rather dark form called *satira* or *satura,* a mixture of mirth and menace. The very first true satirist was

Gaius Lucilius (180-103 B.C.). He wrote 30 books of satires. Because of his nobility and wealth, he could indulge in dark satire with impunity. His style ridiculed high-ranking officials regardless of the severity of Roman law penalties for libel and slander. Politicians and high officials were vilified as crooks, blowhards, cuckolds, swindlers, deviants, misers, and bores. Later, Horace and Virgil followed with equally provocative satire. New faces such as Petrarch introduced sonnets, and soon Boccaccio and Dante followed suit. Eventually, the satire was considered a literary landmark and masterpiece. The appearance of Shakespeare, Milton, Wordsworth, and Keats filled out a cast of satire geniuses. Not to be either pushy or satirical, perhaps there may be some good reading opportunities.

Today we see satire and sarcasm as regulars in both literature and live comedy. Because freedom of speech is no longer associated with imprisonment or death, at least in most civilized countries, actors, politicians, singers, wealthy people in business, and other notables are roasted with innuendo and disclaimers. Satire on television is replete with stories, brief skits, simulations of current events, and stand-up comedy. I find it delightfully entertaining, calming, and spiritually uplifting. I strongly urge you to experience its hilarity and its subtlety. True freedom of speech allows us to laugh and make fun of each other while capturing the inner essence of life's foibles.

POLITICAL HUMOR

It seems that we are always at the twilight of another contentious political debate and election. Humor is often the equalizer and palliative treatment of choice. There is an abundance of political jokes. I chose a couple that resonate with levity and laughter. Significant political figures wrote them. Needless to say, political wit could quickly fill volumes.

"If you can't convince 'em, confuse 'em."
—*Harry S. Truman*

"Good leaders not only need strong backbones; they need strong, funny bones."
—*Senator Elizabeth Dole*

MY FAVORITE HUMORISTS

"The most lost of all days is that in which one has not laughed."
—*Nicolas Chamfort*

During my lifetime, I have been blessed with having so many truly talented humorists in my world of laughter. I've collected volumes of books, articles, movies, and DVDs. I've been fortunate to attend stand-up comedy, watched wonderfully witty television appearances of the best of my era, as well as having seen slapstick comedy and even the silent movies of Charlie Chaplin. In the process, I've collected thousands of jokes, often sharing them with friends and relatives over the internet. I've chosen some samples of the most famous comics, however far from all-encompassing. Each had his or her unique style. Each entered comedy for personal reasons. Some searched for fame and wealth, while many for emotional relief, stress, or a problematic background. But all shared their imaginations and creativity with gusto to bring laughter and happiness to the entire range of humanity. I'd like to share a comedian's credo written by Red Skelton, a very sensitive, compassionate, and superb comedian, followed by one of my favorite lines.

> *"I live by this credo: have a little laugh at life and look around you for happiness instead of sadness. Laughter has always brought me out of unhappy situations. Even in your darkest moment, you usually can find something to laugh about if you try hard enough."*
> —*Red Skelton*

And I end this chapter with a memorable quote by a very special humorist. It includes both comedy and a touch of satire:

> *"If I have caused just one person to wipe away a tear of laughter, that's my reward. The rest goes to the government."*
> —*Victor Borge*

A more detailed critique including famous comedians and their legendary jokes entitled "HUMOR" is available by going to https://www.drtonycedolini.com/humor

"The happiest people are not necessarily the richest, the most beautiful, or even the most talented. Happy people do not rely on outside excitement for fun. They enjoy the fundamentals, often the very simple things of life. They waste no time thinking that other pastures are greener or yearning for yesterday or tomorrow. They savor the moment, glad to be alive, enjoying their work, their families, and the good things around them. They can bend with the wind and adjust to changes in their lives. Their eyes are open and turned towards others. They are aware, compassionate, have a zest for life, and a capacity for love."

—*Jane Canfield*

CHASING HAPPINESS

During the first waking minutes of the morning, I replenish my soul in the solitude of the moment. I allow my mind to wander, ponder, and excel in creative adventures. It is then that feelings of appreciation, enlightenment, and fascination flourish with a rush of emotions that sends chilling thoughts and visions circling in my mind's eye. I am overwhelmed with the excitement and joy of nostalgic reflections and of what is yet to come. Those quiet moments set the stage for a potentially glorious day. I'm able to let go of the concerns from the night before, and I look forward to delightfully enjoying the renewed feelings of a fresh new day.

"Solitude is where I place my chaos to rest and awaken my inner peace."
—*Nikki Rowe*

Although awkward and embarrassing to admit, my other place of solitude is sitting on my bathroom throne.

I can still hear my frustrated dad outside in the hallway, wanting to use our family's sole bathroom, saying, "The king has been on the throne for half an hour, reading an encyclopedia. Does he think he owns it?"

Those quiet and solemn moments are some of the most relaxing times of the day. I'm not sure if it's the break from a busy schedule or a chance to read, but those 20 to 30 minutes are as refreshing as a walk in the woods or a sensational sunset. Ironically and coincidentally, I have discovered that while on my throne, my resting heart rate is almost synonymous with my early-morning healthy heart rate, the low- to mid-50s. Again, it is a time to allow my mind to wander or a chance to read an informational or inspirational piece saved for those special minutes. Finally, my peaceful solitude slowly returns. I can sit, meditate, dream, and allow the stillness and quiet to overtake me.

My happiest moments are when I can share my most personal thoughts with you and the other special people on my journey. Besides being inspired by cheerful thoughts, nothing makes me more content than sharing those same thoughts.

Pause and take a break from chasing happiness by letting your mind relax and wander, even for a few quick moments. It is a pause that refreshes. Enjoying simple pleasures allows you to appreciate the more meaningful moments—your family, friends, sunrises, sunsets, flora and fauna, other glorious gifts of nature, or a baby's gentle breath.

> *"How could I not be happy and healthy? For 101 years, I have observed every beautiful component of nature and have the most wonderful family I could've ever imagined. I have known many wonderful people and have seen and experienced things I could never have conceived of ever happening."*
> —Mary Cedolini, mother

None of you know how long you will be here. Besides, you are only able to make one journey. Why not make your life one that is fulfilled with joy, satisfaction, and purpose? Make it your duty to do everything during this precious time to bring joy to as many people as you can. Knowing this and pursuing it as one of your goals in life will ultimately bring you supreme contentment. Better yet, the satisfaction that you receive will be of your own personal doing, no one else's.

The Declaration of Independence states that the pursuit of happiness is our inalienable right."

When we neurotically and frenetically pursue pleasure, we ultimately create frustration, fear, resentment, and additional stress. Obsessively chasing enjoyment makes it as elusive as a dog chasing its tail.

John Stuart Mill, frequently reputed to be one of the brightest intellectuals of all time, emphasized that true happiness brings joy to others. He also felt strongly that our emphasis should not only be directed to others but also in making our world a better place to be enjoyed by all. Many others also agreed with him; they include poets, psychiatrists, prophets, philosophers, scientists, and even the Dalai Lama.

Although sometimes difficult, compassion for others is necessary for you to reach nirvana. Practice it by caring and understanding for all people and by not discriminating or showing special favoritism to those only like you.

Again, it is our nation's belief, ". . . *that all men are created equal, that they are endowed with certain unalienable Rights, . . .*"

Happiness does not require a complicated plan or a series of strategies. All you will require is humility. A feeling of being equal, not better or worse than others, helps set your moral compass. Your contentment is made up of all the small things that cause you to enjoy others and the simple pleasures of everyday life. In particular, the overwhelming feeling of a hug, kiss, a walk with someone special, a sunset, a call to a friend, a teddy bear, a security blanket—all priceless!

Wake up each morning and remember that happiness is ultimately *your* choice. You and only you are responsible for your state of mind. Blaming others is denying yourself the ability to choose your thoughts and attitudes, which remain your only personal freedom. You can choose your solitude and peacefulness at any time or any place.

It's not getting all you want but enjoying and appreciating what you have, instead of being frustrated and angry about what you lack. Savoring the morning sun or cloudy skies, sharing lunch with a sibling or parent, these are some of the simple, more meaningful, magical, and nostalgic moments of internal happiness.

I have had the opportunity to visit Third World countries and observe authentic spontaneity. What has always struck me is that no matter how little people have, peace of mind coexists with sparse material possessions. Love supersedes all, and life is love, regardless of circumstances or socioeconomics. The very finest things in life are not material things. Remember, the best things in life are indeed free. Personal freedom is one of those very precious gifts.

HAPPINESS ISN'T

Happiness isn't exclusive to comfort and personal pleasure. It isn't sheer luxury or untold monetary wealth; instead, it is true elegance, without fancy ostentatious display. Real joy equates to deep feelings and unconditional love; it is enjoyment and contentment with whatever life offers. There is nothing more important in life than a true sense of well-being. Why? Because not only does it bring personal contentment, but it brings benefits to the world at large. However, it is not all milk and honey. Day-to-day frustrations and unexpected twists and turns are part of life. Problems will always remain endemic to your life's journey; resolving them and moving forward is necessary before refocusing on more constructive issues. Your life can remain beautiful if you are willing to accept and acknowledge the resolution of problems as your supreme gift.

When you obsessively pursue happiness instead of allowing it to unfold, you convolute it. Rather than chasing it, you add fear, frustration, and anxiety; allow yourself to relax and savor the moment. Realize that there will always be trials, troubles, and tribulations. Each makes you stronger and more eager to enjoy your moments of bliss. Acknowledge that your disappointments are real, but also learning moments. And remember that self-pity, egotism, fear, and anxiety are less noble than cultivating acceptance, love, honor, peace, and loyalty. Your paradise resides within you. Cooperating with life, going with the flow rather than against it, and not chasing windmills will maintain your focus on the present.

Consequently, it will eliminate your preoccupation with the past. Happy people bury their past grudges, failures, and resentments. Happy people adapt to failures without choreographing them as their unfortunate preplanned destiny. By not forcing it and utilizing the tools discussed in this book, good cheer will find its way and besiege you with joyful bliss.

SATISFACTION AND CONTENTMENT

Many authors have equated satisfaction and contentment as the equivalent to happiness. Most would agree that being satisfied with oneself is a form of personal happiness. Joy and contentment result in feeling fulfilled compared to pure egotistical self-gratification, which is often self-defeating because it is often at the expense of another person. Over the years, I have discovered that the only genuine and most sincere self-gratification comes from win/win experiences, when both parties walk away satisfied and content. Coming to a mutually fair and judicious conclusion always results in maximum contentment, satisfaction, and increased trust. If, however, one person takes advantage of another, whether it is business, sex, or a social situation, momentary glory may result, but true guilt-free happiness is never accomplished.

Some people spend a lifetime playing one-upmanship with little interest in sharing, compromising, or agreeing to mutual acceptance. Little do they realize that their character is besmirched and their conscience compromised. Initially, I didn't believe others who suggested, "What goes around comes around." However, enough time and experience have passed that I am now convinced that those most greedy and self-centered end up eventually paying dearly for their transgressions.

Feverishly searching for happiness will not bring it to oneself.

One of my mentors would frequently repeat, "You only obtain something when you can let it go." Trying to possess and overly control every aspect of others leads to isolation and loneliness. However, when you allow life to spring forward, like a surprise party, it begets contentment, satisfaction, appreciation, and ultimately happiness.

"The neurotic builds dream castles, the psychotic lives in them, and that psychologist collects the rent."

—Anonymous

TWO COWS GRAZING ALONG THE ROAD

My professional background included 50 years of counseling parents and children as a marriage, family, and child therapist. I also did extensive work assessing children in regard to learning and behavior. During those five decades, there were massive changes in providing mental health, but it brought new tools and understanding to all areas. The concepts of self-image and self-attitude especially clarified how children and adults mature or are stymied in their personal development.

Employers, teachers, parents, and students all recognize the importance of positive mental health. Your psychological health is ultimately more important than your physical condition. Your mind influences all aspects of your life. It is indeed your human computer and needs constant care. The mind and the body are intimately related and part of a highly-complex system of interacting chemicals and electrical discharges that are either harmoniously balanced or dysfunctional.

Confronting your daily stressors requires ongoing attentiveness, and adaptation. Both success and happiness are states of mind.

Your confidence and positive attitude are keys to your positive mental health.

When you value yourself, you exude confidence and optimism. When you don't value yourself, you focus on the negative. Self-attitude and self-image are the critical components for a positive psychological profile.

People have asked me, what is self-attitude, and what are its essential parts? It reminds me of a picture of two cows grazing alongside a highway, near a tanker truck of milk that had a sign that read Pasteurized, Homogenized, Standardized, Vitamin A added. One cow turned to the other and remarked, "Sort of makes you feel inadequate, doesn't it?"

Like the cows, your feelings of adequacy or competence are certainly the major components of self-attitude.

Self-attitude, also referred to as self-esteem, is your overall perception of your world. It is based on a collage of self-images that lead to your overall feelings and attitudes about yourself. I was then asked what self-image was. Self-image is essentially your personalized photograph album composed of thousands of pictures of yourself. They include you in a variety of activities, such as playing baseball or tennis, doing math, cooking, typing, reading, gardening, relating to others, plumbing, playing the piano, doing fix-up jobs, speaking a foreign language, etc. Each activity then connects your personal feelings associated with each of those activities.

What creates self-image? We are all visual beings. You take these pictures of yourself and retain them from your very first day in your cute little birthday suit, the birth of your conscious mind. Whether it's learning to walk, ride a bike, drive a car, or spell, you continuously take snapshots of every activity. Often, you painfully work through each difficult step. As a visual being, you retain these self-image photos. They soon become home movies of yourself walking, riding a bike, learning how to read or spell, play sports, etc. I still remember those old 8mm movies my folks took. And now, since they were converted to DVDs, my kids can't stop giggling. I'm surprised that my granddaughter Isabella doesn't ask if they were silent movies. During these painful learning processes, you will have encountered many successes and failures. They are called feedback loops. These feedback loops are the building blocks of learning, e.g., falling from a bike, hitting a home run, bumping into objects, or getting an A in math. Each loop becomes a visual memory saved as a self-image and capable of eventual upgrading.

Both photos of your success and failure allow you to shape your behavior and to solidify your thinking. As you walk or ride a bike, you find that certain moves work or don't work. These feedback loops help you change your behavior and upgrade your photo album. Changes occur by making adjustments caused by the information you've gained by your feedback loops. It's no different than that provided by mirrors, scales, or speedometers. Each gives you information for your next action. Your actions are based on how you perceive yourself and whether you choose to change a specific behavior. I can't recall exactly, but I spent a lot of time in front of a full-length mirror mimicking nonsense. Fortunately, no one else was looking!

Ultimately, your goal, like mine, is to convert behaviors into automatic responses called automaticity. But it's a double-edged sword. On the positive side, it helps you ride a bike, spell, walk, and drive a car with a minimum of conscious effort. Negatively, you can drift off to unconsciousness and allow your automatic pilot to take charge. Consequently, when you are asleep at the switch, you can lose control, make careless errors, and sometimes crash!

Many mornings, I wake up and lumber into the kitchen. I'll go into the refrigerator and realize I was looking for the coffee pot. I find myself in a daze, not thinking about what should come next. I aimlessly walk into the dining room or pantry, not knowing why I'm there. Why? Because I'm not fully conscious, and my automatic pilot switch is not turned on. My internal gyroscope is barely functioning. I pass it off as senior moments, but then realize these same behaviors have happened for decades. Yes, the older I get, the frequency does increase because my autopilot is not warming up as quickly as it did.

This reminds me of a story a friend told me. He was approached by his parish priest, who suggested that he should start thinking about the "Hereafter." He said, "Father, I want you to know I constantly am thinking about the "Hereafter." I go into the garage, or pantry or closet, and exclaim, "What the hell am I here after?"

These learning experiences and feedback slowly fixed the perceptions of my world. I felt either good or bad, successful or unsuccessful, competent or incompetent, based upon the feedback. Other experiences also provide these powerful feedback loops both in words and pictures. For example, your parents, relatives, and friends send both nonverbal images and word messages. Certain looks and features soon become either positive or negative. "OMG, either I'm in trouble, or it is ice cream time!" Consequently, I either felt good or bad about people, places, and things based on these continuous feedback loops. These perceptions eventually became my feelings about school, dogs, cats, offices, clothing, and understanding individual differences.

However, there is a major caveat. The extent of the database and subsequent programming can be either enlightening or disastrous, depending on whether your feedback is either extensive or limited. If your primary feedback is dispersed solely from parents or a very small community, your database will be very restricted, finite, and narrow. It is not unusual that limited feedback results in strong biases for racial or ethnic food, or other preferences. Ignorance can be unwittingly bliss. The more opportunities for diverse and varied experiences, the larger and broader your database. This ever-growing database provides you with more accurate and realistic perceptions. I remember many clients that were so naïve, due to their lacking exposure, that they were unable to grasp a range of concepts, only seeing things as black and white. The smaller their database, the easier it becomes to develop biases and irrational fears, like a terror of dogs, spiders, distrust of adults, dentists, a political party, or race. Thus, they become fixed in a narrow-minded psyche.

It is evident today in forms of racism, arrogance, and greed. As a result, I see an extreme range from haughtiness to humility.

Ultimately these multiple learning experiences are combined to become the most critical judgments ever made; that is, the ones you pass on to yourself. It is called self-attitude. Sometimes referred to as self-realization, self-attitude is the overall feeling and words you have about yourself. That becomes a huge milestone in your life.

Personal acceptance is based on all of the feedback loops that you established since your original birthday. Ultimately it becomes your private gyroscope. Self-attitude is then the gyroscopic governor that continually keeps you in this default or status quo state, often without your total conscious recognition.

Henry Ford is often quoted—or misquoted—as having said, "Remember, folks, whether you think you can, or whether you think you can't, you're right!"

Your self-attitude gyroscope might say, "I can learn 12 languages," or it might say, "I can't do math worth beans." It keeps you within your perceived limits, your status quo, whether it is income, status, emotional stability, social relations, or work skills. Self-attitude predicts and perpetuates your performance!

Not only does self-attitude predict and perpetuate your performance, but it also becomes your mirror to the world. Why? Because your attitudes are the direct reflections of your self-images.

Thomas Drier said, "The world is a great mirror. It reflects what you are. If you are loving, if you are friendly, if you are helpful, the world will prove loving and friendly and helpful to you. The world is what you are."

Likewise, if you are angry, distraught, confused, anxious, and fearful, you will perceive the world as angry, convoluted, fearful, and unfriendly. There is no question that your feelings are the reflection of how you perceive yourself, and it reflects your world views.

Self-attitude directly influences the way you perceive and explain events. For example, individuals with high self-attitude might say, "I got the job because I was the most qualified and earned it through my efforts." A person with low self-esteem might say, "I was just plain lucky, being in the right place at the right time."

It greatly influences your expectations. Children with strong positive self-attitude attribute their successes to their ability and hard work; they attribute their failures to a lack of effort. Poor self-attitude children do just the opposite. They attribute their success to luck or destiny, and their failures to lack of ability. Also, since they don't expect to succeed, they put forth little effort, thus convincing themselves that they are indeed incapable.

This self-fulfilling hypothesis creates vicious circular thinking and misleading self-perceptions.

A positive self-attitude gives you the confidence necessary to fail, recover, and succeed without feeling excessively frustrated. It allows you to make decisions and take responsibility for your behavior, whether right or wrong. Even more importantly, positive self-confidence will enable you to love and accept yourself and others. No one wants to feel helpless, worthless, or unhappy. A positive attitude is visually expressed by confidence and poise. Those who possess it feel comfortable and relaxed. Negative and positive self-attitudes are expressed both verbally and unspoken to your outside world.

How does one raise self-attitude?

The way you talk to yourself influences your self-attitude. If you say things to yourself like you are unworthy, dumb, or fat, you will believe it, and struggle to overcome that belief. However, if you say you are attractive, capable, powerful, or dynamic, you will believe and behave this way. The words you say, as well as the pictures you recast of yourself, are your self-image and self-attitude. Changing means you must replace the corresponding image and the associated words and feelings.

Paraphrasing the words of Goethe, "Treat people as they are, and they remain that way. Treat people as though they were what they can be, and we help them to become what they are capable of becoming."

Take some time to think about what you say to yourself; visualize the photos that accompany those words. What words do you say to yourself? Are your words kind or overly harsh, realistic, embellished, or fantasy? Do you regularly praise yourself for your successes, or do you just feel lucky? Can you quickly forgive your goof-ups and move forward, or must you self-flagellate? Do you forget yesterday as a canceled check and tomorrow as a promissory note?

These are the questions you need to ask yourself before restructuring your words and photos.

The components of positive self-attitude include the following:

- a sense of personal confidence
- being in control of yourself
- resiliency and flexibility
- personal contentment and acceptance
- feeling socially and emotionally attractive
- valuing your existence and able to change when necessary

- an ability to evaluate yourself without over-relying upon others' opinions
- a realistic understanding of yourself both positively and negatively

CAUSES OF POOR SELF-IMAGE

The most significant cause of a poor self-image is the feedback received by significant others, namely parents, spouses, relatives, neighbors, or close friends. There is no more powerful or more influential source of either encouragement or discouragement than parents and close relatives. If a youngster frequently receives discouraging and intimidating feedback, they become compounded by negativity and insecurity. Likewise, feedback from other sources, such as peers or teachers, may also reinforce these negative self-fulfilling hypotheses. It is not surprising that the result is a poor self-image. Typically, fear, passivity, insecurity, discouragement, depression, and pessimism result from negative feedback. Conversely, if significant others' feedback is predominantly supportive, positive, and encouraging, the result is a positive self-image. A positive self-image exudes enthusiasm, optimism, persistence, confidence, and courage.

Of all the attributes of a positive self-image, the most critical of all is understanding oneself, liking oneself, regardless of your weaknesses and foibles. My mom would always remind me that it is okay to recognize my goof-ups but to correct the mistakes. She said it is also best to then laugh at yourself when you goof up. She meant that keeping self-esteem intact is equally essential. At age 101, she recognizes her failings because when she messes up, I hear a loud guffaw, followed by, "You gotta sometimes laugh at yourself."

Ultimately, it is the decision to accept yourself. The keys to your success lie within you. Liking yourself allows you to choose your attitude each day; it is bolstered by external and internal support. Since your most valuable asset is your self-image, cautiously guard yourself against others' negative influences and expectations. Never allow someone else, no matter how close, to have the ability to rule your world or tell you how to feel. Set the bar at your level, not that of others. Forget about what they demand of you; instead, follow your own heart. Do not allow others to divert your journey. Remember, you are at the helm and the master of your future.

"Know thyself" is an admonition that will serve you well. It continues to be something I continue to learn about myself regularly. Knowing yourself is difficult because you tend to deny your weaknesses and fallacies. Instead, recognizing your limitations gives you an edge over those who deny them or blame circumstances.

Wow, knowing my strengths and weaknesses allows me to remember that my greatest strengths are also my greatest weaknesses.

One of the most difficult things is to recognize your faults. Instead, acknowledge your flaws, own them, and as needed, correct them and move forward! Being frozen in time simply delays maturity. Ownership opens doors and allows for periodic restarts. Denial and blame simply dig a bigger funeral plot. By analyzing your irrational behavior and personal weaknesses, you obtain wisdom. Obtaining honest, objective information from trusted others can help validate feedback. Having this information also provides the data necessary for change. It takes courage, persistence, and hard work to change.

Self-acceptance is the first step in establishing an exemplary self-attitude. The percentage of people who defeat themselves by self-deprecating statements is alarming. Even more self-deprecating is that terrible four-letter word "can't."

Don't forget to identify your capabilities and those things you can realistically control. Reinhold Niebuhr, the founder of the highly-successful organization Alcoholics Anonymous (AA), certainly espoused this belief.

"God, grant me the serenity to accept the things I cannot change, courage to change the things I can, and wisdom to know the difference."

A compendium on "MENTAL HEALTH AND PERSONAL CHANGE" is available by going to https://www.drtonycedolini.com/mental-health-and-personal-change

"Thanksgiving Day comes, by statute, once a year; to the honest man it comes as frequently as the heart of gratitude will allow."
—*Edward Sandford Martin*

"THE MOON BELONGS TO EVERYONE"

GRATITUDE, THOUGHTFULNESS, THANKSGIVING

Thanksgiving officially comes once a year. Yet, every day is a day to rejoice and say thank you. Giving thanks every day has been a habit I learned from my now 101-year-old mother.

I talked with her earlier this morning, and she said, "Just another beautiful day in paradise. Every day is beautiful in some way, and I give thanks to God not just for another day, but for all of creation."

She went on to say that she says a little prayer each day for having a beautiful family, a wonderful place to live with her elderly peers, the food she enjoys, her success in Bingo, and the friends that she has made over the years. She tends to repeat herself often and almost always restates that she has so much for which to be thankful. "My goal in life is to inspire before I expire, so I go about making people laugh or smile by telling jokes or just paying attention to all these fine folks."

Certainly, gratitude and Thanksgiving are welcomed by all. Thankfulness, along with thoughtfulness, is learned and well worth cultivating and practicing. The development of this ability to appreciate something in everyone is the first step in gratitude. Giving thanks, cheery congratulations, providing compliments, and warm recognition are essential in establishing and maintaining relationships and a positive attitude. Thoughtful people think about others first and revel in helping to inspire them. Being thankful and expressing gratitude creates a mutual bond of enjoyment and shared pleasure. We all know that making others happy allows for the prospering of our happiness. Those who are unable to appreciate and express gratitude negate the pleasure and contentment.

A great mind of the past agrees:

> *"He is a wise man who does not grieve for the things which he has not, but rejoices for those which he has."*
>
> *—Epictetus*

It has become our family tradition that before each November's Thanksgiving meal we each share the things for which we are grateful. Initially, when we started this tradition, it was awkward, not just for the youngsters but also for the adults. Our first immediate family Thanksgiving some 25 years ago resulted in short, almost embarrassing responses. It was clear that this was not an easy thing to address with twelve other people. As each Thanksgiving approached, we reminded everyone that it was time to express our thanksgivings. Soon each person was saying more than one-liners, and some were giving paragraphs of their thanks. As I looked around our large table, I saw many tears shed as the thanks became more emotionally relevant.

Within a few years, the young family members even before dinner were saying, "Let's not forget our chance to share what we are thankful for."

From then on, sharing words of gratitude became more comfortable, tears became more commonplace, and sometimes the words expressed were astoundingly profound. Perhaps if everyone could express thanks every day rather than uttering a canned repetitive phrase of grace or lack thereof, we would instead create a world more profound, more unique, and even more meaningful.

Appreciation is the ability to recognize and enjoy the worth, quality, and importance of someone or something. Appreciating others allows you to open your heart and mind by giving recognition and appreciation for your wonderful life and the many things you might easily take for granted—your parents, friends, neighbors, children, farmers, first responders, and colleagues. You have so much to appreciate, especially your five senses, the ability to see, hear, smell, taste, and touch; freedom of choice, health, food, Mother

Nature, your ease in walking to the market, choice of foods, chats with the neighbors, and your living quarters. These blessings are priceless, and most are free! The list is endless; you could add appliances, running water, cars, trains, phones, busses, electricity, sunrises, and sunsets. Some of your most favorite times of the year, Christmas or Hanukkah, Valentine's Day, Easter or Passover, Ramadan, Thanksgiving, or New Year's, can be celebrated with welcoming smiles, compliments, and heartfelt thank-you cards, emails, notes, letters, and surprise gifts. These are the many things that will remind you to rejoice with a glow of appreciation and joy. All are the things that have made you what you are today. Putting them into simple words can inspire you and forever change your life. Life may not be tied to a bow, but it is a gift that beckons regular appreciation. Showing appreciation is a tool that will serve you well on your journey

As a young child in elementary school, I had an extraordinary teacher in third grade who emphasized the fact that the best things in life are free.

When I went home to share it with my mom, she said, "Of course that's true, and there are songs to prove it, like 'The Moon Belongs To Everyone.'"

Well, since then, it has become pretty apparent that those simple words ring true.

You can't buy the exhilaration at the birth of your children, the butterflies in your stomach as you go out with the new love of your life, your children's performances or special events, breathtaking sunsets, the special homemade gifts made by your child, or the flora and fauna that surround us. We are so fortunate to have these things; gratitude abounds!

> *"Gratitude is not only the greatest of all the virtues, but the parent of all others."*
> —*Cicero (106-43 B.C.)*

Focusing on things that you can appreciate is far more inspiring than digressing to discuss your misfortunes, lost opportunities, mistakes, or have-nots! Instead, focus on your blessings and the people that light you up like the bright stars that shine at night. It's those bear hugs, special notes, warm receptions, kind gestures, heartfelt winks, priceless surprises, unforgettable embraces, or kisses that are both a pause and a cause for pure exhilaration.

As you might expect, I have boxes saved, filled with family events, vacation photos, our children's artwork, Father's Day and birthday cards, letters, inspirational quotes, and many miscellaneous joyful reminders of things past. Periodically, I visit the attic and open a box or two, slowly reviewing and refreshing its contents. Those private moments bring many nostalgic thoughts and gut-inspiring feelings, sometimes accompanied by tears. Deep down, I'm just a forlorn romantic.

My other sons Bob, married to daughter Maria, and John, married to daughter Antonia, have special gifts. Bob almost never fails to comment about something special to almost everyone he sees. Whether it is a shirt, dress, hairdo, jewelry, suit, tie, etc., Bob will also acknowledge and make sincerely warm compliments about how lucky we are in food and wine. His sincere comments invariably will light up a smile on the face of each recipient. He also enjoys sharing memories of nostalgically fun moments. John is gifted musically and shares his talents with all. He is always willing to lend a hand, his pickup, or share his food delights. John also has done a lot of special graphics, posters, and illustrations for our special birthdays, anniversaries, and holiday events. I never worry about a ride to the airport or a place to park my car. Our son Peter is the teddy bear of the family, and he is forever hugging and sharing his confidence-building comments with all of the family members. I can go on and on about my daughters, sons, and grandchildren too. They are included in the preface, foreword, and other chapters as well.

When you are genuinely appreciative and unselfish in your thoughts, you will develop a comfort level that will allow you to appreciate yourself. As you age, you will beckon for unforgettable moments. Sometimes you will have them at your ready. Other times, you will reminisce and remember those special times of the past that will, like a bolt of lightning, run shivers of nostalgic joy up and down your limbs.

Finally, gratitude, thoughtfulness, and thanksgiving have an immediate and long-lasting impact on the lives of others. Recognizing and appreciating others' skills and abilities creates rapport, eventually becoming a cooperative spirit that transcends the immediate and contagiously spreads goodwill and teamwork. All lead to self-confidence and ultimate success at home, in the workplace, and unity among villages. Perhaps the best and kindest thing we can ever do is to provide unsolicited acts of kindness with no expectation of discovery or acknowledged appreciation.

Every day is Thanksgiving

"We don't see things as they are, we see them as we are."
—*Anonymous*

WHAT YOU SEE IS WHAT YOU GET

What you think you see or what you think you hear, you believe. Your perceptions become a reality based on your filtered lens. Your reality is only a projection of your belief system.

Not long ago, I received an email from a friend. The story below exemplifies the variance in viewpoints, even within the same family.

"One day, the father of a very wealthy family took his son on a trip to the country with the express purpose of showing him how poor people live. They spent a couple of days and nights on the farm of what would be considered an impoverished family. On their return from their trip, the father asked his son, "How was the trip?"

"It was great, Dad."

"Well, did you see how poor people live?"

"Oh, yeah," said the son.

"So tell me, what did you learn from the trip?"

The son answered: "I saw that we have one dog, and they have four. We have a pool that reaches the middle of our garden and they have a creek that has no end. We have imported lanterns in our garden, and they have the stars at night. Our patio reaches to the front yard, and they have the whole horizon. We have a small piece of land to live on, and they have fields that go beyond our sight. We have servants and service, but they serve each other. We buy our food, but they grow theirs. We have walls around our property to protect us; they have friends to protect them."

The boy's father was speechless.

Then his son added, "Thanks, Dad, for showing me how poor we really are."

If you tend to be a pessimist, you might think something is impossible, "She can never become a test pilot." On the other hand, an optimist would think that it is possible, "She has all of the skills and abilities to become an excellent test pilot." These examples are not substantially different than the rather trite phrase used, "Is the glass is half-full or half-empty?" As a matter of fact, I recently received a note from a friend who wanted to add a humorous twist to that same dilemma:

"Dear Optimist, Pessimist, and Realist,
While you guys were busy arguing about the glass of
water, I drank it!
Sincerely, The Opportunist!"

Whether you are an optimist or a pessimist, only the walls you build around yourself confine you.

There is no doubt in my mind that two people can look at the same thing and see something different. Is the rosebush full of thorns, or is the beautiful thorn bush full of gorgeous roses? No doubt, perceptions are highly correlated to your prior experiences, attitudes, and personal expectations. Most critical is that no individual will ever rise above their lowest personal expectations. For example, "I can barely get into college and can't possibly expect ever to become a physician." Or perhaps the rooster's percept, "I see myself as superior, confident and in control of the yard." An opposing hungry human's sense might be, "I see that big rooster as a succulent meal." So, what you see depends upon the clarity of the filtered window from which you perceive it.

Because your perceptions are your reality, they predict your behavior. If you perceive your day beginning poorly, you will wish yourself into a day you knew would be a bad one. I remember the comment by little Alexander, when he said, "I could tell it was going to be a terrible, horrible, no good, very bad day!"

Similarly, our expectations are sometimes equally distorted. Many disappointments and heartbreaks are the results of misperceptions. We are all capable of wearing rose-colored glasses. On your journey, you will encounter bouquets of roses that sometimes turn into fields of thorns.

As a young person, I can remember the times I woke up grouchy. My mother would say, "Anthony, did you get up on the wrong side of the bed this morning? I want you to go back to bed and get up on the right side of the bed!"

At that very moment, I knew that she perceived something I hadn't given much thought to. I knew that I had a choice based on my previous experiences. If I didn't go back to bed and change my attitude, I'd have extra chores to do before I could go out and play.

Of course, your subjective observations work in both directions. It was believed that no one could ever run a mile in less than four minutes for hundreds of years. Thousands attempted it and concluded that it was an impossible feat. One man perceived it differently. Englishman Roger Bannister broke the record in 1954. Since then, thousands have run the mile in less than four minutes. As a matter of fact, since 1954, the record has been reduced by seventeen seconds! History is replete with records shattered by those able to see paper walls rather than those made of concrete and steel.

PERSONAL GLIMPSES

When we were first married, Clare and I were in college. We bought a small trailer because funds were extremely limited (8'x 38' or 304 sq. ft.). Most peoples' concept of happiness is a big luxurious house. That perception was certainly not ours then, nor is it now. Anyone can be happy regardless of whether they live in a castle or a hut. For us, it was one of the most exhilarating times of our lives. Yes, living in a tiny trailer the first year and a half of our marriage was delightful.

My wife's extended family owned a prune and cherry ranch. They allowed us to move our trailer onto their ranch property. Uncle Al and my father-in-law helped me construct a small septic system. We were soon living amidst an orchard of fruit trees. This was pre-tech Silicon Valley before it became covered with asphalt. It was once the second most fertile valley in the world and known as the Valley of Heart's Delight. Santa Clara Valley produced the finest stone fruit in the entire USA.

After a glorious cherry blossoming, the trees festooned with thousands of vibrant pink blooms, we began to see the appearance of young cherries. From a distance, these buoyant Bings looked artfully perfect in every imaginable way. My 1965 photos and videos of that crop still transfix our eyes. Not only was it the largest and most luscious crop ever, but each tree was also standing at military attention, proud of its mighty bounty. I felt like Adam picking the perfect fruit for my Eve. I picked a bag full of plump Bing cherries, and we sat in our tiny kitchen, slowly savoring the precious nuggets. As I carefully examined each perfectly-shaped cherry, I noticed something I would never forget. Each large, lush cherry had a small, sometimes infinitesimally tiny flaw. I did not find a single cherry that didn't have a speck or maculation on its surface. That epiphany was dramatic. I had concluded that nothing whatsoever is perfect. It was a glorious revelation of which I am reminded regularly. Not only did it clarify my imperfections, but it allowed me to understand and accept the fact that nothing in nature is without flaws. And sometimes, initial perceptions can also be staggeringly flawed.

How many times since have I realized that my first thought of people and things could be terribly misconstrued? Whether it was an initial negative or positive impression, it was only a matter of time before my feelings were corrected. My wife's family often shares an old Italian proverb, "You never really get to know someone until you've shared a sack of salt with them." It's much like visiting your ophthalmologist and obtaining a new, clearer pair of eyeglasses.

I implore you to be cautious of your first impressions.

Don't make premature judgments until you allow yourself sufficient time and experience to assess an individual's character. Yes, it may even take a bag full of salt. The same recommendation applies to first impressions of automobiles, houses, or other material possessions that you consider purchasing. Remember, perceptions come from within your mind's lens. Your lens and your perceptions can be flawed, especially upon the first impression.

THE STORY OF A VIOLINIST EXPERIENCE

This is a true story that occurred at the Washington, DC Metro station on a cold January morning in 2007. The man with a violin played six Bach pieces for approximately 45 minutes. During that time, an estimated 2,000 people went through the station. Most were on their way to work and could easily observe or hear the violinist. After a few minutes, many middle-aged men noticed the music playing, slowed their pace, but then continued to hurry to meet their schedules. At four minutes, the violinist received his first dollar. A woman put money in the hat and without stopping continued to walk away. At six minutes, a man leaned against the wall to listen to him and then checked his watch and began walking again. At ten minutes, a three-year-old boy stopped, but his mother hurriedly tugged him along. Again, the child stopped to look at the violinist, yet his mother continued to push forward, but the child continued to turn his head the entire time watching and listening to the violinist. This same action was repeated several other times with other children, but each time the parent, without exception, moved forward without stopping. The music continued to play for 45 minutes; only six people stopped and listened for a short period of time. About 20 people gave money but continued to walk at their normal pace. The violinist collected a total of $32. When finished, silence resumed. No one noticed. No one applauded. There was no recognition whatsoever.

Interestingly, the violinist was Joshua Bell, one of the greatest violinists in the entire world. He played some of the most intricate pieces ever written for a violin. In addition, the violin used was worth over $3 million. Just two days before, Joshua had sold out a theater in Boston, where the average price of tickets was $100. His playing incognito in the Metro station was reported by the Washington Post as part of a social experiment about perception, taste, and people's priorities. The questions raised were, are people willing to stop and appreciate exquisite music? Can people recognize talent in an unexpectedly perceived context? The big conclusion was that people don't stop and take a moment to perceive the most beautiful things in their environment, whether it be classical music, flowers, architecture, or natural beauty. They don't seem to perceive the difference between beautiful instruments or beautiful presentation. The newspaper's important question was how many other things are we missing as we hurriedly rush through life?

Leonardo da Vinci once reflected that, the average person looks without seeing, listens without hearing, breathes in without awareness of aroma or fragrance, eats without tasting, touches without feeling, and talks without thinking. Premature judgment is often error bound!

On life's journey, your interactions with culture, religion, politics, education, and other institutions carve out your perceived personal belief system. Be prepared to question your premature perceptions before having them pointed out for you.

PERSONAL GLIMPSES OF PREJUDICE PERCEPTIONS OF IMMIGRANTS AND OTHERS THAT ARE DIFFERENT

Belief systems go beyond the bounds of nature. They can cause harm and create inequality. I hesitated and labored for days trying to determine whether prejudice, xenophobia, and ethnic profiling should be included. Each is built on the perceptions of others, often different from our norm group. We are currently experiencing a resurgence of ethnic and racial hostility. Prejudice now is no longer as subtle as it's been for many years. It is now contentious and direct. I decided to broach this controversial subject for a number of reasons. I must admit that by my generation, our family's third generation in the US, I seldom received blatant discrimination. However, as a twelve-year-old, I had experienced residual prejudice, which I shall never forget.

Sally was a fellow eighth grader at my parochial school. Her family was Dutch but had been in the United States for several generations. I had a puppy love crush on Sally at that time. I would call her and talk for several minutes. Our conversations were very mundane and quite harmless. During one of our talks, I overheard her father say, "You're not allowed to talk to that GREASY DAGO!" It hit me like a rocket blast. Sally was sweet, but her father was clearly xenophobic, and I later learned he was quite a racist. We remained friends, but the message was quite clear, stay away! My budding puppy love and infatuation was abruptly extinguished, but another critical learning moment had just occurred.

Digressing a bit, the revised immigration laws of the 1920s were established to restrict Southern Europeans significantly. According to the Army Alpha test results given to all World War I recruits (and administered only in the English language), Italians, Greeks, Spaniards, Slavs, and Jews were determined to be illiterate, unintelligent, and bordering on learning disabled. Col. Yerkes, the commanding officer overseeing the test administration, later became the prominent Dr. Yerkes. He had received his Ph.D. from Harvard University and eventually became a prestigious professor at Yale University. As a result of his testing, he urged Congress to restrict the feeble-minded Southern Europeans from future immigration. Thus, the severe immigration limitations of the 1920s were based on those same Army Alpha IQ scores, administered in English to non-speaking Southern European immigrants. Ironically today, those feeble-minded American Jews and Italians are now considered among the wealthiest and most successful ethnic groups in the United States. Surprisingly, the Army

Alpha continued to be used, even when I was tested for officer training for the US Army in 1960.

As I reached adolescence and later young adulthood, it became more obvious that some less appreciated my nationality, but it was readily accepted by others. Then, movies such as *The Godfather* and *Goodfellows*, as well as TV series such as *The Sopranos* and *The Untouchables* had an effect. In the process, I received many ambivalent messages about my ethnicity. I was proud to be of Roman stock but embarrassed by the Mafia. I was incensed by Italians' portrayal as sleazy, inarticulate, animalistic, and crude, but proud of my relatives and ancestors. I remained proud of my heritage, culture, homeland, food, art, and scientific discoveries. I was also proud of its history and its persistence, sensitivity, tolerance, genuineness, and democracy.

I remain supportive and sensitive to all ethnicities, but saddened by how each new set of immigrants, whether Mexicans, Vietnamese, Chinese, Jews, Middle Easterners, or Slavs are initially chastised and often unaccepted. Unfortunately, like the rites of adulthood, the rites of citizenship can be dangerous, difficult, and painful.

We as Americans need to hold our heads high, triumphant, and proud of all our heritages. We should, as Americans, reclaim the importance of diversity and the uniqueness of all cultures. *Viva la difference!* We need to continue integrating, appreciating, and honoring all of our fellow brothers and sisters, for it was this diverse melting pot that produced such a great nation. We are indeed indebted to our immigrants.

The statue of liberty conveys that same message: "Give me your tired, your poor, your huddled masses yearning to breathe free . . . Send these, the homeless, tempest-tossed to me, I lift my lamp beside the golden door."

May you have the sense to weigh your thoughts and feelings to understand and accept others as equal yet different. They are to be loved and appreciated as brothers and sisters, as part of our enormous human family.

And please, I entreat you, remember that your perceptions become your reality. That's why you have mirrors and scales to provide you with reality as it truly exists. Live life with your eyes, your ears, and your mind wide open. Education, a thirst for learning, good listening, and valuable feedback will help you adjust your beliefs to be more in sync with true reality.

> *"Doubt is not a pleasant condition, but certainty is an absurd one."*
> —*Voltaire*

On a trip to Southeast Asia in March 2017, I brought a new nonfiction book to read. As it turns out, *The Undoing Project* was one of the most inspirational and overpowering literary pieces I had read in many years. It clarified so many questions I had with my professional training, the state of behavioral sciences, economics, decision-making, and especially perception. It produced yet another grand epiphany, at the age of 75. As a result, I decided to add this summary to help clarify and correct the many misconceptions about reality and decision-making.

I leave you with one of the most significant scientific discoveries of the 21st century. Not only did it reach the stratospheric level of a Nobel Prize, but it also turned the annals of perception and decision-making upside down. Michael Lewis's book *The Undoing Project* is a masterful summation of two highly unlikely intellectual sages' discoveries. Lewis, a gifted writer, is now recognized as one of the most prolific and best-selling nonfiction authors. He points out that the human mind consistently and systematically errs in both judgment and decision-making: the two protagonists, Drs. Amos Tversky and Danny Kahneman were groundbreaking psychologists whose seminal work revolutionized several fields of study far beyond psychology and economics. Their boldly earth-shaking research reversed our contemporary models of intuition and decision-making.

This dynamic duo's bold approach researched the human mind and how it makes decisions. They proved that human perception and decision-making *are inherently fallible and unreliable.* The hallmark of their research was their recognition that pre-determinants such as the Halo effect (first impressions) and premature confirmations are based on false premises, and therefore error bound. The researchers discovered that failing to consider a myriad of additional factors necessary to make accurate decisions becomes blatantly errant. They also added that decision-makers must justify and rationalize their ultimate false choices because of their premature biases. Their research recognized that human error's fallibility is far more critical than simply denying or rationalizing its results. Unfortunately, these "fake truths" continue to be tacitly accepted and acknowledged as facts to the true believers and the unknowing. For example, since 400 BC, Hippocrates felt a strong connection between weather and arthritis. However, after more recent scientific studies, it was concluded that there was no relationship between the two. This, of course, is true of many old wives' tales that remain entrenched in the minds of many true believers.

Tversky and Kahneman's compelling statement is, "The fate of an entire society can be sealed by rewarding or awarding mistakes." In our high-stakes society, such mistakes can be disastrous. For example, a modern example was the lack of measurable facts that resulted in the US going to war against Iraq. Certainly, a verifiable reality is based on proven facts, usually expressed in a mathematical logarithm. For instance, the duo concluded that Charles Darwin was indeed correct. We indeed have an evolving brain that is incapable of processing highly sophisticated logarithmic equations. What they concluded was that individuals create their alternative reality by undoing reality.

This fallible decision-making is frequently done to avoid pain, frustration, and failure. Thus, the Nobel Prize creation of the "Undoing Project." To make reliable decisions, the previously-biased assumptions need to be first undone. This can only be achieved by eliminating spurious perceptions and substituting them with facts. We have learned from these famous researchers that humanity must adopt scientific methodologies, instead of inherently fallible intuitive fake beliefs. Not only our country but also our world is at serious risk when impulsive and unreliable decisions are made based on nonfactual criteria. Danny Kahneman was awarded the Nobel Prize in economic science in 2002.

Again, to restate this critical piece of scientific discovery: impulsivity combined with lack of facts can lead not only to poor decision-making but also to potentially national or international disasters. I beseech you to trust yourself, but please collect as much factual information as possible before you attempt to make important life challenging decisions. Don't rely solely on your observations, impulses, or intuition; buttress your choices with verifiable data. You will be able to sleep much better, knowing you did your very best. Your very future will depend on it!

A more detailed explanation of Tversky & Kahneman's research findings and Nobel Prize is available by going to https://www.drtonycedolini.com/ perception

THORNY
PATCHES

DISTASTEFUL PLEASURES

Certainly not surprisingly, like you, I have dealt with problems my entire lifetime. As a child, most were relatively simple to ignore. The biggies were having to go to bed early. That was easy to solve as soon as I could set up my crystal radio set. Having hidden all the wires on the exposed box springs, I could fake going to bed, then pull out my earphones, cover my head with my sheets and blankets and listen to *Inner Sanctum*, *The Shadow*, *Amos 'n' Andy*, "*Sam Spade*, and *The Adventures of Superman*. Later it was reading comic books under the sheets with a flashlight. That is, until the batteries wore out, and I couldn't afford new ones until they were magically replaced. Of course, there was always being afraid of getting into fisticuffs or not studying for an exam. As I grew older, there were personal challenges in breaking up with a girlfriend or not having enough money to do things with my friends. Those were all necessary landmarks that led to learning moments and sometimes epiphanies.

It wasn't until I was a young adult that real, monumental life-altering challenges surfaced. Looking for the perfect partner to marry weighed on my mind. Also problematic was the Vietnam war and my possible engagement in it. Money and savings were huge problems prior to marriage, and then as we discussed having children, they became gigantic. Having children increased the complexities of my troubles. Nor can I forget the daily work stress and working with parents and youngsters that were even more problematic. Now, being retired, there are the health concerns of family and friends along with making sure the retirement nest egg doesn't disappear, as well as other newly added concerns, such as a pandemic. Yes, hurdles will appear daily. They are sometimes simple ones and sometimes almost irreconcilable ones.

Problems are ubiquitous. There will always be problems as long as there are people on Earth. The seven deadly sins guarantee their existence, particularly greed and dishonesty. As history dictates, corruption, manipulation, power struggles, and lack of conscience are humanity's greatest woes. Your job as a problem solver relies on anticipation, experience, information, intuition, and objectivity. Problem resolution and personal peace will not come from anger or aggression, but from your ability to cope and counteract stress by not harboring them. Critical to conflict resolution is knowing that the quickest way to create an even bigger problem is to either delay or deny it. Some folks simply try to deny conflicts by avoiding them. Delay is by far the deadliest form of denial.

In over seven decades of life, the very simplest, most significant, and the best bit of advice on problem-solving I have ever discovered was a quote by Dr. Robert Schuller:

> *"Again and again, the impossible problem is solved when we finally see that the problem is only a tough decision, waiting to be made."*

Dr. Schuller clearly states that the best way to escape stressful dilemmas is to make a decision. Why? Because it provides finality and closure. Hoping or wishing for things to go away accomplishes nothing.

Decisions are unequivocally the only method for problem resolution.

Anything less than a decision further delays and guarantees continued frustration and failure. Unfortunately, there are no shortcuts in problem-solving other than decision-making. Remember, if you are involved in any predicament, you are both part of the problem and the solution.

I have been asked to be a trustee for both friends and close family in the past twenty years. I have readily accepted because it was both a show of confidence and integrity by the nominator. It may appear to be an easy job, but as I've discovered, it is laden with huge drawbacks. I have invariably found that even in the best of families, there is always a vulture or two circling the wagons. Fortunately, I've been reasonably pleased four out of five times. I've sadly discovered that sometimes it is utterly impossible to please all parties, especially when a family is particularly large. The infighting, old grudges, greed, and differences in perception are staggering. I thought mediating with a couple was difficult but negotiating with a myriad of independent individuals will create premature baldness. I can attest to it!

I cannot emphasize enough how important it is to make definitive decisions and escape problems by action rather than inaction. Solving issues by making specific and unambiguous decisions is one of the three most critical tools you will need on your journey.

Problems are perplexing and often misinterpreted. Frequently with each hurdle, intense emotions can be encountered. Instead of utilizing the scientific method by first identifying the problem, it is often easier to deny it by pointing fingers and blaming them on something else. It is far more important to identify an obstacle and begin to determine possible solutions. Developing various alternatives and focusing on problem resolution avoids misplaced and wasted negative energy. I have found that when anything perplexing persists, it is best to write it down. Objectively putting the pencil to the paper clarifies and makes it easier to identify the issue and create a proactive decision. When that happens, you can feel the heavy weight descend from your shoulders.

What would you do if we had no problems? In reviewing the research literature, several authors have suggested that life would be dull and humdrum. One author suggested that it would be the beginning of societal and individual death. Why? Because humankind is motivated by setbacks! We are inveterate conflict resolvers.

Problems are opportunities in disguise.

A hurdle can turn into a hidden miracle because it may be the bridge to progress. Sometimes, problem-solving causes a rapid learning curve and opens the door to the unforeseen. Every problem has a silver lining because each reveals a hidden opportunity, and each new opportunity affords another magical learning moment. Of course, I'm not suggesting that you go looking for hassles. Instead of seeing them as a danger, regard each as a new challenge, and it will feel much less threatening. Welcome them and celebrate them as part of your new repertoire.

Many of us make the mistake of trying to accomplish too much at the same time. Don't multi-task important issues at the same time. Conquer one at a time. As the ancient Romans might say, "Rome wasn't built in a day." And as Julius Caesar proclaimed, "I came! I saw! I conquered!" He said, first things first. Take these opportunistic gremlins one at a time. Again, remember that problems are opportunities often dressed in disguise.

FACING PROBLEMS

Facing difficulties is required in counseling and achieving therapeutic interventions. I can assure you it is no easy task. My job was always to guide, not try to solve the issues myself. Instead, I provided them tools for self-discovery and intimated that they were in charge of the solutions. It was recognized that I was only successful if I was a catalyst for my clients' success. When they were able to make the necessary decisions, only they were responsible for their victories. As simple as it may sound, many of their quandaries were quite complex. A substantial amount of time was needed to guide them. First is understanding, then accepting responsibility, and finally making the critical decisions necessary for resolution. If they were successful, my intervention turned into a mutual celebration.

Facing problems is far better than blaming, finding excuses, or denying their existence. Crisis intervention is often allowing predicaments to fester before either identifying or preventing them. Also, solving predicaments by crisis intervention is an inefficient means of resolution. Dealing with issues as soon as they are identified avoids allowing them to worsen and become a serious crisis. Running away from trouble does not make them go away. Most crises can be prevented by identifying them early. If anticipated, they can be more manageable. Eliminate them before they fester into a full-blown crisis. Putting a preventive Band-Aid on a cut is far superior to the application of a tourniquet. Making a responsible decision can not only solve a problem but eliminate ongoing stress and the creation of a bigger crisis. Thank goodness for my dear brother-in-law and business partner, Pat. When I'm stymied with a tenant's issue, even after sleeping on it a few nights, I can call him, and we collaboratively solve the problem. Don't be afraid of asking trusted others for a hand when perplexed or stopped in your tracks.

However, some issues require additional time. Time may be needed to develop a more accurate analysis and an unemotional decision. For example, I've often made a decision to solve my personal problem by writing a preliminary response. Instead of calling or sending my response, I would sleep on it. The next day when emotions were not as tender or as likely to be impulsive, I would reread and rethink my original response. Angry or potentially offensive language was eliminated, thus allowing both parties to save face. More often than not my response was significantly altered before it was acted upon. There were many times when my written response and decision were discarded entirely. Expressing strong emotions can be dangerous when one is overwhelmed by unthinking, impulsive, or highly emotional responses. To react with rational common sense, allow time to

incubate your thoughts by pausing and carefully thinking about your response's consequences.

Problems are sometimes donated to us by others.
They find it very convenient to share or pass their troubles on to others rather than solve them themselves.
Determining that their issue is not yours, but one that
was foisted upon you by another creates a different
kind of decision-making. This so-called "sharing" often
calls for walking away or redirecting the problem to the
responsible party, not you.

Another similar difficulty is when I'm attending a
relaxing social event, and out of the corner of my eye
comes a casual acquaintance. It frequently begins with
some benign or banal conversation. Just as I let my guard
down, I'm besieged by a plethora of parenting questions
more suitable for a therapy session. Depending on the
situation, I might make an excuse to cut our conversation short and walk away. If deemed a more serious
issue, I might recommend making an appointment to
further discuss possible suggested resolutions.

AND THE WINNER IS

Without question, the single most common predicament for parents of multiple children is sibling-rivalry.
In all of my years of counseling parents, this was the
most common scourge reported. Parents experience
these "donated" problems almost daily. Siblings' usual
purpose is to gain a parent's attention and set up a

potential victory for themselves. Of course, the object is to cause the defeat to their rival sib. Like an umpire or referee, parents do not have eyes in the back of their heads. Parents often miss the subtleties of these troubling events. Sibs are far more likely to be energized or bored, so they create these temporary competitive crises to force their parents' intervention. If successful, they can quietly but smugly claim victory.

When a parent is thrown into the middle of the fray, they are forced into acting as a referee or umpire. After watching many sports contests, seldom does an umpire or referee win the acclaim or affection of those competing for victory. Instead, parents unwittingly reinforce competition. Being placed in the middle, with no place to go, is a no-win for a parent. If you reprimand one party while extolling the other's virtues, it merely fuels the rivalry; and you can anticipate more future battles. Also, comparing one child to the other will only intensify the conflict.

Words like, "I didn't do anything; he hit me!" or "She won't let me play with it," or "He started it," "How come she got to do it?" abound. Wise parents recognize that most of these problems are simply rivalries and not parent issues. These minor crises are time-consuming and frustrating. Since at least one child wants to throw you into the fray, it becomes a guaranteed win-lose situation. The best solution is to take the object of focus away (e.g., a toy) and identify the real problem, "It looks like you two have a problem." Psychologists, beginning with the seminal work of Dr. Rudolf Dreikurs, have found that the most productive solution is to relinquish the role of referee. Then, direct the predicament to the source—the children! Usually, the best solution is to send the gremlins into a neutral corner, typically a bathroom or a large walk-in closet, requesting that when they solve their problem, the object of focus will be returned.

Sometimes, even more attention is demanded by rowdiness or even becoming physical with one another. If so, let them waste their time, not yours. Simply place them in a time-out, only to return them to the neutral corner for round two or three until they solve their problem! This time-saving device allows children to solve minor issues before major conflicts occur later in life. It saves parents time, energy, and disdain. Perhaps this ounce of prevention will eliminate the need for judges, police, attorneys, and prisons that might be required in future, more complex conflicts. A parent's goal is to respect individual differences, improve children's problem-solving skills, and convey an unbiased egalitarian message to all of the siblings. You now have a new tool to utilize when others foist their conflicts onto you!

A typical example of a sibling rivalry conflict might be, Jim was watching television. His brother, George, came and changed the channel. He said that he had to watch another program at his teacher's request. Jim's mother could very easily have suggested that George watch the requested program and send Jim off to his room. This obviously would have created conflict. Instead, the mother immediately turned off the television, sent them to a neutral corner, and directed them to solve the issues themselves. Within a very short time, Jim and George had worked out a mutual solution, and both were happy. Neither the mother nor any of the children "lost" or felt diminished. Many such incidents occur each day. The conflict can be handled consistently through redirection and letting the children resolve their problems. Dilemmas can be averted, and a mother's or father's day could be much more pleasant. This same approach is effective when two of your friends try to have you take sides. Being put in the position of an umpire or referee is guaranteeing a lose-lose situation.

Another approach to sibling rivalry was capsulized in an Ann Landers column written many years ago. I saved it because it was both profound and precisely conveyed a parent's need to love each child uniquely, unconditionally, and without bias. This is the first and foremost foundation of short-circuiting sibling rivalry and negative self-esteem. Regardless, it will not eliminate sibling rivalry because it is fueled by one-upmanship and momentary victory. In addition, sibling rivalry fits the paradigm of intermittent reinforcement, meaning if you are successful only five to ten percent of the time, like Las Vegas casinos, you continue to put more money into your slot machine. Below is my abbreviated edition.

"*Dear Firstborn, I've always loved you best because you were our first miracle. You are the genesis of our marriage and the fulfillment of our young love. You sustained us through the hamburger years, our earliest mode of transportation—our feet—as well as our small black and white TV. You were new, had unused grandparents, and enough clothes for a set of triplets. You were the beginning.*

Dear Middle Child, I've always loved you best because you drew a tough spot in the family, and it made you stronger for it. You cried less, had more patience, wore faded hand-me-downs, and never in your life did anything first. But it made you only more special. You helped us understand that the world wouldn't collapse if you went to bed with dirty feet. Without you, we would have never survived job changes or the tedium and routine of marriage.

To the Baby, I've always loved you best because while endings are generally sad, you are such a joy. You readily accepted stained milk bibs, the lower bunk, and the baby book with nothing written in it except recipes. You are the link with our past and a reason for tomorrow. You quicken our steps, square our shoulders, restore our vision, and give us a sense of humor that security, maturity, and durability can't provide. You will always be our baby.

Love, Mother

*"Thou shalt not borrow other people's problems.
They can take better care of them than you can."*
—Ann Landers

It is of particular importance to point out that this same paradigm applies to any conflict involving three or more individuals. Dealing with adult problems will also demand handing problems back to the responsible party. It is best to diplomatically refuse to become a participant in a threesome's conflict. Be mindful by not inheriting the unpleasant problems of others. When placed in such an uncomfortable position, I am reminded of my mother's wisdom, "Misery loves company!" and also, "Three's a crowd."

I can't emphasize enough how important it is to love unconditionally, respect individual differences, and recognize there are no favorites. Unfortunately, in my practice, I observed the disastrous consequences of parents who had favorite children and treated them differently. Children from those homes grow up having resentments to their siblings and never forgive their parents' lack of fairness, love, and equality. This applies to almost all relationships, where favoritism alienates others. Remember, we are all brothers and sisters!

CONFLICT RESOLUTION

There are many reasons why problem resolution can be delayed or unsolved. Fear is a major culprit. It includes several types of fear: fear of making mistakes, fear of confrontation, fear of pride or ego, or fear of not knowing what to do. Thus, a delay is a consequence of fright. The first step after dismissing your fear is to conduct a careful analysis of the problem. Provide a clear definition of the issue at hand, like a neurologist determining a brain tumor's location. Sometimes determining the cause is necessary; other times, merely locating and defining the actual root problem is all that is required. The next step is to establish a definitive plan, including, "What is the worst thing that could happen if . . ." At this step, you need to include alternatives. For example, if this action doesn't work, what other measures will resolve the problem? The neurologist might consider surgery or laser treatments or chemotherapy or watch and consult. The third step is to put the plan into action. If non-invasive laser surgery is successful, the other more invasive alternatives become moot. Finally, the results speak for themselves. If one action is unsuccessful, another one will be necessary. It's important to remember that science always trounces guesswork and speculation.

In dealing with personal issues, being able to sit and discuss issues peacefully is far superior to trying to quickly and impulsively resolve them. Without adequate thought, excessive emotionality unfortunately aggravates an already volatile situation. Another major mistake most folks make in working out a personal problem is an attempt for a unilateral victory. No one wants to subjugate themselves to an unconditional surrender.

Compromise is the only solution to a stalemate. Both parties need to feel that they have gained and not lost. Patience, mutual willingness, understanding, and a complete review of the facts are necessary. Agreeing to a mutual understanding of issues is the path to a win-win solution. I can assure you that unless resolution achieves a win-win, there will remain harbored animosity and resentment. Even agreeing to disagree is far superior to a win-lose outcome. Many years ago, my wife and I developed a "saving face" strategy. When we strongly disagreed and reached an impasse, to avoid a win-lose conclusion that would result in a stalemate, one of us would say, "OK, I'm sorry if you're sorry!"

If a problem becomes too complicated or confusing, you may need to seek assistance and counsel. Don't be ashamed or too proud to recognize that objective assistance may be necessary. Being humble by accepting complex issues will help speed your trek. Otherwise, indecision and procrastination will consume you. Remember, dealing with problems rather than delaying them is the optimal solution. The prevention of collateral damage can be achieved by action and the help of your intuitive inner wisdom.

Remember, the very nature of resolving any problem is that either the situation must change or you must change. Changing the conditions of the problem or changing your attitude and behavior remain the two stalwarts of compromise and ultimate conflict resolution.

I find it incumbent to share one more major caveat. Having worked with children for a half-century, I'm amazed at the changes in schools during this span of time. The most common conundrums encountered in the 1960s were primarily discipline problems. Those problems could better be described as misdemeanors; some examples are clothing issues, minor fights, tardiness, cigarette smoking, or bad language. Today in recent surveys, school issues are much more serious, and many qualify as what might be called felonies. They now include drug abuse, suicide, school killings, rape, robbery, gangs, assaults, and guns on campus. As a student or a counselor, I very seldom experienced these more felonious episodes. As a society, we must address these severe changes. Problem resolution of these issues will take a meeting of many minds and many villages.

Perhaps, we live in an insane society because we spend more time mopping up and less time preventing misfortunes. Your approach to troubles should remain preventative and not after the fact.

PROGRESS

After problems have been either resolved or coped with, it's time to accelerate your progress. First of all, the desire to progress is the capital motivation to move expeditiously forward. Also, progress will involve a certain degree of risk. It's like eating an elephant; it needs to be taken in small, bite-size pieces. Progress works the same way; it becomes easier to digest if taken in small steps. Having a purpose, focusing on your plan, and executing it becomes the crux of progression.

Motivation is a commitment to progress and may take years of hard work and careful planning to succeed. Obstacles are guaranteed, and persistence necessary. Impulsiveness and arrogance can destroy progress in seconds. Maturity will aid your development. Yes, you will undoubtedly make mistakes; the key is learning. Like the stock market or any other institution, learning is not a straight upward curve. It always involves interruptions and down cycles. Expect up and downs. Regard the regressions as opportunities. Progress is learning, and it takes remarkable patience and time. Remember Aesop's Fable about the tortoise and the hare.

Uncle Al was one of the slowest-moving people I've ever known. But like the hare and the tortoise, he always won the race. Not only did he live to be 95 years old, but his accomplishments, particularly the lives that he touched, were incalculable. He took at least twice as long to complete a complicated job as an average person. For example, he put in an air conditioning unit in our first house, a mobile home. I watched him meticulously measure, gather his tools, cut holes, nail, install them with screws and metal, etc. As long as I knew him, I never once saw him have to backtrack because of a misstep or mistake. He was incredibly slow but very precise. It might have taken a long time to complete but haste was never allowed to create waste. In addition, he was a perfectionist. When Uncle Al completed the job, it was done impeccably perfectly. His self-trust and personal confidence allowed him to carefully connect all of the dots with no stress or fear of failure. Like Thomas Jefferson and all good farmers, Uncle Al knew that you reap what you sow, and you only get back what you put in. And, like a wise banker, you must deposit before you can withdraw.

Like Uncle Al, success has little to do with competition. Success was far more personal. It was a matter of doing your best regardless of any time restraints. Competing with yourself is far more rewarding than focusing on someone else's achievements. Progress becomes your ongoing and continuous goal and must be part of your life's journey. You will need to break your records, not others. Never deter from going forward and onward. Only death will stop your progress. In the meantime, you will have served humanity by making a better world.

> *"But humanity's greatest advances are not in its discoveries, but in how those discoveries are applied to reduce inequity. Whether through democracy, strong public education, quality health care, or broad economic opportunity—reducing inequity is the highest human achievement."*
> —Bill Gates

Each step towards progress gains experience, knowledge, and moves you up the learning curve. It is a process that never ceases. When asked why he continues to practice four to five hours a day, the famous cellist Pablo Casals replied, "Because I think I am making progress."

Embrace your progress, and also embrace all of the people who support your continuous journey. Your progress will not be in vain but will live on long after your mortality.

PARADOX

One of the most intriguing of all human interactions is the paradox of the butterfly. As I sit here in Pacific Grove, the Butterfly Capital of the World, I'm once again reminded of the butterfly's paradox. The monarch's metamorphosis reminds me of removing the shackles of restraint and letting go of the old to allow for renewal. We allow for a new chapter of our life when we can paradoxically leave the present prison for tomorrow's growth, change and reform. I'm also reminded of some compelling quotes, beginning with the late Maya Angelou:

> *"We delight in the beauty of the butterfly, but rarely admit the changes it has gone through to achieve that beauty."*

As a curious child, I was fascinated by paradoxes. Quite frankly, they were very perplexing. The mind of a naïve child is relatively simple and linear. It was not until many years later that I clearly understood the very real concept of paradox.

I was 28 years old and experiencing my first and only deep depression. Thinking, sleeping, and feeling happy were all a struggle. I had just experienced the most traumatic tragedy of my entire life. My brother Billy was killed in a head-on car accident. Not only had I lost my beloved brother and recent business partner, but I was filled with guilt. Just the night before, I called him to announce the birth of our second child, Antonia. He said he would try to settle a few things and then be on his way to visit his newborn niece. Ruminating incessantly in my head was, "If only I had left him alone that evening, he would still be alive." I was beleaguered by those ruminating thoughts and the ever-present and lingering phantasms of my brother in his coffin.

One day I happened upon a fascinating new book called, "If You Meet the Buddha on the Road, Kill Him!" It was written by Dr. Sheldon B. Kopp, a noted psychotherapist. Admittedly, it was a very esoteric book. As I began reading, I soon discovered that the book was the author's catharsis. Dr. Kopp had been diagnosed with terminal brain cancer. He was dying. The book was his purging. As my mother had frequently iterated, "Misery loves company" became a perfect fit for my depression and his terminal illness. Fortunately, I had not been diagnosed with a fatal disease but instead had severe depression. This rather complex and somewhat convoluted time led me back to both reality and renewed happiness. Kopp's cathartic message was that the only way to achieve anything meaningful in life is to let go of it. Initially, it was difficult to assimilate this rather deep and complex paradox. As time passed, the understanding became my epiphany. His ideas resonated so strongly that it was like wearing a perfectly fitting pair of shoes. It all made sense. Letting go was my salvation. Ironically, Dr. Kopp's catharsis somehow worked for him. By his letting go, he survived another 27 years! Letting go allows one to share, understand, and free oneself from confining shackles.

Over time, I have become fascinated with many paradoxes. My most significant paradoxes are listed below. I have embraced them for my entire life.

Life is filled with paradoxes. When you love someone intensely, you cannot possess them because ultimately they will possess you. Instead, you must let them go. This allows them freedom and wings of flight. Only then will you obtain a truly egalitarian relationship. Your ability to renew your love by letting go gives your love the freedom to soar to new heights, unfettered by the shackles of possessiveness, forced choices, or unreasonable expectations. When your value judgments and unjustified expectations are exchanged for unconditional love, you release the hooks that unthinkably penetrate the ones you love most. Value judgments, expectations, and possessiveness are the ruts that will stall your growth and destroy your most intimate relationships.

Paradoxes are everywhere you look! Mother Nature often defies logic. Paradoxically, push creates pull, resistance causes flight, relaxed muscles give you more strength and less pain; fear is eased by courage.

And finally, paradoxically, if there was no brutality, there could be no sensitivity; if there was no evil, there would be no good; if there was no pain, there could be no empathy. Life remains somewhat of a mystery. However, the yin and the yang of balancing the contradicting forces of nature will forever remain. Thus, paradoxes are necessary to understand your world and your delightful journey on planet Earth. Look for them, understand them, accept them, and make them a part of your every day.

STRENGTHS AND WEAKNESSES

When first mentioned to me by my boss Jim Hastings, some 45 years ago, it was difficult to analyze and assimilate. He said, with tremendous confidence and profundity, "Tony, you must always remember that your greatest strengths are also your greatest weaknesses." It wasn't long before I began looking at my strengths and confirming that they were also my greatest weaknesses. My passion for food and wine caused great pleasure but unnecessary weight gains. My strong emotions brought happiness but also sadness. My curiosity sparked interest but also spelled disappointment. My happy-go-lucky attitude might have been fun, but it unfortunately was noncommittal, passive, and boring. My high standards brought success as well as failure. It became evident that Sir Isaac Newton was right when he said, "For every action, there is an equal and opposite reaction."

Similarly, the Chinese concept of yin and yang also resonates here. I will forever be grateful for Jim's simple analogy of life's paradoxes and the unmistakable parallel that it synchronizes with Newton's Laws and yin and yang's opposing balance. They remain the true and natural paradoxes of life.

Two of my fondest play on words are:

"There is nothing stronger in the world, than gentleness"
            —*Han Suyin*

"We are at our most powerful the moment we no longer need to be powerful."
            —*Eric Micha'el Leventhal*

"Life is truly a ride. Were all strapped in, and no one can stop it. When the doctor slaps your behind, he is ripping your ticket, and away you go. As you make each passage from youth to adulthood to maturity, sometimes you put your arms up and scream, sometimes you just hang on to the bar in front of you. But the ride is the thing. I think the most you can hope for at the end of life is that your hair is messed up, you're out of breath, and you didn't throw up."
—Jerry Seinfeld

STYMIED BY ROADBLOCKS

From a very young age, obstacles were the scourge and bane of my journey. Fortunately, as a child, most of those roadblocks only temporarily stymied my path. Frequently, those roadblocks popped up in the form of an adult. For example, the backyard neighbor who put up a fence to detour our shortcut or the other neighbor refusing to let us set up my dad's Army pup tent in the empty lot a few houses away. But other loving and well-meaning neighbors gently balanced those difficult personalities. My next-door neighbor, a British immigrant I called Aunt Kate, frequently invited me in for afternoon tea along with her homemade molasses cookies. Not to forget Zeke, the man two doors down who offered my dad and me the chance to go walleye fishing at Sodus Bay.

It all balanced out. I was beginning to realize that the stumbling blocks of fear of the dark or not being eager to swim in deep water were easier to ignore than the constant harangue of adults making my life more difficult at every turn. The despised rags man, the doctor chasing me around the house to administer an antibiotic in my hind end, the nun who enjoyed using a ruler on my knuckles when I made a mistake, going shopping with my mother for hours, or not being able to play in the rain were all a real pain! It seemed like I was always fretting from my interactions with obstructive adults.

Your journey, like mine, is guaranteed to be replete with potholes, curves, hairpin turns, and unexpected hurdles that will slow or temporarily stop your progress towards your happiness and success. To navigate your journey, you will invariably encounter many moments of smooth as well as bumpy roads. Your progress can be stalled or accelerated by the unexpected, so prepare yourself.

Obstacles are not only inevitable but also necessary learning moments.

As you approach each roadblock, your perceptions define them as either danger or serendipity. Courageous and optimistic individuals welcome barriers with enthusiasm and willingness to overcome them as valuable opportunities. However, if you perceive every roadblock as a dead-end, you will become frozen in your tracks.

Even the most courageous and motivated undergo periodic failures.

> *"The positive thinker sees the invisible, feels the intangible, and achieves the impossible."*
> —*Anonymous*

I remember the barriers that were faced as I reached adolescence. Those problematic years felt like a vice squeezing me from both sides. My recollections included the emerging awareness of girls, learning how to drive, pubescence, football and baseball, high school classes, money issues, parental restrictions, peer pressure, and more. At that time, they all seemed to be crashing down on me all at once. Yet, little did I know that the real bumps of my journey were barely beginning. The days of honey and calm were over. All of a sudden the small jolts on the road were turning into cavernous black holes.

If you are like me, adversity becomes your motivator, and reality teaches the wise to seek progress rather than perfection. Each struggle develops your strength to continue the journey forward. If there were no ups and downs in your life, you would need to be seen by the local coroner and pronounced brain dead. When you overcome even the slightest difficulty, the journey gains momentum, builds confidence, and enhances optimism.

It would be best if you remembered that you ultimately head in the right direction every time you fall on your face.

The wise, the motivated, and the persistent accept obstacles and eventually overcome them. Keep your focus on your priorities. Set your bar, so these impediments remain only as expected challenges. Recognize that the bumps, curves, dead ends, and wrong turns are required for learning. Follow your heart, forge streams, cross mountains, bridge chasms, and fight injustice. Maintain your focus, wipe away your tears and sweat. Remember, every person, like every seed, has its time clock. Each needs nourishment and support to grow like an acorn's development from seedling to a mighty oak. Encouragement is the converse of discouragement, the lack of courage.

Getting caught in a major traffic jam on your journey will require strength and imagination. Finding new, more expedient routes may be challenging but conquerable. Adjust your rudder by looking at various new alternatives perhaps not previously available to you due to impatience, impulsivity, speeding, or poor focus. Recognize and change these impediments, then forge ahead. If you want to make things happen, chase more windmills, take more calculated risks, face your fears, and redouble your efforts. Lighting your internal fires of inspiration will lighten your load and slay the dragons in your path.

TAKING RISKS

From the day you were born, every day after that, there are risks. Risks are unavoidable. They become your building blocks, stumbling blocks, or you become a blockhead. Problems are the raw materials needed for making men of boys and women of girls. Issues will transcend your immaturity to maturity, your simplicity to complexity, and your naiveté to wisdom.

Think of the hardest, strongest, and most beautiful of all minerals, the diamond. Diamonds are the result of extensive pressure and pain. The severe pressure creates stones born of adversity and humbly hidden from the sparkling beauty they possess. This is the path of the most successful. Unfortunately, the people who confuse the pain of obstacles as their destiny of bad luck are unfortunate. These perceived victims cannot withstand the pressure, stress, and pain of temporary setbacks. Yet we all know that opposition is the energy that helps kites rise, birds fly, and airplanes ascend. Without an opposing force like the wind, you can't get off the ground. Resistance and momentary pain are necessary; it is how you transcend the opposing forces of resistance that becomes their solution.

As you conquer each hurdle, your confidence grows. These new feelings light your fuse, and your inner glow of happiness explodes. It may not be the equivalent of a 4th of July fireworks display, but it surely feels celebratory. As I began facing my fears of lacking money, making a tackle, or catching a fly ball, acing a test, negotiating with parents, and driving in snow, soon my momentum became more evident. The tortoise was beginning to outrun the hare.

Of the many problems, fear is the most ubiquitous and nastiest of all obstacles. It paralyzes your confidence and puts the brakes on progress. It is probably the most debilitating of all emotions. The biggest ruts along the highway of life come from the discomfort of fear, gasping for air while in the grasp of its strangulation. Fear of failure frequently deepens the ruts in the road. Instead of finding a rest stop to relax and reconnoiter the situation, fear will force you to retreat and capitulate. However, the wise and courageous use the rest stops to rethink and replan. Instead of retreating from the barriers of fear, restart your journey with increased resolve to assault each fearful wall with fearless determination.

Besides fears, difficult people remain another major obstacle facing your journey. You will surely be faced with hostile and aggressive types. They are sometimes characterized as Sherman tanks or exploders. Those that are less overt are called snipers. These hostile types will block your progress. You will also be slowed by the complainers and moaners. Don't let these self-appointed victims delay your path. You will need to learn how to hurtle them before you are hooked by their needy demands. The super-agreeable or overt pleasers, as well as the passive-resistant types, are more silent and nonresponsive but also equally toxic. You will need

your psychological defenses to counteract their subtle offenses. Of course, there will be the know-it -alls
and their converse twins, the indecisive stallers. And
don't forget the indomitable narcissists. They will often
confuse and frustrate you until you're able to understand their tactics. If you can identify these obstructive
personalities, you will move more quickly through the
mazes of life's journey.

Also, on your journey, you will never receive total
acceptance. You must learn that you cannot please everyone. It's impossible, so don't get stuck in the pothole
of trying to please everyone. Do your best to be your
best. Don't let others sideswipe you and impede your
progress.

Marcus Aurelius, some 2,000 years ago, summed
it up nicely, with words to the effect that, "Today, I
will meet people who talk too much, people who are
selfish, egotistical, ungrateful, or angry. But I won't be
disturbed, for I couldn't imagine a world without such
people."

Unfortunately, excuses or blaming others for one's
behavior is replete in our society. One of the most obvious means is to take the "easy out," by rationalizing or
finding an excuse to relieve responsibility for inexcusable
behavior. As mentioned previously, you live in a culture
that often rewards its members who feel entitled. Those
who feel entitled believe they deserve the unearned and
unjustified. When they don't receive the expected gifts,
privileges, or special recognition, they feel victimized.

Simply doing, not excusing, moves your journey forward. A frequent excuse is, "that's just not fair!" Reality suggests that life is not fair. It has never been fair. Like the excuses below and rationalizations used to excuse or convey victimization, you will ultimately end in a pothole of stress, depression, and failure.

Some of the most common excuses include:

- "That's not my responsibility."
- "I didn't do it!"
- "It's too hard!"
- "I don't have the time."
- "That's so boring!"
- "I can't!"
- "You let . . ., it's not fair."
- "What do you think I am?"
- "It's not my fault."
- "I was too tired!"
- "I've never done that before."
- "Maybe tomorrow . . .

Think about them, and if any ring bells, take corrective action to avoid excuses and blame. Instead, take responsibility for your actions and move on—work on improving yourself. Don't get stuck or frozen at a detour. With encouragement and support, you will undoubtedly succeed. Remember, discouragement is a lack of courage. Don't give your power away; progress, don't regress!

When my wife and I were rearing our children, the excuse of boredom was never accepted in our home. Anytime we heard, "I'm bored," it was quickly met with a list of things that needed to be done around the house, followed by, "Anyone with your intelligence should never be bored." We could accept mistakes and would listen intently to their interpretations of events, but we could never understand or accept boredom. Giving a list of household jobs to reduce boredom seemed to create miracles. Except for a periodic slip of the tongue, the word boredom was seldom heard.

As mentioned, fear, difficult people, excuses, and ego can be major obstacles. There are also other internal obstructions. For instance, those who are unable to overcome roadblocks may have ghosts remaining in their closets. It may be the remnants of childhood trauma, family dysfunction, negative experiences in school, or neighborhood problems. They may also be the result of accumulated grievances or resentments. We all know individuals whose development was arrested or stuck at a younger age or frozen in adolescence. Blaming parents, relatives, teachers, friends, or schoolmates by not taking personal responsibility for past behaviors will undoubtedly inhibit your progress. Dealing with these unresolved issues is necessary before you can regain your path of progress. It is similar to the metamorphosis of the caterpillar. Becoming a beautiful butterfly means working through the chrysalis patiently before progressing on its extended journey. Accept these setbacks as temporary. Be patient, stop, and solve your problems before they magnify.

Since the beginning of human existence, we have been besieged by the seven deadly sins. Whether it was gluttony, laziness (sloth), envy, lust, pride, greed, or rage (wrath), each of these provocative attractions is like choosing your own poison. Each of the seven sins offers lush, seductive pleasure for you, part of the weak Homo Sapiens species. Whether it is money, politics, lust, ego, greed, envy, laziness, or immortality, humans are humbled by the lure of these temptations. Many cannot resist these sumptuous temptations. Without personal strength, humility, and balance, these tempting impediments will eventually inveigle and overcome you. Although difficult, you will need to gain the strength necessary to avoid the forbidden fruit and other temptations. These temptations can cause your trip to be deadly. They are major roadblocks and detours that could severely delay or halt your journey.

If you go back to the original story of Adam and Eve, you will see humanity's greatest temptation. As a friend once shared, "The problem wasn't the apple in the tree, but the pair on the ground."

> *"Obstacles are as hardy as weeds, they grow everywhere."*
> —*Author Unknown*

OVERCOMING OBSTACLES

Keeping your focus, being determined, confident, and deciding which turns to take on your journey will help. It will move you closer to nirvana. Having a stern resolve and an ability to discriminate minor obstacles from major ones will speed your progress. Having the strength to resist the temptations proffered will dramatically assist you in staying on track. Remember that each temporary setback is paradoxically a necessary step forward.

Eventually, as time passes and you hurtle obstacles, you will begin to anticipate them. As you gain more and more experience in anticipating stumbling blocks, new coping skills develop with each occurrence. Likewise, each victory provides you more strength and confidence in overcoming even more difficult conflicts. Recognizing and accepting disappointments will add to your repertoire. However, be careful not to bypass the small but knotty problems. They can turn into big troubles later.

Your problems and life challenges will not only be eye-openers and major learning events but will assist you in your quest for self-discovery. Each new situation will teach you something about yourself. You will learn to discriminate your struggles from the trivial to the thorniest. You will know how much time and energy that each will require. You will discover that partial solutions can be dangerous because they will backfire and reappear later as significant conflicts. Your strength, determination, stamina, and people skills will all be tested.

Risk requires courage.

In the face of fear, courage can overwhelm the strongest of obstacles. Risk is a necessary ingredient in overcoming difficulty. Below is a poignant and perfect summary of risk-taking. I found it in "Bits and Pieces." The author is William Arthur Ward.

> *"To laugh is to risk appearing a fool,*
> *To weep is to risk appearing sentimental.*
> *To reach out to another is to risk involvement,*
> *To expose feelings is to risk exposing your true self.*
> *To place your ideas and dreams before a crowd is*
> *to risk their loss*
> *To love is to risk not being loved in return,*
> *To hope is to risk despair, to try is to risk failure.*
> *But risks must be taken because*
> *the greatest hazard in life is to risk nothing.*
> *The person who risks nothing,*
> *does nothing, has nothing, is nothing.*
> *He may avoid suffering and sorrow,*
> *But he cannot learn, feel, change, grow or live.*
> *Chained by his servitude he is a slave*
> *who has forfeited all freedom.*
> *Only a person who risks is free."*

The most significant hazard in life is to risk nothing.

If you risk nothing and do nothing, you dull your spirit. You might avoid criticism, suffering, and sorrow, but you won't learn, feel, change, grow, love, and live. Chained by your resistant attitude, you are a slave. You will have forfeited your freedom. Only if you risk are you free.

"Good character is more to be praised than outstanding talent. Most talents are, to some extent, a gift. Good character, by contrast, is not given to us. We have to build it piece by piece—by thought, choice, courage, and determination."

—*John Luther*

A FINELY TAILORED SUIT

My deceased brother-in-law, Nick, often said, "You are either right or wrong, moral or immoral, good or bad, there's no in-between. Societies either agree or disagree." Your character and integrity will depend on recognizing the reasonable moral expectations of society.

Nick and I agreed that balanced individuals appreciate self-responsibility, courteousness, thoughtfulness, decision-making, common sense, integrity, fairness, humor, flexibility, promptness, and a mature conscience. You and only you are the one responsible for your ultimate virtues and vices. However, individuals you meet on your journey will also influence your character development. Choose your associations and relationships very carefully. A chef would never select spoiled or tainted ingredients!

You are not endowed at birth with either virtues or vices. Instead, each is learned and earned over time.

Only nurture develops your values, principles, and morality.

Your greatest assets will be the combination of virtues and values that make up the jigsaw puzzle of your personality. Whether you have good looks, good skills, or a big bank account, none will count unless you have integrity. Without it, you will never reach the top rungs of success and happiness. Your personality is the catalyst that makes for a successful journey, and character is your holy grail! Build on it and protect it at all costs. It becomes your reputation and your future. It is not only your coat of arms but your recorded history book that will remain in the hearts of future generations.

Doing your best will guarantee the development of an exemplary reputation. Being sincere and honest with yourself will ensure your genuineness. However, being aware of yourself also beckons something I learned from a mentor on my journey. As I mentioned, Jim Hastings often reminded me that your greatest strengths are paradoxically your greatest weaknesses. So be kind, generous, and caring, but don't be mindless or trusting to a fault.

Personal integrity is worn like a suit. The choice is yours. It can be forged of armor or tailored from the finest quality wool. You might be uncomfortable in your shiny armor, remaining self-absorbed and arrogant, or you can relax, be comfortable, and humble in your own skin. Like a finely-tailored piece of wool, it must feel good and reflect the beauty and strength that lies beneath. Don't take life too seriously; be patient. The harder you try to make things happen, the less successful you'll become. Development of one's ethics and honor need time to mature. Go with the flow! Be yourself. Don't try to be a secondhand copy. Be authentic, be real, be humble, be patient, visualize positive virtues, and allow your exemplary reputation to emerge slowly.

Remember, character is not given to you; you must build it piece by piece.

> *"Set the course of your lives by the three stars—sincerity, courage, unselfishness. From these flow a host of other virtues . . . He who follows them and does not seek success, will attain the highest type of success, that which lies in the esteem of those among whom he dwells."*
> —*Monroe E. Deutsch*

VIRTUES

Most virtues are interrelated, and kissing cousins to each other. They usually reside in the same house and share adjoining bedrooms. I'll try to group the cousins into various categories.

> *"Contrary to the cliché, genuinely nice guys most often finish first or very near it."*
> —*Malcolm Forbes*

The virtues of thoughtfulness, kindness, generosity, altruism and consideration for others go hand-in-hand. These kissing cousins reflect your attitude. They exemplify your brotherhood and sisterhood with humanity. Random acts of kindness are the epitome of all these related virtues. They are the very cornerstones of love and harmony.

Humility, dignity, calmness, self-respect, pride, and poise are valuable tools and first cousins. Each overlaps the other. These virtues reflect your first impression on others, not your looks. If others see you as humble, calm, poised, and self-respecting, they will want to know you better. These qualities are the "sticky sweet honey" that bond both new and old relationships. Like honey, they attract others compared to the vinegar of arrogance, bravado, or gaucheness.

In retrospect and with immense regret and embarrassment, I must admit that one of my darkest shadows and most significant flaws for most of my early and mid-life was a lack of humility. I rationalized it for years, having grown up in New York State, where trumpeting one's every success was an opportunity for boasting. Another contributor and enabler was my mother. As a child, my mother would clap, scream, and jump for joy as soon as I took my first step, urinated in the toilet for the first time, or when the potty-chair replaced my diaper. Her behavior continued through kindergarten, grade school, sports, and even college. Her modeling of bravado and hysterics was slowly inculcated. Regardless, her behavior was contagious and led to many moments of boast and fluff. It took embarrassing moments of introspection and reflection to conclude that substantial personal change was required to remove this terrible character flaw. My wife and a few intimate friends helped me to understand my misbehavior and its negative impact. For most of the past few decades, I have tried desperately to extinguish the boast and replace it with sincere self-deprecating statements to balance. My hero, Uncle Al, probably the most humble person I've ever known, was my alter ego. I knew that if I could approach even 20% of his humility, it would be a personal bonanza.

> *"Compassion is the desire that moves the individual self to widen the scope of its self-concern to embrace the whole of the universal self."*
> —*Arnold Toynbee*

Empathy, compassion, and sensitivity reside next to the house of kindness. Put yourself in others' shoes by caring, listening, understanding, and sharing. These traits bring people together and bond relationships like super glue.

> *"No legacy is so rich as honesty."*
> —*Shakespeare*

Honesty, integrity, and conscience are all are kin to each other. If you cannot be trusted, who will believe you? If you lack honesty, conscience, and integrity, you will lose friends as fast as the deciduous trees lose their leaves in the fall. The consequences are devastating, and the loneliness sublime.

Recognizing right from wrong, good from bad, is the starting block in developing your conscience. It is your sensor and final filter. I call it my "Jiminy Cricket" because it opens and closes the gates to either your paradise or your hell. It is the captain of your moral compass, your code of ethics and morality. It is unequivocally your judge and your jury!

> *"Trust and loyalty are achieved over time by many actions. but can be lost by only one action."*
> —*Author Unknown*

Fidelity and loyalty are seldom discussed in everyday social parlance. They are like flawless diamonds, sparkling rare, and priceless. Marriage and friendships are sustained and nurtured by faithful and loyal companions. Faithful and loyal companions are sometimes rare; acknowledge and appreciate them regularly.

> *"A noble and courageous man is recognizable by the patience he shows in adversity."*
> —*Pachacutec Inca Yapanqui*

Courage and patience are hard-earned virtues. Courage is in a category of its own. It is indeed a very noble quality. Courage is not the absence of fear but the conversion of fear into action. Courage is an antidote to fear and a steroid of strength. It is the high jumper in overcoming great obstacles.

Patience is a meritorious virtue. It is a priceless tool that provides a pause before action. Patience is an opportunity to think, plan, and decide rather than to impulsively and impetuously act. Self-discipline is a sibling to patience, passing up immediate pleasure in order to achieve long-term gain. Be slow like a turtle, reflective, gentle, and careful to make decisions. Being able to withhold judgment and allowing time to think is far more effective than recklessly reacting. Instead, carefully look both ways before you take the next step, which pays large dividends.

Being a relatively impatient child, I was told many times as a youngster, "Rome wasn't built in a day, and don't forget, patience is a virtue."

> *"If you don't have confidence, you'll always find a way not to win."*
> —*Carl Lewis*

Confidence and optimism are the motivational sparks that ignite you to achieve and conquer your inner and outer enemies. Confidence will spur you forward to question, discover, and conquer the many challenges on your journey. Those individuals with lacking confidence are fearful to ask questions or to move forward. They lack the desire to take chances and prefer to remain passive. I can still remember with consternation those years of passivity.

> *"Humility and respect are the hallmarks of greatness."*
> —*Peter Cedolini*

Respect for others and oneself is a mutual and reciprocal process of recognizing the significance of others. Without love and regard for yourself and others, there would be no respect. Respect is necessary for self-control and self-determination.

In summing up virtues, the following garden poem and metaphors say it far better than I can

A GARDEN FOR ALL SEASONS

First, plant four rows of peace:
Presence, promptness, preparation, and perseverance.

Next to these plant three rows of squash:
Squash gossip, squash indifference, squash criticism.

Then, plant five rows of lettuce:
Let us obey rules and regulations,
Let us be true to our obligations,
Let us be faithful to duty,
Let us be loyal and unselfish and let us love one another.

No garden is complete without turnips:
Turn up for meetings,
Turn up with a smile,
Turn up with new ideas,
Turn up with determination to make everything
count for something good and worthwhile.
—*Author Unknown*

VICES

Like virtues, its antonym, vices, include a long list of adjectives describing shortcomings and flaws in one's moral fiber. We all have vices; unfortunately, we frequently try to deny them. As a husband still in training, my wife was often quick to point out my obvious flaws. Almost needless to say, just as you learn, develop, and expand your virtues, you also learn, develop, and nurture your vices. I immediately remember one of the first vices pointed out by my wife, Clare. She was deadly accurate when she said that I was a risk-taker. Of course, risk-taking has its flipside virtue, just as it has a damaging effect as a vice. After a successful trip to Reno, Nevada, I began to enjoy the risk-taking of gambling. Soon both my wife's aversive conditioning, along with the aversive experience of lost time and money, I was quickly cured of what could've become an obsession with gambling. From the early years of growing up until the present time, vices have been most tempting. With tongue in cheek, many of my more serious flaws have been extinguished, suppressed, or significantly reduced

(I'm hoping that I'm not still in denial). A good friend once said, "We are all sinners, but the best part is that we can repent. As long as you possess free will, you are capable of changing your behavior."

My vices, past and current: smoking, lacking humility, obsessive collecting, impatience, hyperactivity, stubbornness, and periodic tactlessness were just a few of my earlier battles with vice. These battles ensued, and progress was slowly made, but like all problems, I needed a plan. I selected the systematic use of the scientific method to solve my character flaws. The identification of the problem was the first and foremost step. It also was the most painful, since staring a vice in the face is humiliating. Clarifying my behavior and understanding its effects on others was crucial. Determining alternative behaviors was next. For example, using a wrist rubber band and snapping it whenever the thought of a vice raised its ugly head helped extinguish some of my inappropriate behaviors. Each vice needed a plan of action that required repeated reinforcement. It's not easy to abolish the venal temptations and their visceral reactions when the alluring seductions appear. It is necessary to address them and put them in their early graves as soon as they pop up. Most of my vices have now had postmortems. There lingers a few that remain semi-comatose!

The quote below suggests that examining yourself may be the start of your self-renewal.

"Vices are like LEDs; the vices of others shine more brightly than our own."
—*Author Unknown*

As an imperfect human being, I must share some of my most disliked character flaws. My biggest pet peeves are people who are egotistical, greedy, cruel, pessimistic, or cynical. I find them boring and uninteresting. Please avoid these folks because they can contaminate you with their negative perceptions. The EGOTIST who reels sentences laced with repetitive I's and me's; the GREEDY who only find comfort in their pleasures; the INSENSITIVE who are unable to recognize and understand the less fortunate; the CRUEL who enjoy inflicting hurt on others or members of the animal kingdom; and the CYNIC who finds all the flaws in others and none of their own. Avoid them at all costs! If avoidance is impossible, silence can be golden. Remember, their objective is to be acknowledged, recognized, and approved. They bulldoze others to obtain attention and validation. Don't enable it, as it will only further reinforce their destructive behavior. At the same time, I implore you to recognize and develop a plan when any of those vices raise their ugly head.

Finally, there remain a few more vices that have received little attention.

- Try to avoid complacency; it is an antagonist to action. Inaction seldom makes the world a better place.
- Rigidity and stubbornness are vices that can stop a high-speed locomotive.
- Have an open mind by listening and allowing progress to move forward.
- Try to avoid being overly judgmental. However, that does not mean that you need to be best friends with those that are offensive or whose vices outnumber their virtues.
- Greed and gluttony are both unbecoming and repulsive. Try not to overeat, overdrink, over-spend, or overindulge. Those vices have sent many a person to the hospital, jail, or the cemetery. Remember, balance is always the best.

Understand that as time passes, we all capable of change, even daily. Each of us wears many different masks that represent our strengths and shortcomings. Accept people as they are and recognize their differences as important and necessary. If we all thought, acted, and enjoyed the same things, life would be rather mundane. Remember that just as you need a different tool for every task, you will need to interact differently with each individual different from yourself.

COPING WITH DIFFERENT
PERSONALITY CHARACTERISTICS

Personality traits, such as being rigid or flexible, brave or cautious, talkative or taciturn, patient or impatient, sensitive or aloof, are not related to gender, intelligence, or genetics. There may be inborn proclivity to certain characteristics, but most personality traits are learned, ultimately reinforced by experience and contact with others. You develop your persona because you have learned to either enjoy or dislike certain behaviors. Put yourself in their shoes before making final judgments. Listen carefully to people and watch how they treat others. Your observations will help you immensely to determine their overall personality. Have an open heart, but always keep your eyes and ears open.

You must carefully watch your thoughts, words, actions, and habits because they are the raw materials that reflect your persona. The composite will ultimately result in your reputation. Just as you have learned both virtues and vices, you can always change and improve your character. However, without understanding and a commitment to change, you are doomed to repeat your old behaviors. Only you can change your behavior. There will always be others willing to support your endeavors to change. You are the only authentic representative of your personage, and only you can authentically modify it.

Zig Ziglar told a story about a 20th-century hero and Nobel Prize winner, Dr. Albert Schweitzer, noted physician, missionary, philosopher, musician, and peacemaker. As a child, Albert encountered the inequity of his wealth by getting into a fight with someone less fortunate. Although he won, the poor boy said that if he had as much to eat and the other advantages of wealth, he would've easily beat Albert. Soon afterward, Albert did what St. Francis, Mother Teresa, and others born wealthy have done. He dispensed with all of his trappings of fortune and prosperity, and he gave the remainder of his life to his human brothers and sisters. His virtuous life was spent improving the lives of others.

Focus on your virtues and the most memorable moments of your life with the people you love the most—you'll again recognize your many attributes as living and loving others. ENJOY THE JOURNEY!! And remember the following words of wisdom:

> *"A good character is the best tombstone. Those who loved you and were helped by you will remember you when forget-me-nots have withered. Carve your name on hearts, not on marble."*
> —*Charles H. Spurgeon*

PERSONAL GLIMPSES

CAUTION: As I write this, there is one caveat that must be interjected. Intuition is a powerful internal warning system if not overused. It is both a tool that you will need to accept and develop. Some of the finest, kindest, and most caring of humanity have been hoodwinked; they experienced emotional hurt, pain, and even death by not listening to their internal warning system. Like you, their greatest strengths were their greatest weaknesses. Being kind, altruistic, and caring are admirable and noble. However, you must keep both eyes open and listen to your intuition. It has saved me several times from danger, and perhaps death. Had I not listened to my intuition, I may not have had the opportunity to write this treatise. Finally:

> *"Watch your thoughts; they become your words. Watch your words; they become actions. Watch your actions; they become habits. Watch your habits; they become character. Watch your character; it becomes your destiny!"*
>
> —*Frank Outlaw*

"A man's doubts and fears are his worst enemies."
—*William Wrigley, Jr.*

FEAR: FRIEND OR FOE

Chills still run down my spine with thoughts of the boogie man, noises or shadows in the middle of the night, spiders, swim lessons, and the rags man. I, like all children, was very vulnerable to imaginary and real fears.

Fears developed naturally, and others become cemented to memory through experience.

At age two, I found an opening in the wall—a small slot. Just the right size for a kitchen knife. Was that a mistake! It turned out to be an electrical outlet. My mother must have been equally shocked because she repeats the story to the point of triteness. She passionately emphasizes that my hair lit up like a Christmas tree; even my curls spiked! Somehow, I must have felt like I was hit by lightning, because every time I plug something into a socket, I hesitate!

Fear is the foundation for caution, safety, protection, and survival. It provides valuable learning moments, teaches the avoidance of danger and how to cope with risk. Standing up to fear builds confidence and conquers indecision.

Courage is not the lack of fear but the decision to face it effectively.

If you are unable to control fear, it will control you.

It is important to recognize that fear can be rational or irrational as a necessary survival tool or cause serious damage.

There are many causes of fear, such as fear of failure, fear of the unknown, fear of injury, fear of danger, fear of the dark, fear of death.

I will never forget my first swimming lesson. It took place at the local Men's YMCA. pool. For some reason, the macho man instructor, a Tarzan replica, thought that the only way to introduce non-swimmers to respect the water was to throw them in the pool. He would then patiently wait for a survival response. Yes, that day was indelibly etched as the scariest moment of my young life. It was like yesterday! That missing link of a primate proceeded to throw us in one at a time to see what we would do. I panicked and was withdrawn from the pool, shaking and crying. No parent was around to console any of us.

Imagine being thrown in a pool, submerged help-lessly, with no one to catch you, unable to know what to do, feeling an eternity of time, and no one to com-fort you from such trauma. I was inconsolable, shaking, trying to catch my breath, weeping, and disoriented. That episode of having been scared out of my wits is carried with me to this very day. Water has always been a dreadfully ambivalent experience. I love the beauty of the ocean, but I am afraid to go very far into its fury.

To add to this distressing, traumatic event, I had a similar experience at age twelve at the end of 7th grade. I had previously avoided going in water over my belly. A bunch of kids in my religious training class were invited by the priest to go to his family cabin on Canandaigua Lake. Everybody was thrilled and looked forward to it. There was to be a picnic and swimming. I did not want to be a wimp, so I put on my masculine pride face and expressed an eagerness to attend our end of the year party. Most of the guys jumped in the lake and headed to the diving platform about 40 yards from shore. The water level was about eight to nine feet. I swam out, gloriously laughing and enjoying the camaraderie. Everyone was diving off the small wooden deck, so I decided to give it a try. When I came up for air, I panicked and must have gotten the attention of my buddy Sam Pizzo. As I went down helplessly, he jumped in to pull me back to the platform. Deja vu, I was shaking and trying to catch my breath as I worked my way onto the platform. Sam had saved my life! Sam, if you are still alive, I am forever grateful—you were a true hero, and I'll never forget it. Thenceforward I avoided deep-water bathing and forever concealed my irrational fear.

When you are stuck in your self-created quicksand and hesitate, you will be in suspended animation, frozen in your boots. One of the most important things you will need to remember about fear is not to deny it but to accept it and face it. Eventually, this paradoxical "letting go," by sheer acceptance ameliorates its existence. This approach will often avoid standoffs and internal frustration.

Fears are often related to current or past associations. Understanding the origin of your fears can be the initial step in growing out of them. For instance, you might discover that a parent, friend, or neighbor may have enabled your fears. Their fears and related behavior could quickly transfer to you. For instance, seeing adults you trusted avoid heights, tell scary stories about their reactions to snakes, dogs, a dark bedroom, or a possible kidnapper. You might imagine facing those same circumstances and also becoming paralyzed by fright. Simply planting a thought into an impressionable young person can create both rational and irrational fears. Likewise, almost drowning, hearing strange, scary noises at night, experiencing frightful turbulence on a flight, or reading a horror story might make those same fearful associations.

Unfortunately, if not faced, fears can expand and generalize exponentially.

Any time we venture into unknown territory, we experience some degree of fear. When attempting something brand-new, whether it is riding a bike, giving your first speech, learning to swim, flying, or participating in a school play, fear is ever-present. Even the most talented actors, comedians, singers, or speakers express some degree of fear. As paradoxical as it seems, fear is a motivator when viewed from a position of power and confidence. However, fear can act conversely and paralyze you. Nonetheless, with confidence and motivation to succeed, you can overwhelm and conquer your fear of failure.

Also, fear of the future can imprison you and force you to remain living in the past. It also can affect your judgment and confound your decisions. Peace, harmony, and balance can be achieved by controlling fear through courage and confidence. Taking aggressive action is much preferred to being frozen with fear. Taking calculated risks or pursuing opportunities will result in successful progress along your journey.

Blame, avoidance, and procrastination are everyday defensive actions when fear prevails. They are symptomatic of fear. It's much easier to blame others or delay action when faced with the fear of embarrassment, disclosure, or failure. Regardless, whether it is blame or procrastination, you remain stuck in your mental quicksand. Avoidance and procrastination were my waterloos (no pun intended) with swimming and deep water. Giving up by suggesting a plea of poor me as the victim is equally regressive.

Sometimes even physical symptoms cause withdrawal from tenuous situations because fear has won. Fear can cause you to feel weak and helpless, allowing others to come to your aid; they sometimes become enablers. Further, they might provide the momentum for you to remain frozen and helpless in your tracks. Instead, take the offensive; it is far superior to remaining in a defensive and vulnerable position. Plan and use your motivators of confidence and courage to overcome your fears. As mentioned below, everything that you want and need is on the other side of fear.

Some fears can generalize and expand to all strangers, complete darkness, or imaginary superstitions. Learning that certain fears have no reality base is like discovering there is no Santa Claus. It takes time, experience, support, and trust in others to shed fears. It's not easy to relieve and reverse them. Sometimes fears are extinguished in seconds; other times, it may take years.

PERSONAL GLIMPSES OF FEAR

As a child, my mother had several frightful experiences with spiders. She often related to falling into a massive web of spiders and struggling to remove the gossamer mesh. She remembered the spiders crawling all over her. That traumatic experience produced hysterical reactions upon the sight of any spider, especially black widows. Her screams and apoplexy transferred those same fears to me as a young boy. My fear of spiders was relatively intense and carried into adulthood. I could imagine and relive all of her images I absorbed while listening to my mother's frightful experiences.

At age 22, when my bride and I were living on her family's prune ranch, I had another of my epiphanies.

Uncle Al had stopped by and asked if I could help him place redwood stakes under the prune trees. They were listing severely that year from a huge crop. He pulled out the flatbed truck, and we headed for the pile of stakes that had been stacked outside from the previous year. Uncle Al grabbed a pile of about 20 redwood stakes. When I bent over to get my stakes, I couldn't believe my eyes. I was glaring at about fifteen black widow spiders. When I screamed, my uncle came running, thinking something horrendous had just taken place.

He asked, "Are you okay? What's wrong?" I pointed to the black widow spiders. He laughed and said, "Those little things? Are you going to be afraid of those tiny spiders?"

He killed one right after the other with his bare hands and with a series of thumb twists. I couldn't believe it.

Uncle Al killed at least a dozen black widow spiders with only his thumb.

My fear of spiders was cured.

During the years that have passed, I have been initially surprised by some spiders, but with my thumb I've killed most of them, even a few black widows (I don't recommend trying this). With that incident, my hero, Uncle Al, provided the most incredible compression of what psychologists call "successive approximations." This process is usually very lengthy. Successive approximation begins by talking about the identified fears, then slowly introducing a progression of pictures of the targeted fear. Eventually, after weeks of support and reinforcement, the person approaches the feared item, dog, hamster, beetle, spider, snake. Even the most severe fears are cured by this very systematic and timely approach, the successive approximating of the identified fear. Incredibly, my long-term fear of spiders was cured in seconds. Most successive approximations take weeks or months.

Baseball was one of my favorite sports. It was one of the first endeavors that taught me about the elements of fear. Having my nose broken by an errant baseball didn't help. Nor did the first time I faced the best pitcher in our Babe Ruth league, a future pro player. Standing at the plate, I froze as three perfect strikes passed the plate without even moving my bat. What helped was experiencing many more similar events and slowly developing confidence and understanding. Learning to hit the ball and catch it required focus, calmness, and confidence. One of the realities was recognizing that you can get up to bat ten times and only get three hits and still be successful. Learning that was great. Understanding that even the best players make errors and that practice may not make perfect, it sure helped develop my confidence and good baseball skills. Those powerful learning moments proved insightful in understanding both the work ethic and never giving up. Baseball and team sports also provided ample opportunity to learn fair play, value your teammates, the synergy of teamwork, and that winning isn't everything. Baseball, for me, was also very special because my dad was my coach. Even though things were sometimes turbulent during those adolescent years, I valued my dad's efforts to teach by example. Baseball provided a lifetime of learning that will never be forgotten. I don't think I ever formally expressed my appreciation; "Thank you, Dad!"

Once you have recognized your fear and can identify its source, you can apply your strength by allowing confidence, mutual support, courage, and creativity to overwhelm your fear. It is important to recognize that the more one avoids fear, the more fear increases. Meet it head-on.

Face your fears; avoiding, denying, or running away simply magnifies them.

Fear is humankind's greatest challenge, and indeed the biggest obstacle to happiness and success.

Action is the only answer.

Doing the things you fear most, you cannot help but eventually be successful.

Remember that fear does not reside anywhere else except in your mind. Conquering the shadows, the ghosts, the un-slayed demons, and dragons of fear becomes your ultimate choice. Viewing fear from a power position rather than from one of weakness is one of the keys to its demise. Don't see fear as a cause for alarm, but as a natural motivator for action toward your progress. One technique I found very helpful was imaging your worst possible consequence.

What is the worst thing that could happen if . . . ?

Most of the time, you will be able to discover the difference between rational and irrational fears. If it is a rational fear, it can be controlled; if it is an irrational fear, it must be resolved. Changing the inner voices within, along with new affirmations, are necessary to combat fear. Affirmations such as "I can," "I will," "I shall," instead of, "I can't," "If only," "I hate," "That's impossible," "I'm scared," or "I'm weak."

Practicing your affirmations, along with visualizing your new behavior, whether in the car, shower, while exercising, or while facing the morning mirror, is critical. You should spend at least ten minutes a day practicing your new affirmations. Believe it or not, you do not have to believe your new affirmations and the associated reconstructed images firmly. With time and repeated practice, they will automatically replace your old trite negative assertions. It's like spot remover; before it is completely removed, you may need to apply it several times, depending on the stain's severity. Remember the tenet; two conflicting thoughts cannot permanently remain in one's mind. The internal conflict is over when your new actions defy your past habits. Taking steps slowly, carefully, and consistently will eventually add momentum and ultimate success. Small steps eventually lead to giant steps. Don't be afraid to employ your support systems; that is, those people that provide you with encouragement, counsel, and love. They will assist you in developing the new, more confident, fearless you!

Remember Uncle Al and my fear of spiders.

"He who sings frightens away his ills."

—*Cervantes*

BEWARE OF HIGH VOLTAGE

My life was tense and frantic from a sixty-hour work-week, a part-time job as a therapist, coping with a dad dying of cancer, an active community volunteer, a parent of three youngsters, a husband, a writer, an activist, a child advocate, and the inability to say no—all a myriad of high-voltage mid-life stressors.

Research and my subsequent book on stress provided a litany of coping techniques to ameliorate my duress and frustration.

Now, over 40 years since my book's publication on stress, I have accumulated even more information. Since then, my file has grown immensely. My life is not as intense and frenetic as it was in mid-life; however, I must admit stressors have not departed. And frankly, there are days that, even knowing coping skills, my tension sometimes possesses me for some time. I begin each new day with Mom's favorite advice, "Tony, remember, each day is a brand-new gift. Start it out as a fresh new day, not as a continuation of yesterday." Fortunately, a good night's sleep, having a loving and supportive wife and family, taking moments to express appreciation, and some meditation usually calms the turbulent seas.

My current concern is the enormity of information collected before and after that publication, thus my need to add a detailed addendum.

STRESS AS A MAJOR THREAT TO HUMANITY

Stress is an enormous threat to humankind. There is no doubt in my mind that there are more bodily wear and tear and ensuing disease results from the throes of it than any other source. Today tension and subsequent depression are the greatest of all challenges to our civilized world.

Stress is an unavoidable and necessary response to your everyday challenges in your personal and work life. It is ubiquitous and will be with you throughout your life. The incessant attacks, which are impossible to avoid, mean you must learn to develop coping skills. Medical professionals suggest that at least half of all illnesses are related to the effects of stress. They include cardiovascular disorders, anxiety, kidney disease, asthma, peptic ulcers, depression, obesity, immune system disorders, rheumatoid arthritis, and perhaps some cancers. The ancient Greeks discussed the mind and body well over 2,000 years ago. I strongly agree they are both interconnected and inseparable.

"You don't get ulcers from what you eat. You get them from what's eating you."
—Dr. Joseph Montague

A life without stress is neither possible nor desirable. It is a motivator at reasonable levels as it primes you for peak performance at work and play. At excessive levels, stress becomes distress and leads to apathy, depression, and illness. In most people, the symptoms of it disappear as the causes of distress abate. For others, distress becomes a chronic way of life. Stress-related disorders such as peptic ulcers, hypertension, and depression, occur more frequently among high-pressure occupations such as air-traffic controllers, office managers, and helping professionals such as teachers or therapists. It is less prevalent in less stressful professions, such as university professors, sports stars, symphony conductors, CEOs, and VIPs.

Stressors ignite the fight or flight syndrome. Your nervous system is no different than that of your early ancestors. Like your caveman brethren, your body reacts physiologically and automatically to physical or mental tension. Then, as now, with the threat of danger, blood pressure increases, muscles tense, emergency hormones such as adrenaline are pumped into your bloodstream, eyes dilate, heartbeat increases, blood sugar rises, breathing accelerates, and additional blood is pumped into the brain. All of these physiological responses gear you toward action, with one major objective—survival. Unfortunately, the threat to an individual need not be real. At least ninety percent is caused by the "stress of stress," better known as worry, imagining things that will seldom come to pass.

People who experience long-term distress are perpetually tense. Stressors consume and deplete unnecessary amounts of energy, ultimately resulting in disease. It can be as extreme as a tragic auto accident or as benign as a job promotion. Certainly, the more serious and prolonged the pressure, the more profound effect on your body and psyche. Interestingly, the word disease, if separated into syllables, becomes dis-ease. Simply meaning, your body is not in balance or at ease. The Chinese use pictures as their form of writing. Two distinctly opposing symbols express stress in Chinese. One symbol represents *danger*, the other *opportunity*. Either can ignite your body's emergency response.

As danger, stress means a harmful threat that can put the body in a defensive and vulnerable position. Since it is perceived as a danger, it depletes energy and alerts the body for action. It ignites the body's emergency response, causing hormones to flow, muscles to tighten, etc., resulting in harmful wear and tear on the body and sometimes disease.

The other opposing Chinese symbol is opportunity. It has the potential for positive results and, thus, a positive stressor. As an opportunity, this dynamic force is turned into a motivational challenge, an energizer, an opportunity for a person to utilize the hormones, muscle tension, alertness, etc., for constructive use. It creates positive energy.

Paradoxically, children can be both a blessing and heartache, not dissimilar to the paradox of danger and opportunity. Children are a wonderful source of love, happiness, and pride. Conversely, children can, at times, be a major source of frustration, anger, and disappointment. It all depends upon your relative perception, as a positive that energizes you or a negative effect that depletes your spirit.

Not surprising, the iconic pioneers, Dr. Edmund Jacobson, Dr. Hans Selye, and Norman Vincent Peale, all lived well past 90 years of age. According to Dr. Selye, each of us possesses a fixed amount of adaptive energy. It's like the world supply of oil. Once depleted, it cannot be replenished. Stress is, indeed, cumulative. Once accumulated, it becomes destructive to both your mind and body. Everyone has a physiological weakness, whether it's cardiovascular, stomach, kidneys, liver, pancreas, back, or head. If attacked, these weak links eventually break down. Unfortunately, stress in the 21st century is here to stay. It is part of your daily life. Physicians and hospitals can't cure it. The only available solution is for you to understand this phenomenon and learn how to avoid it or cope with it. Snoopy summed it up, succinctly, "Don't hurry, don't worry; just do your best and flush the rest."

BRIEF SUMMARY OF STRESS

Stress is one of life's paradoxes. It is either dangerous or motivating. It can be looked at similarly as the interchangeable forces necessary for your life, yin and yang. Some of its key elements include:

- Stress is finite. Every person is vulnerable. Everybody has an Achilles heel, a breaking point. There is no one able to absorb all of life's negative pressures all of the time. Anyone can be caught short. If you are stress-resistant, you become better at coping and eventually become inoculated to the most stress.

- Stress is relative. Like Einstein's theory of relativity, it is comparable to each individual and each circumstance. To a caveman, it may have been a saber tooth tiger. To a Los Angeles commuter, it might be driving home. To an agoraphobic, it might be walking out the front door. It is relative to each individual and each circumstance and is categorized as your personal perception.

- Stress is cumulative; yes, it accumulates. It increases as additional negative forces are applied. According to researchers, at least 50 percent of all stress is job-related. You have experienced the joy of being away from work or school for a weekend or an extended vacation.

Being away from pressure is less stressful and more enjoyable. It is your safe refuge.

"Your home should be the antidote to stress, not the cause."

—*Peter Walsh*

Having a number of little stressors can create thorny problems that otherwise would not have occurred had they not accumulated. For example, Mondays are often referred to as the most challenging day of the week. The reason is that it is a transition from a relatively calm weekend to a new or old set of problems that were temporarily dismissed during the weekend. Your life events are compounded by work, home, social, and emotional stress.

Stress, no matter how positive, causes some wear and tear upon your body. This is true whether the event is positive such as a birthday, wedding, or negative event such as a death or a traumatic event like a car accident or a divorce. Stress only ceases to exist at death, so consider it a daily part of your life.

Experts agree that the source of psychological tension is from the neck up.

A BRIEF SUMMARY OF THE CAUSES OF ADULT STRESS

During your lifetime, you will encounter many faces of stress. For example, a major study listed the twelve most significant stressors for adults, from most serious to less serious. They are the death of a spouse, divorce, marital separation, jail term, death of a close family member, serious personal illness or injury, recent marriage, fired from work, marital reconciliation, retirement, change of health of immediate family member, pregnancy, and sexual difficulties.

My research and book identified the seven major causes of job stress and many lesser causes. The seven most toxic are briefly identified below but explained in detail in the Stress Addendum. Here are the seven:

1. Communication problems
2. Secondly, and perhaps the prime cause of stress is a lack of personal control.
3. Contact with difficult people
4. Work overload
5. Role conflict is sometimes called role ambiguity.
6. Personality differences of individual
7. The need for personal education

In summary, learn how to be stress-resistant by dealing with difficult people, developing good communication skills, and establishing a clear understanding of your personality, role, and workload. Exercise your mind and body, relax, and enjoy life. Be happy! And remember to learn how to deal with different personality types.

THE SYMPTOMS OF DISTRESS

Like many other neurological maladies such as autism or dementia, distress symptoms are part of a continuum from mild to severe. For example, you can have mild forms of dementia, such as forgetfulness, or very severe forms such as Alzheimer's disease. Likewise, the symptoms of stress are on a similar continuum. It is not surprising that there is a direct and high correlation between the symptoms of distress and the symptoms of low self-esteem and low self-confidence.

It was only forty years ago that Dr. John Kane of the Long Island Medical Center discovered the astounding relationship between distress and depression. An article in the American Medical Journal marked for the first time that the medical profession and now accepted the extremely strong correlation between depression and distress. The symptoms of serious distress are identical to the symptoms of depression.

They are as follows:

- Sadness and hopelessness
- Loss of capacity for pleasure (apathy)
- Loss of sexual appetite

- Denial
- Loss of appetite for food or overeating (eating disorders)
- Anxious and restless behavior
- Difficulty concentrating and some memory-related problems
- Insomnia or oversleeping (sleep disorders)
- Being upset by little things
- Feelings of helplessness and worthlessness
- Withdrawal from friends and relatives

Debilitating depression is at the severe end of the stress continuum. It is the direct result of excessive chronic distress. Some authors have summarized depression as a form of anger turned inward. This is best exemplified by people depressed over the death of a loved one. Inward anger exists because you are no longer able to have contact with your lost loved one. This internalized anger is a result of a lack of closure, also known as unfinished business. You are despondent because you have been robbed of this loved individual. Unfortunately, since this anger is unable to be directed outwardly, it turns into tumultuous inner acid. In a similar vein, when you express outward anger, you are angry at yourself. Striking out at others is far easier to rationalize. Making it someone else's fault is much easier than being upset with yourself. I can't begin to tell you how many times I took my upset out on another until realizing I was furious at myself for allowing the situation to occur. Always look inward first to determine why you are so angry. It will save you many apologies, relationships, and heartaches.

DENIAL

Reviewing the emotional symptoms of distress, the most generic of all symptoms is *denial.* It includes irrational anger or hysterical behavior caused by not accepting that as part of your personality. Procrastination is a form of dismissal by avoiding difficult or unresolved situations. Procrastination simply denies that anything needs to be done, at least not immediately. Irrational fears are another form of avoidance through disownment. It can be as simple as being afraid of animals or needles; or, at the extreme level, agoraphobia. Chronic depression can be a form of denial because it delays the resolution of problems, by remaining in the depths of severe inward anger instead of proactively making a decision. Blame is a form of rejection by denying responsibility; "It wasn't me," "I couldn't help it," "The devil made me do it." Self-destructive behaviors constitute another form of disallowing personal responsibility. From the continuum of self-abuse and self-mutilation, pleasure and happiness are personal denials of distress to the lesser spurning of oneself. Finally, escape through drugs or alcohol is another major form of repudiation. There is no doubt that denial can be the most significant road-block to solving problems and relieving distress.

BRIEF SUMMARY—COPING WITH STRESS

"Tension is a habit. Relaxation is a habit, and bad habits can be broken, and good habits formed."
—William James

Resolving the dangers of stress will neutralize it and extend your life. Recalling that it is a subjective perception, what a person perceives to be problematic—is problematic. It may be a non-event, or conversely, a major crisis to another individual. Your reaction to a perceived event is based on your background, character, and personality traits. However, any reaction to these pressures can be tempered by the development of coping skills. This resiliency, which you will slowly develop, will be critical for your journey. Gaining a set of coping tools will be necessary to combat the many stressors you will face. With these newly acquired antidotes, you will be able to bounce back quickly from the threats of those annoying debilitations.

"One does not have to get sick in order to get better." As humans, we often deal with crises after they explode rather than taking preventative action. Negative stress causes unnecessary wear and tear to your body and mind. If you expend more energy than necessary, you accelerate this wear and tear. You can save that damage by dealing with problems before they fester into crises. By first identifying the problem, that ounce of prevention of anticipating a crisis will pay off handsomely. I'm reminded of a tradition in Cornwall, England, where individuals were tested for sanity. The individuals are brought into a room where a water spigot is dripping, and they are handed a mop. If their first action is to mop up the water, they are judged insane. If, on the other hand, they turn off the spigot and then begin to mop up, they are judged sane. Unfortunately, many people fail to think and plan. They deal with crisis directly instead of going to the root of the problem. It's like weeding. You can get it done only if you get to the root of the problem.

It is especially important to emphasize that positive stress can energize you. Stress is, first and foremost, a perception. Perceiving it as a challenge can turn a possible negative into a positive. Not only is an ounce of prevention worth a pound of cure, but a pound of action is far greater than a ton of reactive passivity. Planning is critical. Remember the adage, "If you fail to plan, you plan to fail." Planning how to contain stress and convert it into opportunistic energy will expedite your travel through life.

The scientific method is a planning strategy that is strongly recommended. Getting to the root of a problem initially by first identifying it is your very first step in establishing a plan. Implement your plan, evaluate it, and then make the necessary course adjustments.

And remember, *"Again and again, the impossible problem is solved when we see that the problem is only a tough decision waiting to be made." Dr. Robert H. Schuller.*

This leads to the three basic means of Coping with Stress:

1. Changing the situation by avoiding it; by taking necessary action on removing oneself from the disquieting environment.

2. Changing your perception about the situation; by turning it around, negating its reality, looking at it differently, or resolving it by making a definitive decision.

3. Changing your state of psychological or physiological arousal (fight/flight syndrome) through relaxation techniques, biofeedback, physical exercise, deep breathing, etc.

In order to embrace the three basic means of coping, the following skills will need to be implemented:

- Adjust your attitude—it is the single most important variable in stress management.
- Utilize your support systems—your significant other, family, and close friends, all will help you.
- Add lots of humor—it is the best antidote to distress.
- Don't be stymied by mistakes—see them as learning moments and opportunities.
- Learn to deal with difficult people—identify them, then develop coping skills.

- Develop detached concern—don't allow your-self to get too intimately involved with other people's problems.
- Relinquish yesterday and tomorrow—stay focused on the here and now!
- Prepare a memorabilia file—a collection of inspirational quotes, photos, stories, memories, cards.
- Learn and practice mind-body relaxation—Tai Chi, yoga, meditation, breathing, stretching.
- Avoid unnecessary judging and gossiping—they will hurt you more than the recipient.
- Give thanks daily—every day is a gift, be thankful, and show it.
- Allow for change—don't be rigid. Be open by seeking as much knowledge and information as possible.
- Exercise regularly, eat healthy, don't smoke—your body is your temple; keep it that way.

STRESS RESISTANT PROFILE

Consider the list below your personal goals. Patiently work to accomplish as many as possible successfully. If you can truly master coping, you will become a proto-typic stress-resistant person as follows:

- Having personal confidence, the feeling of being in control of yourself

- Being resilient and flexible
- Feeling peace and contentment in dealing with most problems and people
- Feeling socially and emotionally comfortable
- Relying upon the accuracy of your perception
- Having enthusiasm for life with sincere quality of love, empathy, and altruism
- Focusing on others but eschewing others' vices of greed, egotism, and self-centeredness
- Accepting others by listening and learning from them
- Allowing experiences to happen rather than run from or deny their existence
- Letting go of the past by facing fears, disappointments, and near tragedies
- Not allowing grudges, old wounds, and resentments to fester; resolve and dismiss them
- Maintaining poise, courtesy, and control, not seeking revenge
- Possessing realistic expectations about yourself and others
- Being patient, persevering, humble, and forthright
- Taking responsibility and apologizing for your mistakes
- Appreciating and complimenting others
- Knowing that making decisions is the only means of problem resolution
- Avoid ruminating

- Sharing, confiding, confessing, and cultivating trust in others
- Learning to accept adversity and problems
- Not allowing others to tell us how to think, act, or feel
- Avoiding escape and denial through excess alcohol or drugs.
- Finding pleasures in work and hobbies
- Keeping active by regularly exercising both mind and body
- Recognize strengths and weaknesses. Greatest strengths are your greatest weaknesses.
- Finally, accept yourself by realistic self-appraisal, both positive and negative.

An extensive compendium on "STRESS" is available by going to https://www.drtonycedolini.com/stress

"Don't worry, don't hurry, do your best and flush the rest."
—Snoopy/Charles Schultz

PLOWING THROUGH WORRY

I can't remember my first moments of worry, but it seems that from an early age, I was always worried about something. I worried about my parents, particularly about their health, especially the fear of them dying. My dad had remained in the Army Reserve and regularly attended meetings and summer camp. I remember him coming home from camp with stories of soldiers being caught in explosions and fires during maneuvers. As a child the stories were frightening. He would describe third-degree burns and even one death. I remember worrying about the rags man. Rumor had it that he would kidnap children and hide them under the rags of his horse-drawn cart. I worried about school, grades, getting into fights, or having a mean teacher who threatened to button my lips together with a safety pin.

In second grade, I had a horrifying experience. A very quiet boy with whom I often walked to St. Ambrose School was found dead in his closet. Supposedly, he was playing cowboys. He was found hanging from a homemade rope noose. Some suggested suicide. Regardless, it left me fearful, especially at night, when I heard strange noises. Worries—yes, my head was like a gas tank filled with toxic thoughts. On my journey, it took decades to realize that worries most often led to dead ends.

> *"Worry compounds the futility of being trapped on a dead-end street. Thinking opens new avenues."*
> —*Cullen Hightower*

Worry is stress's diminutive brother. Bobby McFerrin hit the nail on the head when he wrote his Grammy-winning song, "Don't Worry, Be Happy." He went on to sing, "In every life we have some trouble, but when you worry, you make it double." "When you worry, your face will frown, and that will bring every-body down." A certain amount of concern is a natural and normal part of living. It pushes you to get things done and makes you aware of what would happen if something were not done. In that sense, it means pro-tection but might be better defined as a concern. If we did not fret about insulated electric wires, faulty car brakes, or cars as we cross a busy street, the results could be disastrous.

A concern is meritorious; a worry is wasteful.

Brooding over things can be an irrational percep-tion of a situation. While a rational concern is based on facts, an irrational one is based on misinformation.

An important construct is that you shouldn't agonize if you can't control an event.

> *"There is a great difference between worry and concern. A worried person sees a problem, and a concerned person solves a problem."*
> —*Harold Stephen*

According to psychologist Dr. Elinor Kinarthy, the average person has more than 200 negative thoughts a day. Most of them are worries that involve jealousy, insecurity, cravings for forbidden things, etc. She also points out the depressed individuals have as many as 600 negative thoughts a day. Certainly, you can't eliminate all of the disturbing things that go through your mind daily, but you can reduce the vast number of negative thoughts. When a negative thought begins to surface in your mind, pause, stop what you're doing for a few seconds, and don't say anything because talk reinforces negative feelings. Take a deep breath and inhale as much oxygen as your system can handle. Concentrate on a pleasant, relaxing scene, like a walk on a warm breezy beach. By taking in more oxygen, you flush out your system and lower your level of anxiety. Concentrate on the scene for about two or three minutes for minor concerns and ten minutes for more serious upsets. Continue until the worry or upset decreases. Practice it!

*"If you spend your whole life waiting for the storm,
you'll never enjoy the sunshine."*
—*Morris West*

Yes, stewing over things not only affects you, it can affect others as well. As a younger person, I admired the famous internist and diagnostician emeritus at the Mayo Clinic, Dr. Walter C. Alvarez. He often spoke and wrote about how people spoil their days and unnecessarily shortened their lives with agonizing burdens. He pointed out that certain people worry themselves sick. Worriers want reassurances and typically receive them from their enablers. This usually results in rewarding your troubles. For instance, a bank teller goes to pieces when he sees more than six people lined up in front of his window. This type of person worries about things in advance. Normal concern can easily change to pathological anxiety by brooding unnecessarily to the point that you cannot enjoy life.

*"Worry deprives us of our right to enjoy our life
without giving us anything in return."*
—*Robert Gerzon*

Worry is like the repetition of a broken record, a painful constant unable to stop its mind-numbing tones. However, concern about things is far less toxic and more prescriptive because it can lead to problem resolution. Concern allows for decision-making, which in turn suspends anxiety. This puts an end to the insistent cacophony of repetitive nonsense. Rather than chasing your tail, you catch it and stop that silly merry-go-round. Seasoned farmers seldom spend overtime worrying about their crops. When they think it is time to plow over a field, they do it. Like the farmer, you sometimes need to plow a taxing situation under to allow something better to replace it. Concern through active problem-solving moves your journey forward, while constant fretting is an endless circumlocution. It has been sometimes said that worry is paying before ever receiving anything in return.

> *"Today is the tomorrow that you worried about yesterday."*
> —*Author Unknown*

I can remember many nights awakening at one a.m., ruminating for hours about how I was going to pay my bills that month. Worrying causes the mind to clutch an idea but is unable to let it go. It doesn't help current problems; instead, it rains on today's parade. Unfortunately, it seldom leads you anywhere. Having repeated qualms consistently affects your health as an ongoing stressor, causing wear and tear on your body. Stewing doesn't take away your current or future difficulties; instead, it robs you of today's peace and happiness. I can't begin to count the late evenings unable to relax, thinking about our children when they were either not well or not home yet.

"I am an old man and have known a great many troubles, but most of them never happened."
—*Anonymous*

A part of the everyday human condition is the guilt caused by an overactive conscience. It can occupy a substantial amount of worry. Yikes, how many times I kept questioning myself about something I said may have been offensive or hurtful. However, usually the guilt experienced is unjustified and unearned. We frequently blame ourselves for things that are not our fault. We suffer the tortures of the damned, recounting the "what ifs" and the "if onlys" when in reality, nothing that you said or failed to do would have changed a thing. But, if you are guilty of a miscue, resolve it immediately, with an apology. Don't let unnecessary guilt nibble away at you and eventually eat you up. Reconcile guilt with action, either own it or dismiss it.

"Worry is like a rocking chair: it will give you something to do, but it won't get you anywhere."
—*Anonymous*

DEALING WITH WORRY

"A day of worry is more exhausting than a week of work."
—*Author Unknown*

As mentioned, dwelling over the unnecessary is the most frequent cause of stress and is often referred to as the "stress of stress" because people frequently spend a great deal of time worrying about events that may never come to pass. When positive, it can be better defined as a concern because it has survival benefits. After all, concern primes you to deal with emergencies and allows for the solving of problems. Unfortunately, if you worry excessively for needless hours spinning your wheels, it is because necessary action wasn't taken. Since time is life, negative thinking results in squandered time and destroys a part of your productive life. It's a form of denial because it extends procrastination. Constant brooding is passive delay, a stalled prelude to action. Experts suggest that you should not try to reject negative worries because they will keep hounding you. Instead, they suggest you simply tell yourself that your worries can be deferred until a prearranged scheduled time. Don't deny it; set a time for airing your burdens. You will be surprised by its effects. At that time, determine if it is a real concern or a simple negative fret. When you have designated a time to worry, you will find that most problems will become ridiculously bizarre, no longer worth your precious time.

> *"Real difficulties can be overcome; it is only the imaginary ones that are unconquerable."*
> —*Theodore N. Vail*

Rather than expending excessive amounts of time, you can turn your concerns around by using it as an energizer. You can do this by first making a list of the issues causing you to fret. One example is procrastinating. If you are having difficulty completing a lengthy and challenging assignment by ruminating about it continuously, put it on your list with all of the other items causing you continuous stewing. If you cannot convert any of them into concerns that can be resolved by a decision, write them all down and set them aside for that designated set time each day. Allocating fifteen or twenty minutes a day when you can focus on your woes attentively allows only that finite number of minutes to attend to unresolved worries. If a new worry comes up, write it down for the next day's list. Having a lock-tight compartment scheduled each day to review your list avoids wasting many hours ruminating.

> *"Worrying does not take away tomorrow's troubles;*
> *it takes away today's peace."*
> —*Author Unknown*

Chewing the cud of worry is very much like trying to return to sleep after a period of insomnia. Instead of trying to fight it, go with the flow. Resistance to worries like sleep disturbances only causes you to remain awake. Don't count sheep; turn the resistance energy around; surrender to it by refocusing on all the things you are thankful for or that bring you great pleasure. It will save you many hours of unproductive time.

There are two days every week that you should not despair, fear, or fret:

- Yesterday's errors and difficulties are gone forever.
- Tomorrow is beyond your reach and control.

Until then, don't fret; your worries will remain ephemeral. Conserve your energy by focusing only on the present. Tomorrow's journey has yet to pass, so focus your energy on today. Save the worries for your predetermined time, and you will find this alternative to be helpful, cathartic, and energizing.

> *"Worries are pointless. If there's a solution, there is no need to worry. If no solution exists, there's no point to worry.*
> —*Matthieu Ricard*

> *"Worry does not empty tomorrow of its sorrow; it empties today of its strength."*
> —*Corrie Ten Boom*

These same pundits suggest that you use a similar energizing approach to fears. Fears are clearly a form of worry. You need to see the fears, hear them, feel them, and blow them into such ridiculous proportions that they become magnified and result in hilarious laughter.

For example, you may be afraid of spiders. Visualize them as abnormally grotesque monsters. Then when you see a tiny spider crawling up the wall, you can begin to chuckle. If you recall, my fear of spiders was quickly extinguished by Uncle Al. He went about killing more than a dozen black widow spiders by pressing down on them with his naked thumb, saying, "Tony, you're not going to let those little things bother you, are you?" Although mistakenly conceived, fears under the right conditions can be conquered in short order. Thanks, Uncle Al!

> *"Don't worry about the world coming to an end today. It's already tomorrow in Australia."*
> —*Charles Schultz*

Write down your worries and put them in the box. Then you can mentally let go of them and focus on more productive concerns.

Bertha Adams Backus wrote my favorite poem of worry. Her approach is witty, creative, and metaphorical. Enjoy it:

> Build for yourself a strong box,
> Fashion each part with care;
> When it's strong as your hand can make it,
> Put all your troubles there;
> Hide there all thought of your failures,
> And each bitter cup that you quaff;

Lock all your heartaches within it,
Then sit on the lid and laugh.
Tell no one else its contents,
Never its secrets share;
When you've dropped in your care and worry
Keep them forever there;
Hide them from sight so completely
That the world will never dream half;
Fasten the strong box securely-
Then sit on the lid and laugh.

TOSS OUT YOUR WORRIES, BE HAPPY

What are a worry-free individuals? They perceive stress as challenging and necessary. When appropriate, they detach themselves to the point where they can relax and shut off the world of work and brooding. In that regard, they can recover quickly from the stress of those daunting vexations. They can assert, negotiate, respect, and be in control of their daily existence. They are not immune to stress but are stress resistant. They generally find intrinsic rewards in their work and have a positive attitude about life. They can balance overload situations with breathing periods. They work very hard, but they also know how to play very hard. They are generally physically fit and have a variety of activities in which they actively participate. Their attitude towards play and sex is healthy, and they are not deprived of either. They have a good sense of humor and can laugh at themselves. They laugh with and not at others. They enjoy life by finding pleasure in most things and are not usually upset by little things. I remember my wise dad once saying, "Tony, there are two things in life you will need to remember to be happy and successful. One is don't let the trivial things get you down." There was a long pause, and I said, "What's the second thing?" He said, "Almost everything is trivial." Perhaps that was a rather simplistic way of looking at life. When you really think about it, you often pay far too much attention to the little things, the minutiae. As previously mentioned, worrying is the stress of stress. The things you languish over are usually trivial. As a famous general once said, "We need to pick our battles, making sure that they are strategically important ones, and not get hung up with the dogfights."

"The only uncertainty is that in life you will encounter uncertainties"
—*Author Unknown*

INITIAL IMPRESSIONS

After 78 years of life, I'm convinced that I've encountered every aberrant personality; liars, loudmouths, envious, vindictive, blowhards, abusive, racist, angry, confused, sophisticated con men, narcissistic, rigidly closed-minded, and childish.

I have encountered them all.

Communicating with difficult people is by far the most painful and frustrating personal interaction.

In your travels, understand that everyone has a motive. In the chapter on perception, I reminded you that first impressions and perceptions are inherently fallible. It takes many contacts to determine "real friends." When someone is initially friendly and good to you, be careful. Humans have a very poor record of perceiving initial impressions. This Halo effect causes you to decide either friend or foe immediately. It's important to be reminded that trust must be earned. I'm not suggesting being paranoid about everyone having money, power, or that those who are jealous and competitive have a hidden agenda. But arm's length interactions are always a necessary first step. You may honor your word, but you cannot expect all others to do the same. Your only means of understanding their sincerity is to have many interactions in many settings. Only then will you have a better chance to verify your impressions. When I am enthusiastic about meeting a new friend, my wife occasionally reminds me of her family's admonition, and she says, "Remember, my grandfather said the only way you truly get to know someone is after you have eaten a sack of salt with them." You may decide that he/she has unresolved issues, perhaps prior disappointments, internal anger, financial problems, power needs, unknown addictions, or fear of intimacy. Regardless, be cautious but not paranoid or impolite until enough time has passed that your concerns are allayed.

DIFFICULT PEOPLE

Gently taking the wind out of difficult people's sails is a learned strategy. Until you have had sufficient time and experience with various personalities, you will be unable to adjust your approach to deal with challenging individuals effectively. When your repertoire allows, you will need to begin defining various personality types. You will soon be able to identify the silent, the overly agreeable, the aggressive bully, fawners, complainers, critics, hotheads, etc.

I have found the best descriptors, and the best coping techniques were initially developed by Robert

Bramson. His book, *Coping with Difficult People* in 1981, was an iconic classic. Not only timely, but it was also well-written and spot-on. After considerable observation, study, and research, he has further developed additional tools for different personalities. He remains a leading authority on the awareness of and coping with exasperating personalities. Since his original book, he has written several more, including *Coping with Difficult Bosses*. His original work identified seven different personality types and the techniques of how to cope with each calmly. They include some of the following:

- THE SHERMAN TANKS are those that come out charging like a Brahma bull. Whether physical or not, their demeanor is abrupt, abusive, overwhelming, often arrogant, pushy, and bullying. The best way to cope with these big bullies is to stand up to them calmly without fighting. Don't back down, stay calm, and don't lose your temper. Allow for them to run out of steam, maintaining nose-to-nose, nonverbal delivery. Gain their attention by calling their name. If possible, calmly guide them to sit down while maintaining good eye contact and forcefully making your thoughts known. Do it without arguing or becoming critical and overly offensive.
- THE SNIPERS are not aggressive or bullies but lie behind the weeds and take regular potshots.

Their weapons include *sotto voce* comments, quasi-subtle digs, negative teasing, innuendos, and satirical humor. It is best to smoke them out by acknowledging their snipes, "That sounded like a put-down. Is that what you meant?" Frequently the sniper will act dumb and deny it. After your response, it becomes painful for the sniper to repeat. If he/she instead focuses on your supposed weaknesses, double down and do not capitulate.

- THE EXPLODERS are childlike. These adults cannot control their temper, so they tantrum with an outburst of rage. To cope, allow them to get it out of their system and regain self-control. If they cannot stop, use a phrase like Stop! Stop! or YES! Or RIGHT, followed by, "I can tell that this hit your hot button; I'd like to discuss this further with you, but not this way!"

- THE BULLDOZERS are the absolute know-it-alls. Their superiority can leave people humiliated, frozen, and angry. They are seeking attention and recognition. Unfortunately, these paragons of logic and wisdom are often correct. In order to cope, you will need to get them to listen to a different point of view without challenging their expertise. This can only be accomplished by being prepared, having facts, logic, and statistics to support your position. Listen sincerely without criticizing or interrupting while they proceed to pontificate on their position. This will give you ample opportunity to make your point. Don't contradict but do ask questions. Recognize their need for recognition, and paraphrase what they have said, suggesting your ideas as additional information. Use a questioning approach to clarify errors, inconsistencies, or alternate approaches, a response like, "I'm having some trouble seeing how another approach might not also be effective?"

- THE CONSTANT COMPLAINERS are whiny because they are feeling personally angry, perhaps depressed, or passively resistant. Thus, finding fault by complaining, they shed their anger, usually about trivia, because that is their only known weapon. Their regular frustration needs a regular outlet. By ignoring them and their complaints, things will only accelerate. Acknowledge them by nodding or agreeing and allowing them to finish. Once you have calmly listened and accepted their concerns, you can offer a solution, or you can request to get back to them later. Then make a positive comment about them, the day, weather, etc.

- THE SILENT are those that passively do not participate or share their thoughts. One coping technique is to become quiet, nodding with a pleasant smile. Your silence will give you a personal edge. You can often ask open-ended questions that require their verbal response.

- THE INDECISIVE are the people who can't make up their minds. They are frustrated at decision-making; thus, they become wishy-washy. Coping with them requires using an analytical and logical approach. Help by guiding them to suggest various alternatives. Give them time without pressure. Be supportive and give confidence-building remarks and pats on the back, especially when moving towards a decision.

- THE OVERLY AGREEABLE are very friendly, sweet individuals who want acceptance and approval. Cope by conveying that you like them and you approve of their thoughts. Listen, be sincere, notice things to compliment them about, and avoid conflict while rewarding their original ideas and comments.

SUMMARY

Expect that there will always be a certain percentage of bad apples in the barrel. Difficult people demand different approaches based on their idiosyncratic personalities. These more negative individuals will challenge you at each interaction. Your only means of survival will be your ability to learn coping skills by not stooping to their level but instead equalizing the situation. Fight fire not with fire, but with a fire extinguisher. Your successful interaction will send a message that you will not accept their unacceptable behavior. Your appropriate non-confrontational demeanor will be a far better standard of conduct. Remember that the most important survival mechanism is adaptation. To be successful with a variety of taxing personalities, you will need to adapt your behavior to deal individually with each one. It's like wearing a series of layers of clothing to cope with unexpected weather.

Dr. Robert Bramson wrote,

> *"Let your confidence to cope rest securely on the knowledge that many people just like you have found that coping effectively with difficult people is indeed possible."*

It is important to stop wishing that intractable people were either different or that they would go away. Don't deny their existence; try to understand their anticipated problematic behavior. It is essential to maintain an adult set of behaviors. Avoid their expected childlike or immature responses, challenges, or when they are aggressively acting like a demanding parent. Be sincere, honest, and direct.

> *"Money may find a very special dog, but only kindness will make him wag his tail."*
> —*Author Unknown*

I have found that dogs seem to know how to deal successfully with individual differences in difficult people. They seem to intuit that love will always dominate; resistance finds no success!

"If there are no dogs in heaven, then when I die, I want to go where they went."
—*Will Rogers*

"We always knew drugs could influence brain systems, but we didn't know the same about behaviors."

—*Dr. Kent C. Berridge*

THE FORBIDDEN FRUITS

One subject gnaws at my conscience.

Over 50 years ago, when I initially began my collection of materials, I didn't have the vaguest thought of including addictions. At that time, except for heroin and alcoholism, there was little known of other drugs. Smoking was considered a habit and, in most cases, socially acceptable. The tobacco companies were the primary researchers of smoking, and they found, to no one's surprise, that there was little if any connection between cancer and smoking. However, in the past 30 years, the evidence of smoking addiction and its association with lung cancer has been overwhelming. In addition, behavioral scientists have uncovered many new dependencies. We are now experiencing an emerging addiction crisis in most of our civilized world. Almost daily accounts of various chemical abuses have now replaced my entire lack of awareness and naïveté.

Addictions have become epidemic among both the young and the old. Actually, for many years the subject of addiction has been conveniently denied by me and the general public. Thus, with a certain degree of chagrin and embarrassment, I write this chapter unaware of the many addicting temptations surrounding me for many years. In retrospect, now knowing how one becomes addicted, I believe it could happen to anyone. I certainly have flirted with multiple addictions.

It is easy to get hooked.

I toyed with the addictions of smoking, pornography, drinking, and others. Having attended Catholic grade school, high school, and university, I was subjected to repression, mainly focused on all "forbidden fruits." I had been repeatedly told of the dangers and temptations proffered by the devil. The joys of heaven were unavailable to those who sinned. As an adolescent, I had to confess any impure thoughts as mortal sins. I was fearful of hell, yet curious, primarily because of the continued insistence on denying pleasure. Like many of my religious peers, the thoughts of rebellion and experimentation were strong. Alcohol could have been a temptation but wasn't. My parents never appeared to overindulge. In all of my years, I can only once remember my father either drunk or near drunk.

My reluctance to any form of self-pleasure tended to decrease as my testosterone level increased. Playboy magazine was a new but unaffordable pleasure. However, that didn't stop my thoughts from wandering and wondering; my fantasies were cost-free. Years later, after marriage, sexy magazines and their inherent pornography were easily obtained. I must admit the seductions were enormous, and it was easy to succumb. I could have quickly become addicted because the temptations were almost boundless. I was indeed in the throes of addictive behavior. Smoking, later in life, was more affordable and easily accessible. I had a brother-in-law who always had a cigarette, making it easy to begin a new habit. Soon my behavior became apparent to my wife and young children. They recognized that my indiscretions were on a path to self-destruction. Not only did they present evidence; my son on numerous occasions, would tear up my cigarettes or cigars. After several confrontations with my children, I had to relook at my behavior and reconsider change.

However, my road to a gambling addiction was more quickly short-circuited by both my wife's displeasure and a significant one-time loss of over $500. To me, that was a huge amount of money 50 years ago. I have not spent more than $30 gambling at a resort, cruise, or casino in 45 years! Later, I lost my heavy-smoking brother-in-law to lung cancer. I have not touched a cigarette or cigar since his death. Because of these highly aversive events, there had been a regular need to re-evaluate my behavior seriously. Although temptations were inviting, I've been addiction free for many years. My closest other encounter was my obsession with collecting things, fortunately far less harmful, but still a lot of fun and somewhat addictive.

Today, you find yourself bedazzled by the long list of identified addictions. The number of newspapers, magazines, TV, health letters, Facebook, Instagram, tweets, ads, temptations, and potential compulsions is astronomically staggering. Facebook alone has over 2.7 billion active users, accounting for almost ¼ of the world population. Ironically, Facebook and other social media have created new forms of addiction. A very conservative shortlist of all addictions include:

- Opiates/Prescription Drugs
- High-tech gadgets and miscellaneous electronic gear
- Social Media
- Smoking/Tobacco
- Alcohol
- Sex/Pornography
- Food/Eating
- Cannabis (Marijuana)
- Amphetamines
- Exercise addiction
- Online/Off-line shopping addiction
- Hallucinogens/Illegal Drugs
- Inhalants
- Gambling

Also, there are several obsessions and compulsions such as compulsive stealing, spiritual obsessions, self-punishment/cutting, work-obsessions, and habits, not usually placed in the category of addictions.

One primary definition of addiction is by Stanton Peel; "Addiction is an extreme dysfunctional attachment to an experience that is acutely harmful and that a person cannot relinquish." Thus, addiction remains even after the appeal wanes. Most modern authors separate them into two major categories:

- Substance—alcohol, marijuana, opiates, drugs such as methamphetamines, tobacco, etc.
- Behavioral—sex, social media, exercise, gambling, eating, sports, high tech, etc.

There is no difference between our brain's response to either substance or behavioral addictions.

Embarrassingly I must admit to being addicted or at least borderline addicted to food and exercise. Up until the COVID epidemic and a health scare, I religiously overate and exercised excessively.

As mentioned in a previous chapter, our human brain continues to evolve, yet it remains subject to primitive responses to pleasure and pain. It differentiates the various neural activities by responding with different types of hormones. Neurons firing in specific cranial locations cause the brain to activate either a reward or punishment response. When pleasure is paired with multiple hits to our brain's reward center, the outcome is referred to as the "pleasure principle." Repeated pleasure ultimately sets the stage for habits and compulsions that later can become addictions. Drugs like heroin, cocaine, alcohol, and other dangerous opiates more easily achieve this pleasure principle. Ongoing stimulation of the reward center with higher magnitude dosing strongly bonds the powerful pleasure center with destructive substance abuse.

Neuroscientists have concluded that this paradigm creates the same basic brain response with behavioral cravings such as gaming, sex, exercise, shopping, social media, gambling, etc.

BEHAVIORAL ADDICTIONS

Rather than focusing on drug and substance dependency, I have decided to spend time discussing behavioral addictions since they are more recent and far more prevalent than at any other time in history. It has been reported in the book _Irresistible_ by Adam Alter that, "Half of the developed world is addicted, mostly by behavioral addictions such as phones, emails, sex, video games, TV, gambling, and shopping, work, exercise, etc."

The behavioral addictions unknown in past generations continue to increase at an accelerated rate, affecting children, adolescents, young adults, parents, and grandparents. All affected, either directly or indirectly, are struggling to cope with these new temptations. The current epidemics of opiates, prescription, and non-prescription drugs are the most severe in substance abuse history. The incidence is staggering.

NOWADAYS

Behavioral addictions were not reported before the year 2000. As mentioned above, neuroscientists have concluded that the same paradigm that creates the brain's pleasure principle response from substance abuse is replicated in behavioral habituation.

Both types of addictions are the result of brain stimulation through dopamine releases. Yes, just as drugs trigger dopamine, behavioral prompts initiate the same dopamine production. Once triggered, the rush of dopamine hormone results in pleasure. This vicious cycle of dopamine stimulating pleasure accelerates as more of it is repeatedly needed to continue the pleasure response. Not surprisingly, the highest risk occurs in adolescence and early adulthood. It is a time when teens are most vulnerable to the bombardment of stimuli, when new responsibilities are added to already overflowing hormones. They include sexual identification issues, peer pressure, independence, future careers, relationships, school challenges, academic and sports-related challenges. Teens are not always ready to deal with the bombardment of multiple stressors.

Like alcohol and drugs, behavioral habituations are easier to acquire because they appear more innocently to the naïve. They are more often initially perceived as less destructive than hard drugs. Besides, dopamine is released in smaller doses in behavioral obsessions than substance abuse. It slowly creeps up by gently creating comfort and pleasure while soothing psychological distress and relieving pain and discomfort. Regular bursts of additional dopamine feed the behaviors called love and sex. Thus, it creates a craving for bliss and repetitive reactions. Similarly, other bittersweet compulsive and repetitive actions can become equally bonded, such as nail-biting, hair-pulling, or self-punishment.

Addictions have often been described as similar to breathing. When you cannot breathe, you become more desperate for air by gasping and hyperventilating. Similarly, wanting something that promotes soothing pleasure contributes to its deceptive intoxication. Strangely enough, wanting is paradoxically more crucial than merely liking, even though the wanting is ultimately more destructive. And even if you hate the drug or behavior for hurting you, your body wants its soothing effects. Thus, the craving continues and resumes its physical and psychological hold. Also, even if dependence takes up a large amount of time, one continues to look forward to the next pleasure fix. This dopamine stimulus-response paradigm makes a permanent imprint while maintaining its hold like a mighty python's grip.

Addictions continue long after the less appealing stimuli wane.

No one can turn you into an addict, just as no one can independently cure your addiction.

Nor can anyone relieve your psychological pain.

Your vulnerability and susceptibility are dependent upon your psychological strength and your dopamine response.

INGREDIENTS OF BEHAVIOR ADDICTIONS

Behavioral addictions generally start as little steps leading to significant dysfunction. For example, a gambling or gaming addiction can begin as a trial experience and end up never stopping, always looking for the next big win or the new high score. The pursuit of the big win or score, the dopamine, slowly allows the repetitive behavior to become overwhelming and addicting. For example, if you are addicted to gambling or gaming, there are three significant elements. It begins with total immersion in the game itself. The second element is an achievement or a reward for gaming behavior. Finally, and perhaps most importantly, is the social connection. Simulated friendships or attachments are established by other socially naïve, inept, nerdy, or awkward addicts. It's often an escape from dealing with reality and social discomfort from a life that is not satisfying. Gaming addiction usually is established between the ages of eight and eighteen. Time allocated is typically one-third sleep, one-third school, and one-third gaming. Eventually, other socially-dysfunctional gamers begin to associate and reinforce each other's co-dependency, tending to strengthen and legitimize addiction. Parents often hear, "But all the other kids are . . ."

Sex is another common behavioral addiction, similar to gambling and gaming. Sexual addictions follow a very similar course. Sex, like alcohol addiction, can be the result of repression because it forces secrecy. Consequently, one must go underground. It exacerbates desire, motivation, and urges. Sexual addiction can begin at an early age due to molestation or childhood abuse. Or it can start as naïve exploration and then become immersed in habitual excitement and later abuse. This progression can soon become embedded in the psyche and brain.

Those sexually addicted eventually fall into "misfit" relationships and sometimes prostitution. Once sexually abused, the victims can become pawns having great difficulty extricating themselves from repeated abuse. Soon they develop psychological defenses that protect them from reality by rewarding the behavior with momentary success and perceived pleasure. The same primary manifestations of addictive behavior eventually become clearly visible to preying outsiders.

Numerous research studies have shown the suppression of behavioral addictions to cause preoccupation with the forbidden fruits. Consequently, highly repressive environments cause more exploration and more frequent fervent searches for the forbidden fruit. For example, researchers have found that highly conservative settings have significantly higher numbers of porn-related internet searches and more increased attraction to sexual content. Consequently, the over-emphasis of repressive restrictions constructs an environment conducive to sexual habituation. A combination of rigidity and intense pressure for abstinence and suppression have proven both impractical and ineffective.

Millions of others also suffer from other behavioral obsessions such as shopping addiction, exercise addiction, sports addiction, overwork addiction, high tech, and social media. Most people are familiar with many of these behavioral addictions. We are only just beginning to understand the increasing epidemic levels of high tech and social media obsessions.

HIGH TECH AND SOCIAL ADDICTIONS

There are many tools and information available to understand and deal with most behavioral addictiveness and destructive habits. However, there is a current lack of available data, knowledge, and tools to understand and combat high tech and its associated social enslavement. Currently, cell phones and other electronic media have displaced hands-on or face-to-face communication.

Children, adolescents, and adults struggle to reach socio-emotional maturity amidst the proliferation of high tech and social interference. In the past, there was something referred to as "hardship inoculation." Dealing with adversity assisted in developing maturity and the coming of age. Today, it is apparent that the cell phone, the primary tool used by the youngest generation, has a new flipside (no pun intended).

Not only is the cell phone a remarkable asset, but it can also be a devastating handicap.

As mentioned in previous chapters, one's greatest strength can also be one's greatest weakness. This new high-tech digital device has not only created wonderful shortcuts to learning, but it also short-circuits socio-emotional development and critical thinking. In many respects, this virtual world may be superior, but it also creates many new problems, new coping skills, and massive adaptation. It is not a localized problem but affects almost every country on earth. It has become a powerful and massive quagmire worldwide.

Overexposure to this new electronic opiate poses new challenges for parents, communities, governments, and of course, the individuals who operate them. It is not surprising nor coincidental that opiates like electronics are concurrently the most abused drugs, causing countless substance abusers here in our backyard, the United States.

Electronic devices provide a two-dimensional view of a three-dimensional world. Texting is now the most used means of communication. This messaging vehicle is an abbreviated form of what has not been witnessed since the Morse code and smoke signals. It serves as a far less equivalent to face-to-face interactions. Suddenly, hundreds of hospitals and recovery clinics pop up in almost all states dealing with these latest behavioral obsessions. Some have even predicted that this technological epidemic could be similar if not worse than alcohol addiction. Young children who may have begun their initial use of high-tech paraphernalia as young as three or four, are by age seven or eight on their way to possible addiction. Unfortunately, most parents are unable to recognize or understand these potential perils. Social scientists have now designated new names and labels for each type of electronic device dysfunction. Regardless, you must become aware of the dangers of online/offline usage.

CELL PHONE PRISON

This new virtual world may be very advanced in many respects, but each discovery begets both benefits and dangers. For example, we are now encountering a barrage of data. It is euphemistically referred to as data overload. In the past fifteen years, 1500 EB of data (1 EB or Exabyte equals 1 billion gigabytes of data) have been created. This number represents approximately 20 times the amount of data produced in over 3500 years of recorded history. It is estimated that the number will increase exponentially, perhaps over 30,000 EB by 2022. Data is now the newest pollutant to our modern world.

"There is a technical term for data overload; it's called data exhaust."
—*Author Unknown*

Kent Berridge, a neuroscientist at the University of Michigan, reported that what makes addiction so difficult to treat is that wanting is more challenging to defeat than liking. Wanting is much more robust, big, broad, and powerful. Remember, behavioral addictions have the same basic footprint; dopamine is released, pleasure experienced, resulting in repetitions of the stimulus-response paradigm. This occurs in all varieties of behavioral obsessions. Rather than going into further detail, let it suffice to say that all addictions are distinctly related. Each can result in destructive and painful consequences—all waste valuable time and resources. A debilitating addiction has an impact not only on those affected, but also punishes parents, siblings, and society. Yes, relatives, friends, colleagues, business associates, and our entire society are affected. Coping skills will now require a whole host of new tools. For example, they might include learning the dangers of behavioral addiction, usage time limitations, understanding the interactions of pleasure stimuli, peer pressure, identifying early signs of addiction, electronic governors, developing adequate resources, and parental controls.

CAUSES AND SYMPTOMS OF ADDICTIONS

The symptoms of addiction are not initially seen as abnormal. But, as time passes, day by day, actions become obvious by repetitious patterns that become aberrant and self-abusive. The symptoms are:

- Noticeable social and emotional problems
- Excessive focus or obsessing
- Denial of having an addiction
- Very poor control of behavior/impulsivity
- Seeking out and enjoying self-abusive activities
- Cravings
- Secretive behaviors such as hiding paraphernalia
- Inability to stop self-abusive behaviors
- Psychological, physical, and social withdrawal
- Low self-esteem
- A budding history of abuse
- Depression and lacking affect

Habits are established in a few weeks, but addictions usually take months!

Unfortunately, researchers are currently unable to agree whether addictive self-abusive behaviors are a result of life changes, trauma, DNA, impulsive personality, high stress, social alienation, nonconformist/anti-authoritarian personality, or brain damage.

However, researchers can better understand it by understanding the brain. They have determined that the following affected areas of the brain need further study (they include two that I'm not intimately familiar with): Ventral Tegmental Area (VTA), Amygdala, Locus Coeruleus, Limbic System, Frontal Cortex, and GABA Inhibitory Fiber System. It is also undecided by most social scientists whether this phenomenon can be classified as a disease. The National Institute on Drug Abuse, however, has asserted that behavioral addictions are chronic diseases. As mentioned, most behavioral obsessions begin between ages eight and eighteen.

> *"Recovery is hard. Regret is harder."*
> —*Brittany Burgunder*

OVERCOMING ADDICTIONS

There are several means of overcoming compulsions, obsessions, and addictions. Related to each is the lack of cognitive awareness, often referred to as "cognitive misery." It is avoiding the misery of thinking, similar to how misers avoid spending money. Gratification is so intense that compulsions, obsessions, and addictions remain steely resistant to most interventions. Thus, cognitive awareness remains minimal, while the dopamine reward paradigm prevails at a much higher level. The perception of pain is a vital psychological component that requires conscious awareness

Some of the same basic principles of stress relief can and should be applied to addictions. First and foremost is changing the environment latent with its irresistible temptations. Second, the adoption of new or renewed attitudes through revised self-talk. Cognitive therapies can be very useful. Helping addicts understand the destructive effects of addiction is certainly critical. Also, reversing the pleasure to pain, rather than finding a larger magnitude of pleasure by withdrawing from the addiction.

Researchers have found, for example, pornography is more prevalent in highly conservative and ultra-rigid religious environments. One important caveat is that merely advocating for abstinence and willpower does not work. Suppression and repression only accelerate the urge towards addictive behavior.

Those able to understand and express their thoughts and feelings are far more successful in avoiding the temptations of pleasure.

> *"Quitting smoking is easy. I've done it a hundred times."*
> —*Anonymous*

Relinquishing an addiction is far more three-dimensional and takes many weeks, sometimes months to overcome. The twelve-step program presents good evidence to validate the need for time, patience, and perseverance to break these hardened habits. One must redesign their environment where arms-reach temptations are lessened, tolerated, or absent. Changing by redesigning self-talk reinforces attitudes by not accepting the self-fulfilling hypothesis, "I'm hooked." It is important to recognize that curing any addiction takes longer than establishing it and that everyone has a different timeframe. Time and patience are required. One can rarely reverse an addiction cold turkey.

Finally, support from parents, friends, relatives, and others is crucial for total recovery.

Replacing behavioral habituation with a new and more appropriate behavior can become a real solution. In the meantime, focusing on appropriate social relationships, developing a positive work ethic, and enjoying social gatherings with non-addicted peers are essential steps.

In a groundbreaking longitudinal study of Vietnam War veterans, researchers discovered some most fascinating facts. They identified heroin and marijuana addicts and followed them for years. The findings indicated that those who returned to a family and friends supportive environment where the temptations for drugs were virtually nonexistent were able to overcome their addictions. However, those that returned to drug availability and drug-involved peers remained addicted. The results concluded that returning to the environment and social peers were the most critical variables in either overcoming or continuing an addiction. As I think about this, I'm reminded of habitual criminals. I'm convinced that the surest way to maintain criminal behavior is to continue placing them in environments and peer groups that will foster that habitual illegal behavior. Certainly, the results of this iconic study apply to both substance and behavioral addictions.

"People become attached to their burdens sometimes more than the burdens are attached to them."
—*George Bernard Shaw*

Because behavioral addictions are relatively new, remedies designed to extinguish them are also relatively fresh and in their initial development. There are actually apps available to break habits. For example, the Pavlok approaches were designed by Maneesh Sethi. A Pavlok is a wearable device that can assist in breaking bad habits and behavioral habituation. According to some credible research studying the use of the app, up to 55% of those addicted successfully quit bad habits such as smoking, hair-pulling, nail-biting, exercise mania, mindless eating, etc. It is a device like a wristwatch that rewards good behavior and administers an adverse electric stimulus for problem behaviors. It reminds you automatically when you succeed or fail. It has also been found that a rubber band can provide effective aversive conditioning and at a minimal cost. However, the rubber band relies on attentiveness, discipline, and consistency, often lacking for those addicted.

Parents will need a whole new plethora of tools to combat high tech addictions. Reasonable time usage limits might need to be set every day, rather than allowing a youngster's isolation and excessive obsession with their electronic devices. Abstinence is a poor, if not ineffective, alternative. Promoting youngsters to feel connected and understanding socially attractive and validated approaches in using electronic devices is crucial. Of course, discipline balanced by unconditional love will always remain a mainstay. Indeed, providing supportive feedback that is balanced with a non-judgmental approach will be beneficial, catching the youngster in the act of doing things right rather than over-focusing on negative behaviors. The avoidance of preaching and repetitious negative remarks is vital. The use of nonverbal communication conveys a far more potent message than nagging. Appropriate but not highly punitive consequences allow for productivity, choices, setting limits, and social success. Ultimately, the goal is self-determination by increasing social relatedness and successful family activities that promote active involvement rather than promoting isolationism. Designing an environment that encourages good habits and a healthy lifestyle while avoiding excesses and extremes will help avoid behavioral addiction. Remember, balance is key and a very high priority in every situation.

Other approaches, such as reversing the problem into a solution, can be effective. For example, turning a non-game into a game to extinguish the gaming addiction. This is called gamification. It's like turning the chore into motivation by using rewards such as badges, games, points, and leader boards.

Your health, happiness, social relations, and success are based on your ability to control your behavior and environment. As previously mentioned, if you don't control yourself, someone else will. Back in the day, we had checks and balances that quickly altered our behavior. Below are some humorous snippets using aversive conditioning to extinguish potential addictions. It's a short metaphor about the "good old days." A friend had asked me why our generation had so few drugs and behavioral obsessions. I dug into my various folders and found the following set of youthful "drug" problems. Perhaps a bit extreme, here they are:

- I was drug to church on Sundays
- I was drug to weddings and funerals
- I was drug to visit relatives and family
- I was drug to the bathroom or woodshed when I disobeyed, told a lie, or brought home a bad report card
- I was drug to the sink to have my mouth washed out with ivory soap when I used inappropriate profanity
- I was drug to the backyard to pull weeds and cut grass or face a wooden spoon

There were no computers, no internet, no cell phones, no social media, so there were very few distractions readily available for me to become addicted.

Yes, those aversive drugs will remain in my veins and have affected my daily behavior. They are stronger than opiates and speed. Perhaps if one were "drug" (admittedly less harshly) sometimes, the world might be a tiny bit safer.

Additional information is available by using Google to find sites that offer suggestions or recommended treatments. Remember, being alert, responsible, and proactive will accelerate your journey and overcome all the potentially addictive obstacles along the way.

"By the yard, life is hard; by the inch, life's a cinch."
—*Author Unknown*

THE GRIM REAPER

At birth, you began the long and arduous journey of life. Your first recollections were your parents and perhaps siblings. If you have been fortunate, you have had both parents who loved and shared their lives with you. Eventually, they will leave you as you continue on life's journey. As time passes, many new and important people will enter your life and share their private journeys with you. Most will come and be lost along your circuitous route. Some will make such indelible marks on your psyche that they will never be forgotten. Having had these interactions will also bring you joy and happiness. Those memories will sustain you on the way.

There will be many hellos and goodbyes because the road of life is laden with the unexpected. You will never know when your journey will stall or end. So, live a life of kindness, concern, and brotherly love with all those that have touched your soul along the way. These positive memories will make your sojourn one of purpose and perpetuity. Be prepared for wonderment, but anticipate moments of melancholy, grief, and death.

As a young boy, I experienced two very unforgettable events of death and grief.

Each school day meant a twenty-minute walk to St. Ambrose Catholic School. There were no school busses, and frankly, it was fun, and I looked forward to it each morning. I can't say that about my Cheerios, Shredded Wheat rolls, or cod liver oil before my jaunt. There were always school chums to chat with along Clifford Avenue. I often met a fellow second grader as he approached our block. I'll call him James. He was timid and quiet, but a friendly kid. He wasn't like my two sidekicks and me, always ready for a snowball fight with the kids on the other side of the street or a friendly but loud disagreement about sports teams. Usually, we'd meet up with my chaotic "trouble twins," Jacob and Billy. They would join us on our way, and we could be guaranteed some entertaining, funny antics. James never threw a snowball, but he also never came home with a big black shiner like me. In my photo album, there's still a picture of me with that horrific black eye, taken at my youngest brother Gary's baptism.

To my surprise, one Monday morning, our teacher announced that an unfortunate thing had occurred during the weekend. She said one of our classmates was found dead. All of us were shocked and dismayed that someone we knew was no longer with us. Our teacher, a nun, took out her rosary, and we prayed for our fallen friend. It was impolite to ask for any further information, so we walked home somberly, wondering about our lost buddy. We were extremely curious about the circumstances, and eventually, snippets of news and gossip arrived. James was found in his closet hanging from a noose. We were told that he was playing cowboys and Indians. As a young child, I accepted that news; however, I remain flummoxed by the description given. In retrospect, remembering his passive, sober, quiet demeanor leads me to wonder if it might have been depression. It was indeed my very first exposure to the Grim Reaper. The funeral left most of us sadly mute, with indelible and obscure memories of our vanished dear friend James. Walking to school left shadows of darkness with comments and thoughts of our lost soul.

Personal setbacks are the ingredients of life. All of us, even the most positive and upbeat, have moments of sadness. Like most of life's cycles, periods of unexpected melancholy sometimes besiege us. As young children, most of us experienced the death of a pet turtle, fish, dog, or other pet. These sad moments are necessary for you to prepare for the inevitable sadness of losing a loved one—a parent, spouse, grandparent, aunt, uncle, friend, life partner, or neighbor.

These life lessons can be miracles in disguise because death teaches us life!

It's a cruel, harsh reality on the dark side, but on the brighter side, it creates the gusto, appreciation, and enthusiasm that sustains our appreciation of life's everyday surprises.

My second visit from the Grim Reaper was when I was almost ten. Next door lived my dearest old friend. I called her my Aunt Kate. Her name was Kate Smith, the same name as a television personality everyone loved, and who was best known for singing, "God Bless America." Every time she belted that melody, my eyes swelled in memory of my neighbor, Aunt Kate, and my patriotic feelings. Even today, those sentimental visceral feelings remain.

My Aunt Kate was not only a neighbor or surrogate aunt; she was my confessor, high tea companion, alter conscience, extra set of ears, and dearest neighbor. She was someone a young boy could never forget. I loved my Aunt Kate and, I admit, her molasses cookies, too. Regardless, I also enjoyed her baby blue and purple irises. I would break them off and take them to my Mom and Grandma Angelina. Aunt Kate must have looked the other way because I was never reprimanded for my transgressions.

My mom met Kate while they were each hanging their newly-washed sheets on the backyard clotheslines. Since we lived next door, our single car garages were in the very back of the lots, so all that separated us was a narrow driveway. There were no fences between us, just narrow flowerbeds usually beaming with color. Aunt Kate loved flowers and gardens. We would sit and talk about British traditions and English gardens. She taught me how to hold a teacup and add a tad of milk to enhance our afternoon tea parties. Sometimes I felt like the eccentric Mad Hatter and sometimes like the White Rabbit, "I'm late, I'm late, for a very important date . . ." but that was because of the impetuousness of my youth. I knew it was time for tea as the smell of molasses cookies wafted into my bedroom window. Nostalgic fondness lingers as I recall those special moments. Her soft, melodic British accent still fills my ears and heart with joy.

Aunt Kate shared with me her remembrances of overcast England. After her husband's death, she emigrated from London with her only daughter, Mariam. She lived alone with her daughter, who had also been widowed recently. Mariam's husband died fighting in Europe late in the Second World War. My dad and Mariam worked for Bausch & Lomb and carpooled to work every day, so Aunt Kate enjoyed both mom and my company. And as brother Billy got older, he would also join us for tea and cookies, sometimes hard crumpets.

One dark day in the fall, Mariam announced that Kate had passed. At first, I didn't understand "pass," and then I still didn't believe it. A few days later, and we were invited to the wake. It was a very somber day. It seemed as though the clouds were mourning. Rain and thunder commenced as we anxiously prepared for our viewing. I put on my Easter clothes with a lilac-colored shirt, black tie, and sport coat. Along with Mom, Dad, and brother Billy, we slowly walked next door. In those days, it was very common to have the final funeral showing in the deceased's house. Conflicting thoughts and emotions besieged me. What was it like? Would I see Aunt Kate for the last time? What was I supposed to say or do? What was I going to feel? As I reluctantly entered the house, I could smell the fragrance of flowers—roses, gladiolas, and those baby blue and purple irises.

And there in the coffin was my dear friend.

With trepidation, I moved slowly to the casket. Somnolent, peaceful, with a tinge of a smile, was my Aunt Kate. I was dumbfounded; I didn't know if I wanted to run or hide. It was one of the eeriest feelings ever experienced. My dad had his arm draped over my shoulder, so I had little choice. I simply looked up and followed the others. Eventually, I knelt, said a prayer, secretly threw her a kiss, and solemnly left. I felt somewhat numb and kept having flashbacks of my dearest old friend lying in state in her living room just a short distance from where we celebrated high tea.

To this day, those indelible yet fond memories persist. The Grim Reaper had taken away my special friend. I was no longer going to enjoy tea and molasses cookies with my Aunt Kate.

It's time to face up to the facts of life.

Time is life, and life is time.

When either runs out, your life and your time are forever gone. You learn to appreciate life even more when you lose a loved one. You must realize that death teaches you to live! It creates stark and daunting realities. Each day you have 86,400 seconds of precious time. Every second is a gift of life—waste not! Make things possible before they become impossible.

As Abraham Maslow said on his deathbed, "Please remind them that life is short." Let your loved ones know how important they are to you. If you have problems or disagreements, resolve them as quickly as possible because life is too short to let these entanglements strangle your mind and your most meaningful relationships. Enjoy the time you have with family, relatives, and friends because time is truly irreplaceable.

No one ever leaves our world alive; death is inevitable.

You must accept your mortality. So, let the thought of death remind you to live with compassion, understanding, sensitivity, tolerance, kindness, fairness, and love. You will then leave this world with all of these and much more. Your sacrifices and goodness will follow you forever in the shadow of perpetuity.

My wife's grandmother Marietta said, "You should think of death every day." She was convinced that to appreciate life, and you need to remember the alternative.

ANXIETY, SADNESS, DEPRESSION, AND GRIEF

There are a number of anxiety disorders that afflict sufferers. Approximately 40 million people in the United States suffer from some sort of anxiety. They include fears (phobias), post-traumatic stress, panic attacks, and despondency. If intense anxiety persists, it can lead to a more severe type of disorder known as depression. It often begins with episodes of sadness, such as "feeling down in the dumps." If sadness persists, it can become either chronic or deep clinical dysthymia.

Those who suffer from serious sadness feel that their lives are out of control often have difficulty sleeping, eating, working, relaxing, relating socially, and not enjoying their daily activities.

A life-changing event or loss such as a divorce, death, economic hardship, or lost close relationship can be the initial cause of sadness. Typically, as sadness becomes clinical depression, it does not let up. It becomes incapacitating and affects every part of one's being. Thinking, feeling, acting, and loving become extremely difficult. Lack of motivation, inability to process information, hopelessness, and helplessness become constant bedfellows. Serious thoughts of suicide can become a pervasive reality. It is during these times that the body experiences neurochemical changes. Chemicals such as hormones are released that adversely affect your well-being. They cause a weakened immune system, high blood pressure, and chronic illnesses. In her book, *Medical Myths That Can Kill You*, Dr. Nancy L. Snyderman, Chief Medical Editor for NBC news, reported an article published in The Lancet in 2007 that, "Depression . . . can do more physical damage to someone's health than several long-term diseases."

She also reported a World Health Organization study of 245,000 people involving 60 countries. Its results concluded that after heart disease, dysthymia is expected to become the second leading cause of "disease burden" (a measure of the number of years of complete health lost due to an illness) in the near future.

Similar to despair, post-traumatic shock disorder (PTSD) is another debilitating condition. PTSD is often confused with depression because many of the symptoms are very similar. The US Department of Veterans Affairs reported that 70% of men over 65 had been exposed to at least one post-traumatic event during their lifetime. Many think that PTSD only relates to war or terrorism. However, PTSD can result from a natural disaster, a serious accident, assault, or the death of a loved one. The symptoms of PTSD, like depression, are characterized by re-experiencing the traumatic event, flashbacks, distressing memories, sleep disorders, avoidance of people and places, difficulty concentrating, anger, being easily irritated, experiencing persistent fear, guilt, or shame, hyper-vigilance, and self-destructive behavior, including alcohol and drug abuse. Also included are emotional numbing and an inability to find pleasure in what was once enjoyable.

Sadness and grief are the byproducts of a life of love, devotion, and sacrifice. You only experience these feelings when you genuinely care about others. For the more fortunate, it initially comes after the loss of a prized object or pet. Although difficult and painstaking, it prepares and helps buffer you for the more severe sadness and grief of losing a parent, sibling, spouse, or friend. Regardless, unless a person is a sociopath or is unfeeling, we all experience these high-intensity emotions at various times in our lives. The initial losses of my dogs Blacky, King, and Princess, were indeed painful, but not nearly as painful as the loss of my brother, father, grandmother, in-laws, uncles, and aunts.

ELEPHANT IN THE ROOM

Initially, the pain from your loss feels as though it will go on endlessly. Everyone experiences different levels of pain and grief. We all have different time clocks to recovery. Some, especially those who have recovered from prior losses, recover from future losses sooner than those who have previously suffered a severe loss and were unable to let go of it. We are all different, but the more you realize that life must go on and focus on the living, the more efficacious the recovery. Personally, my longest bout with depression and grief was for three years after my brother was killed. Later, although painful at the time, the losses of other loved ones seemed to heal faster. However, the feelings and memories will forever remain. I am reminded daily of all the special people who are no longer here. My hugs and kisses remain imaginary, but my heart knows they are real.

GRIEF

Grief is the deep mental anguish that results from bereavement, defined as being deprived by death. When a loved one dies, it will have a profound effect on you. The misery lingers on and reminds you of the feelings you had for your lost loved one. No matter who it is, no one ever gets good at dealing with sorrow. Some cry, some become sick, some mourn for months, others for a lifetime. No matter how strong or articulate you are, it isn't easy to share your empathy or sympathy with politically correct words, cards, or letters. Unfortunately, there are few words or catchy phrases that make you feel better, whether it is your grief or someone else's. There are no rules, or right way to grieve and certainly no timetable. Time does not heal all the pain and wounds. You will never get totally over it, but you will learn to live with it. Memories will be your solace. In the meantime, shelter yourself with tenderness and double your love for the living. Brave the bitter anguish and cleanse your mind by being grateful, by remembering all of the many happy moments you spent with those very special people.

COPING WITH DEATH

An ounce of prevention is worth a pound of cure. Being prepared for melancholy by having several antidotes helps combat its pain. Understanding the stages of depression and grief are crucial in providing personal relief. Whether it is related to death, divorce, a serious illness, or a recent tragedy, all follow a similar sequence of stages. When my brother died, initially, I was unaware of what I would experience. My first reaction came directly out of the textbook.

I denied his death.

Somehow, I could not conceive that the tragic event had occurred. My thoughts focused on when Billy and I would see each other again. Some reality occurred at the funeral, but I continued to maintain my fantasy that he was okay and still alive. After many private tears, my DENIAL (stage one) turned into anger. The suddenness of this unexpected fatality made me furious. I questioned myself, blamed myself, blamed the other head-on driver, blamed the roads, and was angry that God would allow such a thing to happen. I was filled with bundles of unresolved ANGER (stage two). Later, I concluded that depression is anger turned inward. Even though this realization occurred many months later, it helped me better understand the despair.

My anger and sadness continued unabated for almost two-and-a-half years. The bitterness slowly combined with ENVY (stage three). I was jealous of all those that still had their brothers and sisters and envious of their happiness. Of course, my anger turned inward and became DEPRESSION (stage four). Then I began focusing on my GUILT (stage five). I started questioning myself and feeling responsible for his death.

Why had I called the day before and told my brother that I would see him soon to celebrate his new niece? Why didn't I suggest he drive during the day when he was rested rather than at night when he might be tired? Finally, after reading many books and articles on death, depression, and grief, I stumbled upon a great book. I was finally ready for RESIGNATION (stage six) and ACCEPTANCE (stage seven). It was finally time to let go of these depressing shackles and accept the reality—Billy was indeed dead, and I could do nothing about it but accept the fact. I'm not sure that RENEWAL (stage eight) is an accurate descriptor for the last stage.

Still, I will say that I could finally focus on living as my first and foremost priority, instead of focusing on my self-pity. I will never forget or fully heal from my brother's death, but Billy's death eventually taught me life. As time passed, I was more able to cope with the loss of other beloved family members and friends. My father, Peter, grandmother Angelina, father-in-law, Gene, godmother, Aunt Rosie, brother-in-law, Nick, mother-in-law, Mary, and later many aunts, uncles, friends, and cousins.

These formidable immigrant Italian family members stand large, loving, intimate, and unforgettable. Please remember the stages, because you too will experience them. Obviously, not a cure, but understanding them will provide you with some protection and prevention.

Many have experienced funeral services after the death of a loved one. I like the term often used to describe people's special communion, "A Celebration of Life." The very term focuses on life, not dreadful death. Frequently, the deceased are memorialized by the clergy or an appointed person. The orator reviews the life, love, merits, uniqueness, and talents of the lost loved one. It is frequently followed by sharing nostalgic moments with intimate friends, relatives, and colleagues. These memories bring back the joyful special moments that will never be forgotten. It brings the community of celebrants together in heart and spirit. Love transposes the men, women, and children gathered into one rejoicing family, filled with the impact of unity. Joining hands, crying together, and embracing becomes contagious. As nostalgic tears flow and families cuddle in a union of solidarity, the feelings become almost overwhelming. Those comforting and shared outpourings allow not only for a special closeness, but also an opportunity to temporarily let go and move forward. It's an opportunity to reclaim unselfishness, brotherhood, and sisterhood. This assemblage of caring people benefits by releasing some of their own pain and sorrow in the process. It is a time of deep reflection and personal renewal because it abruptly wakes you up to the appreciation of life and the living. Strength replaces frailty. Those renewed feelings will forever make their mark.

COPING WITH DEPRESSION

Mental health professionals have made significant progress in the treatment of depression and other anxiety disorders. The first notable finding was discovering the effects of lithium carbonate as a mood stabilizer in treating depression in bipolar patients. This discovery by an Australian psychiatrist, Dr. John Cade, dramatically helped eliminate almost 50% of all hospital beds occupied by very depressed patients. It was then followed by the development of antidepressants, additional mood stabilizers, anxiety relievers, and a new and more sophisticated series of cognitive therapies. Regarding drugs— they need to be taken with a modicum of caution, only after investigating their effects and side effects.

To find relief from your despair, you must identify your symptoms. First and foremost, if you feel the funk of sadness and you can't break out of it, ask for help. Seeking help moves you forward because it's the first step in recognizing the problem and its resolution. It is no different than if you were seeking help for a physical ailment or a broken bone. Make an appointment with your family practitioner. You will be evaluated with blood tests, stress surveys, personality questionnaires. If diagnosed, you may be prescribed medication and cognitive counseling. A physical exam will also eliminate any possible disorders such as an underactive thyroid, prediabetes, drug use, heart disease, or gastrointestinal disturbance. If a physical illness is ruled out, you can proceed to medication and, if needed, appropriate counseling, or perhaps an integrated treatment of both.

Remember, listen to your body and mind because they will alert you when you need to seek assistance. Also, listen to your self-talk to determine if you are sending negative messages to your mind, the central control room of your body. If so, reverse them by substituting positive affirmations.

LIVE A LIFE THAT MATTERS

Most people want to think that their life is significant, not only for their self-worth and personal progress but also for the progress of their family and fellow man. Strive to make your life important to others. Spend more time with family and friends and savor those precious moments. Wear your best cologne or aftershave. Use your special china and wear your unique clothes, instead of saving them for that day that may never come. Smell the roses, enjoy each sunset, and tell your friends your warm inner thoughts. Hug and kiss your loved ones and tell them you love them. Trade your worries for hopes. Cherish each moment. Apologize and mend your fences. Don't be afraid to say you are sorry. And remember Auntie Mame's comment, "Life is a banquet, and most damn fools are starving to death."

The subject of depression, grief, and death are not exactly pleasant. As mentioned in previous chapters, humor is the best antidote to stress. It certainly is a wonderful diversion from pain and gloom.

I would like to conclude this chapter with a story that's allegedly about the wishes of Alexander the Great. Over 2,300 years ago, Alexander the Great summoned his army generals and told him his three final wishes. On his deathbed, he said he wanted the following:

1. "I want the best doctors to carry my coffin."
2. "All of the wealth that I have accumulated, gold, precious stones, and money will be scattered along the procession to the cemetery."
3. "My hands shall be let loose so that they hang outside the coffin for all to see."

One of his generals, surprised by his unusual request, asked Alexander to please explain his intentions. Here is what Alexander the Great had to say:

- "I want the best doctors to carry my coffin to demonstrate that in the face of death, even the best doctors in the world have no power to heal."
- "I want the road to be covered with my treasures so that everybody sees that material wealth acquired on earth will stay on earth and be shared."
- "I want my hands to swing in the wind so that people understand that when we come into

this world empty-handed, we leave this world empty-handed. We pass this life when our most precious treasure of all is exhausted, TIME."

You cannot take your wealth, material things, or an extension of time to your grave. Time is the most precious of all treasures because it is finite. You may be able to produce wealth, but you cannot create TIME. When you share your time with others, you give them a piece of your life. The time spent is paradoxically forever memorialized, but the time itself is forever gone. Since time is your life, it is the very best gift you can ever give to your friends and loved ones. You will be long remembered when your time has ceased. There never will be any possession more valuable than your legacy.

"Anger is an acid that can do more harm to the vessel in which it is stored than to anything on which it is poured"
—Attributed to Mark Twain

FESTERING POISON

During my five decades of counseling, I have known anger, hate, and rage intimately. They are the most potent and most destructive of all emotions. The downside is that they seldom have a useful purpose or a positive outcome. These intense emotions will alienate you from others by fostering embarrassment, defensiveness, and sometimes revenge. They not only hurt others' feelings but can cause injury, alienation, imprisonment, and even death.

Anger, hate, and rage are the leading attitudinal causes of work dysfunction and job loss.

In retrospect, I encountered dysfunctional families and individuals. I dealt with sexual deviants, hostile husbands, and wives who beat and harassed their husbands, emotional and verbal abusers, and, unfortunately, murderers. It is sad to say and share that I had direct contact with two serial killers.

Resentment is the mildest form of ire that can develop when you feel unable to express your thoughts and feelings. The longer resentments build, the more extreme the reaction.

Although resentments can have rational roots, they can grow into irrational anger, hate, or rage if left dormant and unresolved.

If you have not adequately bonded with another, this can be the beginning of personal resentment. Communication or the lack thereof becomes either the means of resolution or the trigger of resentment that can later progress to hate and rage.

Learning how to defuse resentment and various degrees of provocation is an important tool necessary for your journey.

Diplomatically sharing your inner feelings, especially with acquaintances or bonded friends, can be difficult. It is part of the learning curve that comes with all journeys. Carefully choosing your words without undertones is initially difficult. Comments like, "I'm not sure about this," "I have no intention of upsetting you," or, "I just want to clarify something that is bothering me," are means of preparing what you will need to say. Practice will help build your repertoire.

Be aware that every individual can be challenging, so pick your words carefully. I have found that the Sandwich Approach is often effective in defusing conflict situations. This approach sandwiches two strong positive statements with a piece of less edible material (the conflict situation) in the middle.

For example, "You know, I think the world of you. The other day you said something that concerns me. I think we need to talk about it. I know that you are a very sensitive and caring person, so I want us to be on the same track. I value you and our friendship a lot."

This type of approach ensures that you maintain your bonded relationship, which you do not want to destroy. You need to resolve each issue that has come between you. Use this approach wisely, and you will overcome many relationship obstacles. It will also defuse problems that can otherwise easily fester.

Anger, hate, and rage are spectrum emotions; they range from mild to severe—the more severe, the more destructive the consequences. Temper displays are emotional attempts to attack a source of unhappiness. At the extreme, irrational anger has destroyed families, initiated divorces, and devastated close friendships. Medical experts have found it to cause physical and emotional stress and can result in heart attacks and other serious health problems.

Rage is the antithesis of happiness.

Unfortunately, once unleashed, all can paint an ugly personal portrait. If these emotional reactions become a repeated pattern, they can result in character assassination and ultimate social isolation. These momentary foolhardy bomb blasts eventually take a heavy toll on relationships while slowly destroying one's mind and body. All of us have had fleeting displays of acrimonious acid and have regrettably witnessed its adverse outcomes. Apologies are necessary but become futile when a pattern becomes repetitious.

Hate is a first cousin of both anger and rage.

Hate is a learned emotion directed to individuals of religion, race, gender, ethnic group, or political affiliation. It can also be directed at family, friends, and neighbors. Hate is a destructive attitude that begins as a small cancer and slowly metastasizes. This inner rage called hate is either the result of actual experiences or is inculcated through family, friends, or associations. Hate can be as mild as name-calling and gossip, or as severe as verbal abuse, bullying, discrimination, destruction of property, or physical attack. It is usually expressed toward individuals or generalized to target groups. We see it often displayed as bigotry, hate crimes, assassinations, serial killers, or terrorist attacks. Racial, religious, and ethnic hate are the most common culprits. As mentioned earlier, like acid, hate spews its destructive juices on its host and the intended target.

Perhaps it would be helpful to discuss rage and my experience with two serial killers. The first was a youngster who happened to live near my family home. He was referred to me by his school while in first grade. At that time, he was an extremely quiet but intensely angry boy who displayed periodic explosive behaviors. Because I knew the family and had attempted several interventions with no success, I had to recuse myself and refer him to a respected colleague. He performed an assessment, met with the staff and parents, and reviewed

his findings in detail. He found many disturbing characteristics in the child and severe family dysfunction. Like
myself, he made some specific recommendations for
outside interventions. The parents adamantly refused.
For several years, the youngster's behavior continued at
school and in the neighborhood. Similar professional
staff recommendations were made with absolutely no
parental follow-up. It was later detailed in the media
that there was severe parental physical and psychological abuse, intemperate use of alcohol, unrestrained
promiscuity, and other ugly details. It was no surprise
that he had an interminable internal rage, especially
for his mother, that eventually erupted in his attacks
on women. I will spare you the gruesome details and a
glimpse of how some disturbed boys turn into potential
serial killers. He sadly awaits the death penalty.

As a practicing psychologist, I have unequivocally concluded that the three angsts are sometimes
self-inflicted. Angry persons are first and foremost
angry at themselves for the situation in which they find
themselves. Often, anger builds with nowhere to go; it
becomes a potential time bomb. Think about it; when
you are mad, you are mad at yourself. Unable to direct
your rage at yourself or at the real offender, your hostility is unleashed on an innocent other person, animal, or
thing. Thus, without thought, to protect your ego your
frustration is projected onto another human or animal
rather than yourself. Like a brewing hurricane, rage is
simply an internal storm that begins from within. When

untethered, it can destroy all in its path. It is critically important for you to soul search your complex defense systems. Figure out why you are angry at yourself. It is a relatively direct and straightforward method of defusing these homemade booby traps. Once your hostility is understood as your inner anger, you will then be able to redirect or control it. The final result will be a much softer landing. I cannot tell you how many times I discovered that I was irate because of my indiscretion, stupidity, or transgression. Only then was I able to defuse my misdirected exasperation.

Put rage and subsequent regret behind you. It's perfectly okay to feel angry when distressed, but it is far better to stop, think, and, if necessary, count slowly to twenty before responding. Most of us have been so upset that we want to call or write an angry retort immediately. Yes, do put it on paper. Get your anger out but withhold sending or calling for at least twelve hours. If possible, sleep on it. Once your fury has subsided, it is time to reread, rewrite, and redirect your otherwise explosive impulses. It can be helpful to bounce the situation off an intimate friend or relative who can review it objectively and respond more rationally. Remember, the relationship and reputation you save may be your own.

It is crucial that you not overreact. Stay calm; try not to get too emotionally entangled. Be patient and avoid throwing more gas on the fire. My dad reminded me many times, "Don't ever start a fight or argue with an irrational dog. When someone is white-hot with anger, nothing constructive will result." Sometimes it is difficult to walk away or avoid a confrontation. Remind yourself that you will achieve nothing if you are dealing with an irrational animal. Instead, set up a time to reconvene when circumstances are more normal. This is especially true in parent-child conflicts. It will be imperative that you learn to choose your battles carefully!

The second serial killer I encountered was another very sad story. He was a young pre-teen (twelve-and-a-half years old) boy referred to me by the junior high school staff. The largest concern came from the secretaries at the school office. He was regularly running into the office, hysterically shouting for help, near tears, and desperately afraid that some boys would beat him up. I found him an extremely fearful young man who proverbially wore a sign on his back, "Kick Me." He was bright, nerd-like, articulate, ostensibly different from his peers, and lacking social skills. Thus, his peers called him nasty things and enjoyed both knowing and pressing his hot buttons. He was incapable of protecting himself and found his only refuge was running to safety in the school office.

We established excellent rapport. I was now his adult refuge. He was able to share his innermost feelings and history with no hesitation. I realized the more time he spent with me, the less intimidated he appeared. At that point, I sought out an alpha male who could help him with social adjustment. Being associated with a strong, burly school leader, well-respected by his peers, was beneficial to our plan. Yes, he was now under the protective eye of a big brother. Fortunately, this highly-regarded new peer was remarkably cooperative. The three of us became effective in working together in concert. In the meantime, I learned the dark secrets of his mother, for whom he had very fearful and extremely hostile feelings—the lack of a father figure in his life and a mother who was unprepared to provide for his needs. The saddest part of all this was his announcement that he was abruptly moving away after only four to five months of interventions. The staff and I were heartbroken. I still get teary-eyed when I remember our last day. He and I had established a bond that had not been available to him since his grandfather's death a few years prior. He came into my office with a nice leather briefcase.

He gave it to me with tears in his eyes and said, "I want you to have this. It was my grandpa's, and it was very special to him."

About twelve years later, I was contacted and asked to be an expert witness. Again, I will spare you the gruesome details of his attacks on women; by now, you can now better understand boys and how they can internalize rage. That is not to suggest it is always boys or that rage is directed at only women. It can be the converse. The last time I saw him was on death row. I asked that he be unchained so we could chat. He had been sentenced to the death penalty. It was, without a doubt, one of the most excruciating experiences of my entire life.

Choosing your battles and responses is challenging. Feedback and allowing time for your spring to unwind takes practice. Soul-searching, you will be better prepared to express yourself. There will be ample opportunity to deal with real issues that require more appropriate responses to your resentments. Perhaps another person has offended you and spewed their irrational fury, or you are dealt an unsuspecting blow. You must learn to respond with a carefully thought-out and mutually-respectful retort rationally. Controlled anger is a far more appropriate response. I remember a firefighter who once gave me the following advice, "Don't anguish, don't languish, just carefully extinguish the fire."

However, it is important to note that rational anger can also act as both catalyst and motivator. With thought and creativity, negative energy can always be turned into a positive. You can use your angst to propel you forward without needing to share your upset with others. I find that I need a lot of physical exercise when I'm upset or angry. My otherwise negative energy is converted to positive energy. Physicists call this Conservation of Energy, and it is an effective use of outrage. It is similar to the conversion of solar energy into electrical energy. Some individuals use an inflated Bozo or a punching bag to hit when they need to displace their anger. I secretly admit that every once in a while, when exasperation suddenly emerges, and no one is in the car with me, I roll up the windows and scream as loud as I can. I find that I become suddenly relaxed and refreshed. I have religiously told my children and clients that it is far better not to take your wrath out on another person, only on a suitable non-living thing.

When I disagree with family members, friends, or occasional acquaintances, I mentally label it a "urination contest." At that point, I make every attempt to shut it down from proceeding to a destructive conclusion. This type of contest is always adversarial competition, and if hooked, results in a no-win situation. Besides avoiding such a confrontation, time is saved, and relationships are salvaged. I can't emphasize enough the importance of preventing conflicts.

Finally, don't let anger consume you. It is a destructive emotion that can ruin your health, poison your disposition, and banish your friends. Use it judiciously, but always understand that it is created internally and can have destructive powers. However, your bubbling fury can also motivate and energize if transformed into positive energy. If rationally applied, this power conversion will resolve problems calmly and resolutely.

FROM MY REARVIEW MIRROR

I find the topic of age both fun and poignant. Although my favorite quotes tilted towards the golden years, my first inclination was to focus on youth. Ironically, it was then that I realized my last winter's journey is, conversely, your early spring. I was looking backward to your future—like looking at my rearview mirror! After much deliberation, it made good sense to share the regrets and gratitude of my entire journey from finish to start. It was also important to emphasize connecting with your elders, not just for companionship, but for wisdom and empathy. Much can be learned by interacting with the older generations. Parenthetically and as a disclaimer, I must admit I also learned some things unexpectedly. For instance, just because a person is elderly doesn't mean they're grouchy or impatient!

Throughout my life, I have been extremely fortunate to have had a grandmother who adored me, as well as many aunts, uncles, and neighbors with whom I maintained close and intimate relationships.

I am so appreciative of the remarkable contributions to my learning curve from both the very young and the very old.

Every day I walk past a large number of photos of deceased relatives on the various walls of our home. I momentarily will stop, pick out one, and quietly say to myself, "I love you, thank you so much."

I don't believe I have ever shared that information with anyone until now.

You, the young whippersnappers, adolescents, or young adults, the following will give you a real look through the knothole of aging. Real-life examples, thoughts, and feelings to better prepare you for the long journey.

Age, like time, is both uncontrollable and finite. No one knows when they were conceived or when they will succumb to death. Life on Earth is transitory.

All life begins and ends.

Immortality, although an exhilarating fantasy, cannot coexist on planet Earth. Age is paradoxically both relative; "I don't feel 78," as well as fixed "My birth certificate verifies that I was born in 1942."

All of a sudden, I'm seized with the realization that I've never been this old before!

I've got to finish my bucket list.

I need to smell more flowers, visit more places, fish more streams, eat more banana splits, see more sunsets, visit more museums, and laugh more with my loved ones.

And, before I succumb, I need to finish this book!

I need to allow myself private time to cry and mourn my lost family, friends, and colleagues. I must contact lost friends, repay lost favors, forgive both mine and others' transgressions, and appreciate the beauty that Mother Nature provides me.

Please remember, *growing older is a gift and a privilege denied to many.*

OLD MAN

For thousands of years, humankind has looked for the Fountain of Youth. Storytellers have shared their ideas with each new generation. Perhaps, someday there might be cloning. Maybe then we will return and start life over. Until then, we can only fantasize.

I need to emphasize that life can be only as exciting as you make it; indeed, not every moment, but often. Your hopes and dreams allow you to be whatever age you choose. Thinking young avoids the calamity of narrow-mindedness, grumpiness, and sadness. Free will, a young outlook, and gratitude for life will keep you young-at-heart.

Celebrate life rather than succumb to it.

Enjoy it, because every day is a gift.

A good friend sent me something that I saved just for you. You will probably need to read it over and over again and put it in your virtual toolbox. Indeed, whoever wrote this meant it for regular review, knowing that we all occasionally forget. Your youthful thinking will require repetitive reminding by rereading. I prescribe it as a regular pause to refuel your attitude and determination.

HOW TO STAY YOUNG

1. Try everything twice. On one woman's tombstone, she said she wanted this epitaph: "Tried everything twice, loved it both times!"
2. Keep only cheerful friends. The grouches pull you down!
3. Keep learning: learn more about the computer, crafts, gardening, whatever. Never let the brain get idle; an idle mind is the devil's workshop— and the devil's name is Alzheimer's!
4. Enjoy the simple things!
5. Laugh often, long and loud. Laugh until you gasp for breath. And if you have a friend who makes you laugh, spend lots of time with him or her!
6. The tears happen: Endure, grieve, and move on. The only person who is with you your entire life is yourself. *Live* well while you are *alive!*
7. Surround yourself with all the things you love, whether it's family, pets, keepsakes, music,

    plants, hobbies, or whatever. Your home is your refuge!

8. Cherish your health; if it is good, preserve it. If it is unstable, improve it. If it is beyond what you can improve, get help!

9. Take responsibility but let go of unnecessary weights. Don't take guilt trips. Take yourself to the mall, even to the next city, state, or foreign country, but *not* to where the guilt is!

10. Tell the people you love that you love them at every opportunity. "I love you, and you are so very special!"

11. Forgive now those who made you cry. You might not get a second chance!

And remember, lost time can never be found. So be kinder than necessary, for everyone you meet is fighting some kind of battle. As age descends upon you, realize how much remains undone. That thought sparks the motivation to act before time recedes to oblivion. Since you are probably not on the back nine, think about your older parents, relatives, neighbors, and those you meet. Those that are in the winter of their life need your understanding, support, and love. Whether you like it or not, you'll be there soon enough.

Don't wait to become kinder and less critical of yourself.

Maintain meaningful relationships with your loved ones and friends. Read, play, and work with enthusiasm!

Take long walks, keep your body fit and healthy, and eat without excessive fat or salt. Let go of broken hearts, pet disasters, mistakes, and life's required failures. Be strong, positive, compassionate, fun, and considerate. Expect grey hair or baldness, forgetfulness, pain, and wrinkles. Most of all, protect your freedom by making choices without fear of reprisal.

It is also critically important that you avoid self-imposed limitations such as expecting the loss of vigor for life, developing disabilities, or degenerative diseases; if unable, you will eventually capitulate and succumb. One author called it *time neurosis*, which was described as more handicapping than physical or mental dysfunction. Once again, the temptations of fear are at work. Those psychologically dysfunctional ideas will cause you to be old, sick, and infirm. These self-fulfilling hypotheses can cause overnight grey hair and weary legs, as well as the anticipation of imminent death.

It is very important to understand that you have only one round trip on your journey. You don't get second chances or free rides. Once completed, all your unfulfilled hopes and wishes are forever gone. Start preparing by initiating a bucket list of all the things you hope to accomplish during your lifetime. They become the motivational fuel to move you forward on your journey. You can add, delete, and correct that list as you gain more clarity and maturity. Attempt to schedule your bucket stops and starts as early as you are capable of reaching those milestones.

May you be fearless and persistent.

May you be surprised at your capabilities and progress.

You will overcome obstacles, and new adventurous opportunities will be on the horizon.

SOME THOUGHTS ON THE TEEN YEARS

You will need the following information, whether you are a teenager or a future parent. For generations, adolescents have been criticized and condemned for their poor manners, rebelliousness, selfishness, and wild, raucous behavior. The word teen is a derivative of old English, meaning vexations. Every generation has experienced the unpredictable vexations of youth, particularly the teen years.

Your teenage years are a time of sexual awakening, preoccupation with peers, identity crises, and a rush of hormones. It is a period of developing social, emotional, political, and personal awakenings. And, most importantly, your adolescence is a persistent striving for individuality, autonomy, and independence. Your teenage mind is whirling and struggling for an understanding of yourself and establishing an identity. It is the most unbalanced period of your existence. Breaching childhood and assuming adulthood is laden with obstacles and supreme challenges.

As a parent, you will never know what to expect from your teenager, from unintelligible music, new forms of slang expressions, outrageous-looking clothing, piercings, tattoos, slovenly bedrooms to new hairstyles. I have seen parents apoplectic and discouraged at their adolescents, wholly bewildered by these unexplained behaviors. Most arrive at this momentous period of parenthood unprepared for this challenging time, but it is equally—if not more—painful and challenging for the teenager.

Both parents and teens will undoubtedly wonder whether they will survive these volatile and tenuous years.

As a parent, you should slowly start meting out independence by marrying more freedom with commensurate responsibility. Guiding, not controlling; skillfully managing, not micromanaging, are key. Riding the waves and letting go, although extremely difficult, will ultimately put the onus of responsible behavior on your beloved progeny.

Surviving those teenage years is certainly not simple or easy. My generation saw the rise and eventual fall of Haight-Ashbury, accompanied by the beatnik and hippie revolution. I cannot think of a more turbulent time when sex, drugs, and the Vietnam War were occurring contemporaneously. They were explosive, dangerous, and deadly years. Yet, I am convinced that teens and parents of today feel that things are even worse now.

Yes, the beat goes on, what goes around comes around, history is repetitive!

During those turbulent times, I knew many peers who were far more into that "hippie" scene than I was. Almost all are now respectable citizens, reputable lawyers, doctors, teachers, principals, entrepreneurs, public safety officers, and corporate leaders. Those wild love children of yesteryear have become our quiet, placid, and well-balanced conservative neighbors and friends. There are few things more gratifying than seeing their metamorphosis into responsible adulthood, albeit with a home mortgage, car payments, playful involvement with toddlers, and volunteering for community events. You may be there sooner than you think.

Yes, there is no question that the teen years are very volatile times; however, with time, things eventually move back to the center. Whether the stage of your journey is at the teen years or parenthood, please anticipate and be prepared.

Below is a litany of ideas and potential items you might consider adding to your bucket list or virtual memory. Include those that you feel are life-fulfilling and fit your journey. They might provide you a time of joy instead of waiting and regretting your final days. Erma Bombeck died in 1996 in San Francisco, California, a relatively short distance from my college digs. She was one of my early heroes. I appreciated her quick wit, humility, intellectual depth, and creativity. Her creative column provided suggestions that were nothing less than inspirational. They were my morning energy drink! She focused unpretentiously on real life and not on the mundane. She ingenuously made fun of herself and shared her insights. Her intuitive awareness of everyday life and its vexations was nothing short of genius. As a tribute to Erma, I share her final bow to humanity. Her thoughts remain ageless, applicable to whatever your age. Also, in honor of women's history, it is a tribute and an honor to share the memory of a lady who lost her fight with cancer but left behind a formidable legacy.

IF I HAD MY LIFE TO LIVE OVER

I would have gone to bed when I was sick instead of pretending the Earth would go into a holding pattern if I weren't there for the day.

I would have burned the pink candle sculpted like a rose before it melted in storage.

I would have talked less and listened more.

I would have invited friends over to dinner even if the carpet was stained or the sofa faded.

I would have eaten the popcorn in the "good" living room and worried much less about the dirt when someone wanted to light a fire in the fireplace.

I would have taken the time to listen to my grandfather ramble about his youth.

I would have shared more of the responsibility carried by my husband.

I would have never insisted the car windows be rolled up on a summer day because my hair had just been teased and sprayed.

I would have sat on the lawn with my grass stains.

I would have cried and laughed less while watching television and more while watching life.

I would have never have bought anything just because it was practical, wouldn't show soil, or was guaranteed to last a lifetime.

Instead of wishing away nine months of pregnancy, I'd have cherished every moment and realized that the wonderment growing inside me was the only chance in life to assist God in a miracle.

When my kids kiss me impetuously, I would never have said, "Later. Now go get washed up for dinner." There would've been more, "I love you's." More, "I'm sorry's."

But mostly, given another shot at life, I would seize every minute, look at it and really see it . . . live it, and never give it back. STOP SWEATING THE SMALL STUFF!

Don't worry about who doesn't like you, who has more, or who's doing what. Instead, let's cherish the relationships we have with those who do love us.

—Erma Bombeck (Written after discovering she was dying of cancer)

We can all appreciate Erma's love of life. Her insights, humor, humility, and unpretentiousness, combined with her contributions to humanity, make her another true American icon. As age descends upon you, please realize how much remains undone. That thought should spark your motivation to act before time recedes to oblivion.

CENTENARIANS AND NONAGENARIANS

I write this so that you can see life backward, from the end of my journey to the beginning of yours. Hopefully, you will pick up some cues and tools you can employ to get to that magic age. There have been many studies of the elderly who live in this world for 100 or more years. They found the trait most common among them was their continued engagement with life. These oldsters worked in their gardens, had ongoing relationships with neighbors, friends, and children, and took an interest in world events and local activities. They loved humor, were silly and fun-loving. They expressed their emotions by crying and laughing instead of focusing on their troubles or vulnerabilities. They engaged the present each precious day. I have personally only known three centenarians. The first was Aunt Sara L., who passed away at age 102. The description above fits her to a tee. She loved to laugh and giggle, seldom complained, worked diligently in the kitchen and yard, and always displayed her inimitable smile. She was a love; she loved others dearly and, not surprisingly, was truly adored by all.

Anecdotally, I've also had the pleasure to know Jim W. He works out at the same athletic club as I do. He's currently 102 years old and until recently still makes his pilgrimage to the gym three days a week, albeit with a cane. His most outstanding characteristics are a frequent loud chuckle, an open and razor-sharp mind, an incredible awareness of the current world, and local affairs. He also remains physically active and has a daily thirst for more knowledge.

Of course, I'm reminded of my dear mother, who recently turned 101 years old. She also has a great sense of humor, a love of life, a devotion to family and friends, and has a keen interest in politics and current affairs. She's always sharing current events and says her role in life is to inspire others and bring them laughter.

Another hero in my life was Uncle Al. He died a couple of years ago at 95. He was the consummate role model. He was loved and respected by all who knew him. His major characteristics included being a profound raconteur, a supreme and compassionate teacher of culture and tradition. He had a great sense of humor, was playful, always kept busy, was unpretentious, kind, and the most caring person I've ever known. All of the nonagenarians that I have known had wonderful senses of humor, vitality, resilience, and a zest for life. Most importantly, they were all young at heart and very spirited. I recently lost another nonagenarian, Ralph D., age

95. Again, he comes from a similar mold, a composite of the centenarians and nonagenarians mentioned above.

Take note, these personal characteristics, research data, and anecdotes sketch a vivid picture of some of the traits necessary for a long, fulfilling, and happy life. Aim to fill their shoes.

I once received testimonials about centenarians. I want to share this nostalgic story with you. I think you will find it insightful, inspirational, and amusing:

The longest confirmed human lifespan on record is held by Jeanne Louise Calment. She lived to be 122½ years old. Somehow her fate was improved by her genes and lifestyle. Madam Calment was born in Arles, France, in 1875. At the age of fourteen, the Eiffel tower was built, and she reportedly met Vincent van Gogh. Her description of him was that he was dirty, badly dressed, and disagreeable. At 85, she took up fencing, and at age 100, she was still riding her bike. At 114, she starred in an autobiographical film and had a hip operation at 115. When she was 117, she finally gave up smoking, having started at age 21 in 1896. She didn't give it up for health reasons, but because she was almost blind. Her independent spirit would not accept asking someone to help her light up. At 90, she called her lawyer, who agreed to pay her a monthly allowance (2,500 Francs) conditioned on his inheriting her apartment upon her death. Upon his death 30 years later, she was still alive, so his widow was legally bound to continue paying the agreed allowance.

Human life expectancy has increased more in the last 100 years than it did in the previous 200,000 years of human existence. In 1900, life expectancy in the U.S. was 47.3 years; in 2000, it was more than 74 years. The aging mind does change. It bestows some gifts, but there are also some neurological realities to the aging brain. Neuroscientists have documented some changes in brain function. As you approach the winter of your life, you will undoubtedly experience neurological changes, such as the changes I am currently experiencing. They include some difficulty focusing, slightly slower processing speed, and some forgetfulness. Don't fret. If you anticipate them, they will be transitioned as normal and expected age-markers. Once again, your attitude is of critical importance. However, if we look at recent research, people who feel years younger than their chronological peers are less likely to die, as compared to those who felt older than their years. Feeling young at heart is a symptom of being physically healthy. Remember, your perceptions are your reality. If you want to live to be 100, the American Medical Association (AMA) clarified the following characteristics as consistent with those who live to be 100 or older. They include an easy-going disposition, a quick and witty sense of humor, and the desire to keep physically and mentally active as much as possible. If you choose to follow these guidelines, you might extend your journey to at least a century!

GROWING OLD IS MANDATORY
GROWING UP IS OPTIONAL

As you know, storytelling was the principal means of transmitting information to future generations. It was THE tool of learning for thousands of years. The raconteurs of the past were the college professors of today. I would like to keep that tradition intact by sharing another inspiring story. Below is a beautiful story that was written by an unnamed author. I received it as an email from an old friend. It is so precious, and it needs to be shared and appreciated by all.

"On the first day of school, our professor introduced himself and challenged us to get to know someone we didn't already know. I stood up to look around when a gentle hand touched my shoulder. I turned around to find a wrinkled little lady beaming up at me with a smile that lit up her entire being. She said, 'Hi, handsome, my name is Rose. I'm 87 years old. Can I give you a hug?' I laughed and enthusiastically responded, 'Of course you may,' and she gave me a giant squeeze. 'Why are you in college at such a young, innocent age?' I asked. She responded, 'I always dreamed of having a college education, and now I'm getting one!' We became instant friends. Every day, for the next three months, we would leave class together and talk nonstop. I was always mesmerized listening to this 'Time Machine' as she shared her wisdom and experience with me. Over the course of the year, Rose became a campus icon, and she easily made friends wherever she went.

"At the end of the semester, we invited Rose to speak at our football banquet. I will never forget what she said. Frustrated and a little bit embarrassed, she came to the microphone and simply said, 'I'm sorry I'm so jittery. I gave up beer for Lent, and this whiskey is killing me! I'll never get my speech back in order, so let me just tell you what I know.' She cleared her throat and began: 'We do not stop playing because we are old; we grow old because we stop playing. There are only four secrets to staying young, being happy, and achieving success. You have to laugh and find humor every day. You've got to have a dream. When you lose your dreams, you die. We have so many people walking around who are dead and don't even know it. There is a huge difference between growing older and growing up. If you are 19 years old and lie in bed for one full year and don't do one productive thing, you will turn 20 years old. If I am 87 years old and stay in bed for a year and never do anything, I will turn 88. Anybody can grow older. That doesn't take any talent or ability. The idea is to grow up, always finding the opportunity to change. Have no regrets. The elderly usually don't have regrets for what we did, but rather for things we did not do. The only people who fear death are those with regrets.'

"She concluded her speech by courageously singing 'The Rose.' She challenged each of us to study the lyrics and live them out in our daily lives. At the year's end,

Rose finished the college degree that she had begun all those years ago. One week after graduation, Rose died peacefully in her sleep. Over 2000 college students attended her funeral in tribute to the wonderful woman who taught by example, that it is never too late to be all that you can possibly be and reminded us growing older is mandatory, growing up is optional! Not only was Rose inspirational, she was the embodiment of a great mind and the fountain of eternal wisdom!"

—Author Unknown

I received the following email several times from several different people. After reading it carefully, it appeared as another traditional story worth sharing, a keeper. Read it thoughtfully, for there are many compelling messages.

Remember, you are still on the first hole of your journey. Now is the time to think about your parents and grandparents while reading it. There is a subtle but cogent series of empathetic axioms.

AND THEN IT IS WINTER

"You know, time has a way of moving quickly and catching you unaware of the passing years. It seems just yesterday that I was young, just married and embarking on a new life with my mate. Yet, in a way, it seems like eons ago, and I wonder where all the years went. I know that I lived them all. I have glimpses of how it was back then and all of my hopes and dreams.

"But here it is, 'the back nine' of my life, and it catches me by surprise. How did I get here so fast? Where did the years go, and where did my youth go? I remember seeing older people through the years and thinking that those older people were many years away from me and that I was only on the first hole and the back nine were so far off that I could not fathom it or imagine fully what it would be like.

"But here it is. My friends are retired and getting grey. They move slower, and I see an older person now. Some are in better and some worse shape than me, but I see the great change. Not like the ones I remember who were young and vibrant, but like me, their age is beginning to show, and we are now those older folks that we used to see and never thought we'd become. Each day now, I find that just getting a shower is a real target for the day! And taking a nap is not a treat anymore, it's mandatory! 'Cause if I don't on my own free will, I just fall asleep where I sit!

"And so now I enter into this new season of my life unprepared for all the aches and pains and the loss of strength and ability to go and do things that I wish I had done, but never did! But at least I know that though I'm on the back nine, and I'm not sure how long it will last, this I know; that when it's over on this Earth—it's over.

"Yes, I have regrets. There are things I wish I hadn't done; things I should've done, but indeed, there are many things I'm happy to have done. It's all in a lifetime.

"So, if you're not on the back nine yet, let me remind you that it will be here faster than you think. Whatever you would like to accomplish in your life, please do it quickly! Don't put things off too long! Life goes by quickly! Do what you can today, as you can never be sure whether you're on the back nine or not! You have no promise that you will see all the seasons of your life, so live for today and say all the things that you want your loved ones to remember, and hope that they appreciate and love you for all the things that you have done for them, in all the years past! Life is a gift to you. The way you live your life is your gift to those who come after. Make it a fantastic one. Live it well! Enjoy today! Do something fun! Remember, it is health that is real wealth and not pieces of gold and silver!"

—Author Unknown

Lastly, live well, but don't ignore the hard work, persistence, and perseverance that you'll need to take on your travels. You will need to keep adding to your toolbox all of the things necessary to sustain you.

A PERSONAL GLIMPSE AND FINAL COMMENTS

What goes around comes around; perhaps a trite phrase but often accurate. When I was growing up, my parents and my friends had learned to economize and save. They grew up under the dark clouds of the Great Depression of the 1930s. Like most, my parents seldom threw out things. My mother washed plastic dishes, forks and spoons, cleaned soiled aluminum foil for reuse, and all of our shoes were resoled and reheeled, as long as they barely fit us. Buying new things was a luxury; we needed to use every last thing until the bloody end. There were occasional times when mom wasn't looking that I would throw an item away, especially old reused tin foil with holes in it, but rarely. Dad would fix and repair almost everything with tape, glue, or old used parts. I seldom remember my dad going to a mechanic. If he had the tools, it was fixed. We rarely went to restaurants, to a car wash, or on a long trip. However, we often looked forward to a candy bar, shaved lemon ice, or a stop at a local ice cream parlor.

Cars, buses, and an occasional train were OK, but never an airplane. Leftovers were almost guaranteed at many meals if we had had company or food remained unfinished. I unabashedly brought a brown bag with leftover liver and onions, roasted peppers and Italian sausage, or a liverwurst and mustard sandwich. I could usually tell my lunch from the others by the dense saturated olive oil stains on the outside of the bag. Then, a quarter for a movie was a reward for the many expected chores. Conservation and savings were of extreme importance, and you never knew when the next crisis might occur. After the recent Depression and World War II, most families feared the inevitable, another unexpected disastrous event!

As I look around today, I see a resurgence of reuse, recycling, and doggie bags. We are once again finding that resources and energy are becoming more scarce and expensive. I see parents sharing non-gender designated duties and children earning privileges for chores and good grades. In some respects, we have gone full circle from the more hedonistic times of the recent past. What I also see is more parent involvement, yet more fear of things lurking outdoors. I also see much less corporal punishment and more humane consequences. I see more understanding of racial, ethnic, gender, and sex differences. Yes, there is progress; but some regression. I believe parents need to be less solicitous and that more emphasis should be placed on individual responsibility. I believe we still need to develop more cooperation and less polarity; more responsibility and less coddling; more altruism and less greed; more concern for others less fortunate; and less narrow-mindedness. These, my fellow journey members, will be your challenges. Proceed on your journey with a determination to keep making our world and our future generations proud of you for having aged with grace, distinction, and a positive attitude.

THE
CLASSROOM
OF LIFE

"Happiness is a way station between too little and too much."
—*Channing Pollock*

BALANCE

How many times have I heard my wife, Clare, remind me, "My dad always believed in moderation; it was our family's maxim."

In a healthy marriage, there is a constant need to adapt to mutually make life more balanced. I knew there were several behaviors that needed attention. You did not have to be a rocket scientist to realize I was a husband in need of basic training. In retrospect, there was no doubt that to have a cooperative and peaceful life together, my obsessive behaviors needed to be addressed. Clare leans more towards moderation in her life choices, while I tend to be more excessive and obsessive.

One of the first issues was learning to choose clothing with more complementary colors—those that matched, rather than my more garish selections. As time passed, my gambling at Lake Tahoe, smoking, and my enjoyment of "mashing the gas pedal" surfaced, then later, my obsession with excessive collections, magnanimous eating, or my messes accumulated around the house. They undoubtedly needed attention for compatibility. I was initially resistant and pushed back. After some deep thinking and action, eventually most of my excesses wangled into a semblance of balance. If you want a happy marriage, you first need to do some insightful introspection, especially by listening to your partner's feedback.

I say this with all sincerity; I firmly believe that women mature faster than men and appear to have more common sense.

All husbands and wives are in basic training during the early years of their relationship. Periodically, you may find it necessary to take a refresher course.

Life without balance is like walking a tightrope without a balancing beam. On your journey, you will need to employ many specialized tools. Like life, they will require learning and many trials and errors. Life is often a delicate equilibrium between work and play, joy and sorrow, school and home, family and friends, eating and dieting, and a whole host of other combinations. To bring harmony into your life, you will need to learn how to equipoise your activities. Excess is not good, but abstinence is not much better. The daily temptations you face will cause you great concern, frustration, and ambivalence. Learning balance will equip you with a quality of life that ensures happiness and success.

What equates to the definition of quality of life? The ideal equilibrium would be providing time for yourself and the many other priorities in your life. My father-in-law, Gene, would frequently declare,

"Everything in moderation." Surely, he was right, but how do you define moderation? We know that too much sunshine is dangerous; however, we need it for the production of Vitamin D. How much is considered moderate? We know that water can drown us internally as well as externally, but what is an optimal balance? We know that excesses of food, alcohol, fat, drugs, vitamins, partying, etc., are all potentially dangerous, but we have great difficulty understanding how much is optimal or in excess. We also know that the total exclusion of certain foods, like fats or alcohol, vitamins, social activities, etc., can also be quite troublesome. Everyone struggles with the terms of moderation. Learn what is right for you!

Finding balance was an ongoing struggle. Defining my priorities helped designate time for each of my highest priorities. For instance, my highest priority is family. Like me, you will need to decide in rank order with who and how often you should spend your time. School or work was usually another high priority. Working around those schedules needs careful consideration. Obviously, commute time, time to shop, time to eat, time to visit, time to socialize, time for exercise, and relaxation time all needed my consideration. Rationing became a difficult set of decisions.

And as you know, having a happy and compatible marriage is another important priority. My goals of happiness, calmness, and personal satisfaction were part of that equation. Times devoted to those things were not selfish, but necessary.

Don't feel guilty if you schedule "me time." You have as your top priority to be responsible for yourself. However, being responsible does not mean being selfless and losing track of taking care of your personal needs. You cannot expect your other activities to be quality time if you do not reserve some quality time for yourself. For me, it's always been a juggling act. Sometimes I must cheat myself of time, but I frequently scheduled dead time for recreational activities. "Me time" usually was during early morning or on weekends. I find that working out is one of my most beneficial times to relax and withdraw from the intense interactions and frenzy of a typical day. It not only provides for a healthy diversion, but it helps balance work, play, and health. I enjoy calm and quiet activities such as hobbies, writing, collecting, reading, watching sports events, or sometimes doing nothing! Although often very challenging, I make every effort to avoid distractions and interruptions while attempting to focus on only one thing at a time. Achieving the equilibrium of calm and quiet is challenging but necessary, and only you can control it. Shortchanging yourself is regrettable. Only you can achieve balance.

Maintaining control and focus creates a lifestyle of equilibrium. Many authors have coined the term serenity, that calm and entirely peaceful state of meditative nirvana.

Our Universe is a complex system of equilibrium. Our planet Earth has maintained a consistent and relatively harmonious course around the sun since time immemorial. Everything in our Universe moves in a rhythm called equilibrium. Not only is this true of our solar system, but it is also true of our human moods. Planet Earth relies on this stability of nature; conversely, extremes are always brought into harmony. Mother Nature creates fog to cool inland's high temperatures; she creates earthquakes to settle internal stress; she allows for tornadoes and hurricanes to combat extremes of high and low-pressure systems. Our Earth carefully maintains this natural balance 24 hours a day. Yet we, as simple humans, have difficulty understanding these somewhat capricious acts of God. Mother Nature's primary purpose is to maintain her equilibrium.

You have probably heard terms like, "What goes around comes around" or, "When someone gets something for nothing, someone else gets nothing for something." These are short epigrams extolling the moderation of actions. One of Newton's laws states that for every force, there is an equal and opposite force. Balancing forces creates equilibrium. Wall Street knows that in the stock market, for every dollar earned by someone, someone else loses a dollar. Things always level out. Seneca summed it up with facility two thousand years ago, "Everything that exceeds the bounds of moderation has an unstable foundation." Perhaps even more simply, all things are maximized by moderation.

Look for the truth and good in all of earth's cracks and crevices, and you will find peace and calm.

When you take the time to think about life and realize the true meaning of happiness, like Mother Nature, you must maintain a natural balance to find true happiness. Overeating is as destructive as eating too little; drinking too much water can be as dismal as dehydration; working or exercising too excessively can be as devastating as remaining an inveterate couch potato. Overextending yourself and intruding into others' heads or bodies can also be as caustic as total passivity. An analogy that applies is our use of automobiles. Having extensive first-hand experiences with automobiles, I have learned through lessons of over- or under-use. For instance, if we race the engine repeatedly, it wears out. If we allow the vehicle to sit unattended for long periods, the brakes leak, gasoline and gaskets deteriorate, and fuel lines clog like plaque in arteries.

Again, moderation and balance are nature's SOS call to slow down and enjoy life. The most exemplary is peace and calm. Enjoying nature is an excellent means of finding relaxation. One of the calmest, quietest, prettiest, and most relaxing ways to establish equilibrium is a walk in nature. It is medicine for the mind and body. No greater sense of well-being can be achieved than surrounding yourself in a forest of trees or walking along a creek path. Trekking through Mother Nature's Garden of Eden will renew your energy, clear your mind, lower your blood pressure, and reduce your stress. Relax and enjoy the splendor of nature's flora and fauna, showered by the sun and lightly shadowed by the surrounding trees. You need to be realistic by recognizing that life has natural vexations each day. Whether it is expending energy, motivation, expectations, work or play, balance and moderation allow for the equalization of not too much or not too little, but just the right amount.

There are tracking apps currently available. If you prefer high-tech, go for it. Perhaps a little old-fashioned, I still use a daily calendar, a to-do list, and a planner. I can't say that things are always even-keeled and work out perfectly, but using those tools helps me remember appointments, meetings, activities and include "me time," even though it may not be necessarily just for me. I purposely clock in some "me time" into my to-do list. It typically includes enjoying activities with my extended family, going places with them, especially out to dinner. I consider this very important "me time." Even ten or fifteen minutes of it at different times of the day can be refreshing and inspiring.

There is no substitute for longer uninterrupted quality time, but any break can work wonders. Regardless, maintaining personal time is essential and transformative. With it, life becomes less laden and more in equilibrium when you do not exclude yourself in your daily equation.

Live a life of balance and moderation, and your journey will remain exhilarating!

"The greatest discovery of my generation is that a human being can alter his life by altering his attitudes of mind."

—*William James*

ATTITUDE, ATTITUDE, ATTITUDE

From the time I was a tiny tike, my mother's words echoed like that of an unusually large Asian gong, "Tony, attitude is everything!" Now at age 101, there is seldom a conversation that doesn't somehow relate to her admonition on expressing a positive demeanor.

Attitude is to personal happiness and success what location is to real estate. It is the heart and soul of positive mental health. Your mental state is the gyroscope of your future and the guidance system of your longevity. It is the runway to reaching your highest altitude. For hundreds of years, there has been a dichotomy of semantics regarding one's disposition. Those that are known as optimists have a rosy or optimistic view of their world.

On the other hand, pessimists are those that possess a skeptical and cynical look at their world. Admittedly this is a rather simplistic dichotomy, but it establishes the continuum of perceptions, from one extreme to another. One of the significant researchers of this dichotomy is Martin Seligman, Ph.D. from the University of Pennsylvania. His findings concluded that optimists contribute to positive personal health, while pessimists contribute to their poor health. He and other colleagues found optimists are generally more successful and pessimists less fortunate.

Pessimists tend to explain their difficulties as personal and permanent; optimists see their problems as either temporary or opportunistic. Optimists see their lives as a series of challenges that could be successfully overcome. Their mantra is, "I can; let me show you." Pessimists are frequently discouraged by obstacles and more commonly conclude, "I can't." Pessimists over time through disappointments develop associations of words and images that create their self-proclaimed prophecy. However, optimists foresee their challenges as fun and exciting. Pessimists saw challenges as difficult, fearful, and anxiety-provoking. These self-fulfilling prophecies often result in the exact direction they perceived. Their results are either success or defeat because their initial thoughts were bonded to their final action. More often, optimists act in constructive and planned movements. Pessimists act with ambivalence, hesitance, and passivity. They anticipate the difficulty that they were convinced would be inevitably encountered.

Attitude includes your cognitive thoughts and perceptions. They embrace what you see as difficult or easy, possible or impossible, as well as the myriads of other positive and negative values that you place on things. If you are an optimist, your leaning is generally hopeful, inspiring, progressive, adventuresome, energetic, sanguine, and idealistic. If you are a pessimist, you are frequently apathetic, mistrusting, cynical, grim, critical, very conservative, conforming, and fearful of change or the unknown. Pessimists find safety in remaining status quo. They are often the masters of criticism and sarcasm.

Optimists lack fear, see adventure and opportunity, and are active participants in life. They ignore the danger, are persistent and persevering. They see the glass as half full, see sunshine behind the clouds, look for discoveries on the horizon, see friendly foes, and always look for the pot of gold at the end of the rainbow.

However, I almost forgot about the realist. He or she provides the perfect balance. It is not unusual that pessimism and optimism can be so ingrained that they can become extreme. The extreme optimists take unnecessary chances because they are fearless. Extreme pessimists can become so fearful that they withdraw from society and become hermits. The perfect balance is a realist who observes life as a challenge but thinks and prepares before making decisions, without being frozen with fear and inaction. Realists are generally happy, calm, relaxed, and confident. They have a generally optimistic attitude but are aware of the possibility of the unexpected or danger.

The formula you should seek on your journey is balanced, not overly optimistic, or too pessimistic. You will meet many individuals who are full of either positive "fluff" or, conversely, filled with negativity. You will need to decide the happy medium that will provide you with reasonable doubt yet not scare you to death with the impending danger that the sky is falling.

As you awaken each day and gently brush the sand from your eyes, you are magically inspired by all the possibilities that exist within the next 24 hours. Knowing you have the power to transform each day, you can choose the things that will provide enthusiasm and hope. I have often heard others suggest that if you alter your attitude, you can ultimately change your life.

There is growing evidence that optimistic people have a lower risk of disease and premature deaths than pessimists. In one study, those over age 50 who viewed aging as a positive experience lived an average of seven and a half years longer than pessimists. Statistically, that's considered to be a very significant leap forward. Further, it was noted in one study that optimists seek and follow medical advice and live in ways that prevent illness and thus have a positive impact on their immune system.

Eventually, the wise realize that their circumstances are only improved after readjusting their attitudes. Many inspirational speakers emphasize that you either control your mood or it controls you. How often have you been in situations where shop owners, bosses, neighbors, or relatives have not learned this lesson? The results are lost business, bankruptcy, depression, and sometimes suicide. I can recall several people who lost their jobs even after guidance and advice because they refused to understand that their flip approach and lack of concern for their clients/employees were career-ending. I can immediately think of someone who was fired three separate times and never "got it"—of course, it was always somebody else or the circumstances that caused it.

The key to mediocrity and remaining at the status quo is to compare yourself to someone else. A more positive attitude builds personal power and momentum as your confidence grows internally. As you gain wisdom, you recognize that your way of thinking is indeed contagious. Listening to others lament, complain, and feel sorry for themselves allows for your contagion. As a boy, my mother reminded me regularly that "Misery loves company." It is so easy to get hooked into someone else's depression or feelings of helplessness.

Conversely, it is just as easy to adopt someone's enthusiasm and optimism. Bonding with others of similar positive energies creates a powerful kinship of reinforcing synergy. Eschewing the conversational traps of politics, religion, ethnicity, sexual preference, or race avoids confrontation. Your avoidance of controversy sustains enthusiasm, confidence, and positiveness. As a dear friend and fellow winemaker once shared, "Always see your wine glass as half-full, not half empty."

Confidence and enthusiasm are byproducts of your attitude and can either expand or contract. For example, if asked, "Can you learn to speak three languages?" A positive thinker would say, "Of course I can, if I so choose." A pessimist would answer, "No, I can't." Attitudes of fate, fear, sadness, and discontent hold you back from gaining control of your perspective. You cannot control Mother Nature; however, you can and must control yourself, especially your attitude.

Ironically, today I received an email that illustrated the ability to take the same negatives conveyed by the sarcastic and critical pessimist and easily convert them into a realistic and optimistic message. Below are the contrasting attitudes:

A famous writer was in his study. He picked up his pen and began writing. He wrote, "Last year, my gall bladder was removed. I was stuck in bed due to this surgery for a long time.

"The same year I reached the age of 60 and had to give up my favorite job. I had spent 30 years of my life with this publishing company.

"The same year I experienced the death of my father.

"In that year, my son failed his medical exam because he had a car accident. He had to stay in the hospital with a cast on his leg for several days. And the destruction of the car was my second loss."

His concluding statement: "Alas! It was such a bad year!"

When the writer's wife entered the room, she found her husband looking dejected, sad, and lost in his thoughts. She carefully and surreptitiously read what he had written, and silently left the room and came back shortly with another piece of paper on which she had written her summary of the year's events and placed it beside her husband's paper.

When her husband saw that she had written a response, he read her thoughts of the year's events.

She wrote, "Last year I finally got rid of my gall bladder, which had given me many years of pain.

"I turned 60 with sound health and retired from my job. Now I can utilize my time to write better and with more focus and peace.

"The same year, my father, at the age of 95, without depending on anyone and without any critical conditions, met his Creator.

"During that year, God blessed my son with life. My car was destroyed, but my son was alive and without permanent disability.

In the end, she wrote, "This year was an immense blessing, and it passed well!" Notice, all of the same incidents, but different viewpoints!

Moral: In our daily lives, we must see that it's not happiness that makes us grateful, but gratefulness that makes us happy. There is always, always, always something to be thankful for.

Thanksgiving is indeed a daily celebration.

ATTITUDE IS EVERYTHING

An attitude is the one thing that you always have available in every circumstance. It is your choice; you have control over whether you want to convey positiveness or negativity.

KEYS TO A HEALTHY ATTITUDE

There are a number of keys to obtaining a healthy attitude. The first and foremost key to the development of a positive attitude is self-awareness. When you recognize your perceptions of the world are either healthy or unhealthy, that becomes your very first step, awareness.

- Realizing where your fears, anxieties, or worries originated brings clarity and self-responsibility to problem-solving and ultimately personal change.
- Obtaining feedback from trusted friends, colleagues, and relatives create the basis of introspection and self-change. As you recognize the specific areas of personal growth needed, you will avoid denial and instead take full responsibility for your thoughts, feelings, and actions.
- The next step is to become assertive, which gives you the courage to establish and pursue worthwhile goals. Be your own best advocate.

- One of the biggest obstacles is becoming overly judgmental. Introspectively judge yourself; avoid projecting your judgments onto others. The cost of judging others most often results in frustration—and failed relationships.

Reframing your comments and goals with simple affirmative statements is far more constructive to bonding your relationships with others. For example, "I will become more tolerant and understand my husband, son, daughter, or neighbor." "I'll say at least two compliments every time we are together." "I will bite my tongue every time a negative thought or judgmental statement enters my mind." Or, "I will look for and find some beauty in everyone and everything."

Monitoring your input and output is key to a healthy, positive attitude and achieves positive mental health. However, always be reminded that you will need to fully accept and forgive yourself before you can accept and forgive others.

Savoring each new day, you can realize the preciousness of each second, as a gift of time. Be thankful for knowing you have the sole responsibility and power to choose your points of view no matter the constraints.

A much older friend gave me some good fatherly advice, "Go for it and give it your best! Remember, you don't need to be a professional to build a great product. Amateurs started Google and Apple; professionals built the Titanic!" Attitude remains 98% of everything!

SOME TRUE STORIES OF A
HEALTHY ATTITUDE

Vice Adm. and former VP candidate James Stockdale, a Congressional Medal of Honor winner, spent seven years in a Vietnam P.O.W. camp. His salvation and key to survival were to change his attitude. He said, "In my case, locked up and hungry, never knowing when I'd be called next for more torture, the tension was unbearable. I realized that I couldn't allow myself to waste precious time and energy, worrying about what might happen next. To prevail, I had to find a way to take charge personally. I would stand up and challenge them. Courage is endurance in the presence of fear. It is proactive, the very antithesis of passive worry."

Viktor Frankl comments in The Will to Live, "We who lived in concentration camps can remember the men who walked through the huts comforting others, giving away their last piece of bread. They may have been few in number, but they offer sufficient proof that everything can be taken away from a man but one thing: The last of human freedoms— to choose one's attitude in any given set of circumstances, to choose one's own way."

The two stories above acknowledge that every 24 hours are precious gifts. Your disposition and choices are critical in appreciating and orchestrating each day's magical gifts.

Yes, attitude is indeed 98% of everything!

"If music be the food of love, play on!"

—William Shakespeare

FUEL FOR YOUR JOURNEY

The definition and understanding of love are both elusive and relative to each type of relationship. There are so many meanings that it defies a simple singular description. Everyone has felt this emotion, yet it comes in many different shapes and sizes. It can be the love of a child, adult, pet, and even inanimate objects. We have all heard children say they love pizza or spaghetti or an adult says how much they love their dogs or cats. We talk of loving our wife or our neighbors, family, country, or sibling. Yes, there are many variations of the theme and various intensities, forms, and degrees. Love's intensity can be further described as infatuation, affection, intimate, routine, fake, enduring, playful, selfless, puppy, forlorn, or unrequited. Each represents a distinct form very different from the others. Many spend their lives seeking it, while others bask in its sunshine. Not surprising, there are many contrasting perceptions regarding its definition.

Fortunately, but not by serendipity, my life has been filled with love. First, it was my mother's, almost over the top because she was denied pregnancy for a number of years. My father was less demonstrative but was usually able to express it as unspoken and nonverbal. Of course, there was my darling grandmother Angelina's, my godmother, Aunt Rose, and other aunts, my godfather, Uncle Orlando, and other uncles, my neighbor and tea partner, the inimitable Aunt Kate, some accepting neighbors, and dear friends. Later, my wife and children and more new relatives, friends, colleagues, and secretarial staff. It seemed like it was an ever-expanding family circle. The list is almost endless. My biggest challenge was learning how to return it in kind. My regrets are that lacking time sometimes prevailed. There are so many nostalgic memories and photos that ruminate peacefully in my mind's eye, as I lay in bed early in the morning. Sadly, many of them are now gone, but never to be forgotten.

As mentioned previously, the best things in life are free. They are the intangibles, gifts freely available. Love is the most alluring one of all. It is the most talked about and the most commonly-used word in literature. It is found in fiction, nonfiction, legends, soap operas, religion, philosophy, songs, ballads, poems, myths, and metaphors. The Greeks and Romans had their gods of love and sex—Venus, Aphrodite, Cupid, and Eros. Cupid's arrows are replete in paintings, sculptures, scenes, valentines, and other expressions of art.

Many are regularly reminded that 1 Corinthians 13:4 –7, which defined it almost two millennia ago as: *"Love is patient, love is kind. It does not envy; it does not boast, it is not proud. It is not rude, it is not self-seeking, it is not easily angered, it keeps no record of wrongs. Love does not delight in evil but rejoices with the truth. It always protects, always trusts, always hopes, always perseveres. Love never fails."*

Although adequate and generic, a universal definition of it remains elusive. Yet it unequivocally remains the most important human need, often a mysterious obsession.

No matter what your definition, love is necessary for survival. Many studies verify our need for it and its direct relationship to success and happiness. As a graduate student, I cannot forget the early studies conducted in the Boston area. The conclusion was that orphaned infants would self-destruct if not held or enamored during those critical initial months of infancy. Social scientists have consistently found strong correlations between parental rejection, lack of affection, and inability to provide love and its strong relationship to socially inappropriate, felonious, homicidal, and self-destructive behaviors.

A MOTHER'S LOVE

My mother, grandmother, and wife have on several occasions mentioned the very special love a mother has for her child. Each expressed their feelings somewhat differently, but invariably the twinkle in their eyes was soon gently bathed by unexpected moisture. Each remembered and reminisced the special moments of childbirth and the delightful moment of the first cry and holding their newborn for the very first time.

To this day, my 101-year-old mother says, "You will never know how much I love you. I love you more than you will ever know; of course, son, a mother's love is different."

My grandmother, who had less command of the English language, said it more succinctly "I love my son Pete so much! I hope God bless him always!"

My wife regularly tells our children how much she truly adores them and says, "I love you to the moon and back. I love you, oh, so much."

Or perhaps her mother's comment: "I love you a bushel and a peck." There is nothing more special or more important to a child than a mother's deep affection.

ROMANTIC LOVE

The most talked-about type of love is romantic. It has been the subject of poems, letters, plays, and books for millennia. It is the most publicized, yet to many, the least understood of all. It is relatively easy to understand the feelings one has for a pet. It is more difficult to comprehend the true depth and type of feelings that individuals have for each other. For centuries passion between adults has been manipulated or embellished. It's been hot and cold, ambivalent, and capricious. However, some authors have captured it in the most eloquent of terms.

WHAT IS TRUE LOVE?

Romantic love is boundless passion! Love is internal butterflies and a fluttering heart! Love is a song, a heavenly dream, a touch of honey, and a fragrant flower bouquet! Love is the glimmering glow of the stars! It is the sunrise! Love is a mysterious mix of magic and joy! Love is ecstasy and exhilaration, the mightiest of all emotions.

LOVE AND MARRIAGE

It is hard for me to forget the song lyrics, "Love and marriage, go together like a horse and carriage . . ." In his book, _Love_, Gregory Godek said there were ten important ingredients in a truly loving relationship. They include trust, patience, commitment, communication, friendship, flexibility, forgiveness, intimacy, humor, and an outward expression of affection.

After over 56 years of marriage, I agree heartily, but I would add two major components: tolerance and acceptance. In any relationship, one needs to accept as non-judgmentally as possible the other person. Without non-judgmental acceptance, you cannot learn to tolerate and understand the differences of your beloved. My first naïve marital issues included burnt food, squeezing the toothpaste from the top, tardiness, and tidiness. It was not long after that I commented that I really liked it burnt, and then I bought separate toothpaste tubes and learned to be fashionably late! Tolerance has benefits! Others may choose different alternatives, but it is the best to choose your battles rather than lose the war; or the special relationship you have with your very special love. I believe Charles Darwin would call this behavior adaptation—tolerance and acceptance are necessary for marital survival.

Allowing your ego, your lack of acceptance and tolerance, or your need to control your spouse to prevail will inevitably result in ongoing conflicts, and worse yet, divorce.

Marital love is delicate and needs constant sustenance. Renewing a marriage before it becomes stale and humdrum is critical. Marriage is like a fresh spring garden. It needs tender loving care, regular weeding, and ongoing maintenance. It needs nourishment and precious doses of refreshing water. It can't be ignored, or it will slowly shrivel up and expire.

Here's one last glimpse of true marital love. Percy and Florence lived to be 105 and 100 years old, respectively. They celebrated their 80th wedding anniversary, which set a Guinness book record for the longest marriage on record. They attributed their long union to their nightly ritual. They would kiss and hold hands, refusing to go to bed in anger. They admitted that there were times when it was not so easy but love and perseverance prevailed. May you enjoy even a small part of their longevity, legacy, and loving marriage.

LOVE OF FRIENDS

Love of friends does not possess all of the characteristics of maternal, romantic, or maternal love. It is unique in that it resembles warm, caring feelings rather than being passionate or motherly. You don't feel the same towards your best friend as you do with your mother or your lover. Friends express their love unhesitatingly by helping and making each other happy. They are sharers, concerned confidants, and kindred spirits. Many consider friends to be similar to fraternal warmth, less passionate and intense but characterized by affection, companionship, and kinship. Being enamored with others is as contagious as a flu epidemic. Spread it, be an active carrier.

FAMILIAL LOVE

Similarly, the bond that begins at birth is different from friendship. There are many types of familial love. It can be fraternal or sisterly between brothers and sisters or grandparents, cousins, aunts, uncles, and even close friends referred to as family. Typically, familial love is based on the fact that there is continued contact from birth to later life. This bonding can have dramatic effects.

Most of us have very fond feelings for our family. There is usually a very special affection for a brother or sister or a cousin. Certainly, if grandparents are actively involved, a very close bond is established. It is frequently referred to as magical. Grandparents can often take a more objective hand in the rearing of their grandchildren. Sometimes they have even more influence, especially during the tender years of adolescence. Those fortunate enough to have an extended family have supplemental support systems only available to them. They can usually rely on their extended family for advice, modeling, sharing, learning, and love. Although I was only able to have one living grandparent throughout my young life, I found it one of the most secure, confidence-building, and memorable experiences of my existence.

As a grandparent now, I find that special role to be supreme. It is a role that comes with new responsibilities but has unlimited rewards. Whether you are a son, daughter, cousin, aunt, uncle, godparents, grandparent, or parent, you have a special role in a child's life. This role must be taken seriously, responsibly, and thoughtfully. I sincerely believe that this is one of the most important and rewarding roles anyone can play during another family member's lifetime.

Once you have been exposed to love and have begun to reciprocate, the very next thing is to learn to love and appreciate yourself. Without these feelings, it becomes impossible to express to others. Your internal glow also allows you to ignite the spark in others. If you don't love yourself, you have no foundation to share it with others.

There are many days that the words of the late motivational speaker Dr. Leo Buscaglia resonate with me. He said, "Remember, the opposite of love is not hate; it is apathy." It certainly does not take a rocket scientist to determine that there are serious consequences if apathy replaces this deep emotion. This lack of inner feelings results in a shadow of a person. You cannot show or expect love if your fuel tank is empty. It is not surprising that cold-blooded killers, child abusers, or hatemongers lack the Golden Rule and its required love. If you cannot express this tender emotion, you will be unable to construct a relationship and instead will result in self-destructive behaviors.

> *"There is no difficulty that enough love will not conquer."*
> —*Emmet Fox*

Whether it be the words of Mother Teresa, Leo Buscaglia, or Sophocles, the message is clear: it starts at home, and without it, we can only expect conflict, crime, death, or war. If there is anything we need to share in this world, it is love!

HUGGING AND KISSING

Hugging and kissing are explicit expressions of love. They are the key ingredients to good health and longevity. When I met my wife, I discovered the magic of hugging and kissing. My family might put an arm around you momentarily, or my aunts might give you a peck on the cheek, but they were not fervently demonstrative. On the other hand, my wife's family always had a bear hug and a sincere kiss on your cheek. It didn't matter what your gender; you received it tax-free! Soon, it became a habit. Surprisingly, although I was a tad dazed initially, it soon became our ritual, too. Now, not only do we continue to express it freely, it is becoming more acceptable in current social parlance. There is nothing more warm and inviting than a big hug and sincere kiss on the cheek.

Turning to children—there is something very special and heartwarming about children's love and their perceptions of it. After more than five decades of helping these precious cherubs, I have heard so many priceless expressions. If only I had captured them like Art Linkletter on his show, "Kids Say the Darndest Things!" There are few things more exhilarating than hearing the genuine thoughts of young children. I want to share some of the precious thoughts of young children sent to me by a colleague who also has worked with children for many years. They were taken from a group of professionals. They asked a group of four- to eight-year-olds,

"What does love mean to you?" It will be difficult for you to hold back warm feelings and the subsequent emotional and visceral reactions you'll have when you think of these children and your childhood.

"When my grandmother got arthritis, she couldn't bend over and paint her toenails anymore. So my grandfather does it all the time, even when his hands got arthritis, too. That's love."
—Rebecca, age 8

"Love is when a girl puts on perfume, and a boy puts on shaving cologne, and they go out and smell each other."
—Karl, age 5

"Love is when you go out to eat and give somebody most of your French fries without making them give you any of theirs."
—Chrissy, age 6

"Love is what makes you smile when you're tired."
—Terry, age 4

"Love is when my mommy makes coffee for my daddy, and she takes a sip before giving it to him to make sure that the taste is okay."
—Danny, age 7

"Love is what's in the room with you at Christmas if you stop opening presents and listen."
—Bobby, age 7

"Love is when you tell a guy you like his shirt. Then he wears it every day."

—Noelle, age 7

And one final note, Dr. Leo Buscaglia once talked about a contest he was asked to judge. The purpose of the contest was a find the most caring child. The winner was a four-year-old child whose next-door neighbor was an elderly gentleman who had recently lost his wife. Upon seeing the man cry, the little boy went into the old gentleman's yard, climbed onto his lap, and just sat there. When his mother asked him what he had said to the neighbor, the little boy said, "Nothing. I just helped him cry."

Some thoughts to remember: Love is what makes the world go round, so please remember—Love is magic. Love is necessary. Love is to be shared. Love is never to be forgotten. Love is grand. Love is endearing. And may the loves of your life continue to brighten your way. It provides the fuel for your journey toward a life of happiness

"A man of genius makes no mistakes. His errors are volitional and are the portals of discovery."

—*James Joyce, Ulysses*

BLISSFUL BLUNDERS

It seemed that during the first third of my life, I qualified as the master of mistakes. During those years, I was under the impression that missteps were bad and self-defeating. As time passed, I discovered them to be feedback. Now I'm convinced that they are often golden opportunities. So, I guess all that fuss was just part of the painful learning curve.

Mistakes and momentary failures are not only lessons that teach success but are the cornerstones of ultimate happiness.

So, what I initially thought of as defeats or major stumbling blocks are really feedback, new beginnings, and subsequent epiphanies. It was my genesis to eventual independence, freedom, and success. It's your turn now!

If your journey is mistake-free, you will have a long and arduous trip to Nirvana. Make your miscues and failures early, then watch them work magic for you. Take responsibility for your failures because later they will result in your triumphs and successes. Once you accept yourself as the responsible party for your behavior, you permit yourself to be imperfect. At that point, you will know that you are still okay. After each fall, you can pick yourself up, discard the old behavior, and attempt a new strategy. Remember the scientific method: Identify the problem and then try various alternative strategies. The scientific method's prime principle is not the generation of hypotheses, but rather the testing through trial and error. Also, remember that most scientific discoveries started with a mistake. Your creativity is limitless. The important thing is getting back up after falling. Don't admit defeat but remember the immortal words of Edison searching for the very first light bulb, "I have not failed. I have just found 10,000 ways that don't work."

Close the steel doors of the past. Don't dwell on the past; focus on the now and your next step. Occasional missteps are the price we pay for improvement. They are like the minor bruises incurred learning to ride a bike. They are not fatal but forgiving. These painful mistakes will become your major learning moments. They are the doors to discoveries and new levels of maturity. Just think how dull life would be if it lacked the excitement of discoveries and the rewards that follow.

From every blunder, you will gain something new, resulting in less chance of a repeat. The most sophisticated, elegant, learned, and wise are more mistake-prone than those less sophisticated and mundane. It is our human fallibility that allows the wisdom of learning by "practice." Riding a bike, skiing, or playing sports means hurts and bumps. Getting back up and mastering a sport develops courage and character. There is not an Olympic athlete, writer, scientist, or President, who has not been rejected or failed in achieving prominence. No one becomes eminent by total success or total failure. Even the most espoused of all basketball coaches, John Wooden, said, "The team that makes the most mistakes will probably win." Likewise, how many famous writers send out their books to publishers only to be repeatedly rejected? At least twelve publishers initially dismissed some of the biggest bestsellers. The journey is indeed bumpy but bountiful. Paradoxically, the most respected individuals are the result.

No one enjoys making mistakes. Everyone tries to avoid making them, but you can't simply avoid slip-ups any more than you can stop time. Many have turned out to be major discoveries. Most major scientific discoveries started with flubs. Virtually every discovery occurred because of a wrong turn en route to a carefully planned destination. These miracles of irony have revolutionized medicine (Madame Currie, Alexander Fleming, and Louis Pasteur), transportation (Charles Kettering); advanced electricity (Luigi Galvani and Thomas Edison); opened the skies (Galileo Galilei and Hans Lippershey); and discovered continents (Christopher Columbus, Amerigo Vespucci, James Cook, Juan Cabrillo, and Vasco da Gama). Without these daring and courageous people, we may still be in the dark ages. The person who never makes mistakes remains motionless and powerless.

That same energy required to write a book with accurate information and knowledge may create misinformation and promulgate ignorance. Unfortunately, in school we learn that making errors is bad. Instead of focusing on what's wrong, you need to focus on what is right, to appreciate our percentage of success, not the percentage of failure. Then you can celebrate your mistakes as progressive feedback, not utter failure. Disappointingly, the concept learned is that to err is patently wrong, which is unequivocally erroneous. Thinking that erring is wrong produces a negative self-attitude that avoids blunders, thus fearing future attempts. This kind of attitude undermines creativity and personal progress. Fear destroys the seminal and germinal phases of creativity.

> *"The quickest way to success is to double your failure rate."*
> —*Thomas Watson, Founder of IBM*

FAMOUS AND SUCCESSFUL PEOPLE

In the annals of time, there remains no doubt that successful people make more mistakes than their less prone peers. In reading the biography of Thomas Watson, founder of IBM, it became transparently clear that he endured failure after failure on his road to incredible notoriety and success. The immortal words of the founder of IBM (above), and of Soichiro Honda, founder of Honda Motors, "Success is 99% failure." Both give credence and support for harvesting errors as major stepping stones to ultimate success and happiness. Their sons followed in their footsteps, and thus perpetuity was preserved for what became rock-solid blue-chip companies.

The most successful are those that not only recover quickly from mistakes but do not waste time wallowing in self-pity. They don't rehearse their errors. They reverse them! The feedback received by these hardy individuals allows them to bounce back after digesting the critical components of their misconstruction. That feedback provides the data to plan and restructure the changes necessary for their next systematic attempt. Most average individuals are frozen by fear and afraid to move forward. Fear of failure is an immense problem for many. It usually stops and thwarts even the smallest of efforts. It is the strong, motivated, and near fearless individuals that are energized by blunders. Each mistake is a lesson in learning. These learning moments are the catalysts that will catapult you to your future success.

Thomas Edison was one of America's biggest heroes. His biography is most interesting. Edison is the holder of more patents than any other individual in American history. When he began school, he was promptly asked to leave due to his poor behavior and excessive curiosity. His teachers felt he was low in intellect and difficult to control. Before disaster struck, his mother decided to home-school him. She had an overwhelming influence that transcended his wildest expectations. She supported him unconditionally, and he excelled because of it. For instance, by age ten, he had already developed his chemistry laboratory. His love and appreciation of his mother's undying faith and devotion to him prompted these comments:

> *"Success is 10% inspiration and 90% perspiration."*
> —*Thomas A Edison*

> *"Results! Why, man, I have gotten a lot of results!*
> *I know several thousand things that won't work."*
> —*Thomas A. Edison*

It took Thomas Edison approximately 10,000 attempts before getting his first bulb to maintain light. Now, that was indeed an education! Thus, it is not surprising that other famous individuals like Mozart had either a mother or another special person who believed unquestionably in his creativity and intellect. Emotional support and encouragement early in life can have dramatically positive outcomes. Interestingly, most luminaries were relatively poor students, and many were considered to lack talent. Sir Isaac Newton, Albert Einstein, Thomas Edison, and Wernher Von Braun all did poorly in school, particularly mathematics. Walt Disney was told that he lacked creativity or good ideas. Ludwig van Beethoven and Franz Schubert were considered mediocre and lacking true talent. R H. Macy failed at least seven times before having a successful store.

The Red Baron, Manfred von Richthofen, crashed on his first solo and nearly washed out as a pilot. He couldn't control his plane, and the plane crashed nose-first. After a second attempt, the aspiring pilot's examiner graded his performance as unsatisfactory and flunked him. It was his third and final attempt that won him his wings. Later, he and his Fokker triplane downed 80 allied planes in dogfights. This was an aeronautic achievement never again to be repeated.

What about Abraham Lincoln, one of our greatest presidents? He failed in business several times, had a nervous breakdown, and was defeated at least seven times in major political elections. Yet, he courageously persevered and went on to become the most quoted American President of all time. Mistakes and momentary defeats are the building blocks of character and success. They are inspirational events of momentous proportions.

FOR ALL YOU BASEBALL FANS

Those that excel in sports, especially baseball, know that they can't hit a home run every time. Some of baseball's greatest heroes are very candid and humble concerning their records. Babe Ruth held the major-league strikeout record for 30 years. He struck out 1,330 times yet hit 714 homers. He had a lifetime batting average of .342.

He was considered by many as the best baseball player of all time. So, for every single home run hit, he had to strike out two times. That doesn't even include all of his other 2,873 base hits. In addition, he was also a pitcher who had a lifetime ERA of 2.28.

Willie Mays broke Ruth's strikeout record with 1,526 strikeouts. He hit 660 home runs and had an overall batting average of .302. He also made 24 All-Star appearances. Neither Ruth nor Mays worried about their strikeouts. Instead of being worried or paralyzed by fear, they knew that nothing ever happens until you take action, persevere, and accept momentary defeats.

Most people think success and failure are opposites. On the contrary, they are both products of the same phenomenon. Boston Red Sox first baseman Carl Yastrzemski (3,419 hits, .285 lifetime batting average) suggests, "The activity which produces a hit may also produce a miss; if you want the hits, be prepared for the misses." Lou Gehrig, one of baseball's all-time best players, had 2,721 hits, 493 home runs, and a lifetime batting average of .340. His career was cut short by what is commonly known now as Lou Gehrig's disease. His most famous quote was, "Fans, for the past two weeks you have been reading about the bad break I got. Yet today I consider myself the luckiest man on the face of this earth. I might have been in ballparks for seventeen years and have never received anything but kindness and encouragement from you fans . . . So I close in saying that I may have had a tough break, but I've got an awful lot to live for!" This giant of baseball was often referred to as indestructible, a "Gibraltar in cleats." Although he was able to get one hit for every three at-bats, an incredible feat, many feel that he hit more emotional home runs than any other man in the history of baseball.

WISDOM THROUGH THE AGES

The sages of the past knew that success and happiness result from a learning curve similar to the vicissitudes of the stock market. Just like the losses and gains of each trading day, life's mishaps are kissing cousins to the ups and downs of Wall Street. We come to wisdom through failure. We learn through our losses.

The wise know that experience dictates learning. It is only the foolish who repeat failure without a scintilla of learning. Turn your mistakes into advantages, not disadvantages. Having fought an uphill battle means sliding down that same hill with motivational momentum. We must always scale obstacles on our way to success. Experience is what you gain from life's inevitable mistakes.

The key to working through failures is what you learn each time. Sometimes it takes several similar mistakes to learn a lesson thoroughly. Whether it takes two or more of the same slip-ups, if a learning moment occurs, don't fret, because everyone has a different learning curve, time clock, and unique approach to learning and ultimate retention.

One of the quickest shortcuts to avoid the pain of failure is by learning vicariously from others' mistakes. Why walk many miles to your destination if you can bicycle three times as fast? Keep alert by watching others; you will expedite your journey by learning from their blunders. Also, it's always better to proceed forward by asking as many questions as necessary to shortcut your journey.

Exasperated and frustrated by mistakes, we need to identify whether they are intelligently planned failures or simply dumb thinking errors. If they continually repeat themselves, they can be easily classified as dumb mistakes. When learning doesn't occur, slip-ups have a much higher probability of being repeated. By trial and error, smart mistakes teach you a lesson and assist in the development of maturity. Don't complain about the smart ones. Dumb mistakes, however, usually include denial or blame. Finding a scapegoat denies the error and instead focuses the blame on somebody else. Nothing can be learned; thus, exasperation and frustration are its byproducts. Intelligent failures allow you to profit and correct your course of action.

Expect mistakes and failures.

They will buffer your reaction to their recurrence. Focus on solutions, not excuses. Don't react to a mistake as a crisis; instead, accept it as an opportunity to learn and move forward. Acceptance of errors causes renewed excitement and the courage to continue unabashed.

I can guarantee you that you do not have enough fingers and toes to count the failures you will encounter on your journey. If you make a mistake, accept it.

Don't be fearful of mistakes. Learn from them.

Forget yourself, let go, and move on. Misjudgments may be painful, but they are painfully instructive! Put a notch in your belt as a victory, not defeat.

A mistake is not the end. It is only the beginning.

Your attitude allows you to perceive them as repairable disasters and stepping stones to paradise.

"In every walk with nature, one receives far more than he seeks."
—*John Muir*

GOTTA LOVE
MAMA NATURE

Mother Nature is the most magnificent, yet the most menacing phenomena of all things known on Earth. The miracles and beauty of nature surround us. Notable artists have made many attempts, yet none can reproduce the inimitable quality and beauty produced by Her. Consequently, no attempts by people have ever succeeded in reversing or duplicating the quality, precision, balance, or beauty of nature's originals.

As a therapist, I'm always reminded that nature is far less expensive than therapy.

There is no better place to visit for personal peace and balance than a dense green forest; climbing a hillside replete with wildflowers; walking in the sand of a secluded beach; roaming through a field of tall bright green grass; watching a sensational sunset. The magic of nature is almost anywhere you turn. Open your eyes, smell the fresh air, and feel the mild breeze across your face.

You live in a very organized universe governed by the laws of nature. What fascinates me most is that these laws of nature are highly correlated with human behavior that have direct application to our actions. Many of the laws of physics replicate those that you as humans need to understand, assimilate, and follow.

For instance, Newton's First Law, "Every object persists in its state of rest or uniform motion in a straight line unless it is compelled to change that state by forces impressed on it." Your force or an external force is needed to either cause action or reaction! Does this sound vaguely familiar to human behaviors? Motivation? Decision-making? Momentum?

Newton's Second Law, "Force is equal to the change in momentum per chance in time. For a constant mass, force equals mass times acceleration." Doesn't human behavior depend on the size and force you apply? Again, does this sound familiar? Generosity? Politics? Money? Greed? Good will?

Finally, Newton's Third Law, "For every action, there is an equal and opposite reaction." Again, this is indeed very familiar. For every one of your forces there may be an equal and opposite reaction. Anger? Retribution? Kindness? Attack? Gratitude? It can be a response to a derogatory comment or even the beginning of a full-scale war.

As time passed, I continued to be amazed by how many laws of physics have a direct relationship with human behavior. For example, "Two things cannot be in the same place at the same time without causing disharmony." Our Earth and its universe depend upon harmony, balance, and rhythm. When you experience rhythmic imbalance or disharmony, you will also experience human conflicts and problems. It is not by accident that the Chinese symbols for disharmony are two adult women and a man under the same household roof. Leon Festinger's definition of cognitive dissonance, like Newtonian physics, suggests similarly, that the human mind cannot have two conflicting beliefs without causing mental disharmony. Sound familiar? Dilemma? Frustration? Stress? Depression? Decision making?

After studying anatomy, I was overwhelmed by the human body's complexity. It is astounding! Your body can survive with a large proportion of internal organs removed. You can lose your stomach, spleen, 15% of your liver, 80% of your intestines, one kidney, one lung, and virtually every organ from your pelvis and groin area and still live! The acid in your stomach is strong enough to dissolve razor blades or a nail! Our feet have 500,000 sweat glands and are capable of sweating up to a pint a day! Your body has enough iron to make a 3-inch nail! Your nose is capable of remembering 50,000 different scents! It is estimated that you have 60,000 miles of blood vessels! Your brain can hold five times more information than an encyclopedia! Your human-computer operates on the same amount of power as a 10-watt bulb! Three hundred million of our body cells die and are reborn every day! The tooth is the only part of the human body that cannot reproduce itself!

Mother Nature's creations are not only beautiful but highly complex and inexplicable. Their maternal God of Nature, like Leonardo DaVinci's Mona Lisa, has left us with an inimitable smile. Yes, it decided to make it easier for us to smile rather than frown. According to anatomists, it takes only seventeen muscles to smile and 43 muscles to frown! And on a more humorous note, she gave humans two ears and only one mouth. Perhaps it was an attempt to make a defining statement. Taking her statement one step further, our ears were made double and always open, while she made only one mouth, and it was capable of closing.

It was not surprising that primitive man and later Native Americans worshiped Mother Nature and her creations—wind, water, fire, and air. She amazed them as well. They recognized the oneness of the universe, the incredible power of Mama, and her endless delights.

The stature and power of nature should never be questioned. We have all witnessed the forces of hurricanes, earthquakes, tsunamis, and volcanoes. Mother Nature reminds us regularly that she is in charge, and humanity cannot control her. There is no doubt that Mama will always impose its forces and its order upon Earth. However, she is indeed, capricious. Weather and natural disasters are always at the discretion and control of Mother Nature. You, the most intelligent organism on Earth, remain unable to tame her or change her decisions. You must always remember that our landscape allows us to plant corn or wheat but does not guarantee it will receive adequate irrigation or ever be harvested. It may provide a bounty of honey but does not throw it into the arms of bears. You must always recognize that nature allows flowers to bloom, trees to provide fruit, rain to irrigate, and the sun to provide heat and light. You are subject to her order, harmony, integrity, and forces. She will forever reign. Don't attempt to challenge your inimitable Mama, so cooperate, and learn to live with nature by "going with her flow."

Perhaps the most remarkable of all is that Nature surrounds us at all times. You need not buy an entry ticket for all of its glory, grandeur, and beauty. Her Majesty simply provides free admission.

I cannot overemphasize my respect for Mother Earth. After having experienced a 7.1 earthquake, a notable hurricane, ocean swells equivalent to a "perfect storm," a deluge of rain, and sandstorms that stopped our airplane flight, I'm thoroughly convinced. Whether the incredible beauty of a Hawaiian sunset, the mighty Iguazu Falls and Niagara Falls, the immensity of the Rocky Mountains, the gorgeous glaciers of Patagonia, the miracles of birth and the sounds of a newborn, the feel of gentle raindrops, birds chirping, a gentle breeze, or monkeys in the wild—all here on Mother Earth

Please, I beg you to respect her, appreciate her and all of her wonders. Love her and thank her, rejoice, for your life will forever blossom in her unspeakable glory.

INSTINCT, DNA, AND INTUITION

One can only be amazed and aghast at what Mother Nature provides us. Our family loves the Monterey Bay Peninsula. Walking in the nearby streets of Pacific Grove, California, the trees are beautifully adorned and abounding with monarch butterflies. It is an exhilarating example of the world of nature in action. These butterflies go through extensive birth and rebirth cycles. They travel thousands of miles south into Central and South America before returning to the very same place their ancestors have inhabited for millennia. Similarly, migratory birds travel and return thousands of miles each fall. They also return to the same habitat that they had left the year before.

My initial experience with hunting dogs some 55 years ago left me puzzled by their instinct. As a graduate student, I volunteered to take high-risk teenagers pheasant hunting each fall. After teaching safety and general hunting procedures, we would make our way to the city dog pound. There we would find an array of potential hunting dogs. Usually, the dogs were young and inexperienced in upland game hunting. Most of the dogs had reached puberty, yet they made poor house pets because of their hyperactivity and innate curiosity. Regardless, we would teach the dogs to heel and follow routine hand signals. Most were initially impatient and impetuous. However, within a few weeks, they learned basic skills and were off to Willows, California, to Fr.

McGoldrick's private pheasant reserve, gratis of the good Padre.

Although somewhat rambunctious, each year the dogs would obey and eagerly run into the rice fields with gusto, without any apprehension. With the use of a lengthy rope as a leash, we would allow them to make horizontally parallel runs in order to adequately cover the field and allow everyone an opportunity to bring back at least one of nature's wonders, the ring-neck Mongolian pheasant. Each year, without fail, their instincts would prevail; soon, the dogs were sniffing, chasing, and eventually holding the bird at point, anticipating a reward for their hard work. After three days of relatively intense hunting, we would have many legal hunting limits and future meals for all participants. We were all impressed and thankful for the uncanny performance of man's best friend. We had no difficulty selling the dogs to anxious hunters wanting a trained hunting dog. The proceeds went to help allay our costs. After many repeated performances over the years, there was never a doubt that the dogs possessed instinct. Somehow Mother Nature had mysteriously installed in their genetic code the aggregate learning conveyed by past generations. That genetic code was obviously transferred into their DNA and, in turn, passed through each parentage. It is no wonder that as time passed, their pedigrees possessed more code, which further enhanced their skills, and future generations enjoyed more and more special benefits from their increased acumen.

There remains not a single doubt in my mind that you, being human, also inherit instincts. Is it no surprise that those never schooled to read or write for hundreds of generations score lower on reading, academic, or IQ tests? Is it not surprising that some families excel in academics, others in sports, others in the arts? Unfortunately, others have come to different conclusions. I don't believe it takes a genius to understand instinct as an internal mechanism of stored experiences transmitted by DNA and available by pre-conditioned talents in certain areas. Nor does it take a rocket scientist to determine that you also have hidden instincts readily available to assist and enhance your decision-making skills.

Many people call that intuition.

I am unequivocally convinced that heredity and DNA will eventually offer us untold and perhaps unbelievable information about their role in both susceptibility and causes of physical health, mental health, personality characteristics, and natural selection. Just as Charles Darwin connected the dots to evolution, researchers and scientists will soon begin connecting the dots to relationships previously unimagined or dreamed possible.

PERSONAL GLIMPSES

I can never forget the time I experienced my subconscious signaling a nagging fear of danger.

We were at a restaurant in a less attractive area of town. Our family was accosted by two rather seedy individuals who asked for handouts. The entire time I was very uncomfortable and having very strange, unknown feelings, causing me fear and anxiety. After finishing our meal, yet still feeling apprehensive, I gathered my family and asked them to wait a few additional minutes. Then, for the very first time, I guided them. We all walked in the middle of the street towards the dark parking lot at the rear of the building. As we approached the parking area, we could hear voices, screams, and someone being hit with a blunt instrument. These same two men were now the assailants of an innocent chef, who had ventured outside for a smoke. They were beating and striking him with a sixteen-inch piece of steel rebar.

My purposeful dalliance, not wanting to leave too soon, had saved our family as well as the chef's life. The two had waited for us, but since we had delayed our departure by ten minutes, they had grown impatient. Instead, they decided to attack the innocent chef. When we saw the attack, we yelled, "POLICE! POLICE! POLICE!" The attackers scattered immediately. We reentered the restaurant and called 911. The police arrived promptly. The next day, we were notified that they had found the first culprit immediately and later found the second. If I had not listened to my instinctive intuition, I rather doubt that I would have ever started this book.

HISTORY

This rather short digression on history will be succinct and to the point. History has a strong sense of repetition. It teaches you preparation and implores you to carefully review the past and understand how it can be repeated either positively or negatively. Like intuition, it prepares you for the unexpected. The study of your past can ultimately determine your success or failure. It is your early warning system that, combined with instinct and wisdom, will either provide you freedom or place you in shackles. Only you can create your future by respecting and recalling the past narrative. Remember that history is an epic that chronicles the past. It allows you to understand the present, avoid repeating past calamities, and to structure your future.

The past has a strong sense of repetition. The time and circumstances may be different, but the results are usually very similar to prior historical occurrences. Therefore, I entreat you to take history very seriously. For some strange reason, humanity tends to quickly forget the conditions that may have caused the last cataclysm. For instance, if you live in earthquake country or the path of past hurricanes or live in areas of high-incidence problems, protect yourself from these unpredictable reoccurring events. As mentioned previously, "an ounce of prevention is worth a pound of cure," whether you are talking about feeling confident of the strength of your residence to disaster or your own personal safety. Always have an escape route, supplies to sustain the lack of utilities, water, and food. Mother Nature does not typically give detailed warnings of her unpredictable forces. You cannot rely solely on your instinct and intuition. It is necessary for you to prepare and plan in order to avoid an ultimate disaster. Just as history applies to acts of God, it also applies to geopolitical, national, and local politics and leaders. Be alert and prepared for corruption and the abuse of power. Consequently, I believe that if you know history, it can bolster your intuition, instincts, and decisions.

Periodically look back, but don't get stuck obsessively looking through your rearview mirror! Keep your eyes focused on the road.

Understanding humanity, the richness of our past, and the centuries of accomplishments are critically important. However, just as history prepares us for the future, it also reminds us that people have remained relatively similar to what they were 100, 500, 1,000, or even 2,000 years ago. Just as in the past, there remains a vast variety of characters whom you will encounter in your lifetime. Some will possess many fine qualities, others the most deplorable of human characteristics. These very repulsive and aberrant behaviors will represent the same excesses as the seven deadly sins—greed, gluttony, lust, envy, rage, sloth, and arrogance. You can be assured that at least five percent of any population will contain these deviant personalities. Again, recognizing and understanding their existence helps prepare you for the kinds of experiences you can expect to encounter in a lifetime. Be prepared. There is no doubt that you will encounter and have challenging interactions with them during your lifetime.

Periodically look back, but don't get stuck obsessively looking through your rearview mirror! Keep your eyes focused on the road.

SOCIAL INTELLIGENCE

People need people. To live successfully, you will need to relate and cooperate with other people. Yours is not a life of solitary existence. You were born into a society, not the solitude of a deserted island.

Life requires regular social interactions with family, friends, neighbors, and strangers. It was fun when I was young and naïve—before learning the hard way to monitor my big mouth! As a young boy, my parents frequently corrected me for using the wrong words or sometimes not being respectful and polite. The more correcting there was, the more I became self-conscious of what blurted from my lips. There were many episodes with family, neighbors, and new acquaintances that my folks sent me to my room for or demanded that I apologize for the way that my words came tumbling out. Also, I found it difficult speaking in a large group or in front of a person of importance.

When I became flummoxed, I started stuttering. I was so nervous that the words in my head were all stacked up. Because of their backup, they were stuck. I could feel my throat gulping and resonating as I tried to extricate a word or phrase. My lips were vibrating as if they had acquired a new form of Parkinson's disease. I felt like crawling under a boulder. To this day, I don't know how and when my stuttering stopped. All I remember was that I was about ten or eleven when it disappeared. I suspect that I had finally matured and gained confidence. I became more aware and less fearful, more calm and more peaceful. Even today, if I need to give a large group presentation, my stomach is deluged with monarch madness. Sadly, I once recall stopping in midstream and excusing myself when the butterflies overran my gut and flooded my head. By adolescence, developing individual and small group social skills finally became relatively effortless. It was the large groups that continued as my greatest challenge.

Social skills, aka social intelligence quotient (S.I.Q.), are the ability to facilitate and negotiate your relationships effectively. Successful interactions are as important to you as your mental and physical well-being. Building beneficial relationships is required for support, stress reduction, and a successful career. Gaining good friends can buffer your moods and provide you valuable feedback. They help clarify your thoughts and feelings, as well as share their own. Your convivial relationships can become mutually-trusted confidants. They can help bolster your confidence and increase your communication skills. As mentioned throughout this book, friends are a critical source of communal support for stress relief.

Developing social skills will add valuable new tools to your toolbox.

You develop your *savoir faire* through your communications; it includes both verbal and nonverbal types. Your verbal communication conveys credibility and trust when it is open, honest, clear, and concise. Equally important is your ability to listen attentively and then share your inner thoughts and feelings with empathy, sincerity, and sensitivity. Nonverbal communication includes eye contact, posture, the position of arms and legs, attitude, gestures, physical distance, voice intonations, and facial expressions. Like most things, practice makes perfect. If you question your non-verbal skills, you can practice with a mirror or make videotapes of yourself.

Establishing new social relationships begins with your initial conversation. Begin by paying a compliment or making a positive observation. All can be positive introductions and a comfortable starting point. Remember to talk about neutral subjects, and don't talk too much. The best compliment you can pay another is to be a great listener. If comfortable, disclose your personal information; however, try not to get too personal too quickly.

To extend a conversation without being a question machine, you can ask things like, what do you like? Tell me about your . . .? How did you . . .? How long have you . . .? What are your plans for . . .? Stay away from controversial and inflammatory comments, especially politics and religion. Remember to wear a smile, maintain eye contact and remain at a comfortable distance.

When appropriate, gracefully end the conversation and express your desire to continue again at a later time. If starting and maintaining conversations is difficult, join a support group, and develop your skills in a comfortable and secure environment. Be aware that different social and cultural skills are required for various ethnic contexts. Casual interactions are very different than those in professional or business relationships. Also, be reminded that social skills can be taught, practiced, and learned, so start practicing as soon as you can. A mirror or recorder are great tools. If shy or fearful, consider joining Toastmasters International.

Many sociologists believe that S.I.Q. is more important than standard academic intelligence. Psychologist Dr. Edward Thorndike coined the original definition of Social Intelligence (S.I.Q.) in 1920. He related it to the ability to understand and expand human relations. Today the generic definition of S.I.Q. is a person's competence in relating appropriately and successfully with others. It applies to all interactions and collaborations with family, business associates, friends, neighbors, colleagues, and the general public.

It is essential to point out that high social aptitude is not limited merely to the ability to interact successfully, but also includes the ability to process the information being shared with clarity, preciseness, and understanding. The keys to these skills include at least the following: having situational awareness, active presence, a genuine personal connection, authenticity, clarity, and empathy. Social intelligence should also include good judgment, responsibility, insight, flexibility, and integrity.

The key elements of social intelligence are either taught or learned in everyday social contexts. Instruction, exposure, practice, feedback, more practice, and more exposure allow for your inculcation of these major ingredients.

S.I.Q. is the culmination of good character traits taught by parents, relatives, teachers, mentors, authority figures, clergy, neighbors, and friends. Through modeling, direct instruction, and practice, you will learn to be socially successful. These experiences will teach you the difference between acceptable and unacceptable social behaviors.

Complex communication is also acquired vicariously by observing others and their inter-relationships. Finally, thinking before speaking allows you to censor your words to achieve maximum social benefit.

The bottom line is that your best personal experiences and job insurance require a reasonably high S.I.Q. It includes the ability to understand others, maintain sensitivity to individual differences, respect others' feelings, and provide clarity in all social interactions. Having people skills by getting along well with others, developing cooperation, and respecting individual differences are the keystones to S.I.Q. Unless you are a hermit, no one is exempt from the daily challenge of social relationships.

You can find socialization in books of etiquette, but it need not be stiff and formal. Cheerfulness and effective acculturation need only be appropriate and sincere. It requires empathy and the ability to delay verbal impulses. It includes courtesies, cooperation, honesty, and sharing. Maintain an understanding that others are always equal and need to be given your due respect.

So, surround yourself with people who provide cheerfulness, support, inspiration, and intellectual challenge. All will promote a rich relationship that will enhance your sociability. One major study found that those who engaged with friends three or more times a week had less than a 6% chance of reporting depression and social isolation. Those that interacted only every few months had twice as much risk.

We know that social support buffers stress. Researchers have found a strong correlation between relationships and one's sense of happiness. Not only do bonding relationships improve both mental and physical health, but it also extends longevity. Conversely, neuroscience research has found that being alone or living a hermit existence is fundamentally difficult because it is far more stressful.

To achieve your goals, maximize your social skills by making your interactions win-win. Be kind and encouraging, honor your promises, bite your tongue, express your thoughts with clarity and brevity, make good eye contact, and exude a positive attitude. Be sensitive to the fact that everyone is different, and some may be experiencing temporary pain. Be yourself, do your best, and chuck the rest.

THE ENGINE
THAT COULD

One of my first childhood disappointments was my inability to qualify for Little League. During the late '40s, a Saturday Little League try-out included catching ground balls, fly balls, throwing, and batting. It was merely a pass/fail; you either qualified for the spaces available, or you went home with the hope that you might be eligible the following year. I didn't make the cut and was crestfallen. After a few sobs, I was more determined than ever that I'd be ready next spring. I practiced in the rain, snow, and sleet, and the following spring, I was ready! As my reward, I was recruited to the New York Yankees Little League Team. What a prize, being part of my friend Bill Jackson's team, managed by his dad! My obsessive practice continued throughout that season. I was fortunate, my fellow players were equally motivated, and we often got together on non-game days. We won the league! That year I hit seven home runs—admittedly they had no fences, so if you got a ball past the outfielder, it was a cinch to make it home. Regardless, I was proud and happy; my persistence and perseverance had paid off. With that victory under my belt, I was on my way to duplicating my feat. I can't ever say I was born with raw talent, but I soon learned that determination would outrun untapped talent.

Later, mastering my feeble mechanical ability not only verified my prior baseball conclusion, but also propelled me to new frontiers. It was replicated many times thereafter, each resulting in a new epiphany. Probably the most earth-shocking of all occurred during my freshman year in college. Like my baseball try-out, my poor writing and grammar skills placed me in "Bonehead" English. It was a stigma that I frequently visualized as a dunce wearing a cone-shaped black hat sitting in the corner of the classroom. It was such an embarrassing black eye, then, only to be regularly reminded by my dormitory mates. Once again, the creatures of determination, like the phoenix, were resurrected. Not only did I work my way out of it, I proceeded to go on to the next two semesters of English with, well, not A's, but all above average grades. It took another fifteen years for my epiphany of having written and published my very first book. It wasn't easy, and I needed a lot of help from my peanut gallery, but it happened and is now replicated for the fifth time! Don't ever be afraid of failure. When you are handed lemons, savor the lemonade!

Persistence differs slightly from perseverance. Persistence is the ability to continue regardless of success or failure. Perseverance is the ability to meet obstacles and failure, continuing to move forward, using these setbacks to create additional motivation. Both are wonderful tools that can maximize your talents and skills and enhance your journey.

Dr. Benjamin Bloom, a distinguished educational researcher from the University of Chicago, researched top artists, athletes, and recognized scholars. His data defied the expected. Most people predicted that those with natural gifts were concert pianists, Olympic swimmers, sculptors, tennis players, mathematicians, and research neurologists would become the most brilliant and gifted producers. Instead, based upon anonymous interviews of top performers in each of the six fields studied, the results were eye-opening. Bloom and his researchers found that the top performers maintained their dedication, even after encountering frequent failure. A long and intensive process of encouragement, nurturing and training, persistence and perseverance were the most significant predictors of notable success, not natural gifts. Mathematicians often said they had difficulty in school and were rarely the best in their math classes. Athletes said they experienced numerous failures early in their competitions. They all admitted to repetitive practice, hard work, and intense focus.

In almost all cases, their parents played key roles, usually by fostering early exposure to learning or sports. Very few parents were themselves distinguished in the ultimate careers of their offspring. However, they recognized their children's curiosity, interest, and drive, so they allowed them to experiment, question, and investigate their areas of interest, even though it absorbed many hours. The parents emphasized hard work and competition with their children. Most notable was that their parents strongly encouraged them to do their very best at all times. However, it should be mentioned that these parents wanted their children to have very normal childhoods, even though they unselfishly spent time and money continually shuttling them to and from lessons.

All were characterized by many hours of practice and incredible tenacity and stamina, and all became highly distinguished in their careers, not just "average achievers."

PERSISTENCE

Persistence is defined as continuing to doggedly plod one's way toward an objective. This ability to sustain passionate efforts eventually will pay you huge dividends if you develop profound motivation. Many authors, artists, scientists, and scholars have credited determination as the significant factor in their notoriety. They include Thomas Edison's many thousands of attempts to invent the very first light bulb, or Michelangelo's Sistine Chapel and his incredible marble statue of "David." For the Sistine Chapel, he endured seven painful years of being held by a scaffold while painting on his back. Additional examples are almost endless.

Below are the wise words of highly-successful individuals:

> *"Our greatest weakness lies in giving up. The most certain way to succeed is always to try just one more time."*
> —*Thomas Alva Edison*

> *"Success seems to be largely a matter of hanging on after others let go."*
> —*William Feather*

If you persistently pursue quality and attempt to do your best, it is usually rewarded. Stick-to-itiveness has been one of my finest qualities. My former roommate is still surprised by my resoluteness and hell-bent attitude in further developing my writing skills. We both had the unenviable distinction of taking "Bonehead" English as freshmen at the University of San Francisco. Not only did we not receive credit for the course, but we also shared the embarrassment of being boneheads in our native language. It seems that when I'm down, I fight back by doubling and tripling my motivation and determination. I was determined to be more proficient at writing and grammar, my two weaknesses. In both cases, I was repeatedly told I lacked the innate skills to be successful. Admittedly, I only had an ordinary ability, but I became incensed and motivated rather than face defeat. It was the spark that fired the ovens of persistence, perseverance, and determination! It later took me more than ten years before my very first publication.

I am also indebted to my uncles, Al & John. Both not only shared their knowledge and mechanical skills, but also inspired me to believe that I could accomplish things I had never even dreamed possible. As I toiled under their supervision, both conveyed important lessons—do the job right the first time by using the right tools, don't be afraid to stop and ask questions, pause when frustrated, be patient, and sleep on problems you can't quite figure out. Most importantly, don't ever give up. Just keep going until the job is done right. It took me an entire summer to overhaul my 1954 Ford engine. It later took me twelve years to restore a 1930 Graham-Paige automobile. It included the restoration of the body, rumble seat, interior, and all mechanical parts, including driveline, transmission, and engine. Nothing is as motivating or tiring than having a challenging long-term goal and the unfinished closure it entails. Fired also by the determination that I had been tagged inept and unable, I doubled down and then doubled down again and again. It was a combination of those two powerful motivating energies: persistence and perseverance that finally took me over the top!

To be driven, unrelenting, and relentless, you will need to steel up your confidence, strengthen your courage, maintain your determination, engender encouragement from your mentors, and allow enthusiasm to infuse your every muscle. With those tools, you can conquer any task. You will feel internally like the King of the Mountain, inwardly smug and ebulliently successful, while you remain outwardly humble.

PERSEVERANCE

Perseverance, like persistence, is not inborn. It is a learned personal attitude. Anyone can develop it, but it involves blood, sweat, and tears. Probably the most exemplary person in American history was our 16th President, Abraham Lincoln. His rare grit and pluck eventually catapulted him into worldwide recognition and rendered him an American hero. This tall, rather homely icon suffered defeat after defeat. He failed in business several times, he was repeatedly defeated in local legislative elections, he lost several loved ones, and he suffered a nervous breakdown. Not only was he defeated in an election to become a local legislator, he was defeated in his bid to become Speaker, Elector, Congressman, Senator (twice), and Vice President. Our sixteenth president must have read and followed the advice of our sixth president, John Quincy Adams, who remarked, "Courage and perseverance have a magical talisman, before which difficulties disappear and obstacles vanish into air."

There is one more tale to share about our granddaughter, Antonia. I initially hesitated to add this story, fearful that it would sound like bravado, hokey, syrupy, or haughty, mainly because it is real and sometimes surreal. It is the epitome of persistence and perseverance. Her parents and brother had transferred to Scottsdale because of our son-in-law's work. We would visit them in Arizona almost monthly. At about age two and a half, my wife and I noted her difficulty with verbal communication. When we talked on the phone with her, she would often say, "What?" In person, she was more likely to express herself non-verbally. When we were ready to leave after a delightful weekend, she would put her head down sadly but not utter a word. We took note and continued to observe a lack of verbal facility. Fast forward to first grade, our little Antonia, with her parents and our prompting, requested that the school evaluate her. It was soon verified that our darling had significant auditory processing problems. With the school's help, her mother, a first-grade teacher, and my special education teacher wife, she was bombarded with supportive special learning curricula.

Antonia was a perfect candidate. She was extremely cooperative, hard-working, persistent, and, yes, persevering. Almost nightly, her mother worked with her, sometimes until late hours. The schools she attended were superb. She received special resource assistance in elementary and high school. Everyone loved her and admired her work ethic, stamina, and a positive attitude. Because of it, she eventually began getting better and better grades. That feedback only not only vaulted her determination but created a momentum

I have never seen before. After high school, she was accepted to the University of Arizona and qualified for special assistance as necessary. However, by that time, she was able to wean herself from needing intensive help and only received help as required for certain classes. Emotionally, I share the miracle at the end of this rainbow. After four years and a baccalaureate degree from the School of Education, Antonia completed her studies with a perfect 4.0 grade-point average. During those four years at the university, she never received a grade lower than an A. She graduated Summa Cum Laude! On top of that, she received a California state teaching credential. She is currently doing what inspired her most, teaching elementary school children, proudly reciprocating the gifts given to her by former educators and mentors.

As both an observer and a participant, I can assure you that if you remain patient and hungry with mojo, willing to persist and persevere, you will be able to climb Mount Everest, win an Olympic medal and find an occupation that you adore. You will soon find yourself in the fast lane.

"Time is the totality of LIFE."

—*Anonymous*

THE MOST VALUABLE NATURAL RESOURCE

As a youngster, one of my most puzzling and frustrating issues was time. It seemed like it was always working against me. It was time to go to bed, to get up, straighten up, wash your hands, eat, go to school, come home, come in.

When I saw the movie *Alice in Wonderland,* the puzzle was partially solved, but the frustration lingered. The strident announcement by the White Rabbit, "I'm late, I'm late for a very important date," languished in my ears for hours. I was betwixt and between the Mad Hatter, nutty as a fruitcake, a raving lunatic, and the mysterious White Rabbit who was hysterically obsessed and neurotic. I was able to relate to the words, but my internal sensations were filled with fear and anxiety. Eventually, I discovered that time was either my savior and saint or my nemesis, the Prince of Darkness. It could be my ladder to freedom or my staircase to despair. I remained perplexed by it because there was never enough, too much, or the world was staying still.

We are all born with a finite amount of time.

No one knows when it will end, only of its beginning.

There is no commodity more valuable than time. Unlike any other natural resource, it cannot be controlled, bought, or sold; it cannot be reproduced or changed. It is a constant that has no controls. It is indeed irrecoverable. You can continue your journey as long as time is your ally. Mishaps and wrong turns can be corrected, while time lost is forever gone, never to be returned.

Each day you have the same amount of time as everyone else in the world. How you choose to use each precious moment is purely your sole decision. As your journey continues, you will magically discover that each decision you make will solve the frustrating problem. The fact remains, each of us has the very same 24 hours each day.

Many people have equated time to a gift of money, or an hourglass of sand, or a bank of saved funds, or a jar of marbles. Each metaphor points out the finite amount we possess, and the wisdom needed to extract optimal benefits from this unique resource.

The following metaphors represent a gift, your 86,400 seconds in each day. How you spend this gift of time depends on you. You can wisely expend it with prudence and good judgment or waste it like drunken gamblers.

This story was written by Jeff Davis, who was listening on his ham radio one Saturday morning and heard the voice of K9NZO say: "You see, I sat down one day and did a little arithmetic. The average person lives for about 75 years. I know some live more, and some live less, but on average, folks live about 75 years. Then, I multiplied 75 times 52 when I came up with 3900, which is the number of Saturdays that the average person has in his entire life. It took me until I was 55 years old to think about all this in any detail. By that time, I had lived through over 2,800 Saturdays. I got to thinking that if I lived to be 75, I only had about 1,000 of them left to enjoy. So I went to a toy store and bought every single marble they had. I ended up visiting three toy stores to round up 1,000 marbles. Every Saturday since then, I've taken one marble out and thrown it away. By watching the marbles diminish, I found that I focused more on the really important things in life. There is nothing like watching your time here on this earth run out to help get your priorities straight. Now, let me tell you one last thing before I sign off and take my lovely wife out for breakfast. This morning I took the very last marble out of the container. I figure if I make it until next Saturday, I have been blessed with a little extra time to be with my loved ones. It was nice to talk with you, Tom. I hope you get to spend more hours with your loved ones, and I hope to meet you again someday. Have a good morning!"

Tom had listened intently to the message. He had planned to do some work that morning but instead went upstairs and woke his wife up with a kiss. "Come on, honey, I'm taking you and the kids to breakfast. Hey, can we stop at a toy store while we are out? I need to buy some marbles."

Every day is a gift; make it count!

Another unknown author had written about a very special prize. It was found in Bear Bryant's wallet after his death in 1982. Bryant, the most famous of all football coaches at the University of Alabama, said:

"Imagine that you had just won the following prize in a contest: Each morning, your bank would deposit $86,400 in your private account for your personal use. However, the prize had some rules. The rules included everything you didn't spend during each day would be taken away from you. You may not transfer money into some other account. You may only spend it. It's important to know that the bank can end the game without warning; at any time, it can say, "Game Over!" It can close your account forever!

"What would you do if you had money left over on any particular day? You could buy anything and everything you wanted, not only for yourself but for loved ones as well. Even for people, you don't know because you couldn't possibly spend it all on yourself, right? You would try to spend every penny and use it all because you knew it would be replenished the following morning, right?

"This game is real! Shocked? Yes! Each of us is already the winner of this prize. The prize is time. Each morning we awaken to receive 86,400 seconds as a gift of life. And, when we go to sleep, any funds remaining are lost forever. What we haven't used up that day is forever lost. Yesterday is gone, never to be regained. Each morning the account is refilled, but the bank can dissolve your account without warning! So, what will you do with your 86,400 seconds? Think about it and remember to enjoy every second of your life because time races by so much quicker than you think. Take care of yourself, be happy, love deeply, and enjoy life! Here's wishing you a wonderful and beautiful day. Start spending and remember not to complain about growing old. Some people never get that privilege."

I'm not suggesting that you rush through life overworking and becoming a workaholic. It simply means the planning and judicious use of your time. Certainly, work, fun, relaxation, adequate sleep, and genuine respect for time are important. Don't take them for granted. And, as mentioned earlier, your life's journey will provide plenty of bumps and obstacles. You will have great days and bad days. Yet, it is so wonderful to be on the right side of the green, surrounded by relationships and conversations! Life is precious, and knowing that, if you only had three months to live, you'd recognize that life is indeed glorious. Yes, life is like an hourglass. Each day, grains of sand pass through its neck. Treat every day as a very special gift, as Carl

Sandburg suggested, "Time is a sandpile we run our fingers in." It doesn't matter what you're doing at that moment; the sand slowly continues to pass, one grain at a time. You solely determine the true value of time. The fleeting moments, days, and years can be respected and appreciated or defecated into darkness.

THE VALUE OF TIME

The value of time is priceless. As mentioned, it is your gift of life. Yes, finite, but worth spending as wisely as possible. It takes most individuals many years to understand and appreciate the gift. Being aware that we are all on temporary loan and have no control over this, it must be judiciously and carefully managed. We are simply provided free rent until our lease runs out.

Most importantly, until you begin to value yourself, you will be unable to value your time. The clock of life is set only once to live, love, and enjoy until the final bell ends it all. Your allotted time is the most important and the most valuable possession you will ever be given. I will never forget the immortal words of Mrs. Davidson, my sixth-grade teacher. At the first report card review, she told my parents, "Anthony is definitely college material, but I'm finding that his biggest problem that may work against him is that he wastes a lot of time in class." Then, for the remainder of the year, perhaps with my parents' encouragement and regular reminders, "Anthony, you're wasting time . . ." To this day, I reflect on those words. If I feel my day is proceeding unproductively, Mrs. Davidson's memorable words ring in my ears, with my internal voice abruptly evoking, "Yes, damn it, she was right!"

Remember that every day can either be taken for granted, or you can give it all you've got. What should be feared is not the next 24 hours, but what you will do during those gifted hours. Reaching for and doing your best is far more beneficial than selfishly letting it go with minimal interest or effort. Never put off living your best every sunrise. Don't allow yesterday or the fear of tomorrow to affect your today. You will need to guard your every moment before it becomes your vacant past.

Being conscious of each minute, each hour, and each precious day keeps them from slithering away. You may not control the never-ending ticking, but you are still the only person who can control your use of every second. You will only remain the pilot of your journey as long as your clock continues ticking.

Personal relationships take time to gain and even more to maintain. Very serious relationships take far more time. Love at first sight may be a first impression and a major moment, but it may simply be an infatuating attraction. More exposure is required for love to truly magnify and conquer. It is both the most inexplicable and intangible natural resource of all. Spending time with those you dearly love and care about is the best use of this special gift.

Time is indeed the miracle of life. Without it, there is eternal darkness. The miracle of life begins with the ecstasy of birth. It is the magical moment of indescribable emotions of joy and fulfillment. The ultimate purpose of creation is the start of a new life clock and the mysterious miracles of a new beginning.

THE TIME TRAP

As a young rambunctious child, I was frequently reminded that "patience is a virtue." It took decades for that thought to sink in and make sense. Also, I was similarly reminded that "haste makes waste." It didn't take long to understand my haste. It took much longer to slow down and avoid unnecessary mistakes. Certainly, patience and better planning are required for ultimate success and happiness. My learning curve resulted in many false starts, frequent cleanups, and regular discouragements. I was a slow learner. Perhaps you will learn from my mistakes. I can never forget the immortal and paradoxical words of Uncle Al, "When I go slow and take my time, the job goes faster." He assisted many in making his behavior a model and a personal life lesson. Ultimately, with time and experience, his approach to tasks became a proven fact. Uncle Al may have been slow, but he seldom made mistakes. I eventually saw this wonderful human tortoise as surprisingly far more efficient than anyone else I've ever known.

Time demands patience. Rushing does not allow you to think and plan. Haste truly does make waste! Hurrying is almost sure to cause you multiple mistakes. Quality seldom results from a rushed, frenetic environment. Good things take time. Dealing maturely with it is like pregnancy; both require supreme patience.

Who can forget the frantic White Rabbit in Alice in Wonderland, or his incessant chant, "I'm late, I'm late, for a very important date." Yes, we Americans seem to lead very busy lives, filled with the hustle and bustle and now fueled by rapid technological "timesavers." Everyone is busy, so very busy! If not texting, it is cell-phoning, video gaming, or multitasking while fighting commuter traffic. We are all so crazy busy! Personal contacts, visits to family, neighbors, or friends, even holidays need to be rationed and carefully planned, often months in advance, to avoid conflicts. Few people want to live this way, but it has become a mutually-dependent means of living. Offices, busses, trains, and airplanes are replete with laptops, cell phones, tablets, or other electronic devices. They often interfere with genuine human contact. We often hear "time is money." Somehow, we have let materialism often interfere with real living. Time is life, and life is priceless! All of us have only a finite amount of it.

Since my quasi-retirement, I often wonder how I ever had the time to work ten hours a day. We all are in the same glue, and it is indeed a sticky problem. I'm amazed at my grandchildren and their schedules:

dance lessons, gymnastics, softball, soccer, special summer camps, spirit practice, scouting, music lessons, performances, etc. It makes me tired, just thinking about
it. Thank goodness, as a parent, all I can remember is
the fun of taking them to sports events, swimming,
dance lessons, gymnastics, a hobby, a monthly Indian
guide/princess meeting. The rest of the time, other
than chores, they were free to play, ride bikes, and visit
with friends. Playdates, what were those? When I was a
youngster, after chores all I knew was to make sure to
be back by sundown. Many choices taught me how to
plan and use my precious moments. I learned to guard
it like a junkyard dog. I commend parents for their
worthwhile pursuits, especially community service, but
it tires me thinking about keeping up with this regimen.
When asked, most people are not only busy; they feel
anxious or guilty when they are not working or doing
something constructive.

I make every attempt to remain without guilt and
unmolested by too many obligations. Sometimes I'm
even successful! When sticky scheduling problems arise,
I attempt to avoid making impulsive decisions, but usually only delay them temporarily. Somehow, I deny their
existence so I can sleep on them. This allows an opportunity to clarify, digest, and invite my subconscious to
provide a solution. It often feels fresh and best the next
morning. They can usually wait until I'm ready. Some
problems go away with time; others can wait until they
have been ripened by rationality. What could be more

important than writing a book that touches every nerve and funny bone, rather than dealing with one's mundane obligations? Occasionally I reminisce about my childhood, when my free time was replete: surfing my set of encyclopedias, reading comic books, making snowmen and snowballs, or playing cowboys and Indians. It was fun, spontaneous, and very relaxing. Some idleness is indispensable and as important as breathing. Why get your muscles taut and spastic? Why not relax, smell the coffee, and focus on the worthwhile. Paradoxically, taking breathers is necessary for completing any job.

Allow your creative spirit to rise above life's stressors, so that inspiration can both endure and multiply. The greatest of man's creations, interventions, technological developments, and masterpieces were accomplished by creative accidents, usually in an open, relaxed, and friendly environment. It's important to set a good example for families and friends by scheduling periodic mental health breaks, such as watching a sports event, having lunch, or a small party. It's fun as well as intimate human contact. And most importantly, short breaks provide for the maintenance of extremely worthwhile relationships. It is indeed a wise, not wasted use of time.

At age 78, I'm currently a relaxation junkie, taking naps, having lunch or dinner with friends, going to movies, playing bocce ball, or having a pleasant phone conversation with a relative or friend. If a friend calls and wants to get together for wine or snacks or visit a local exhibition or museum, the answer is usually a resounding yes!

Time is life, and it is indeed short.

Life is to be shared and enjoyed with others.

If my wife wants to go wine tasting in Napa, take a cruise, visit distant relatives, we pool our funds and do it. There's no time like the present—who knows what lies ahead? So, make it possible before it becomes impossible. Who knows how many marbles are left inside the jar? Seldom do we lie around for hours watching TV or just doing nothing. Walking or exercise, usually with others, by far trumps passive do-nothingness. However, having private alone time is important to recharge my batteries; by meditating, reading, writing, imagining, or quietly saying thank you while staring at Mother Nature's creations. Yes, I'm a sinner, too. I do get up early each morning to check my emails. I cull them to avoid excess and then send the special ones to my friends to be re-shared. And, yes, as a sinner, I do call my mother while driving and talking. It is usually hands-free; regardless, it's my mother! I'm reluctant to share any more of my other transgressions.

CRAZY BUSY

The scarcity of time reminds me of our recent four-year drought in California. Circumstances forced people to rethink their extravagant water use, just as the shortage of time forces you to rethink its extravagant waste. In addition, it also allows you to examine your priorities. Psychologists, sociologists, and physicians remain worried that our overly-busy schedules have undermined and caused many recent health problems. The feelings of constant rush contribute to both work and family stress. Many professionals feel that anxiety and depression are the major causes of modern disease and disability. Certainly, it causes sick day absences, job dissatisfaction, and disability claims. The cost to businesses results in many billions of dollars of wasted money. All of the various artificial reasons to be in a hurry create a constant obsession to find more things to fill one's day. Slow down, remember that life is short.

Yes, crazy busy! Yet, it's not what most people want in their lives. In contemporary society, parents working, meetings, long work hours, being on call are all commonly rampant in our 21st Century. Most of us accept it, yet it is mostly self-imposed. We have great difficulty saying no, so we fill our calendars with excessive obligations. It's almost like an addiction, not allowing free time, yet feeling driven to fill every slot available. Activities with friends and neighbors are choreographed, very similar to the play dates set for children. Even the latchkey kids of our previous generation had several hours after school to unwind and pursue spontaneous activities. Spontaneity is now being replaced by a rigid structure, usually a carefully assigned agenda added to a phone or electronic calendar. Little room is left for relaxing in between. It's no surprise that people want to escape, either physically or mentally. Post-traumatic stress, drug abuse, anxiety, and depression are increasing almost exponentially. Our frantic escape behavior is often a result of being crazy busy, fear, and the avoidance of loneliness. However, the current pandemic has helped folks change their minds and lives by rethinking the concept of "crazy busy."

On the contrary, now that I'm retired, I've earned the classification as the proud member of the "Purgatory of the Lackadaisical and Idle." Unfortunately, it has taken many mistaken years to reach some balance in life. I go to bed at a reasonable hour, exercise every day, refuse to talk on the phone until I feel like it, visit or have lunch with friends and relatives, regularly share worthwhile email articles or jokes, take naps, often leave my cell phone at home, enjoy taking trips, running errands, or writing parts of a chapter only when motivated and inspired. I control the pace of my day unless I need to help or volunteer help to friends or family. Woven throughout this book, it is clear that my ultimate goal is to focus my time and full attention on those closest to me, those I love and cherish. And perhaps by sharing my thoughts, experiences, ideas, and feelings, I might inspire some others that life need not be frantically frenetic.

During my college years, I worked at the American Can Company. At my first real job, I frequently witnessed a number of workers virtually "killing time." I have never been able to understand that type of mentality. Why would grown men simply stand around and enjoy doing nothing? Most people, including myself, find waiting and idleness a waste of precious moments. Both are unproductive, aimless, and worthless expenditures that devalue time. I especially dislike standing in line or traffic. It can be very frustrating. It took years to discover that waiting is a solemn gift. And being worried about waiting adds even more stress. I eventually became convinced that dead time could be used in many productive ways. In the past 20 years, I seldom forget to bring a folder of reading material. For example, when I'm waiting in the doctor's office, it may be a vocabulary folder from my Italian class; or health letters from various medical universities, or an article from a periodical, or a short story, or a bundle of collected jokes and quips. The wait goes by quickly during those windfall moments, plus I've learned something new. Realizing that is a gift of time. A mental attitude that can replace frustration or boredom.

Time is so precious.

Why waste it?

TIME WASTERS

There are many ways to waste time. They include multitasking, procrastination, failure to plan, lack of motivation, distractions, anger, tardiness, boredom, irresponsibility, perfectionism, obsessions, and wishful thinking, such as "if only," complaining, living in the past, equivocating, etc.

One of the most common time wasters is attempting to do too many things at once. It is frequently referred to as multitasking. It causes a person to go in different directions simultaneously, thus diluting the major task at hand. Multitasking simply adds insult to injury by piling on additional tasks, adding new problems, making more mistakes, added frustration, distractions, and more unexpected decisions. The stress is sometimes unbearable because it overburdens and overwhelms even the most capable. We all know that progress demands patience and a willingness to proceed one step at a time with focused attention. Rome certainly wasn't built in a day. It took many years, progressing from one brick or column. Similarly, a house demands a foundation, followed by the placement of each piece of lumber.

Another time waster is procrastination. Projects that can be easily postponed usually are. Allowing time to slip away because you are distracted by side issues takes your focus away from the present. Not being adequately prepared, not having the correct tools, and becoming angry with your tools delays and often stops your progress. Relaxing and taking breaks are necessary for completing tasks. But continued procrastination simply avoids the present and finds excuses to delay and deny moving forward. Avoid putting off things when they can be accomplished today. Beginning a project, rather than delaying it, eventually begets closure. Once you are able to start, your desire and motivation will be sparked, thus providing the momentum for ultimate completion.

I had a cousin whose elderly wife developed cancer and eventually succumbed to it. Unfortunately, many of her desires, particularly travel, were unfulfilled. During visits to his home or hospital, my cousin would repeatedly say, "If only I had . . . If only we had . . ." He was financially well-off and could do all these things he wished "if only." His wife often suggested her bucket list, but he just couldn't take himself away from his daily duties. His wife died, but the "only ifs" continued. It's sad to see healthy people avoid the mutual pleasures that sustain intimate relationships. Remember, it's never too late to do the right thing, even if it means compromising your daily schedule to bring satisfaction to the most important person in your life. Don't spend your life living, "If only I had . . ." or under the tag name of "I wish I could have . . ." Learn from others' mistakes; it's a huge timesaver!

Lacking motivation, also commonly known as laziness, can be an additional time waster. If you lack motivation and feel tired or incapable of moving forward, your lack of confidence soon destroys your attempts toward purposeful action. Thus, when you waste time, you degrade yourself, add additional stress, and delay your progress. It is necessary to rest, relax, and restart as soon as you feel tired, frustrated, or distracted, and then you will be able to restart your engine and proceed at full speed ahead.

Some people are perennially late. They are either unaware of time, unable to plan, or insensitive to others who must wait for their dalliance. This can cause frustration for those waiting and may mean missing the curtain go up. Regardless, it is another time waster as well as potentially socially gauche.

Anger and animosity are also major wastes of time. When you become angry, you are no longer able to truly focus because your limbic system is set into high gear, and emotions soon destroy patience and rationality. When you begin to take out your anger on your tools, it's time to quit. Deciding to take temporary detours can postpone a project and allow us to restart refreshed and eager to continue. For many years, when I was frustrated or angry at someone, I would take a temporary detour. I would go jogging or get under one of my old cars and crank away! Once I burned off my frustration and anger, I could settle down and return, fresh, motivated, and with renewed enthusiasm. There were many occasions during the jogging or cranking that I would realize what part of the problem caused my anger. Often, I would understand that I was part of the equation. Sometimes it was forgiveness and an apology. Other times it was getting a good night's sleep. With help from my subconscious, I was usually able to achieve relief and problem resolution.

Being mired in the past is yet another major time consumer. It often results in unfulfilled hopes and desires. Living your life in reverse accomplishes nothing.

Living in the past and allowing it to impact your present only produces chaos and regrets. Instead, learn from your past transgressions, and replace them with revised strategies that move forward, not backward. The weight of yesterday does not need to be carried into today's fray. These reflections of your past can place you in an imaginative dream world that creates a major waste of your time. However, fantasizing and daydreaming can sometimes be a pleasant temporary pause and a beneficial break from reality. But, spending excessive time dwelling on unfulfilled dreams or wishing, "if only I . . ." are disruptive time wasters. The "wishbone" is only meant for hapless romantics!

Living in the past not only will date you but often makes you a bore. Your relatives, close friends, and associates will find you not just dull, but an anachronism not unlike an extinct dinosaur. Enjoy the excitement of today. The past serves no further purpose other than reminding you not to repeat it. Bury it!

A more detailed account of TIME MANAGEMENT & TIME-SAVING STRATEGIES is available by going to https://www.drtonycedolini.com/time-management

WE ARE FAMILY

For years, I have thought long and hard, trying to determine the one human rule that reigns over all others. Again and again, I come full circle. Perhaps the shortest and simplest is the Golden Rule, "Do onto others as you would have them do unto you." It remains the only truly universal truth necessary for peace and civility.

Together, we could eliminate irrational anger, enemies, and wars.

Indeed, on Earth, we are all family. No matter what your beliefs, religious, political, or scientific, we are all family. Barry Commoner said that the first law of ecology is that everything is related to everything else. Either we work together by combining our forces, or we work against ourselves and cancel our energies. Cooperation and commitment to humankind foster the concept, We either sink or swim together. We either celebrate our mutual success or capitulate by eliminating each other.

As I look around, I see constant conflict, divisiveness and stalemates, whether it is our own Congress, the current conflicts in the Middle East, or the insidious division in our country and the countries represented by the United Nations. Why can't we agree with the fact that we are all family? Isn't the Golden rule still golden? Aren't Dr. King's simple words, "We must learn to live together as brothers or perish together as fools," sufficient to claim us as one world, rather than factions and fractions of a dysfunctional family? These power struggles are like a rocking chair: it gives you something to do, but it gets you nowhere. Coming together is the beginning, remaining together is progress, and cooperating is the ultimate success. I recognize that you may judge my thoughts as pie in the sky, an idealistic Utopian vision. Admittedly, they are idealistic, but the survival of humanity lies in the balance.

Perhaps the words of others may help convey the same basic message. Let's first look back millennia and then chronologically follow their wisdom through the ages.

Since the beginning of time, almost all cultures developed their own sets of Golden rules. Each culture and religion had its individualized interpretation of acceptable behavior. It was stated in biblical times: "Do onto others as you would have them do unto you." Generally, it was accepted that if individuals treated others with courtesy and respect, they, in turn, would reciprocate with equally positive actions. Thus, if followed, you could be ensured a peaceful world.

Unfortunately, as time passed and populations grew, conflicting amendments were added. For example, the phrase, "An eye for an eye, a tooth for a tooth." In other words, if you happen to be a nonbeliever or critic of the current cult, you might be subject to even more severe consequences such as punishment or death. As cultures continued to emerge, disparate interpretations abounded. Each new twist contained a new caveat. Although almost everyone would agree with the Golden Rule's original spirit, not everyone's actions followed its basic tenets. Unfortunately, there is a sociological truism that seems to apply. "The longer an organization exists, the further it gets from its original purpose." This certainly applies to religions, politics, social orders, forms of government, economies, and ideologies. Regardless, human survival requires a simple agreed-upon creed for humankind to follow to gain and maintain long-term peace and happiness.

The Golden Rule is the epitome of wisdom. If there is one principle that you should incorporate into your daily life, it is treating others as you would prefer to be treated. Just as your body and your mind need exercise each day, your social conscience needs exercise as well. If replicated universally, it would create world peace. It may sound idealistic but think of a world that operated on this very simple premise.

Ruth Benedict, noted anthropologist, was intrigued by the differences in cultures. She sought to uncover the civilizations that flourished, as opposed to those that failed. She found that the people that thrived were those who understood the concept of cooperation and mutuality. Working toward a common good is far superior to working against one another. She concluded that high synergy societies had more creativity, productivity, and longevity. It is no surprise that the longest uninterrupted and most successful democratic republic was The Republic of Venice. It lasted over 1,100 years. The Republic of Venice was based on the democratic principle of restricted terms for all offices, top to bottom, chosen by representatives of the entire community. It was also predicated on synergy, creativity, mutual responsibility, cooperation, and shared productivity. These principles avoided corruption and undue influence. R. Buckminster Fuller, world-renowned for his synergistic designs, said that Spaceship Earth rests upon the mastery of synergistic effectiveness of all humanity.

Certainly, by working together, we can celebrate each other's successes as well as our own. Many spiritual leaders have proclaimed the same. And many of our generals, statesmen, and presidents have shared their thoughts on cooperation and synergy.

> *"Unity is the great need of the hour, and if we are united we can get many of the things that we not only desire but which we justly deserve."*
> —*Martin Luther King, Jr.*

Everyone is connected to this planet and part of our one big family. We all live in a village and are responsible for our own immediate family. In turn, we are accountable for our village, and it is responsible for the broader citizenry community. If each of us cooperates, and families cooperate with their community, we can ultimately solve many of our world's problems. By combining forces with the population at large, we can accomplish incredible things.

You must realize that your actions alone can have a domino effect that can spread widely, perhaps even globally. Unity is indeed necessary because there is power in numbers. Each act of kindness brings comfort to others, and this chain effect multiplies exponentially.

Realizing that there is strength in numbers, you need to make conscious decisions to join with others for your common good. One voice added to another's voice will develop the sound of a nuclear explosion and may perhaps be more powerful. Adding, not canceling; multiplying rather than dividing; larger numbers, willing to join hands, will overcome the biggest of Goliaths.

The peace and happiness of future generations require your courage and cooperative action.

To achieve peace and happiness, you must recognize and respect individual differences in countries, cultures, races, religions, political beliefs, ethnicity, and individuals. It is both your right and your obligation. You cannot possibly expect that we should all be the same, nor would it be even remotely desirable. If you truly believe in justice and equality for all, you must understand that it is not just another banal bromide or trite cliché. Respecting differences is necessary for humankind's survival.

I cannot forget my childhood fascination with Abbott and Costello. They remain famous for two parodies that will forever live in my memory as insightful and illuminating. Both men were gifted humorists. The parody below is considered a true American classic. It exemplifies the paradoxical and sends an unmistakable message.

EVERYBODY, SOMEBODY, ANYBODY, AND NOBODY

"This is a story about four people named Everybody, Somebody, Anybody, and Nobody. There was an important job to be done, and Everybody was sure Somebody would do it. Anybody could have done it. But Nobody did it. Somebody got angry about that, because it was Everybody's job. Everybody thought Anybody could do it. But Nobody realized that Everybody wouldn't do it. It ended up that Everybody blamed Somebody when Nobody did what Anybody could have done."

I would also like to share a brilliant reply from Mahatma Gandhi when he was asked by a reporter, "What do you think of Western Civilization?" His response was, "I think it would be a good idea."

I choose to end this book with a powerful story, which I paraphrased from Robert Fulghum's book, *MAYBE (Maybe not)*. It is one of the most compelling stories I have ever read. The story is centered on what the author called the myth of the impossible dream. He strongly advocated, "When we cease believing this, the music will surely stop. The myth of the impossible dream is more powerful than all the facts of history." It is an insightful and heart-rendering tale. I encourage you to read and re-read it. It will be your final homework. Hopefully, you will pass the baton to your world-mates. As the author suggests, you will never regret or apologize for the belief that you, and you, alone, can successfully share this charge with your brethren. The world needs to stop what it is doing and hear the music. It will be more powerful than anything humankind could conceive or create. Read on: (excerpted and edited from *Maybe (Maybe Not).*

In the year 2050, in a large Eastern European city, at a central square, there remains a bronze statue. It does not represent a soldier, politician, general, scientist, or decorated war hero. It is a statue of an unknown musician playing his cello. This cellist is their national hero. This original story occurred during a civil war there when hatred and polarization were at their peak. No one was either safe or immune. Anyone disfavored due to a different religion, ethnicity, skin color, or political party, were maimed or killed. Soon everyone was an enemy of everyone else. Old or young, male or female, strong or weak, those that didn't die were treated like animals in the ruins of what was once a beautiful city. All except one man; a cellist. He came each day to a particular street corner, dressed in formal black evening attire, and sat in a charred chair, playing his cello. He knew that at any time, he might be beaten or shot. Yet, for 22 days straight, he played his music. As it turned out, his music was stronger than hate, mightier than fear, and filled with courage and confidence. As time passed, other musicians, inspired by his spirit, eventually took their instruments and sat beside him. His courage became so contagious that anyone who could play a musical instrument found their place near him. After 22 days, the hate and fighting stopped.

It's a nice story, and inspirational, unfortunately our world hasn't been able to work this way.

Many might assume that music would have little effect on rage, hate, and wars in our real world. However, Vedran Smailovic disagreed. In a New York Times magazine dated July 1992, his photo appeared in Sarajevo, in front of a bakery where bullets and mortars were raging. At that site, 22 people had been killed in late May 1992, waiting for bread. And there was Vedran playing his cello. Unfortunately, history reports this was not new to Sarajevo; this city dealt with hate, rage, and war for centuries. Yet, for 22 days, Vedran braved bullets and mortar rounds to play Albinoni's profoundly moving Adagio in G Minor. He had constructed his music from a manuscript fragment found in the ruins of Dresden after WWII. For some unknown reason, the music had survived the fire-bombing and complete devastation of Dresden.

What he did was true; it was real! Neither the bread-line, mortar shells, nor bullets are fiction. It was the heroic act of an ordinary citizen.

Yes, unexpected miracles that overcome tyranny and evil do occur.

Somehow music was triumphant over the horrors and ravages of war. Was the madness of this man playing his cello able to quell the bombs and bullets? This Pied Piper was not calling out the rats that infested the city. No, he was addressing the rats which infested the human spirit of Sarajevo. Vedran Smailovic was a very real man who changed history! He did it with the only possession he had, his beloved cello.

His informal shrine is a place of honor among Serbs, Croats, Muslims, and Christians alike. They all recognize his name, face, and fame. They, regardless of religion or ethnicity, place bouquets where he once played. It is with great hope that humanity emulates Vedran and overcomes tyranny and war. TV, newspapers, and the public have come to commemorate Vedran Smailovic, his music, courage, and passion for peace and brotherhood. Millions have read about him.

Who among us can say that world peace cannot be realized? The impossible dream is real, and you and others can change history. As Robert Fulghum suggested, "In my imagination, I lay flowers at the statue memorializing Vedran Smailovic, a monument yet to be built, but may be." Meanwhile, in his place of honor, a cellist plays in the streets of Sarajevo.

I implore you to share Vedran's deeds with others and keep his spirit and the spirit of unity and peace alive.

May the music play on.

"If you do not take an interest in the affairs of your government, then you are doomed to live under the rule of fools."

—Plato

FREEDOM NOT TAKEN FOR GRANTED

Never in my lifetime had I witnessed more chaos and more dysfunction than I have in the years both preceding and including 2020. Corruption and chaos have become ubiquitous in government, politics, and financial markets. It has come in the form of prejudice, greed, racism, polarity, and extreme capitalism. Consequently, our society encountered an untold degree of stress from the leaders of government, finance, and our political system. Quite frankly, I believe that the many red flags I witnessed in this chaotic and corrupt environment spurred me on to write this book and specifically this chapter. Initially intended for my family and close friends, it became incumbent upon me to share my thoughts, observations, and historical precedents with you, my worldly brothers and sisters.

Born in the outskirts of a small city among striving middle-class, second-generation immigrants, sprinkled with scattered farms, I grew up in a predominantly multi-ethnic congenial community and attended Catholic grade schools, high school, and eventually a Jesuit University. As a child, I was generally easy-going, notably compliant, non-obtrusive, but very curious, and frequently rambunctious. When I reached preadolescence, I developed a skeptical and even more pronounced curiosity combined with a questioning mentality. I usually needed far more answers than those provided. At that time, a Google search was not available or even remotely conceived of. I relied on my set of encyclopedias, school learning, libraries, and periodicals. I particularly questioned the rigidity of religious and governance beliefs. Because of my parochial thinking, I honestly didn't quite understand how corruption should restrict my freedom and independence.

I vaguely perceived corruption and dysfunction but could not put my finger on it. I watched and listened during my younger years but could not comprehend all the conflicting nuances and obscure observations. Mixed among all of these conflicts was enthusiasm for clarity. Fortunately, I was surrounded by kind and loving relatives, neighbors, friends, and role models who were far more accepting of the current conditions. It was obviously their "normal," and taken for granted.

Perhaps my most fortunate advantage was my freedom. I was able to travel on my bike, take a bus to pursue my varied interests. Unless weather conditions didn't permit, I could be off on my own to libraries, magazine racks, and newspaper stands or be with friends until dark. I was seldom questioned by retailers about my free use of their periodicals, newspapers, or books. Likewise, except for chores, my home was a free ticket to endless choices. Learning was taking place whenever the opportunity was available. I especially spent endless hours on the "throne," sitting with an encyclopedia, newspaper, or library book on my lap. As I read, there were many conflicting opinions. Yet as time passed, I began forming my ideas about politics, religion, and corruption. You might say it was full hands-on. I was beginning to recognize the consequences but not comprehending its causes. There were times I shared my new beliefs with those close to me. Needless to say, my thoughts were not always appreciated, and verbal penalties were served aplenty when I bridged counter-beliefs. Perhaps it was clairvoyance? It was the very beginning of the second-most important epiphany of my later life. For years it remained a work in progress. That is why it remains such an important task to share my thoughts.

At age sixteen, my world was transformed with a new city, fresh experiences, diverse new people, renewed adjustments, and a brand-new beginning. I was a high school senior with a new job, new friends, a non-parochial high school, and a budding future. Being a teenager, I was now dealing with an unexplored environment and dawning hormones, a mélange of myopic and prescient perceptions, refreshed *raison d'etre*, and increased responsibilities. In retrospect, I hadn't realized how insular I had become. Now I was beginning to truly understand how corruption, stereotypes, and labels could restrict one's freedom and independence. All of a sudden, I was experiencing an untried type of personal freedom. I no longer was constricted by those old labels, stereotypes, or narrow thinking. In retrospect, without realizing it, I had inculcated a false parochial belief system. I had believed myself to be less capable, smaller, and more insignificant than my real potential. In many respects, I had allowed myself to be unwittingly pigeonholed and confined to a belief system that was not only unrealistic but grossly stereotypical, one that I had previously been unable to slip out of its well-established attitudes. My former feedback and beliefs had placed me into a nice, neat box fastened by a tight-fitting ribbon. It was called the "status quo." This constrictive set of attitudes that I had unconsciously and unwittingly believed was patently fallible. It was now an opportunity for explosive epiphanies to correct the old false perceptions and replace and expand them with more realistic ones.

At that time, my mind still did not fully understand corruption, greed, politics, government, or the financial world. Each year, I would read, see, and experience more of the real world, not just my previous small parochial micro-world. Sometimes it was frightening and often difficult to finally accept the realities that truly existed. I learned that a percentage of people would consciously do anything, regardless of negative consequences, to get what they wanted. They with impunity could rationalize their transgressions as necessary for their aggrandizement.

As Sir Thomas More and Machiavelli so poignantly suggested 500 years ago, humanity's corrupters included money, property, ego, and personal power. I finally realized the value of Plato and Aristotle's thoughts and warnings. Yes, it was the same old thing, just replaced by a flock of new actors. That is why it remains such an important task to share two iconic sages of the past. They will help illuminate the potential dangers of your journey ahead.

It was an untrodden type of freedom. I was now thousands of miles away and free to think without the former influence of unrecognizable corruption, especially my narrow thinking of what in retrospect was a very constrictive set of beliefs. When I read the book "The Rochester Mob Wars" by Blair Kenny, I was shocked by the enormous level of fraudulent and unethical activity that had surrounded me in my first sixteen years. According to the author, organized crime was more prolific in Upstate New York than in any other part of our country. There were many accounts of deceit and dishonesty by judges, police officers, politicians, labor leaders, and city officials. It took the FBI, the State of New York, and a federal crime commission more than two decades to finally gain control of the massive crimes committed. Hundreds were arrested and dozens sentenced. Some were sent to very lengthy federal prison terms. Finally, clarity replaced the cloudiness of the past.

To my surprise, I recognized some of the surnames. One turned out to be a younger cousin I had lost contact with after moving to California. Fortunately—although I had a subtle suspicion of unscrupulous activity—it did not fully register at that time. Years later, another cousin visited our family and shared very intimate information. During those sixteen years in Rochester, my father, a true straight shooter, always protected us from the information he knew so very well. As my father lay on his death bed in the last few weeks, he confessed to the extensiveness of corruption he witnessed during his first forty years. He said it was corruption that motivated him to move our family to California.

No wonder my new home in San Jose offered a much less clouded environment where payoffs and clandestine backroom dealings seldom existed. Yes, local business dealings, real estate development, and city contracts had some degree of greed and dishonesty, but it was far less frequent than in my sixteen earlier years. I remain confident that our local community remains resistant to my former environment. San Jose is far worthier of approbation, whether compared to my prior home, Washington, DC, and other localities of greed, power, and financial control.

It leads me to an iconic quote worthy of sharing:

"Those who cannot remember the past are condemned to repeat it."
—George Santayana

For many years, I searched for the most idealistic locus and the most egalitarian, honest, and ethical habitat. During that search, I read a diverse array of nonfiction and metaphorical fiction. I was impressed with four significant works in college that have withstood the tests and trials of time. Chronologically the books that were head and shoulders above anything else I read were: *Il Principe* by Machiavelli (1532), *Utopia,* by Sir Thomas More (1516), and the more recent *1984,* and *Animal Farm,* both written by Eric Arthur Blair under the pen name of George Orwell.

After encountering our current dysfunctional government and political system, I decided to reread each of those books. Although written many years ago, they still offered timeless information and a better understanding of greed, corruption, and dysfunction. I want to share with you what I gleaned from both Machiavelli and Sir Thomas More. It is some of the most critical information you will need for both understanding and protection on your journey forward.

IL PRINCIPE

Machiavelli's *Il Principe,* (The Prince) is not only timeless but highly instructive, and quite frankly, on point. Written over 500 years ago, it was like reading today's political summary in our local newspaper. Machiavelli's understanding of politics was uncanny. At that time, his writing was not only innovative but the very first publication of political philosophy.

His treatise was in direct contrast to the ethics of the dominant Catholic doctrines of both that time and even current times. Machiavelli discussed the rise of governmental and religious "princes" who abused their power and justified their actions. The author dissected the politics of the day as operating on the sole premise that the end justifies the means. Whether by heredity or subjugation, monarchies and oligarchies ignored the good. Instead, they adopted corruptive means to gain and maintain their tyrannical form of government.

Machiavelli extolled the model of Republics for their ability to share and distribute power democratically and not allow foreign nations to gain influence over their government. In contrast, monarchs once in power found it easy to subjugate their citizens as servants and control their lives. He felt that monarchial bloodlines needed to be broken. He discussed the means of ending the excessive power of tyrannical princes. The same analogies were made of those who usurp power and crush their opponents. However, reforming an existing order is both difficult and dangerous. Even for those remaining subjugated, resistance to change is always formidable for fear of any new order.

Consequently, to remain in power meant death to resistors. Thus, the accumulation of more wealth to support armies and mercenaries was necessary to do the dictator's dirty work. Cunning, cruel, and immoral deeds were required to either quiet or execute dissidents to maintain power. Those despots who hesitated in their ruthlessness failed. At that time, the Medici and Borgia families were great examples of politics, especially as they related to the powerful and corrupt Vatican. Machiavelli warned that the populace needs to be aware of those like the Medici and Borgias, flatterers, and cunning in their pursuit of control. His last chapters conveyed the need for the Prince in power to be virtuous and keep his word, yet also be able to abandon those virtues when necessary to maintain control. Nor should a Prince be excessively generous, because it instills greed in his subjects and exhausts the treasury. It was far better to be a miser and be somewhat feared than overly loved. All were based on the original premise, the end always justifies the means.

Do these 500-year-old writings ring true to today's political chaos? Does it provide you with a better understanding of your current state of affairs?

I suggest that you arm yourself with as much information, knowledge, and wisdom as you can withstand. Understanding the past should help illuminate potential future dangers and arm you for the journey ahead. It will be a means of survival and provide for your successful continuation without too many abrupt stops and detours that you would have otherwise encountered.

UTOPIA

Sir Thomas More, also known as St. Thomas More, was an English statesman, lawyer, philosopher, humanist, and author. He wrote his first and most famous book, *Utopia*, in 1516. Refusing to take an oath of supremacy, loyalty, and acknowledgment of King Henry VIII as the supreme head of the Church of England, he was decapitated in 1535. Over 1,000 miles away, independently, but not coincidentally, he and Machiavelli were in sync with their intense feelings regarding the tyranny of rulers.

Utopia introduced More's strong sense of social justice. Like *The Prince*, Sir Thomas's book shared his thoughts about rulers, especially monarchs of inherited lineage. Sir Thomas was admired as a man of strict principle, a believer in fairness and justice. His Utopia was an imaginary island where individuals were respected, treated fairly, and cooperated for their common good. It resembled an ideal life that existed in many monasteries at that time.

Sir Thomas More and his fictitious Utopians abhorred the concept of property, money, tyranny, and war. They felt that not only did those concepts corrupt but also controlled the lives of the ruler's subjects. Anyone who attempted to rebel against the prince, was punished severely, usually by death or abject poverty. These despots stacked their courts with judges who enforced ancient laws that justified their actions to incarcerate or hang petty thieves. Sir Thomas More established the fact that corrupt rulers caused poverty. The minor crime such as the petty theft of bread, became the only means rulers were able to judge and imprison an unruly subject. They certainly could not empathize with the peasant's need for survival. Sir Thomas wrote, "As long as there are money and property, I cannot think that a nation can be governed fairly, happily, or justly because all will be divided among the few, the rest left miserable."

His idealistic and humanistic Utopia had fewer laws, was well-governed, and had a well-conceived Constitution, where the rewards of virtue and equality prevailed. This ideal island served the public more than the rulers by having a sincere interest in quality, modesty, balance, and humility. Utopia lacked ostentatious excess and had a rotating leadership similar to that of the Venetian Republic, the very longest of all forms of government—the only democracy to exist for 1,100 years successfully!

Sir Thomas More's ideal world of Utopians was a seminal idea of a simplistic society able to structure their existence democratically with a decentralized government made up of rotating representatives, something that our foundering fathers had envisioned. Their terms were short, thus regularly allowing the attraction of new blood, not despoiled by old hidden agendas. Utopia had no property, money, or lawyers. It required the labor of six hours per day. Property and money were eschewed as corrupters. Exchange of goods was the primary means of trade, and it substituted for money. Gold and silver were only common in pots, pans, utensils, shackles; only used for everyday functions, which diminished their need for greed, possessiveness, or value. Silk, gold chains, and fancy clothes were looked upon as ostentatious and only worn by fools. Utopians spent most free time reading and learning rather than dressing like plumed birds of prey. They studied Greek, Latin, music, logic, astronomy, weather, chemistry, religion, ethics, and the virtues of happiness. They felt that the greatest treasures were intangible, such as truth, a good conscience, virtue, and health. He described the Utopians as happy, free, cheerful, and dedicated pursuers of knowledge, something every conscientious American dreams of becoming.

Paradoxically, the practice of Utopians, such as ease of divorce, euthanasia, married and female clerics, was contrary to the Catholic Church edicts. Deep down, Sir Thomas More was a pragmatist who preferred cooperative problem-solving, justice, honesty, professional ethics, modesty, and minimalism.

I hope that these historical snippets of the past will convince you that history does indeed repeat itself, and if you allow it, you will be subjected to its reoccurrence. I strongly encourage you to take heed of the affairs of government. Otherwise, you will be doomed by the fools of déjà vu.

A detailed review of George Orwell and Michael Lewis "GOVERNANCE" is available by going to https://www.drtonycedolini.com/governance

DIGNITY AND HONOR

"Learning makes a man fit company for himself."
—*Thomas Fuller*

ENLIGHTENMENT

Learning is the foundation of knowledge, the child of teaching, and the institution of education. I find it like starting a bank account at birth and regularly making deposits. Over time, the deposits compound, and soon the numbers become exponential, yielding huge benefits and dividends. The results provide your satisfaction, gratitude, wisdom, and happiness. These daily deposits expand your mind while keeping you young, alert, and wiser. Not only does learning expand your horizons, but it also begs for more. It excites your curiosity and encourages you to seek more places to imagine and perhaps visit. Knowledge is the fuel of the mind, just as exercise and food are the fuels of your body. Obviously, like vision, gleaning information only occurs when the mind and eyes are open. It requires time and patience.

Keeping your mind open allows you to fill it with all the tools you can gather.

I was impressed by Robert Fulghum's book, *All I Really Need to Know I Learned in Kindergarten.* In retrospect, he was correct that our kindergarten teacher initiated much of our early learning. Like Fulghum, I can thank my wonderful kindergarten teacher, Mrs. Mason, for teaching me how to play fair, not hitting others, cleaning my messes, putting things back where they were initially found, saying you are sorry, washing your hands, teaching us to have balance in our life by painting, singing, playing, working, dancing, skipping, and taking a 20-minute nap! She also taught us the value of friends, sticking together, looking both ways, and helping others. In kindergarten, we also learned that animals and plants don't live forever; they all die, and so do we. Those of us who started our education with a masterful instructor like Mrs. Mason had a great start on learning and have appreciated the value of a good education.

Like your journey, obtaining wisdom will never end. As time passes and your experiences grow, it becomes evident that the more you learn, the more you realize there are infinite amounts of additional knowledge yet to be savored. You will also learn that there are many types of learning. John Wooden, probably the most successful basketball coach and teacher of sports, said, "I created eight laws of learning; namely, explanation, demonstration, imitation, repetition, repetition, repetition, repetition, and repetition." Whether it is acquiring an additional sport or mastering a new science, you must read for the explanation and digest it to move forward with success. You not only learn the subject at hand but must overlearn it. Overlearning is what Coach John Wooden called repetition, repetition, repetition, repetition, and more repetition. Overlearning will assist in making your future worthwhile and sustainable.

Keeping your mind open helps build and fill your toolbox. However, if your mind is closed, you will be living in a limited world of four empty walls; you will shrivel up because that which does not grow shrivels up and eventually dies. One of life's greatest certainties is your ability to learn and grow. It is one of the very few human certainties in this world. Some suggest that they only include death and taxes. However, I remember Dr. Leo Buscaglia's presentation on life. He said, "Life is change, and change is life!" He continued, "Without change, there would be no life because change is necessary for growth and survival."

The process of daily learning is a constant encounter with new ideas and concepts. Many people take it for granted and don't realize that not only is it essential for knowledge, but it is the essence of adaptation and change, the very keys to survival. These include successful assimilation, memory, and retention. Learning comes naturally but knowing the nuances of it will further expand and enhance your adaptation and survival. Challenging new ideas will not only be enlightening and thought-provoking but will open new vistas and unlock stilted opinions. This unique learning will undoubtedly accelerate your journey.

KNOWLEDGE

Knowledge is the by-product of learning—digesting the information and converting it to usable fuel for discovery. Combined with a conscience, it provides you the freedom to think and act responsibly rather than impulsively. It liberates you from the shackles of ignorance. Without knowledge, the action becomes inane, accidental, scattered, or inconsequential. Knowledge is not only power, but it enables you to stretch into becoming more worldly and wise. It allows for your slow transformation from ignorance to wisdom.

Please keep in mind that, like your life travels, you are always on a wisdom journey. Hindsight will periodically meet you on the road. There will be temporary destinations on your travels, but your search will always be for truth.

Knowledge can never be taken from you; it will free you from the bondage of ignorance.

While I was in college, I met many influential minds. However, I learned that some of the mightiest minds could also be terribly ignorant and socially inept. These super bright students were knowledgeable, had massive warehouses of stored information, and could repeat almost verbatim the works of other great minds. Yet some were intolerant, bigoted, parochial, insensitive, and ignorant of others less able. Not only did they spew racial expletives, but they had no patience for others unlike themselves. Knowledge does not guarantee wisdom. My first few years in college were eye-openers and provided another major epiphany. I was awakened and immersed in a world I hadn't realized existed.

The most compelling universal truth applies to all humanity and an important destination on your journey. As I mentioned, perhaps the most important universal truth of all humankind is, "Living as loving brothers and sisters in peace rather than conflict" It bonds perfectly with the Golden Rule. If only these truths could be realized, wars would be nonexistent, and harmony would prevail. Many other truths will be found along your journey.

EDUCATION

Education isn't just an institution. It begins soon after the first swat on your butt and subsequent primal scream. Proper education is the development of conscience, an open mind, common sense, fairness, responsibility, and appropriate decision-making. It is the antithesis of ignorance!

Education isn't memorizing facts or figures soon to be forgotten. It is inspiring the spirit of learning and lighting the torch of mental Olympics. Education is acquiring and remembering what counts. Included in any worthwhile curriculum is the knowledge required for common sense choices necessary in making responsible decisions.

Education is limitless. It reminds you of your past, defines your present, and it creates your future. It expands your knowledge, motivates your desire for curiosity, and answers your questions. Education makes you more fit for life because it helps discriminate, judge, evaluate, and understand life's nuances. Education allows you to gain wisdom from your experiences, which you will need to learn outside of the classroom.

There have been many reports of false news by the media. You should be cautious about believing everything that is read or seen on TV. It's important to remember that newspapers and televisions rely on advertisements, and advertisers are wealthy and yield great power. Advertisers sometimes encourage embellishment and even dishonest newscasting to garner financial benefits, especially for the owners. Likewise, the wealthy owners themselves often prefer false information to gild their treasuries further. So, carefully discriminate, be cautious, and verify questionable information.

TEACHING

Life teachers continuously surround you. Teaching expands your experiences and interactions with others. It represents your daily lessons in life. You are an agent of education, whether directly through words or indirectly through imitation, observation, or modeling. The power and scope of instruction are endless. You eventually become a piece of each of your former inspirational teachers. There are no socioeconomic barriers to teaching. We can learn from the homeless as quickly as we can learn from the most erudite.

Necessity is the mother of invention. You will learn many things because they will be necessary for your daily survival. However, you will know even more from the most unlikely of teachers. It will be from people you find disgusting, repulsive, and destructive. This type of learning will not necessarily be in your best interest, but it will teach you valuable lessons about life. You will especially learn an enormous amount from those that are quite different from yourself. Due to their lack of education, they will teach you what you will not want to do or say. Quite the contrary, they will have taught you what to avoid.

You can derive learning from every event, whether positively or negatively.

I recall as if it were yesterday—It was 1960, and I was seventeen years old and started my first year of college at the University of San Francisco. At that time, I was a pre-med student in a relatively intense program. I can never forget the altruistic words of a fellow pre-med student named Joe Addiego. He was an earnest student who possessed a facile and quick mind. He also had the wisdom of a seasoned professor. There were moments when I didn't understand a particular lecture or reading assignment. Joe never hesitated, helping to explain it without the least bit of resistance. I also remember his comment, "When I review an idea or concept with you, not only do I help you better understand it, but I digest it and remember it even better." Although we lost contact more than a half-century ago, I am confident that Joe went on to be a profoundly outstanding physician and a talented teacher. Ironically, I went on to be an educational psychologist.

I am thoroughly convinced that a teacher can change a life in minutes. Teachers can indeed modify eternity! Each of us can remember that special teacher, those memorable words and unique insights that helped us overcome fears and discover new possibilities. Those special moments are never forgotten, and they continue to resonate with warm and fuzzy feelings upon their recollection. You will owe your success and happiness first to yourself and secondarily to those transforming teaching events. Each provide both freedom and independence. Sharing with others is a profound means of teaching, and we learn so much in the process. In retrospect, I can recall most poignantly the faces, names, and effects left by three elementary teachers, two high school instructors, and five university professors who will reside in my heart forever! THANK YOU, your gifts will forever be appreciated!

Excellent teachers are like gourmet chefs preparing a table of delectable dishes. These fine teachers invite their students to taste and discover new and exciting flavors without undue pressure. However, like all professions, a few teachers try to force-feed and proselytize instead of allowing choice and freedom. I remember Leo

Buscaglia's experience with a wise monk, who told him, "Don't walk in my head with your dirty feet, a dead teacher cannot teach life . . ." Many years before, Henry Seidel Canby suggested that "Arrogance, pedantry, and dogmatism . . . the occupational diseases of those who spend their lives directing the intellects of the young." I can never forget my third-grade teacher, a nun who was pointing to her habit, said, "Anthony, you open your mouth one more time, and I'll take this safety pin and button your lips." I admit it worked, I learned, but I did so fearfully. There will always be teachers who take their job too seriously. Instead of offering delectable dishes, they want to force-feed students—no differently than force-feeding geese to enlarge their livers. However, many unsung heroes in the classroom provide quiet miracles every day. These inspirational souls are the salt of the earth. They need to be praised as much as they offer praises to their students.

EXPERIENCE

Throughout my life, I have been besieged by the trite quote, "Experiences are what you get when you expected something else." There is no doubt that those immortal words were on point. Experiences are necessary and very important. They promote many new learning moments. Some of the most poignant discerning experiences were the most embarrassing and the funniest in my lifetime. Like when I learned not to eat too many beans or pretending that ex-lax was chocolate, "borrow-ing" something that didn't belong to me, or as a teen, saying or doing something that would make me want to crawl into a hole. We've all been there and never forgot-ten those emotionally-charged events. The most salient issue is that we seldom, if ever, repeat those experiences. A prudent person soon learns to gain vicarious experi-ence by observing others.

THINKING

Social scientists have convincingly concluded that our thoughts are our very being. What you think you are or will soon become. Cognitive therapists have been remarkably successful in altering one's negative thoughts and replacing them with more appropriate verbal sub-stitutes. Choosing our thoughts defines us as happy or sad, realistic or fantasy-based, loving or resisting, fear-ful or courageous, healthy or hypochondriacal, winner or loser, etc. If we wallow in being a bona fide victim, we will undoubtedly become victimized. If we feel love and are liked by others, we will be liked and loved by them. However, if we feel fearful and undeserving, we will find ourselves without friends and afraid to connect to others. Marcus Aurelius summed it up, "Our life is what our thoughts make it."

Some people act without thinking. The average person makes over 1,000 decisions a day. If decisions are made without thought, you will succumb to the computer truism "garbage in, garbage out." Thinking is both incredibly powerful yet laborious and pain-laden. Thinking is indeed what few people do, and why it is the toughest of all mental tasks.

Thomas Watson, the founder of IBM, was known for having a rather compelling but straightforward sign placed in his employees' offices. It was displayed in large, bold capital letters, saying, THINK!

RESEARCH FACTS

Researchers, especially educational psychologists, have studied learning extensively. It is well recognized that our eyes play a significant part in obtaining information and memory. In my own experience, I found that acquiring knowledge is multisensory, seeing, hearing, feeling, and touching simultaneously. Along with repetition and re-teaching, it is considered the best means of memory retention. Although there is a certain amount of variance, our visual sense accounts for approximately 85% of learning, while auditory accounts for 10% and all other senses account for 5% of retention.

It was no big surprise to me that in recent years, the myth that intelligence was solely verbal and mathematical skill has been summarily dismissed. As a matter of fact, the brain has at least eight types of learning intelligence. They include musical-rhythmic, visual-spatial, verbal-linguistic, logical-mathematical, bodily-kinesthetic, interpersonal, intra-personal, and moral–existential. Surely, intelligence is not made up of only language and mathematics. If you can develop each of these eight intelligence areas, you will undoubtedly add more balance, gain more knowledge, experience, and have more success in your life.

Knowing the facts of retaining information is an important part of your learning. Having the knowledge to enhance and maximize the retention of information will be extremely helpful. Knowing this will maximize your retention. For instance, scientists have found that after going to a lecture, taking a class, or hearing a body of information, within one day your retention level is 84%. Within five days, retention is 50%; within 16 days, it is 2%. However, if you review the material six times within those 16 days, there is 65% retention. If you review the same material and share it by teaching it to another, retention can reach beyond 65%. Want A's? A review will get you there.

Forgetting information is normal and allows you to delete rather than retain inane and unnecessary data. Thus, you need to empty your brain's registers simply as a regular human activity. This is not very different than deleting the cookies that accumulate in your computer registers. This type of housekeeping maintains balance and allows for additional retention.

When you get to my age, memory recall becomes more difficult but not necessarily symptomatic of disease or senility. They indicate an age-related slowing down of memory's information processing. I have certainly noticed "senior moments." Insufficient word recall, name recall, or forgetting things (e.g., car keys) have noticeably increased as I've grown older. I especially have had great difficulty acquiring a new foreign language. In conversing with my contemporaries, we are all convinced that normal aging is quite dramatically the primary variable that affects memory. You are not there yet, but be advised, be prepared.

Studies have shown that learning training, like physical training, is helpful as you reach these golden years. Mnemonics help improve short-term memory recall and ferret out facts, meanings, and words. The use of mental pictures to associate with names and words also helps your memory. Utilizing rhymes, repetition, rehearsing, using acronyms, musical associations, chunking or clustering data in groups of three or four, and structuring (e.g., using key hooks) are practical means of retention. Also important is being confident and relaxed. Don't think like Chicken Little that the sky is falling; be comfortable, relaxed, and maintain your confidence. Also, word games like Scrabble, crossword puzzles, and playing cards keep your mind and your focus sharp. These mnemonics will aid you both now, as well as later when you are better prepared for age-related memory issues.

Similarly, acquiring high-tech tools like computers and scanners or utilizing Google searches will help keep your brain remain fit. So will crafts, gardening, hobbies, and social groups. Remember, "An idle mind is the devil's workshop," and the devil is dementia.

In summary, without taking learning, knowledge, and education seriously, you will be unable to build a strong foundation for your journey. Make sure your mental switch is on. The brain, your toolbox, will need to be filled with various kinds of learning tools. These devices are some of the most valuable tools in your toolbox. Continue to add as many of these strategies as you are able. You will find them to be the most significant personal assistants on your journey.

"The children now love luxury. They have bad manners, contempt for authority, they show disrespect for their elders and love chatter in place of exercise. Children are now tyrants, not the servants of their households. They no longer rise when elders enter the room. They contradict their parents, chatter before company, gobble up dainties at the table, cross their legs, and tyrannize their teachers."

YOUR MOST PRECIOUS UNDERTAKNG

The above was allegedly written over 2,400 years ago by Socrates. Does it sound any different than some of the comments heard at social gatherings today?

Children are still children. And that's what makes them the supreme challenge of your lifetime. Children are not only our future; they are our present and our past. Children are the most wondrous gift anyone could receive. Whether you are young or old, you will eventually become a parent, aunt, uncle, or a significant nurturer. I have been amazed at the transformation that takes place upon the birth of a child. It transforms parents, aunts, uncles, neighbors, and grandparents. It can be one of the most magical epiphanies of your lifetime. If you choose to be a parent or become an aunt, uncle, godparent, or neighbor, you will need to sober up to the fact that what you say or do will affect each child's future and eventually society. The birth of a child is a true blessing or can be a potential disappointment. This enormous responsibility is reflected in your influence on the development of a child. There can be no greater reward or more severe punishment than being a parent or significant other. To ensure world harmony, you must take this responsibility very seriously. You must make every effort to preserve the child as the most precious undertaking of your gift to society and its future. Love, kindness, and respect are the keys to happiness, which always begins with your family unit.

PREAMBLE TO CHILDREN

I have written this book for you, the youngsters and young adults who have embarked on the most important journey of all, your life. My goal was to provide you a passport and roadmap to the many stops, pauses, bends, and turns on your voyage to enlightenment and success. I have remained your rock of Gibraltar, supporting and cheering you along the way. I know that on one of your many stops, you may choose parenthood—a mighty choice, but not one that can be taken lightly. If you determine that you want to become a parent, I hope you are prepared for the challenges and responsibilities required for such an ominous decision. There is no other subject that I feel more confident in sharing. After spending a half-century working with children and parents, it occupies the most profound part of my heart.

There is nothing more sacred or exhilarating than seeing your child grow from a whimpering, highly dependent bundle of joy to a fully functioning, independent, and responsible blessing to this earth. If you make that choice, your work is cut out for you. However, I can unequivocally assure you that my many years of training, experience, and practice will provide you a 24-karat guide to follow. There remain a few strategies that, if followed, will make you a proud parent. Every strategy provided has been tested against time for many millennia. They have been witnessed by my own eyes over 50 years of diligent work with children, parents, and fellow professionals. The strategies are the hallmark of thousands of professionals spanning centuries. This has been the most serious work I have undertaken. Like a vaccine, it has been studied for centuries by dedicated scientists who have probed it and experienced thousands of trials. Although not a 100% perfect cure, the vaccine allows for a life of vitality, happiness, and fulfillment.

If you choose parenthood, you will find that being a mother or father is the most challenging role you will ever assume, yet it will become the most inspiring and rewarding of all. In the meantime, please continue your journey to enlightenment and success.

ADOLESCENCE

Adolescence is a topic that cannot be neglected because it is the most difficult and the most remembered. All adults have experienced it. Quite a number of years ago, while in graduate school, I remember a slightly off-color comment by Dr. Thomas Tutko, a friend and nationally recognized sports psychologist. He jokingly said, "Adolescence is a parent's penance for having had sex." At the time, it was funny. After three children, it was spot on! If you think that the childhood years were difficult, you will soon learn that adolescence is several quantum leaps more enlightening and painful.

Early adolescence is the beginning of cataclysmic collisions of physical, emotional, intellectual, social, and spiritual events! It's a time for the appearance of zits, over-development or under-development, awkwardness, and hours of bathroom recreation fixing or finishing things. Most teens are unhappy with the recent changes in their physical looks. Adolescence is the onset of increased putdowns by oneself and others. Mood swings become the standard rather than the exception. Raging hormones and peer pressure contribute to emotional shifts. It is a period of passionate feelings and mixed emotions. Words are equivocal or dotted with excess emotion. In addition, there are many hyperboles such as "always," "never," and, "everybody," but they are also laced with challenges like "All the other kids can . . ." followed by a plethora of "Whys?" The term teen comes from the old Anglo-Saxon word "teona," meaning vexations or bewilderment. Not only is it painful and bewildering to parents, but it is also frustrating, vexing, and perhaps more stressful to the teen. As a result, parents can sometimes feel the tightening tendrils of a python slowly cinching their body like a vice. On the other hand, teens also feel they are in the dark vortex of a menacing maelstrom.

This is a time when the apron strings are cut, and parents become a lesser priority. It's a time when family values are questioned, and friction becomes a regular prescription for conflict. These ongoing battles reflect the push towards independence. Teenagers want freedom and refuse to be treated like babies. Parents are accused of being overly protective and unable to see the real world. Unfortunately, teens can have unrealistic ideas of the world around them. Concurrently, parents are at a loss because they are seeing dramatic changes in attitude and feeling a loss of control. However, attempting to regain control is antithetical to any reasonable resolution of adolescence. Thus, the sparks begin to fly.

Teens think they know everything about the birds and the bees. Yet their information and knowledge are often incomplete, inaccurate, dangerous, and unrealistic. In the meantime, teenagers are strongly influenced by their peer group, diluting family influence. There is no way that either parents or teens can ever avoid these turbulent times. Parents can only temper these difficult years by understanding, not falling prey, throughout this highly volatile period.

The teenage years are indeed a time of confusion, indecision, and collision. It is the beginning of a lifelong journey of self-discovery. As their minds and bodies are changing, teens finally begin looking deep within themselves, searching, learning, growing, and changing into their very new and different autonomous selves. This internal voyage will begin an ongoing struggle to define their character, personality, and attitudes. It will be very challenging but also very valuable and meaningful. It is the search for the "real me." It is a time when parents are confused and often ready to criticize the self-centered, self-absorbed, self-dominated teenage behavior they are now witnessing.

Parents are less apt to shower compliments and positive thoughts on these now bewildered monsters. However, finding fault or making disparaging remarks seldom produces harmony. These remarks fuel the sparks of rebellion rather than promoting budding independence. Instead of moving closer, negative comments cause more psychological distance, a metric of achieving independence. Going with the flow, applying honey rather than vinegar will serve everyone better than full-scale war. Silence sometimes is golden, but having reasonable limits, especially those transitioned from earlier years, will help. Nonverbal and clear-cut consequences for transgressions will be far more victorious than futile verbal fisticuffs.

Yes, teenage language, hair, clothing, footwear, jewelry, accessories, and music is often quite different, perhaps even bizarre. In addition, there may be less respect shown than previously. Not all teenagers will adopt these trappings. Regardless, they are the signals and red flags of either mild or radical resistance. The budding teen is sending a message, "I'm no longer a child. I am a maturing individual looking deeply to define myself and my new identity, hopefully, as a young adult." They are awakening to find a revised personal philosophy, seeking truths, looking for answers and direction, searching for balance. You, the parents, are equally bewildered and must take time to think and remember your epiphany during those turbulent years. Only then can you begin to understand and provide a modicum of guidance without excess criticism and rage.

I can honestly say I knew many during my adolescent years who went through several years as hippies during those turbulent 60s and 70s. Not surprisingly, most are now some of the more conservative and proper people I know. Yes, the music, behavior, dress, and mood were rebellious and bizarre. Yet, those "love children" have become the standard-bearers of our current society. They are parents and grandparents, like you and I, able to meet problems and deal with daily responsibilities. There is nothing more exciting nor more painful than watching the metamorphosis during the struggle to adulthood and eventual responsible citizenry.

There will be many opportunities for you to stop and think about this period of turbulence. As a parent of teenagers, I often relied on the guidance of an astute sage, Galileo: "You cannot teach man anything; you can only help him find it within himself."

A comprehensive and detailed explanation on PARENTING & CHILD REARING is available by going to https://www.drtonycedolini.com/parenting-and-child-rearing

THE TASTE OF SOAP

Going back some 60 or 70 years, I can't remember my first faux pas, but there were hundreds, maybe thousands made over those years. I do remember my stomach twitching every time I realized I had stuck my foot in my mouth. They were always the wrong words to use. When I let the cat out of the sack, I immediately wanted to crawl under a boulder. I must admit there was no difficulty picking up on others' non-verbal reactions, facial contortions, blank looks, or obvious disdain. Those responses eventually became blatantly sensitive and humiliating to me.

I just didn't know how to censor my thoughts before they arrived as a devastating tsunami.

Even after an apology or clarification, it was too late. I still felt embarrassingly foolish. I am sure that I lost friends and, indeed, credibility during those naïve and immature moments. I was undoubtedly a relatively slow learner. My verbal diarrhea continued unabated for quite some time during those early years. My parents were aghast at some of the garbage that came leaking out of my rather big mouth. It was especially problematic when a new friend, neighbor, or boss happened to be at our house. I might hear a word that sounded sophisticated or contemporary, then repeat it and regrettably find it miserably missed its mark. Sometimes it was slang or an unwitting dirty word. Sometimes, it was out of context, and sometimes a judgmental pejorative. Occasionally, my utterances were simple things like fat, ugly, homely, midget, stupid idiot, ass, and, of course, many far worse.

Probably my more judgmental comments received the biggest reprimands from my parents, relatives, and neighbors. Yes, I must admit to recognizing the taste of soap and the many trips to my room. I can only guess that yours truly, Mr. Loquacious, turned a lot of heads and stomachs, too. During those trial years, I slowly listened and learned. As time passed, instead of opening my mouth to change feet, I began to censor more of my verbal output, especially interrupting less. The other lesson that was slow to learn was listening. After repeatedly being told, "Remember, you have only one mouth and twice as many ears," I was cajoled to either change or suffer. My listening and communication skills were challenging but learning took hold after experiencing the many emotionally-painful consequences. To this very day, I still make a periodic faux pas. The only difference now is that I'm quicker to pick up on the non-verbal cues and immediately clarify what I originally meant. To me, it remains a very sensitive area that requires constant vigilance. As Mark Twain might say, "It is sometimes better to keep your mouth shut and let people think you are a fool than to open it and remove all doubt."

After millions of years, Homo sapiens have evolved into a status uniquely different than any other species. We not only have a highly developed and sophisticated brain; we can communicate in expressive language; not a single language, but multilingual means of communication. As with all unique gifts, language represents both opposing spectrums. It can develop relationships filled with love and intimacy as quickly as it can create vociferous enemies filled with hate, enmity, and revenge.

Words, therefore, can be salutary or dangerous.

A long-term relationship can be shattered or enhanced by only a sentence or a few uncensored words. They can build, or they can destroy because they are the mightiest of humankind's verbal tools. Words have Herculean strength. Once uttered, they cannot be retrieved or unsaid, only swallowed. Attempting to correct utterances as soon as possible is ultimately far more beneficial than eating them as crow later. Use words wisely to think, organize, inform, create, build, and store for later use. They will ultimately become your greatest ally or your fiercest foe.

We all recognize that a single sentence can make your day or kill it. Conversely, reading a simple sentence such as a quote can immediately improve your mood. Certain phrases, especially those that are inspirational, can have a dramatic effect on your attitude. I have filled this book with many simple sentences from wise people. Each has the potential to have a monumental impact, and that may change your life. Quotes have the power to inspire you to think more deeply about life. Perhaps these cogent quotes might motivate you to a richer understanding of others as well as of yourself. Sages past and present share their treasures with those willing to listen, explore, and expand. Each day you are presented with challenges and obstacles. Taking a moment to find a wise phrase brings revised vitality to life's daily bumps and allows the phoenix to arrive each new morning with renewed energy and a new perspective. Pick the most meaningful ones and place them in your toolbox. Once mastered, they can be a lifesaver, especially when responding to another's challenging retort. I keep hundreds in my tickler file and review about 50 of them each week. They are often my perfect antidote.

As a child, I repeatedly heard, "sticks and stones will break your bones, but words will never hurt you." It took many years to understand that this statement is blatantly and unequivocally false. Another example of false news. It is easy to fall prey and naïvely accept short phrases that purport wisdom and truth. Careful thought and discrimination should be given to each "old person's tale."

You should be vigilant, knowing that words can be weapons far more destructive than stones. Understanding this will aid your choice of words and assist in your selection of close friends. Learning to communicate successfully requires understanding the quality and power of language. Listening becomes the impenetrable armor of your youth. Careful listening to the comments of others should precede your life-defining decisions about them. Caution will assist and forever alter your journey.

Guarding your comments and carefully monitoring what you say will expedite your journey towards happiness. Make every effort to say what you mean and sincerely mean what you say. This allows you to graciously take responsibility for the things you utter. I wish I could say that making inappropriate comments was never one of my problems. However, as a teenager and young adult, I was amazed at some of the remarks that exited my mouth. I can't tell you how many times I bit my tongue; it must now be laden with scars. Those were the days. If I didn't restrain myself—I'll say it again—I was likely to open my mouth only to change feet! It was only after the feedback and support of concerned but befuddled others that I was able to obtain honest responses. With their feedback, I slowly learned a more appropriate language. After years of trial and error, the foot and mouth disease has diminished. Fortunately, my feet don't fit into my mouth as quickly anymore.

My mother, a wonderful woman, had episodes of the same dreaded disease. There is little doubt that there is a strong hereditary connection, not only DNA, but modeled and learned. Carefully choose your words.

Make them tender and tasteful. Otherwise, you may later need to eat them. Please take my counsel seriously; it will save time, embarrassment, and pain.

President Harry S. Truman was at heart a farm boy from Missouri. He felt most comfortable talking in very common language to his Missouri farmer constituency. When President Truman discussed fertilizer, he used the word manure, frequently much to his subordinates' dismay. When his wife Bess was asked if she might help Harry stop using such an offensive word, she paused and, with a loud sigh, responded, "You would be amazed at how long it took me to get him to start using the word manure!"

COMMUNICATION

Communication is the sending and receiving of messages. However, this simple sending of messages doesn't guarantee a successful transmission. Sincerely sharing your thoughts, feelings, and preferences is critical for effective connections, mutual understanding, and trust. It first requires the ingredients of trust and good listening. Poor communication is usually the result of poor listening. By being supportive, a good listener, and nonjudgmental, you will develop implicit trust and enhanced communication, the foundation of personal relationships. However, many obstacles interfere with optimal transmission. They include your physical environment, psychological state, past experiences, attentiveness, preoccupation, current perceptions, fear, rejection, and defensiveness. Emotions such as anger, fear, melancholy, or overexcitement frequently muddle your ability to transmit effectively.

Conversations can begin as civil discussions and then turn into conflicts. Language, like most physical phenomena, spans a huge continuum, from brief and unemotional to lengthy and salutary, or from brief and mildly angry to blatant hostility. Verbal advice can be a welcome sermon with innate wisdom and diplomacy, or it can be a boring monologue of dictatorial do's and don'ts. Always be alert to recognizing positive conversations from harangues. Avoid allowing yourself to be a party to chaos, hostility, boredom, or rigid proselytizing. Live so that your actions and words defy others' attempts to draw you into conflict. You can withdraw or disagree with grace and not lose face. Afterward, you will feel proud of having been stronger, wiser, and more adaptable.

POSITIVE AND DESIRABLE WORDS

Ideally, you want to leave others with your best thoughts. Consequently, you need to select and express your best intentions of encouragement and love, as well as your deepest and most tender feelings. It is often difficult to choose the language that expresses your deepest emotion. It takes time and practice to develop those skills. You will want to feel the positive power of words and their intimate effects on others. It is called "affect." In a small book I wrote and published many years ago, "The Effect of Affect," there were many examples of expressing emotions verbally and nonverbally. The impact of your statements is more potent when your body also expresses them enthusiastically and with emotional sincerity. To both loved ones and friends, your affect can become the cornerstone of eternal memories. Like the power of quotes that sustain thousands of years, your congruence of carefully selected remarks and the delivery of sincere body language will have priceless impact.

Sharing words of encouragement, compliments, praise, and respect are means of finding the best in others. Giving sincere compliments provides positive recognition of other's behaviors, feelings, or dress. Compliments typically are short-term acknowledgments. It's like taking a bath; once a year isn't enough, you need to do it often. This is why you should be giving loving compliments often and regularly. When passion moves you, don't delay. Say it with all your heart!

Hearing these words of inspiration are like blaring trumpets: they billow joy and create euphoric hearts, overflowing with love, peace, and happiness. They give thanks and resonate with jubilation. These positive messages include the most powerful force of life—love! They have the greatest impact on the heart—encouragement! These inspirations provide one of life's biggest sustainers—hope! They inject the most contagious of spirit—enthusiasm!

TOXIC WORDS

Without reservation, your most powerful verbal tool is your ability to say to yourself, "I CAN!" Yes, these are the two most potent words of your entire vocabulary. Conversely, the expression "I CAN'T" is the most destructive and debilitating in the English language. Preeminently, the slogan is short but deadly accurate, "Success comes in "CANS"; failure comes in CAN'Ts!" Norman Vincent Peale, Zig Ziglar, Norman Cousins, and most motivational speakers have declared CAN'T as toxic and deadly. CAN is able to accomplish, while CAN'T surrenders to failure. All things are possible with an open mind willing to say I can. There is a long laundry list of nonbelievers who refuse to believe in new possibilities. Perhaps at the pinnacle was a director of the U.S. patent office, who made the following statement, "Everything that can be invented has been invented." Wow, would he be surprised by the hundreds of thousands of new patents since his statement was made in 1899. There have been millions of individuals who choked success by their lacking faith in the simple phrase, "I CAN!"

In a similar vein, the words possible and impossible are also very potent. Progress can be stalled, further delayed, or stopped when the toxic element of impossible is presented. For example, "We will never have a car that operates without a driver." "A flight to Mars, that's simply comic book stuff," or "Regenerating organs like a heart, liver, or kidneys is nonsensical science fiction." These are killer statements to budding creativity.

Negative thinking shuts doors, creates fear, destroys dreams, and diminishes imagination and creativity. These are the very same values that created our wonderful country! Our prowess in robotics, medicine, high tech, and other scientific discoveries, was and will continue to be the result of an "I can" and "It's possible" attitudes. Keep your mind open, explore, be curious, and don't succumb to negative comments.

COURTESY

Lace your communications with courtesies. Some of the most appreciated phrases you can share are common courtesies like, please, thank you, you are welcome, congratulations, you remembered, I appreciated that! Being polite and grateful is always welcomed. Another aspect of successful communication is the ability to sandwich a positive statement both before and after stating a concern or problem. It is also important to note that if the criticism is necessary, I always try to place it between layers of chocolate praise. Almost every serious letter I write has a positive beginning, followed by a problem or issue that needs attention, and ends with a positive comment.

An example might be, "I have greatly appreciated your help with this project. Your input and feedback have been invaluable. Can you send me the notes you borrowed last month? I'll need them soon for a speech I'm giving. It is always a pleasure working with you. You are indeed a wonderful friend."

DESTRUCTIVE AND UNDESIRABLE WORDS

There are many forms of destructive and undesirable words. They come in various types and forms. Some of the singular ones of least importance are the pronouns ME and I. It is easy to identify the egocentric and selfish by the number of I, Me, and My utterances. You can also tell more about people by what they say about others who are not in attendance.

Similarly, be cautious of the inveterate flatterers. They can prey upon the naïve with empty promises. Likewise, be careful of those who talk in excess. Their messages are boring, thus negating their over-the-top messages. For the same reason that we limit ourselves, we must restrict those whose communications are filled with fluff, repetitive nonsense, or egotistical demagoguery. Also, be keenly aware of your own responses; for example, if you are easily bored, you may be equally boring to others.

Most importantly, be especially cautious of those who make constant excuses for their behavior, for they are irresponsible. They take refuge being the constant victim of circumstances. They tend to blame others, such as family, friends, schoolmates, and teachers, but never blame themselves. To them, it is always someone else's fault. Eventually you may be the person they will blame in future transgressions.

Perhaps the most dangerous pariah of all communication is the gossiper. Decades ago, in one of Dear Abby's columns, a reader shared some sage advice. Bruce Fassinelli was from upstate New York, not far from my birthplace. He had shared with his Rotary International group a four-way test of gossip. It included these four questions: "Is it the truth? Is it fair to all concerned? Will it build goodwill and better friendships?" and "Will it be beneficial to all concerned?" By asking these questions, you will avoid the unnecessary verbal venom inflicted on others. Besides, it will help you maintain your integrity. Needless to say, mudslinging, name-calling, and character assassination are the essence of gossip. Avoid at all costs being a participant in a gossip group.

Interestingly, Socrates some 2,500 years ago had a similar three-filter test. First filter, "Have you made sure that what you are about to tell me is the truth?" The second filter, "Is what you are about to tell me something good?" The third filter, "Is what you want to tell me going to be useful?" Socrates answered, "If what you want to tell me is neither true nor good or even useful, why tell me or anyone else?" And now a bit of levity: History tells us the joke was on Socrates. It explains why he never found out that Diogenes was having an affair with his wife!

ACTIVE LISTENING

Like a wonderful spouse, listening is the better half of communication. Learning to be a good listener is very hard work. It takes a great deal of practice, skill, and open-mindedness. The effectiveness of your attempts to communicate are not only the words and meaning of your transmission, but your intentions, body language, inflections, sincerity, or conciseness. It is equally important that your communication is heard by the listener. Unfortunately, it is possible that the recipient may be preoccupied or judgmental.

Sharing your most personal thoughts, problems, challenges, or intimate feelings is difficult. As mentioned in previous chapters, obtaining verbal feedback is the most effective means of personal change. However, in regard to optimal communication, it is better defined as "active listening." This verbal feedback comes from the listener who, by actively reflecting comments, shares his/her interpretations to you. It is like an interpreter carefully listening and then translating a foreign language. The active listener succinctly reflects the heart of the intimate message. If truly sincere, active feedback will further bond a relationship like super glue. In addition, it will also unlock the steel doors of one's deepest emotional safe.

Active listening also applies to you. When you listen carefully to others' feedback and accept their reflective feedback, you have added a powerful tool. Accepting and acting on trusted feedback is the most significant building block of self-change and self-actualization. Without honest, objective, clarifying information from trusted others, you will flounder in confusion and limit your personal growth. With it, you will not only grow and become an even better person, but with course corrections, happiness will be your reward. Remember, you can't further develop or change without objective feedback. That's why we need mirrors, scales, speedometers, tape recorders, photos, home movies, and especially friends.

Listening is one of the most crucial yet difficult skills in communication. A good listener must focus on both the explicit and implicit meanings expressed. Good listeners must also understand body language, unspoken words, attitudes, and possible hidden agendas. If the listener jumps to conclusions, is thinking of what to say next, or frequently interrupts, the conditions for successful conversation are breached.

Getting answers to questions and summarizing comments are also necessary to ensure accurate reception. Assuring that you have received the complete message is equally helpful. Unfortunately, many people fail the test of good listening. It has been my experience that to ensure good listening for complete understanding, you must not only practice it regularly, you must also set the example. This is verified by periodically summarizing in a few words the speaker's meaning. Reflecting the key points is the epitome of active listening. It ensures accurate transmission. For example, "Alice, you are sad because your friend John upset you and you don't know what to do. It sounds like you'd like me to help you think through an appropriate resolution to this knotty problem." You will usually receive a quick response indicating the validation of your effective listening.

Responding by reflecting key elements of a sender's message guarantees that you are actively listening. It encourages you to go on to develop further what the sender is willing to share. It is crucial to understand that reflective responding is nonjudgmental. No matter what is shared, no inference of either right or wrong should be conveyed by the listener. Active listening is simply a means of reflecting the thoughts and feelings of that particular moment to avoid verbal shutdown. By evaluating, instructing, judging, or giving unwanted advice, you will no longer remain neutral. Instead, you tilt the scales and can abruptly close down further disclosure. Your ability to help a friend in need will be immediately curtailed. For example, "I think it's kind of dumb to be concerned about such a stupid thing." End of conversation!

Any degree of discounting the sender will guarantee the termination of future intimate conversations. Even worse, it will infuse distrust and perhaps an unwillingness to have further discussions. Instead, a neutral and supportive reflection might be, "Alice, you sound like you're very upset about the fight you had with your boyfriend." An invitation to further explore the sender's feelings and concerns has just been sent; trust and respect will result. Listening, like imitating others, is one of the sincerest forms of flattery. Everyone loves to be heard, copied, and recognized. It is a wonderful compliment; use it often.

An old but helpful reminder is that you have one mouth but two ears. I know I've mentioned it before, but not only should you spend twice as much time listening, but it is twice as important that you listen intently. In addition to your ears, listening is a multi-dimensional process where your eyes, body, hands, and hearts are intimately involved. Understanding body language is an important part of listening. By carefully observing body language, you will slowly master the multi-dimensional components of language and listening. Armed with your newly assimilated learning, you will be able to make quantum jumps in your interpersonal relationships. In the process, your social intelligence, emotional maturity, and social support will be immensely enhanced.

One final thought: reading is a form of listening without the assistance of your ears. It is considered the best means of expanding your vocabulary, which in itself has multiple benefits. Focusing your listening attention on reading will not only vastly extend your knowledge but will transform your life.

SILENCE IS GOLDEN

In some social situations, silence can be as effective as eloquence. You can certainly make a significant statement with your golden words. But at other times, you can overwhelm with silence. It can be in the form of silent criticism, lack of agreement, silently making a point, or avoiding conflict. Silence can speak much louder than verbiage! It is almost impossible to refute.

If you are wise, take a very deep breath and say nothing when a point needs to be made by your complete silence. This will allow the other person to reflect on his/her last statement. You have just made a more powerful statement without uttering a single word!

Silence is not always golden. There are times that silence is tantamount to surrender. Allowing destructive ideas to flourish can create disharmony, division, and sometimes death. Also, not responding to a loved one or someone in need can be problematic. Listen carefully and act prudently; you will not regret it.

SPEECHES/ LECTURES

If you need to give a speech or lecture, remember there are significant steps you'll need to be aware of. First and foremost, prepare! Know your audience and make your salient points with emphasis and passion. Be aware and tactful towards others' differences. Speak softly but directly, and more importantly, avoid preaching.

Remember the old saw, "The secrets of successful public speaking are be sincere, be brief, and then be seated." It is best to keep your words simple, sweet, and short because the greatest art in speaking is to know when to stop.

"When you're good to others, you're best to yourself."
—*Benjamin Franklin*

RANDOM ACTS
OF KINDNESS

As a child, helping my neighbor, Mrs. Kate Smith, was one of the most rewarding acts that I remember. Helping the 80-year-old English immigrant not only brought the brightest smile to her face, but it also brought an even bigger one to mine. Regardless, I knew that I might be invited that afternoon for high tea and molasses cookies. Although initially prompted by my parents, letting little old ladies have my seat on the bus or assisting another senior across the street produced strong, positive visceral feelings. Those warm, welcoming feelings persist to this day when an act of kindness spontaneously occurs.

Possessing unselfish regards for the welfare of others is called altruism. It is a humanistic virtue in almost all societies, religions, and cultures. Many studies strongly suggest that this type of social support promotes physical and mental health. According to Dr. S. Leonard Syme, professor emeritus of the UC Berkeley School of Public Health, "The importance of good social relationships for health has now been shown in almost every study ever done." Some studies suggest that the most significant health benefits come from providing social support to others rather than receiving it.

Unexpected and unsolicited acts of kindness are the ultimate of altruism. On the flip side, it is equally important that you not become an enabler in the process of assisting others. Enabling can destroy confidence and independence while reinforcing dependency. This is a tightrope you must alert yourself to at all times. It is best to be a guide or mentor, assisting but not an unnecessary crutch. Benevolence is both noble and wise. It promotes confidence, motivation, and independence.

As I've gotten older, it is still a gut-rending pleasure to see the joy of others in response to the simplest act of kindness. I've learned that not only is it easy to be kind, but it also takes away your everyday stress and redirects your focus. It allows you to refocus on the needs of others instead of yourself. Someone once said that the test of generosity is not only how much you provide, but the profundity of what you receive in return.

Instead of bemoaning your fate, you reap rich benefits by focusing on others. It is far better than ruminating about your problems. Lending a hand to your fellow man takes the stressful weight off your shoulders. Doing so transfers negative energy to positive energy. The results of such a transformation are amazing. It is very similar to taking positive solar energy and transforming it into the electrical energy needed to run your household lights and appliances. Scientists call it conservation of energy. By dividing your success, you multiply another's happiness!

Compassion is having empathy, sensitivity, and concern for others. Compassion and kindness are kissing cousins. Everyone experiences major disappointments and misfortunes in their lifetime. Compassion for others allows the opportunity to listen, share, and care to alleviate their suffering and pain. Wanting to help the sick, hungry, homeless, and troubled is meritorious and reflects brother and sisterhood's supreme essence.

Your future and the future of humanity rely on cooperative caring and kindness for each other.

Denying, preaching, being indignant, or insensitive reside in a callous mind and soul. You can always test another's sincerity by observation: if their only benefit in assisting others is to help themselves by personal aggrandizement, it is not altruism. Helping others is like investing $10 and getting $1,000 in return.

Unfortunately, we live in a world where greed sometimes prevails. Greed is a disease that interferes with giving aid to the genuinely needy. The greedy want to multiply their fortunes as if it were their divine right. Yet none of them will ever be able to take their bankroll any farther than their gravesite. Fortunately, many understand that a fulfilling life is made up of the unselfish charities that fill others' lives with joy and happiness. I am extremely impressed with the Gates Foundation. Bill Gates and Warren Buffett have pledged 99% of their entire fortunes to medical, educational, and social research, as well as providing direct assistance to those in need. There are now over 200 extremely wealthy philanthropists who have also pledged their fortunes to the Gates Foundation. This generosity is spelled ALTRUISM in bold capital letters. Bravo!

Many of us are so very thankful for our health, family, job success, friends, etc. It only takes a walk through your closest city to discover that war, mental illness, health, abuse, handicap, family background, and lack of confidence has influenced the lives of the homeless and less fortunate. If you ever have an opportunity to sit and talk to these sad, desperate folks or talk to a social worker whose caseload is bulging with these less fortunate, you will realize how very fortunate you are indeed. My middle daughter, Antonia, is a social worker. She has shared many stories about her many experiences. The stories would cause even a stoic to bawl a hat full of tears. The cases of physical and sexual abuse, schizophrenia, post-traumatic stress disorder, family abandonment, and mental cruelty are astounding. She devotes her time, energy, and money to assist these forsaken folks. Few truly know and understand their past or plight. Unfortunately, there are always the fakes, charlatans, and con men who disparage the truly unfortunate. Caring adults frequently do not know if their food, money, or handouts go to good or evil. We do know, however, that food kitchens and homeless shelters are generally legitimate. Either volunteering time or donating money usually goes to them directly. Please recognize the realities of the less fortunate and provide your kindness before time runs out for them or for you.

PERSONAL GLIMPSES

As I look back, I'm reminded of my hobby of collecting hats. Initially, I bought hats to protect a bald pate, and later to remember a special event or a memorable vacation spot. So, I began collecting various kinds of hats. The collection grew and grew. Every time I put on a hat, it brought back the nostalgic memory of the place or circumstance. And now it serves as a beautiful metaphor, reminding me of all the kinds of hats we wear in life. As most of us have experienced, it's fun and exciting to change hats frequently. It relieves boredom and provides a truly needed service. We are all blessed by rotating hats and thus taking on new roles. Sometimes we wear the hat of an educator, counselor, or spiritual leader. Other times, we wear the hat of a philosopher, listener, or healer. We frequently wear different hats as a good neighbor, nurse, or doctor. It is not uncommon to wear the hat of a negotiator, police officer, firefighter, peacemaker, environmentalist, protector, soldier, builder, repair person, soulmate, parent, or grandparent. They are all recurring roles that many of us play. The best part of wearing these hats is that life is not dull. It is exhilarating and rewarding. Each hat gives you a different role and different responsibilities with your family, friends, country, and world. Changing hats sparks the energy that provides meaning and purpose. It is your singular contribution to making the world just a wee bit better. Keep the hats coming! The Mad Hatter obviously knew his purpose in life!

There have been many instances of a stranger coming forth anonymously and performing an extraordinary act of kindness. Just think, if you could do the same for another and inspire them to reciprocate a similar kind deed for another, it could become an ongoing momentum of synergy. Unlike a chain letter, it would provide a model for others to observe, maintain, and magnify! Think about it. It only takes one person to push the first domino.

ROAD TRIPS
OF LIFE

NOSTALGIC
REFLECTIONS

I will never forget the day our granddaughter Isabella asked, "When you were kids, did you go to school in a horse and buggy?"

Initially, my wife and I were baffled by her question. Upon reflection, I can understand it was probably difficult for our granddaughter to place her ancient grandparents in an era with modern conveniences. I did share with her that our cars were quite different. They were big, bulky, made of hefty steel, and were gas-guzzlers. They caused massive amounts of pollution, frequently spewing green or yellow fumes. To make our headlights brighter, we pressed a metal button on the left side of the floorboard. Also, on the far-right side of the floorboard was another round metal button. You pushed it to start the car.

Later a much smaller, round starter button was part of the dashboard. It was called an ignition switch. Keyed ignitions didn't show up until later. All cars had manual transmissions that required the driver to move a shift lever to change gears. Most cars had three gears forward and one back. There were no seatbelts, airbags, or other safety features. There were no turn signal lights when you turned, so you had to roll down the window—manually!—regardless of the temperature, rain, or snow, and use your arm to alert others that you were making a right or left turn. There were no special features like air conditioning, power steering, disc brakes, airbags, cruise control, electric windshield wipers, or any of the other features we have today. At that time, to think of a car able to drive itself was science fiction material. Cars were fundamental (and accidents profound), usually only one to family, and predominantly a means of transportation to work. The only good thing was that you usually could buy one new for about $800-$1,000 and a luxury car for $2,000.

On another occasion, our granddaughter asked about the food we ate when we were growing up. She queried my wife and me, asking, "Did they have places like McDonald's or Jack-in-the-Box?"

I said, "No, we didn't have anything called fast food. Our food was slow and almost invariably prepared at home. Our family couldn't afford to go to a sit-down restaurant, and there was no fast food except for TV dinners. Mom would go to the store and buy fresh ingredients for that night's dinner. Your grandma cooked every day, and we, as a family, sat down at the dining room table to say grace and proceeded to eat a homemade meal."

My brother and I rotated either setting or clearing the table. At the table, my mom frequently reminded me that the children in other countries were starving.

I was told that whatever I took and put on my plate, I should eat and not waste. Before I was allowed to get up from the table, I asked to be excused. We would bring our dishes and silverware to the sink. Sometimes we were denied permission because mom or dad wanted to discuss something with us before retiring to either homework or a rare television program. Every evening represented a very similar routine.

As a young boy, I was fascinated by our only major means of entertainment—the radio. A neighborhood friend had told me about a "crystal radio" that he had assembled from a kit. Somehow, I earned enough money to visit the local hobby store and promptly purchased my very own radio kit. I raced home, strung copper wires around the bed's metal frame, which made their way to my headphones hanging on the side of my bed. Within a few hours, I was listening to my homemade radio. While others slept, I enjoyed many hours listening to radio shows like *Inner Sanctum*, *Perry Mason*, *The Shadow*, *Sam Spade*, *The Thin Man*, *Amos'n Andy*, *Crime Doesn't Pay*, *Dick Tracy*, and *The Fat Man*. That was great fun, and many nostalgic memories remain.

I was also asked about television, and my grandchildren were surprised that there were only a few channels and very limited programs available. Cable TV was nonexistent. They were shocked to hear that my first television didn't find its way into our home until I was about eight years old. Our first TV was no more than nine inches in diameter, and the screen was only

black and white. Our sole TV channel usually had programs until evening and then signed off until the next
morning. I still remember that repetitive sound and
the strange black and white test pattern that remained
until morning.

Of course, as time passed, there were many follow-up
questions, and each time we shared our childhood experiences. I distinctly remember our grandchildren's faces,
filled with astonishment and dismay when we told them
that times were very different than what they have experienced. For instance, we usually had to earn almost
everything special, except for our clothing. My wife said
she was expected to make some of her clothes or wait for
hand-me-downs from her cousin Rosanne. They were
shocked to hear that I started working at age eleven. I
shared my 60-hour work week and that at age eleven, I
received a total of five dollars for an entire week's work.
I also shared my experience in delivering newspapers
at 5 a.m. My Friday nights were filled with collecting
25 cents from each newspaper customer. Often in the
winter, it was dark and near or below zero degrees. It
cost approximately five cents a paper, and I was able to
keep about one cent. I was thrilled when a customer
gave me a quarter tip. Fortunately, I was able to pay
100% of my high school tuition. By age sixteen, I was
working at the American Can Company in San Jose. It
was my first truly meaningful job, and it was my very
last menial job.

Well, life was quite different in the 1940s, '50s, and '60s. Over the years, my wife and I have shared many nostalgic memories about growing up during that era. My childhood was indeed very strange to our children and grandchildren. Our house was substantially smaller than what they have experienced as children. We had a one-car garage with only a single car. We didn't have credit cards, except perhaps a metal embossed card issued by Sears, Roebuck and Company, only to be used at their store and no other. Besides my feet, my bicycle was my primary means of transportation. My Schwinn Black Phantom bike was the most exhilarating of all the presents I had ever received. I cried and was utterly speechless when my dad presented it to me. Never in a million years did I expect such a phenomenal gift. For weeks I was in the clouds, savoring and basking in delightful jubilation of my prized possession. My bike got me to baseball practice and games, to the store, to my friends' houses, fishing at the Bay, going downtown, delivering newspapers, visits to the recreation hall, and any other place within a five- to seven-mile radius. As a child of eight or nine years, I was free to leave the house early in the day and did not need to return until dark. The streetlights were our signal that we were late and in big trouble. We weren't afraid of being kidnapped, molested, or injured. We felt invulnerable and quite capable of acting independently. We all knew how to change a tire on our bikes. I always had a patch-kit with me. After removing the tire, it allowed me to rough up the inner tube, grab a rubber patch, and with pressure, glue it over the puncture. I still remain aghast about riding my bike at night without light with no identified bike lane. I recall frantically peddling home in the dark, heavy rain falling, hearing and feeling cars within inches of me, and periodically tires splashing water from pothole puddles. I would come home late, shivering and wet from top to bottom—soon to be scolded for being late and having made poor choices!

We walked to school in the rain, sleet, and snow and usually enjoyed it—however, not uphill both ways. There were never school buses. We walked with our friends and had ongoing conversations before, during, and after school. As previously mentioned, one teacher, a religious nun, surprised me one day. She looked at me with a very stern face and said, "Anthony, if you open your mouth one more time, you see this safety pin? I will pin your lips together with it." After that, I was petrified and forever cautious. Fortunately, I returned to my old ways in the following years. It was painful for me to sit all those hours without an opportunity to socialize. During my education, it was not unusual to receive corporal punishment. I must admit that I escaped most of the time but experienced a ruler over the knuckles in grade school, and in high school, a rubber hose to my bottom. Things were indeed different then. You won't find discipline like that administered in today's schools. Our teachers and principals ruled; my parents supported and complied with them. Fortunately, very rarely, a telephone call home was made. If so, the consequences would be disastrous.

The only telephone we had could only be engaged by taking the receiver off the hook. An operator would then ask for the number you wished to call. Initially, it was only four digits, but later the number was preceded by two letters. She would then connect us. There was no such thing as a private line. We shared our telephone with several other people; it was called a "party line." If another party used the line, you could not call out until they were finished. As a curious young boy, I would occasionally lift the receiver to listen to one of our shared party line members' conversation. It was always interesting to hear what other people were thinking or doing. Later we would have a telephone upgrade that included a rotary dialing system, where we could easily dial the number using our pointer finger. As you might imagine, there was very little privacy. When I was on the phone, there were frequent reminders from both my parents and the other shared parties to hurry, that other people needed to use the phone. Phone calls were short, concise, and to the point. Seldom were we on the phone more than a few minutes.

My parents and all of our neighbors had recently experienced the worst economic depression of the 20th Century. We were just beginning to climb out of the Great Depression. Families were very cautious about their spending. Frugality was the order of the day. Since we were among the emerging middle class, we needed to conserve our money as much as possible.

Consequently, we seldom went out to eat. We bought clothes sparingly and often wore hand-me-downs that extended the life of our used clothing. Shoes lasted as long as possible. They were frequently repaired with new soles or heels. Clothes were washed at home, first by hand and later by the contraption that allowed them to be squeezed semi-dry between two rollers. It was called a wringer washer. I'll never forget our first Bendix washer. It automatically washed the clothes but needed to be installed in a cement casing because of its noise and the torque in the spin cycle. We never had a clothes dryer, so my mother would hang our clothes on a line outside. Sometimes when the weather became frigid, the clothes would freeze on the line, stiff as a board. I would laugh as my mother took them inside. Since we didn't know any better, life was wonderful. I couldn't conceive of things being any better. I didn't have the foggiest idea of what was to occur in the future.

Growing up, we saw home deliveries, but very different from the ones we see today. We had milk delivered to our front door. It had rich, thick cream sitting at the very top of the glass quart bottles. This was a real treat. If your mom didn't catch you sipping the heavy cream on top, you still might get caught with the large thick white mustache on your face. We had ice delivered to the house until we had a refrigerator. Later, it was finally great to open that Philco refrigerator door and pull out something to eat. We also had men with horses and flatbeds, going from house to house, selling various things. I especially remember a fruit and vegetable man. He would display his items and sell them directly to my mom or dad. Initially, we had a coal furnace. A truck would pull up, put a funnel-like tube at our basement window, and drop a load of coal down the pipe. Years later, we switched to oil. An oil delivery truck would fill the new tank, which had replaced the coal bin in our basement. All these deliveries were exciting to watch. We would even stop our playtime.

I especially remember being very fearful of the "rags man." Parents and neighbors somehow concocted a myth that he might put you in his cart and haul you away. We were told that if we didn't behave, he would toss us in under the rags. He was supposed to be feared and avoided. You could hear him from afar, his cart and horse clanking down the brick-laden streets. I didn't stick around to find out! However, his job was only to collect old clothes and rags so that they could be recycled. I'm not sure why we believed that myth, but maybe it was because he was rather dirty, unshaven, and disheveled, and so was his cart and horse.

Yes, we recycled everything. We saved newspapers for Boy Scout fundraisers. We saved and reused tin foil. My mother used a soda pop bottle with holes in the cap when she ironed because there weren't steam irons then. We used paper bags until they fell apart. My brown school lunch bags often had grease stains on them. It was not unusual to find waxed paper liverwurst, greasy cutlet, liver and onions, or pepper and sausage sandwich in those stained brown bag lunches. We recycled food, too! Nothing was wasted. Our dog Blackie was the end of our food chain.

There were very few things that we were unable to reuse.

We always had people going door-to-door selling encyclopedias, vacuum cleaners, and brushes. I can still vividly remember the Fuller Brush man with his many accoutrements hidden inside his many coat pockets, gesticulating as he pulled them out one by one. Most of the time my parents politely refused, but sometimes they would listen to their spiel. We did buy a set of encyclopedias, brushes, and a vacuum cleaner. Dad worked at Bausch & Lomb and rotated our car with others in his carpool. By today's standards, gas was reasonably inexpensive, but almost everyone conserved as much as possible. Vacations were a family affair, often taking my grandmother or cousins with us. We traveled by car to vacation spots, usually no more than a few hundred miles away. It was not until I was fifteen years old that we traveled by train to California to visit my mother's brother. It was that trip that predicated our future as a family. After visiting California, my dad and mom decided that we were going to move 3,000 miles away. It sounded like fun, but I knew it was going to be a difficult transition. I would be leaving my friends and from the only area that I had ever known. Also, I was sixteen and about to get my learner's permit, and eventually my driver's license. That was all I could think about then. Little did I know that the girl next door in California would be my partner for more than a half-century.

My grandchildren asked what kinds of toys or activities were popular then. I told them that I liked to play with a cork popgun and later with my own real Daisy BB gun. We used to eat candy cigarettes and drink little wax-coated shaped bottles with colored sugar water in them. Later, we would go across the street to the gas station and pull small bottles of Coca-Cola through a maze of bottles and then out a small opening from the refrigerated vending machine. They were only a nickel each. It was especially fun when it was hot on a humid summer day. We played with our Radio Flyers wagons; we tightened our roller skates with a key, frequently falling as we chased each other. We played mumblety peg, cops and *robbers*, superman, jacks, checkers, chess, cards, and board games like Monopoly. I can never say I was ever bored; however, I was sad when it rained or snowed and when I saw lightning flashes among the dark clouds. During those days, we would gaze through the window because we were restricted from going outside. There was always something to do on those days, including tormenting my brother, Bill. On Saturdays, he and I visited the movies. As a younger child, it was cartoons, but later, we watched two full-length movies for 25 cents. Newsreels about current news events invariably preceded the shows. As I became older, I remember diners with table jukeboxes playing either 78 or 45 records. For a nickel, you could choose a song, press a button, and magically a record would go into a rotating disk, and the song would play for a few minutes during our dinner.

That was about the time that I decided to use butch wax or Vaseline on my hair. I will never forget my dad frequently warning me that I would lose all my hair if I continued adding gobs of that stuff on my hair. It didn't take long! By age 25, I was becoming noticeably bald. In the summer, it was cool to have a crew cut on top and regular hair on the sides—a "crewcut with sides." For the rest of the year, it was very important to have a pompadour in front with a ducktail in the back. With all of the primping, those preadolescent years soon began to focus on the opposite sex. All of a sudden, girls were attractive. Never before had a coeducational conversation been more important. As puberty continued, girls became my prime focus. On Sundays, my friends and I would go to the movies, primarily to meet girls and socialize. It was a big deal to meet as many girls as possible and sit with them during a movie. Perhaps not as important as football, it became a competitive sport for many of us. In the meantime, school had lost some of its luster, and we all looked forward to our weekends, especially with the newfound girls. When I began to drive, the local theater was soon exchanged for a drive-in. The movies were quite tame in comparison to today's flicks. We seldom saw violence; there was no profanity and only closed-mouth kissing. Sex was very subtle, and nudity or even near nudity was nonexistent. The only scary movie I remember seeing was Alfred Hitchcock's *Psycho*. It was a far cry from today's bloody horror movies.

I can't say that we lived in a puritanical society, but times were different, especially mainstream media. Then, New York State allowed individuals to drink at age eighteen. Ironically, we did engage in some drinking, but there was seldom a time when we abused alcohol. Drugs were unheard of, and marijuana was considered to be absolutely the bottom of the barrel. At age fifteen, when I visited California, I was shocked to understand that some people were already experimenting with weed. Even though I was generally very adventuresome, I avoided associating with any users and maintained a very conservative posture. Drugs and alcohol were taboo. However, my actions were not always saintly. For instance, I was politely asked to leave my local church's Sodality Group because of my "lacking Christian values." Yet, I attended Aquinas Institute, a Catholic High School, and considered myself quite religious and moral. As my adolescence proceeded, I slowly concluded that those turbulent years were a war of hormones and extreme emotions!

My dad took a leave of absence from Bausch & Lomb in January 1959 and proceeded to San Jose, California, to find a job. He ended up taking a position as a nuclear engineer at the General Electric Nuclear

Energy Division there. In June of 1959, at the end of my junior year in high school, we packed up and took a three-and-a-half-day train trip to California. The rest is history that you will find scattered throughout this book.

I have hesitated and labored for hours, trying to determine whether prejudice, xenophobia, and ethnic profiling should be included in this book. We are currently experiencing a resurgence in ethnic and racial hostility. Discrimination now is no longer subtle but contentious and direct. So, I decided to briefly broach this subject for a number of reasons. I must admit that by my generation, the third generation in the United States, I seldom was the object of blatant prejudice. However, as a twelve-year-old, I saw and heard blatant racial slurs, as well as ethnic pejoratives. I also experienced subtle residual discrimination, which I can never forget.

As mentioned, by the time of my generation, attitudes towards Italian-Americans had shifted from blatant repudiation to tacit acceptance. However, my grandparents' and parents' generations had endured serious recrimination from the then status quo. The German and Irish immigrants had just reached levels of success and acceptance, even though they had also endured prejudice. Ironically, it was often the last accepted immigrants who were usually the most loudly outspoken. Waves of Italians, Greeks, Jews, and other

Southern Europeans started arriving at the turn of the 20th Century.

Consequently, my grandparents, dad, and mother were subjected to both direct and indirect prejudice. They were referred to in the media and their communities as wops, (from the southern Italian dialect *guappo*; also an acronym for With Out Papers), greasers, dagos, and garlic-breathers. These labels clearly differentiated them from society's acceptable members. They were now pariahs occupying the lowest rung of the social ladder. These last arriving immigrants were often pigeonholed as undesirable aliens who were taking away jobs and property only deserved by regular citizens, regardless of naturalization. In carefully reviewing the past, no ethnic group other than the original settlements of Great Britain and France were ever initially accepted into American society. That is unless you were a true native American!

As I reached adolescence and later young adulthood, it became obvious that my nationality was less appreciated by some but readily accepted by others. Then with movies such as *The Godfather* and *Goodfellows*, as well as TV series such as *The Sopranos* and *The Untouchables*, I received many ambivalent messages about my ethnicity. I was proud to be of Roman stock but embarrassed by the Mafia. I was incensed by the portrayal of Italians as sleazy, inarticulate, animalistic, and crude. However, I was proud of my heritage, its culture, and its scientific discoveries. I was also proud of its history of persistence, sensitivity, tolerance, and genuineness. I remain supportive and sensitive to all ethnicities but saddened by how each new set of immigrants, whether Mexicans, Vietnamese, Chinese, Jews, Middle Easterners, or Slavs, are initially chastised and often unaccepted. Unfortunately, like the rites of adulthood, the traditions of citizenship can be challenging and painful.

We as Americans need to hold our heads high, triumphant, and proud of all of our heritages. We should as Americans reclaim the importance of diversity and the uniqueness of all cultures. Viva la difference! We need to continue integrating, appreciating, and honoring all of our fellow brothers and sisters. We are indeed a nation of immigrants who have labored to make our exemplary nation the most democratic and most egalitarian in all of history. And as our Statue of Liberty inscription conveys, "Give me your tired, your poor, your huddled masses yearning to breathe free, the wretched refuse of your teeming shore. Send these, the homeless, tempest-tost to me, I lift my lamp beside the golden door."

Certainly, there were things I wished were different and mistakes I wish I could have reversed. But, as I think retrospectively, it was a good life, a chance to learn, change, and pursue my dreams. Sometimes it was the very worst of times, but mostly the best of times; I have very few regrets. After all of my antics, I am so thankful to have had the opportunity to remain on the right side of the green and a chance to share this story lovingly. I sincerely hope you enjoy it, take away some tools, and gain some insights. May your life be as fulfilling!

"Inch by inch, life's a cinch, yard by yard, life is hard."
—Author unknown

RANDOM THOUGHTS ABOUT LIFE'S JOURNEY

The best things in life are indeed free—family, friends, smiles, hugs, kisses, love, pleasant memories, laughter, sleep, and Mother Nature. Tongue in cheek, family—it maybe not exactly be free, there are upfront costs! My 101-year-old mother frequently reminds me to celebrate each day as a Thanksgiving gift. She remains my ambassador of goodwill and also for the senior community in which she resides. The testimonials by her peers reinforce my subjective feelings.

Life is an endless series of ups and downs. Comedian Phyllis Diller notes, "Life is a do-it-yourself kit, and the minute you find that out, you're on your way." The comic character, Maxine, quoted Virginia Satir, "Life is not the way it's supposed to be. It's the way it is. The way you cope with it is what makes the difference." It isn't tied with a bow, but it is still a gift.

The way you live your life is your gift to those who know you and those that come after you. Life goes by so quickly. So do what you can each day because you never know what tomorrow may bring. You must remember that when life is over, it's over; at that point, it's too late! Your ticket gets punched, and the journey terminates.

Henry Thoreau called the art of living the highest form of all the arts. Life is made up of continuous experiences, like the sand as it passes through an hourglass. The unforgettable moments you have with your loved ones, the smiles on children's faces, the hug from a friend, and completing a challenging task, are all part of the tiny successes that make life fulfilling. Taking pleasure in every day is the pinnacle of happiness.

Each day on life's journey, you add a new memory. Sometimes it's not the most thrilling or exhilarating. But each memory is a building block of learning, understanding, coping, responding, and reacting to each situation. Appreciating the fact that you may trip and stumble along the way only adds to your character. We are all imperfect beings, and thus all are sinners. We all err and commit transgressions. It's impossible to be perfect. Of course, life doesn't always work the way you intended. If there were no mistakes, no pain or suffering, you could not learn to appreciate its true meaning. It's impossible to be happy all the time. Life, like Mother Nature, will throw you curves, not that different than unexpected weather. You, too, will need to weather life's curves and bumps along the way.

Whether the weather is fraught with clouds, incessant snow, or a Hades' heatwave, you must learn to understand and cope with life's realities. Reality should never be substituted by fantasy or magic. Weathering each storm teaches you valuable lessons. Sometimes making lemonade out of bitter lemons can result in a very sweet lesson. Indeed, life is a series of unexpected personal tests and challenges. There have been many attempts to explain various views on life. Here are a few:

In your quest for a life of true happiness, and always looking over your shoulder or through a rearview mirror, you will never find it, because by then, you have just passed it up. If you focus your sights with a telescope or binoculars, you are looking far beyond what is immediately in front of you. The present will soon become your past, and your future is too far off. If you don't embrace the present with both arms, it will be as elusive as a pig slathered with fat. Remember, the best things in life are free. You can only find happiness by adjusting your attitude; it is your gyroscope, your GPS, your heart and soul, and your ticket to freedom.

Leo Rosten was a gifted writer. In his *Free Mind*, he commented, "The purpose of life is not just to be happy, but to matter, to be productive, to be useful, to have it make a difference that you lived at all." The truth is that you can accomplish all of these things and be happy and prosperous. He further stated, "We must forever oppose hysteria and error, even when error is wrapped in patriotism, even when an error is embraced by those we like, we must learn that those we like are not always right, and those we don't like are not always wrong, and that an idea has nothing to do with who is for it or who is against it. We must learn to seek change without violence. Always change and never violence, not even in words, much less in deeds. We must try to understand men by reconciling ourselves to the fact that most of us never really mature. We simply grow taller. We must meet fanaticism with courage and idealism with caution. We must be skeptical of that which is promised and not proved. We must be strong enough to be gentle."

Leo espoused balance, moderation, healthy objectivity, and change for the betterment of our world. His words were simple concepts, yet they have profound roots. We live in a veritable paradise and have so much to be thankful. The freedoms we possess are second to none. The choices available are endless, whether they are education, work, food, living conditions, technology, social availability, etc. You must also strive to help others who have fewer choices due to poverty, handicap, age, accident, or other circumstances. Working towards common goals by helping others less able creates balance and real life.

Having patience and time to think allows you to see life as a meaningful and lengthy journey, not a quick sprint to personal success. Recognizing all the elements of life and its journey are the stepping-stones of this book. Each chapter will encapsulate many of the whistle stops along your circuitous route called life.

Below is the definition of life often attributed to the person who personified it, Mother Teresa:

Life is an opportunity; benefit from it.
Life is beauty; admire it.
Life is bliss, taste it.
Life is a dream; realize it.
Life is a challenge; meet it.
Life is a duty; complete it.
Life is a game; play it.
Life is a promise; fulfill it.
Life is sorrow; overcome it.
Life is a song; sing it.
Life is a struggle; accept it.
Life is a tragedy; confront it.
Life is an adventure; dare it.
Life is luck; make it.
Life is life; fight for it.

Over the years, my friends must have been sent at least twelve copies of the letter below. The latest one sent was a beautiful copy done in calligraphy. It was written by an octogenarian by the name of Nadine Stair. She has a very poignant message extolling what she would do if she had a second chance at life.

"IF I HAD MY LIFE TO LIVE OVER"

"I'd dare to make more mistakes next time. I'd relax, I would limber up. I would be sillier than I have been on this trip. I would take fewer things seriously. I would take more chances. I would eat more ice cream and less beans. I would, perhaps, have more actual troubles but fewer imaginary ones.

You see, I'm one of those people who was sensible and sane, hour after hour, day after day. Oh, I've had my moments. If I had it to do over again, I'd have more of them. In fact, I'd try to have nothing else, just moments, one after another, instead of living so many years ahead of each day. I've been one of those persons who never goes anywhere without a thermometer, a hot water bottle, a raincoat, and a parachute. If I had to do it again, I would travel lighter than I have. If I had to live my life over, I would start barefoot earlier in the spring and stay that way later in the fall. I would go to more dances, I would ride more merry-go-rounds, I would pick more daisies."

Some two thousand years ago, the poet Horace urged his fellow Romans to seize the day, "Carpe Diem." Robin Williams, as an inspirational English teacher in the classic film *Dead Poets Society* convinced his students to live extraordinary lives of passion, with a strong desire to make their lives both meaningful and purposeful. "Sine Qua Non" or "without which, not" completes Horace's thought; that without seizing the day, you will instead allow the day to seize you. May your life become a legacy of love, sensitivity, integrity, responsibility, kindness, helpfulness, fairness, and honor. If so, you will have bestowed the world your perpetuity.

THE FINAL JOURNEY

"We are mere journeymen, planting seeds for someone else to harvest."

—*Wallace Thurman*

PLANTING THE SEEDS

My intent in writing this book is to help facilitate your personal growth by providing you with the tools, knowledge, and wisdom on your travels. I want to plant the seeds of enlightenment that will provide a road map and expedite your journey. My goal is to allow you to enjoy your life to its fullest. The road signs are in the form of quotes, anecdotes, and personal glimpses of both ancient and modern worlds. Please feel free to share the thoughts and suggestions provided, especially those of the erudite minds of the past. My other objective is to help you find your path forward as I look back upon my life. So, as I'm looking through my rearview mirror, you can be looking through your front windshield, navigating each intersection along the way. It sounds a little confusing, but my rearview mirror is now much cleaner; my hindsight becomes 20/20! As a bonus, my guidance is free and comes with unconditional love and support.

"Again, you can't connect the dots looking forward; you can only connect them looking backward. So you have to trust that the dots will somehow connect in your future. You have to trust in something—your gut, destiny, life, karma, whatever. This approach has never let me down, and it made all the difference in my life."
—*Steve Jobs*

As much as many would like to believe it, there is no such thing as a "self-made" man or woman. We are all dependent upon each other for help to support and correct each other's mistakes. We are all interconnected. We need our brothers and sisters to nurture our bodies and minds. Without each other, real happiness would not be possible.

Your life's journey will always be a work in progress. The travels you undertake will be similar to the Amazon River, ever-winding and twisting, turning into new territories, new adventures, and many new challenges. Of course, there will always be things you would have preferred not to do or encounter. And you will give up some skin when compromise is needed or when you fall along the path. There will be disagreements, reconciliations, and times to let go. Your decisions will mark the turning points, detours, or dead ends along the trail. Life's trip will surely be filled with a range of intense feelings and emotions. It will include frightful and delightful moments, joy and sorrow, fantasy and reality, love and rage, happy hellos and sad goodbyes, salutations and disappointments, welcome homes or unexpected farewells. You can also expect to have sensational victories, yet other times, have feelings of loneliness and loss. Regardless, you'll need to be patient and calm and remain confident throughout your journey. I could not imagine it without all of these elements.

> *"Patience, child, patience. Remember, life is a journey. Remain calm; all is within reach; all you have to do is show up every day, stay true to your path, and you will surely find the treasure you seek."*
> —*Jackson Kiddard*

If you travel light, without being burdened by extra weight, you'll mature more quickly in a more positive manner. Let go of the burdensome, drop your grudges, your mistakes, your mistaken beliefs. As each day and year progresses, you will be able to see more rainbows and less fog. You will gain knowledge and wisdom while savoring every step.

> *"If you wish to travel far and fast, travel light. Take off all your envies, jealousies, unforgiveness, selfishness, and fears."*
> —*Glenn Clark*

Don't be afraid to take notes on your travels. Save them; the words of inspiration that ignite your spirit will also speed your journey. Don't leave your most precious reflections on the altar of dust. For this is the bountiful wisdom you will have painstakingly earned. Save them and share them all with as many as possible. Some day you may want to plant your own special seeds for others to harvest. Your purpose in life is not getting everything you like but sharing it with others through kindness, gentleness, love, and wisdom.

> *"The universe isn't invested in you getting what you want. It's invested in you experiencing what's necessary for your enlightenment."*
> —*Marianne Williamson*

Your choices will determine your next turn. Each outcome can temporarily shackle you with fear or extricate you to freedom. Win or lose, you will have achieved insight. Experience is priceless and often lifesaving. Don't sleepwalk through life; stay alert and follow the beacon of light forward from the haze. Grab the rudder, check your compass, and begin moving forward. Soon it will be full speed ahead. Make fun out of life by enjoying each precious moment. Your sunshine will brighten and inspire others who resist life; welcome them with open arms. Anonymously perform random acts of kindness; they will add to others' sunshine and nourish your soul as well.

> *"I have a clue how my story will end, but that's all right. When you set out on a journey and night covers the road, that's when you discover the stars."*
> —*Nancy Willard*

As you may recall *The Station* by Robert J. Hastings cited earlier, I'd like to close with some of my additional interpretations and thoughts about your station.

Yes, during your travel, you will often clamor, "Are we almost there, Dad?" And Dad will answer, "No, not yet." Then, at sixteen or eighteen, your assumed stations are a driver's license, freedom, and a car. At nineteen or 22, you are swept with new emotions and idealism. You will be asking questions about governance, the environment, war, poverty, racism, altruism, and "Where am I, how much further?" At 30 or 40 or 50, you will be focused on a house, a new car, a job, a family, finances, the plight of the world, and lots more. At 50 or 60 or 70, you will be asking, "When will I retire? Am I almost there?" No doubt, you will continue your journey, stopping at temporary stations along the way. As you reach your retirement years, you will continue pacing and questioning about the next stop.

But maybe, you will have concluded by then that there is no final station.

So, you will finally be struck with my revelation. Life is beautiful! You, like me, will reminisce of all the mountains you've climbed, the deserts you crossed, the delicious desserts you've eaten, the fabulous family you have supported, loved, and enjoyed, the environment you helped save, the neighbors and strangers you comforted, the sunrises and sunsets you have witnessed, the oceans and rivers you've traveled, the tears of joys, the tears of those lost, the many hours of laughter and giggling, and the many other delightful memories that will besiege you. As you slowly drift into somnolence, you will redeem yourself and your fellow brethren. For you now deserve the honor of perpetuity and the joyous rewards of success and happiness.

NOTE FROM THE AUTHOR

I have received one very persistent personal criticism that has echoed in my ears for over a half-century. My wife, children, and even my grandchildren have classified me as an inveterate collector. I collect antiquities, coins, woodcarvings, panda bears, books, plates, paintings of nature, and scrimshaw. With a tinge of emotional discomfort, I must admit they occupy our house, including the attic and three offices. There are also boxes of memorabilia, letters, notes, quotes, and creeds, too. My embarrassment actually caused me to buy a book on collections versus hoarding. To my surprise and relief, the final verdict was I am a collector, not a hoarder. However, my embarrassment is exacerbated every time I think of Mahatma Gandhi. When he died, there was a photo of the totality of his personal possessions—shockingly, they didn't even fill a shopping bag.

Typically, especially in periods of sadness or times of transition, I would seek out these various creeds and inspirational quotes from the collection saved for the past fifty-plus years. Over the years, I developed deep respect and reverence for these mighty mentors and their classic creeds and poignant eloquence. It sometimes took hours or days to review them. Depending on my mood or needs at that time, I wrote selected annotations of phrases or comments. They became my mantra for weeks or months. I would keep them in my car and read their messages at traffic lights or commuter stalls. I'd review them over and over again. Soon I had developed individual folders that contained different categories of motivational and inspirational creeds. I'd rotate them in my tickler file so that they were always handy. They became invaluable while waiting for doctors' visits, standing in line, waiting for events, or just stopping at a vacant parking spot to wind down and transition before returning home from work. The priority of each folder changed with time and mood. However, over time I read with anticipation the entire collection many times. To this very day, I can find in my "tickler file" a contemporary folder containing medical information, short stories, quotes, and inspiring thoughts. Usually reviewed just before retiring for the evening, I use the new accumulation of inspirational tidbits to relax, clear my mind, and end the day with a touch of satisfaction.

ABOUT THE AUTHOR

Tony Cedolini, Ph.D., was born in upstate New York in 1942. At age sixteen, his family moved to San Jose, California, where he still resides. He married his wife, Clare Marie De Rose, in 1964, and they had three children. Dr. Cedolini has worked with children and parents for more than 50 years. He spent most of those years in private practice as a licensed educational psychologist and marriage, family and child counselor with his wife at their Educational Associates office.

Dr. Cedolini first earned a bachelor's degree and a master's degree from San Jose State University. After extensive research, his book, *Occupational Stress and Job Burnout* was published by Columbia University's Teachers College Press. It became the vehicle for his Ph.D. dissertation in educational psychology from Columbia Pacific University. He is also the author of two previous educational books. His first, *A Parent's*

Guide to School Readiness, was published in 1971, his second, *The Effect of Affect* in 1975, and *Occupational Stress and Job Burnout* in 1982.

After a 35-year hiatus, and 51 years of research, he completed his latest book called *Passport—Your Journey to Wit, Wisdom, and Inspiration* in 2018. It was directed toward and published for his extended family and friends. Throughout his career, his research in the area of psychology and mental health was documented in various professional publications and newspapers as author and co-author.

In addition to devoting five decades to working with children and their families, Dr. Cedolini also has maintained an interest in various organizations outside of the mental health field as well. He was co-founder and on the board of directors for Lyceum of Santa Clara County from 1971 to 2001, where he continued to serve as a consultant. This Silicon Valley non-profit organization is self-supporting and relies on parent participation and professional volunteers. It provides after-school enrichment classes for intellectually-gifted children that otherwise might not be available to them. For the past 50 years it has been responsible for some of the high-tech talent that has come out of our Silicon Valley. In addition, he enjoys reading, collecting coins and antiques, classic cars, woodcarvings, travel, and winemaking. He has been semi-retired since 2017.

You can dive deeper into many of the topics covered in this book at: https://www.drtonycedolini.com

"WISDOM OF THE AGES" https://www. drtonycedolini.com/wisdom-of-the-ages

"HUMOR" https://www.drtonycedolini.com/humor

"MENTAL HEALTH AND PERSONAL CHANGE" https://www.drtonycedolini.com/ mental-health-and-personal-change

"PERCEPTION" https://www.drtonycedolini.com/ perception

"STRESS" https://www.drtonycedolini.com/stress

"TIME" https://www.drtonycedolini.com/ time-management

"GOVERNANCE" https://www.drtonycedolini.com/ governance

"CHILDREN" https://www.drtonycedolini.com/ parenting-and-child-rearing

"CREEDS" https://www.drtonycedolini.com/creeds

"PITHY PROVERBS" https://www.drtonycedolini. com/pithy-proverbs

Made in the USA
Columbia, SC
17 June 2021